The Epistles and the Apocalypse

The Epistles and the Apocalypse

Commentary on the Holy Scriptures
of the New Testament
Volume III

Archbishop Averky (Taushev)

Translated from the Russian
by Nicholas Kotar

The Apocalypse is translated from the Russian
by Hieromonk Seraphim (Rose)

Edited by Vitaly Permiakov

HOLY TRINITY SEMINARY PRESS
Holy Trinity Monastery
Jordanville, NY

Printed with the blessing of His Eminence,
Metropolitan Hilarion First Hierarch
of the Russian Orthodox Church Outside of Russia

Commentary on the Holy Scriptures of the New Testament:

The Epistles © 2018 Holy Trinity Monastery

The Apocalypse © 1985 St Herman of Alaska Brotherhood

Compilation © 2018 Holy Trinity Monastery

Third Printing 2023

HOLY TRINITY
SEMINARY PRESS

An imprint of

 HOLY TRINITY PUBLICATIONS
Holy Trinity Monastery
Jordanville, New York 13361-0036
www.holytrinitypublications.com

ISBN: 978-1-942699-18-7 (hardback)
ISBN: 978-1-942699-19-4 (ePub)
ISBN: 978-1-942699-20-0 (Mobipocket)

Library of Congress Control Number 2017963205

Scripture passages taken from the *New King James Version*.
Copyright © 1982 by Thomas Nelson, Inc. Used by permission.

Psalms taken from *A Psalter for Prayer*, trans. David James
(Jordanville, N.Y.: Holy Trinity Publications, 2011).

Scripture passages quoted in the Apocalypse section are extracts from the Authorized
Version of the Bible (*The King James Bible*), the rights in which are vested in the Crown,
and are reproduced by permission of the Crown's Patentee, Cambridge University Press.

CONTENTS

For we cannot but speak the things which we have seen and heard.

(Acts 4:20)

For I have not shunned to declare to you the whole counsel of God.

(Acts 20:27)

For I think that God has displayed us, the apostles, last, as men condemned to death.

(1 Cor 4:9)

Therefore, brethren, stand fast and hold the traditions which you were taught, whether by word or our epistle.

(2 Thess 2:15)

 EDITOR'S PREFACE

This book is the third volume of the commentary on the New Testament Scriptures by the ever-memorable Archbishop Averky (Taushev), who was the rector of Holy Trinity Orthodox Seminary and abbot of the monastery in Jordanville from 1952 until his repose in 1976. This volume includes the commentary on the Epistles of St Paul, the General Epistles, and the Apocalypse (Book of Revelation). Like the two previous volumes in this series, this commentary emerged from the transcript of Vladyka Averky's lecture notes for the courses in the Scriptures of the New Testament, which he taught at Holy Trinity Orthodox Seminary between 1952 and 1955. From 1957 to 1959, these lectures were published as an appendix to the Holy Trinity Calendar, and in 1974, they were reprinted in book form.

In his short essay "On Reading the Gospels," St Ignatius (Brianchaninov) encouraged his readers: "Do not content yourself with unproductive reading of the Gospels; strive to fulfill its commandments, read it with deeds." We can see this maxim as equally relevant and true for Orthodox readers who strive to read carefully the writings of the Holy Apostle Paul, the apostle of the "whole world" (St John Chrysostom) who eloquently proclaimed through his letters the eternal gospel, which he received "not according to man ... but it came through the revelation of Jesus Christ" (Gal 1:11–12). The commentary by Archbishop Averky, which is offered in this volume, seeks to guide a modern Orthodox reader toward careful, attentive, and fruitful reading of the Epistles of St Paul and other apostles: St James, St Peter, St John, and St Jude. In his introduction to St Paul's writings, Vladyka himself emphasizes a need for Orthodox Christians to peruse and study these writings, since they reveal to the reader that Christianity is "not merely a system of belief, an acceptance with the mind of certain known truths, but ... an entire way of life by faith." To show the depth and relevance of St Paul's letters today, Vladyka Averky always emphasizes the moral and pastoral aspects of the Scriptures: indeed, these commentaries emerged as lectures addressed to the Jordanville seminarians, many of whom became pastors of the Church tending to the spiritual flock of the Russian diaspora. At the same time, Archbishop Averky's approach is thoroughly patristic: the reader will see Vladyka constantly turning to the wide array of the Church Fathers for the elucidation of one or another particular verse, especially to the commentaries and expositions of St John Chrysostom, Blessed Theophylact of Ochrid, Blessed Theodoret of Cyrus, and others. The reader will also find how deeply indebted Vladyka's lectures were to the voluminous Scriptural commentaries of St Theophan the Recluse (1815–1894), an enormously influential spiritual figure of pre-Revolutionary Russia.

Having been produced in the genre of classroom lectures, Vladyka Averky's commentaries were naturally lacking references and endnotes, both in their original Russian publications and in later reprints. This English edition, however, has been supplied with endnotes to the works of Church Fathers and contemporary writers wherever direct quotations from these sources appear in the commentary. For the convenience of readers in locating specific references, more recent English translations of the patristic works are cited when possible. All material in the endnotes for Archbishop Averky's commentary on the Pauline and General Epistles was produced for this English edition by the editorial staff of Holy Trinity Seminary Press.

This third volume of Archbishop Averky's commentary on the New Testament also incorporates the translation of his commentary on the Apocalypse, accomplished in the 1970s by another influential figure in American Orthodoxy, Hieromonk Seraphim (Rose; 1934–1982). Fr Seraphim's translation was published in 1985 as *The Apocalypse in the Teachings of Ancient Christianity* by St Herman of Alaska Brotherhood (Platina, CA) and is reproduced in this volume with minor editorial emendations. As in its first edition, this new publication likewise includes the text of the Apocalypse, to be read together with the commentary, as well as Fr Seraphim's footnotes supplying additional patristic references, in addition to the commentary of St Andrew of Caesarea, on whom Archbishop Averky primarily relied.

We sincerely hope that this English edition of the Scriptural commentaries by Archbishop Averky will further inspire Orthodox faithful to regular, scrupulous, and attentive reading of the Holy Scriptures, interpreted through the lens of the Orthodox patristic, liturgical, and spiritual tradition. May we be inspired to turn constantly to the sacred, salvific words of Scripture and, by the grace of God, may we be revealed as "not mere hearers of the spiritual sayings, but also as the performers of good works" (Liturgy of St James).

Holy Trinity Seminary Press
September 9 (22), 2017
Saints Joachim and Anna

The material here offered consists of a series of summary lectures for the course on the Holy Scriptures of the New Testament, which I taught at Holy Trinity Orthodox Seminary in Jordanville, NY, between 1952–1955.

Being a seminary lecture course, this overview relies heavily on such secondary works as the *Commentary on the Apostolos* by Bishop Michael (Luzin; 1830–1887), and the commentaries on the Pauline Epistles by St Theophan the Recluse, as well as on the collection of articles by Matvei Barsov (d. 1896) and several other prerevolutionary seminary textbooks, including ones by Archpriest Michael Kheraskov (1836–1901), Alexander V. Ivanov (1837–1911), Archpriest Nicholas S. Alexandrov, and others.

This volume, like the others, has as its purpose the instruction of the word of God for all lovers of Scripture in the proper interpretation given it by the holy Orthodox Church. This is especially necessary here in America, where even among Orthodox Russians the virulent preaching of Protestant sectarianism confuses many, turning them away from the right path.

I ask my readers to forgive all omissions and insufficiencies of this volume of my work, covering them with your love and prayers for my soul.

—Archbishop Averky

 CONCERNING THE APOSTOLOS

THE MEANING OF THE TERM "APOSTOLOS"

The second part of the New Testament consists of holy books that usually are united, at least in their liturgical usage, under the general term "Apostolos" (*Апостол* in Russian or *Apostolos* in Greek). The word *Apostolos* means "messenger." This name was given to the disciples of the Lord Jesus Christ, sent by Him to preach the Gospel to all mankind. Just as the name "Gospels" now indicates the written word (originally the oral preaching) concerning the life and teaching of the Lord Jesus Christ, the term "Apostolos" refers to the extant writings of Christ's apostles, including their deeds, lives, and teachings. This division of the New Testament into two parts—the Gospel and the Apostolos—is of ancient provenance. We find this division and the name "Apostolos" in the writings of St Irenaeus of Lyons, Clement of Alexandria, and Tertullian. (This volume of the *Commentary on the Holy Scriptures of the New Testament* series covers part of the Apostolos.)

THE CONTENT OF THE APOSTOLOS

Even though in the first centuries of Christianity many books appeared bearing the titles Acts, Epistles, and Revelation, the only authentic and canonically recognized books are the following (twenty-three in number):

1. The Acts of the Apostles
2. St Paul's Epistle to the Romans
3. St Paul's First Epistle to the Corinthians
4. St Paul's Second Epistle to the Corinthians
5. St Paul's Epistle to the Galatians
6. St Paul's Epistle to the Ephesians
7. St Paul's Epistle to the Philippians
8. St Paul's Epistle to the Colossians
9. St Paul's First Epistle to the Thessalonians

10. St Paul's Second Epistle to the Thessalonians
11. St Paul's First Epistle to Timothy
12. St Paul's Second Epistle to Timothy
13. St Paul's Epistle to Titus
14. St Paul's Epistle to Philemon
15. St Paul's Epistle to the Hebrews
16. The General Epistle of the Holy Apostle James
17. The First General Epistle of the Holy Apostle Peter
18. The Second General Epistle of the Holy Apostle Peter
19. The First General Epistle of the Holy Apostle John the Theologian
20. The Second General Epistle of the Holy Apostle John the Theologian
21. The Third General Epistle of the Holy Apostle John the Theologian
22. The General Epistle of the Holy Apostle Jude
23. The Book of Revelation (the Apocalypse) of St John the Theologian

In this collection of writings, Acts is a book of historical record, the Epistles of St Paul and the General Epistles are instructional in nature, and the Revelation of St John is a book of prophecy.

[In his Thirty-Ninth Festal Epistle, St Athanasius of Alexandria also mentions that "there are other books besides these not indeed included in the Canon, but appointed by the Fathers to be read by those who newly join us, and who wish for instruction in the word of godliness." Among such books, he mentions the *Didache* (Teaching of the Twelve Apostles) and *Shepherd of Hermas*. Aside from those books, St Athanasius mentions the so-called apocryphal (i.e., hidden, secret) books, which are "invention(s) of heretics," who attribute them to the apostles, "so that, using them as ancient writings, they may find occasion to lead astray the simple." Following patristic witness, the Church rejects the pseudo-epigraphical (fabricated) and apocryphal (hidden, esoteric) books that claim apostolic origin but do not reflect the authentic apostolic doctrine. The faithful are discouraged from reading those books, as their reading can bring spiritual harm.]

PART I

The Epistles of the Holy Apostle Paul

THE SIGNIFICANCE OF THESE EPISTLES AND WHY THEY ARE SO DIFFICULT TO STUDY

Of all the writers of the books of the New Testament, no one has done more to interpret Christian teaching in written form than Apostle Paul, who wrote fourteen epistles that have survived. These writings are so important that some have fairly called them a "second Gospel," and they have always attracted attention, both from the Fathers of the Church and from the enemies of Christianity. The Apostles themselves, as we see in 2 Peter, were no strangers to these instructive words of their "beloved brother Paul" (2 Pet 3:15), younger in terms of his conversion but equal to the rest of the Apostles in the spirit of his teaching and in his gracious gifts.

Many Fathers and teachers of the Church wrote commentaries on the Epistles of Apostle Paul. Comprising a necessary and important addition to the teaching of the Gospel, the Epistles of the Holy Apostle Paul must be the subject of the most attentive and zealous study for every Christian theologian. In addition, one must never forget the incredibly exalted character and depth of the Holy Apostle Paul's theological thought, as well as the uniqueness of his voice, which is sometimes so idiosyncratic that it is difficult to understand to the fullest extent. Even such great interpreters as Chrysostom, Jerome, and Augustine paused in amazement. These epistles reflect Paul's extensive education and deep knowledge of the Scriptures of the Old Testament, as well as his profound interpretation of Christ's teaching of the New Testament, the fruit of which was an entire series of new words and expressions of dogmatic importance and moral-instructive character that belong exclusively to St Paul, such as "to be buried with Christ," "to put on Christ," "to put off the old man," "the laver of regeneration," "another law in my members, warring against the law of my mind," and so many more. Every epistle contains truths both of the dogmatic and moral aspects of Christianity, because Christianity is not merely a system of belief, an acceptance with the mind of certain known truths, but it is without doubt an entire way of life by faith.

ST PAUL'S WRITINGS IN THE CONTEXT OF HIS LIFE

The Epistles of Apostle Paul are the fruits of his apostolic zeal; his teaching, expounded in them, is a reflection of his life. Therefore, to better understand his letters, we must carefully study his life and fully understand the character of his personality. There is no need to enter into the fine details of his life, which we know well from the Book of Acts. Instead, we should reflect on the internal aspect of his life that, by the words of the apostle himself, served for him as the source for answering many questions of Christian dogma and morality.

THE LIFE AND PERSON OF THE HOLY APOSTLE PAUL

"I am the least of the apostles, who am not worthy to be called an apostle, because I persecuted the church of God. But by the grace of God I am what I am, and His grace toward me was not in vain" (1 Cor 15:9–10). This is how the great Apostle to the Nations (the name by which the church remembers him) spoke of himself. Gifted by nature with rich intellectual talents, he was raised and taught in the strict rule of the Pharisees, and by his own admission, he was more successful in following the Jewish ritual law than many of his contemporaries, for he was a zealot of the traditions of his fathers (Gal 1:14). When the Lord, Who chose him from his mother's womb, called him to the apostolic ministry, he dedicated all his energy, all the power of his great spirit to preaching the name of Christ among the pagans of the entire civilized world of that time, but only after suffering much sorrow from his fellow Jews, who had become blindly obstinate in their opposition to Christ.

While studying the life and labors of the holy apostle in the Book of Acts, one cannot help but be amazed by his incredible, limitless energy. It is difficult to imagine how this man, who did not have a strong constitution (Gal 4:13–14), could have endured so many difficulties and dangers for the glory of the name of Christ. It is especially amazing that the greater these difficulties and dangers, the more ardent his zeal and energy, like steel hardened in the forge. Forced to recall his difficulties for the edification of the Corinthians, he wrote the following:

> In labors more abundant, in stripes above measure, in prisons more frequently, in deaths often. From the Jews five times I received forty stripes minus one. Three times I was beaten with rods; once I was stoned; three times I was shipwrecked; a night and a day I have been in the deep; in journeys often, in perils of waters, in perils of robbers, in perils of my own countrymen, in perils of the Gentiles, in perils in the city, in perils in the wilderness, in perils in the sea, in perils among false brethren; in weariness and toil, in sleeplessness often, in hunger and thirst, in fastings often, in cold and nakedness. (2 Cor 11:23–27)

Comparing himself with the other apostles and humbly calling himself "the least" of them, St Paul could in all fairness maintain, "but I labored more abundantly than they all, yet not I, but the grace of God which was with me" (1 Cor 15:10). Truly, without the grace of God, no ordinary man could undertake such labors and perform so many deeds. As brave, direct, and indomitable as Paul was in his conviction before kings and lords, he was equally decisive and sincere in his interaction with his fellow apostles. One time, he even rebuked Apostle Peter when that great apostle acted inappropriately in Antioch (Gal 2:11–14). This fact is important, moreover, because it clearly contradicts the Roman Catholic teaching concerning Peter's position as "prince of the apostles," the vicar of the Lord Himself (for which reason popes bear the title "the Vicar of the Son of God"). Would Apostle Paul, the former persecutor of the Church of Christ and the last of those called to the apostolic ministry, have dared to rebuke the very vicar of the Lord Jesus Christ in the apostolic assembly? This is completely unlikely. St Paul rebuked Apostle Peter as an equal, a brother admonishing a brother.

Apostle Paul, initially bearing the Jewish name Saul, belonged to the tribe of Benjamin and was born in the Cilician town of Tarsus, which then was well known for its Greek academy and the education of its inhabitants. As a native of that city (or as a descendant of Jewish slaves freed by their Roman masters), Paul had the rights of Roman citizenship. In Tarsus, Paul received his primary education and, perhaps, became acquainted with pagan education, for in his speeches and epistles, one can easily see his familiarity with certain pagan writers (Acts 17:28, 1 Cor 15:33, Titus 1:12).

He received his higher education in Jerusalem in the famous rabbinical school of Gamaliel (Acts 22:3), who was considered an expert in the Law and who, despite his belonging to the sect of the Pharisees, was a free thinker (Acts 5:34) and a lover of Greek wisdom. In this school, according to the Jewish custom, the young Saul learned a trade (tent making) that helped give him financial independence in his later life (see Acts 18:3, 2 Cor 11:8, 2 Thess 3:8).

The young Saul, apparently, was preparing to become a rabbi, and so immediately after the end of his education, he showed himself to be a strong zealot of the Pharisaic traditions and a fierce persecutor of the faith of Christ. It is possible that he witnessed the death of Stephen (Acts 7:58, 8:1) and then received the official authority to persecute Christians even beyond Palestine, in Damascus. The Lord, seeing in him a chosen vessel, appeared to him in a vision on the road to Damascus, calling him to the apostolic ministry. After being baptized by Ananias, Saul became a zealous preacher of the same faith that he used to persecute. For a time, he traveled to Arabia, and then returned to Damascus to preach the Christian faith.

The anger of the Jews, astonished by his conversion to Christ, forced him to flee to Jerusalem in c. A.D. 38, where he joined the community of believers. After yet another attempt of the Jews to kill him, he returned to Tarsus. From there (c. A.D. 43), he was called by Barnabas to go to Antioch to preach. He then traveled with Barnabas to Jerusalem with aid for those suffering from famine (Acts 11:30). Soon after his return to Jerusalem, commanded by the Holy Spirit, Saul and Barnabas undertook their first missionary journey, which lasted from A.D. 45 to 51. The apostles preached all across Cyprus, from which moment Saul, after converting the local Roman governor Sergius Paulus, was named Paul. Then they established Christian communities Antioch of Pisidia, Iconium, Lystra, and Derbe—all cities of Asia Minor.

In A.D. 51, St Paul took part in the Apostolic Council in Jerusalem, where he ardently spoke against the necessity for pagan converts to follow the ritual observances of the Law of Moses. Having returned to Antioch, St Paul, together with

Silas, undertook his second missionary journey. At first, he visited the churches already established in Asia Minor, and then he traveled to Macedonia, where he established communities in Philippi, Thessalonica, and Berea. In Lystra, St Paul met Timothy, who would become his favorite disciple, and from Troas, he continued his journey with St Luke, the writer of Acts. From Macedonia, St Paul traveled to Greece, where he preached in Athens and Corinth, remaining in the latter for a year and a half. From there, he wrote his two Epistles to the Thessalonians. This second journey lasted from A.D. 51 to 54. In A.D. 55, Paul traveled to Jerusalem, visiting Ephesus and Caesarea along the way, and from Jerusalem, he traveled to Antioch (Acts 17, 18).

After a brief visit in Antioch, St Paul began his third missionary journey (A.D. 56–58), beginning with the churches in Asia Minor, as he did in his second journey. Then he established the base for his ministry in Ephesus, where for two years he preached daily in the school of a certain Tyrannus. From there, he wrote his Epistle to the Galatians, in response to a disturbance in that community caused by the heresy of the Judaizers, and he wrote the first Epistle to the Corinthians, in response to a letter sent by the community concerning certain local problems. A disturbance against Paul caused by the silversmith Demetrius forced the apostle to leave Ephesus, and he returned to Macedonia. On the way, he received news from Titus about the state of the Church in Corinth and the positive effect of his first epistle, and Paul wrote his second Epistle to the Corinthians, giving it to Titus to take back to Corinth.

Soon he visited Corinth himself, from where he wrote his Epistle to the Romans, intending, after visiting Jerusalem, to travel to Rome and farther west. Having parted with his Ephesian flock, he traveled to Jerusalem, where his presence caused a riot among the Jews, and he was taken into custody by the Roman authority, ending up first under the jurisdiction of the proconsul Felix, then later Festus (A.D. 59). In A.D. 61, Paul, a Roman citizen, appealed to Caesar.

On the way to Rome, his ship capsized at Malta, and so the holy apostle arrived in Rome in the summer of A.D. 62. The Roman authorities treated him with great respect, and he was not hindered in his preaching. The account of his life in Acts ends here (Acts 27–28).

From Rome, St Paul wrote his Epistles to the Philippians (with gratitude for the money they sent to him through Epaphroditus), Colossians, Ephesians, and Philemon, who lived in Colossae, on the subject of his escaped slave Onesimus. All four of these epistles were written in A.D. 63 and were sent with Tychicus. In A.D. 64, Paul wrote his Epistle to the Hebrews.

The subsequent fate of Apostle Paul is not entirely clear. Some believe that he remained in Rome and was martyred by Nero in A.D. 64. However, there are reasons to believe that after his two-year imprisonment in Rome, Paul was set free, and he undertook a fourth missionary journey, which seems to be suggested in his "pastoral epistles" to Timothy and Titus. After defending his case before the Senate and emperor, St Paul was probably freed and again traveled throughout the East. Having spent some considerable time in Crete and leaving his disciple Titus there to ordain presbyters for all the cities of Crete (Titus 1:5)—which suggests that Paul consecrated Titus as Bishop of Crete—Paul traveled throughout Asia Minor, from where he wrote his Epistle to Titus, instructing him in the responsibilities of a bishop.

From this epistle, it is clear that Paul planned to spend that winter (A.D. 64) in Nicopolis (Titus 3:12) near Tarsus. In the spring of A.D. 65, he visited the other churches of Asia Minor, and in Miletus, he left the ailing Trophimus, who was the alleged reason for the riot that resulted in Paul's first bonds (2 Tim 4:20). It is unclear whether Paul traveled through Ephesus, as he himself said that the presbyters of Ephesus would no longer see him (Acts 20:25), but he, apparently, consecrated Timothy as Bishop of Ephesus at this time. Then Paul traveled through Troas, where he left his cloak and some books in the house of a certain Carpus (2 Tim 4:13), and then he went to Macedonia.

In Macedonia, he heard about the rise of certain heresies in Ephesus, and he wrote his first Epistle to Timothy. After spending some time in Corinth (2 Tim 4:20) and meeting Apostle Peter on the way, Paul traveled with Peter through Dalmatia (2 Tim 4:10) and Italy to Rome, where he left Apostle Peter and continued farther west (A.D. 66) to Spain, as has been assumed from ancient times (Rom 15:24) and as tradition agrees.

There, or after his return to Rome, he was again imprisoned and eventually martyred. There is a tradition that after his return to Rome, he even preached at Nero's court, converting the emperor's favorite concubine. For this he was taken to trial, but by God's mercy he was spared "the mouth of the lion" (2 Tim 4:17), that is, being eaten by lions in the Coliseum, though he remained imprisoned. From these "second bonds," he wrote his second Epistle to Timothy, inviting him to come to Rome for a last meeting, sensing his imminent death. Tradition tells us nothing about whether or not Timothy managed to find his teacher alive, but it does tell us that the second imprisonment was not long in duration. After nine months of imprisonment, he was beheaded, as befitted a Roman citizen, not far from Rome. This was in A.D. 67, in the twelfth year of Nero's reign.

By looking at this summary of Paul's life, we can see that it was divided into two distinct halves. Before his conversion, Saul was a strict Pharisee, a fulfiller of the Law of Moses and the tradition of the fathers, thinking to justify himself with the works of the Law and with a zeal for the faith of his fathers that bordered on fanaticism. After his conversion, he became an apostle of Christ, completely dedicated to spreading the good news of the Gospel, joyful in his calling, but still mindful of his own helplessness in fulfilling this exalted calling without God's grace, which is why he constantly ascribed all of his successes to God. The very act of his conversion is described as exclusively the work of the grace of God.

The entire life of Saul before his conversion was thus a delusion and a sin, leading him not to justification, but to perdition, and only the grace of God saved him from this pernicious delusion. From that moment, St Paul tried only to become worthy of this grace of God and never turned aside from his calling. There was not, and there cannot be, any consideration of his alleged merits. All of it was God's work.

Being the complete reflection of his life, St Paul's teaching, as revealed in his epistles, is founded on this essential thought: "man is justified by faith apart from the deeds of the law" (Rom 3:28). However, this does not mean that St Paul rejected the significance of one's own personal efforts in salvation, that is, good deeds (see Gal 6:4, 1 Tim 2:10, and others). The "deeds of the law" are not "good deeds" in general, but the ritual observances of the Mosaic Law.

One must firmly remember that Apostle Paul had to constantly battle the Judaizing heresy during his ministry. Many Jews, even after their conversion to Christianity, considered it necessary for all Christians to carefully follow the ritual observances of the Law of Moses. They deluded themselves with the proud thought that Christ came to earth only to save the Jews; therefore, the pagans who desired to be saved had to become Jews first, that is, they had to be circumcised and follow the Mosaic Law to the letter. This delusion so significantly hindered the spread of Christianity among the pagans that the apostles were obliged to assemble in A.D. 51 in Jerusalem. This Apostolic Council canceled the requirement for Christians to follow the Law. However, even after this council, many Judaizing Christians continued to firmly hold to their previous views and later separated from the church entirely, creating their own heretical assembly. These heretics, opposing St Paul personally, sowed confusion within the church, always taking advantage of Paul's absence from this or that local church. Therefore, St Paul was forced to constantly underline in his epistles that Christ is the Saviour of all mankind, both the Jews and the Gentiles, and that man is saved not by the fulfillment of the ritual works of the Law, but only through faith in Christ.

Unfortunately, this formulation of St Paul was perverted by Luther and his followers by their insistence that he denied the significance of good works for salvation in general. If this were so, St Paul would not have written the following words in his first Epistle to the Corinthians: "Though I have all faith, so that I could remove mountains, but have not love, I am nothing" (1 Cor 13:2), for love is best expressed by good works.

THE NUMBER OF EPISTLES WRITTEN BY APOSTLE PAUL

The Church considers Paul to have written fourteen epistles, although in ancient times there were some doubts as to Paul's authorship of Hebrews. These epistles are printed in Bibles in the following order:

1. Epistle to the Romans
2. First Epistle to the Corinthians
3. Second Epistle to the Corinthians
4. Epistle to the Galatians
5. Epistle to the Ephesians
6. Epistle to the Philippians
7. Epistle to the Colossians
8. First Epistle to the Thessalonians
9. Second Epistle to the Thessalonians
10. First Epistle to Timothy
11. Second Epistle to Timothy
12. Epistle to Titus
13. Epistle to Philemon
14. Epistle to the Hebrews

The epistles are not arranged in a chronological order. Rather, the epistles are listed in order of importance and length, as well as the comparative importance of the churches and individuals to whom the letters were written. After the epistles to seven local churches, four epistles to three individuals follow, and the Epistle to the Hebrews is placed last because it was the latest to be accepted as canonical. Usually, these epistles are divided into the following categories: (1) those of general Christian content, and (2) the pastoral epistles. To the latter belong the epistles to Timothy and Titus, because in these Paul describes important foundations and rules for proper pastorship.

Some passages in the epistles (such as 1 Cor 5:9 and Col 4:16) give rise to the opinion that Paul had written other epistles that are not extant: another Epistle to the Corinthians and the Epistle to the Laodiceans. However, it is unlikely that these letters were lost, considering the care with which the early Church preserved the writings of all apostles. In any case, the extracanonical texts known under the name of "3 Corinthians" and "Laodiceans" have shown to be much later fabrications. There was also a correspondence with Seneca attributed to Paul, but it is also not considered to be genuine.

THE SIGNIFICANCE OF THE EPISTLES OF APOSTLE PAUL AND THEIR SUBJECT MATTER

The epistles of St Paul have great importance in the New Testament, because in them we find a profound and multifaceted revelation and exegesis of the truths of the Gospel. Acknowledging his favorite topics of discussion—such as the relation of the Old Covenant to the New, the corruption of human nature, and the only possible means of justification before God (by faith in Jesus Christ)—one can safely say that there is no single point in all of Christian dogmatic theology that is not founded on, or at least supported by, the Pauline Epistles. Therefore, no one can call himself a true theologian without assiduously studying these writings.

The greater part of each epistle is built along the same plan. They begin with a greeting to the readers and gratitude to God for His providential action concerning the city or person to whom the epistle is addressed. Then, the epistle in question is usually divided into two parts—dogmatic and then moral instruction. In conclusion, the apostle usually mentions issues pertaining to the community in question, makes recommendations, tells of his personal situation, expresses his good wishes, and sends words of peace and love. His vivid and vibrant language reminds one of the language of the Old Testament prophets and is proof of his profound knowledge of the Holy Scriptures.

CHAPTER 1

The Epistle of the Holy Apostle Paul to the Romans

THE ESTABLISHMENT OF THE ROMAN CHURCH AND ITS DEMOGRAPHICS There is no precise historical record concerning the founding of the Church of Rome, so important in the Church's history. All we can say is based on suppositions, even if they are very likely. Apostle Paul himself wrote in his Epistle to the Romans that among the Roman Christians some believed in Christ even before he did (i.e., Andronicus and Junia) and that the faith of the Roman Christians was well known throughout the world (Rom 1:8). In the *Recognitions of Clement*, we find that even during the Lord Jesus Christ's earthly life, news of Him reached the Romans and inspired not only wonder but faith as well. This is not so incredible, especially if we remember that from the time of Judea's subjugation by Pompey (63 B.C.), many Jews began to move to Rome, and later they had their own personal quarter in the city. They traveled to Jerusalem for the feasts as was required, and so they could have easily spread word of all they saw to Rome.

On the day of the Descent of the Holy Spirit, as St Luke witnesses in the Book of Acts, Roman Jews were present in the crowd that saw the miracle (Acts 2:10). Among these Romans, some could have believed and been baptized, and these could have then become the establishers of the first Roman community. The question then arises: to which apostle can the Church of Rome's establishment be attributed? The tradition of the Roman Church tells of Peter's arrival in Rome in A.D. 43 after his miraculous deliverance from prison, and his subsequent residence as bishop of Rome for the next twenty-five years until his martyrdom in A.D. 67. However, this tradition does not agree with other historical facts. There can be no doubt that Peter was not in Rome during the time that Paul was imprisoned there and wrote some of his epistles. If St Peter was bishop of Rome during that time, would St Paul have dared instruct a flock that was not his own when he wrote his Epistle to the Romans? And if he did consider it necessary to write to the Romans under Peter's episcopate, Paul would have at least referred to St Peter as the bishop of Rome.

Moreover, St Paul said concerning himself that he did not have the custom to "build on another man's foundation" (Rom 15:20) or "to boast in another man's sphere of accomplishment" (2 Cor 10:16). St Paul would not have had such a fervent desire to preach in Rome if St Peter was already there. Consequently, St Peter was not in Rome until the end of Paul's first imprisonment. It cannot be that St Luke, who wrote of Paul's arrival in Rome in Acts, would not have mentioned that Apostle Peter was in Rome at the same time. Thus, there can only be one conclusion: St Peter only resided in Rome after St Paul's first imprisonment, that is, not long before his own martyrdom.

Who then was the founder of the Church of Rome?

We must assume that the Roman community was established by the disciples of St Paul. In the end of the Epistle to the Romans, St Paul greets a long series of people who were close and well-known to him. Who were these people, and how could Paul—he had yet to visit Rome—know them so well? Doubtless all of them were Jews exiled from Rome by Claudius and dispersed throughout Greece, Macedonia, and Asia Minor, where they would have had ample opportunity to become acquainted with Paul. Some of these people were converted by him, others became his fellow laborers in the faith. After Claudius's death, they returned to Rome and became the spiritual founders of the Christian community in Rome. This also explains why Paul had such an ardent desire to travel to Rome to harvest the fruits of his disciples' sowing.

The tradition that the Church of Rome was established by Peter can be explained thus: the first believers in Rome were among those converted on the day of Pentecost, having heard Peter's fiery words. They naturally considered Peter to be their spiritual father. Added to this is the fact that St Peter was martyred in Rome.

The members of the Roman community were initially Jews for the most part, but later many pagans joined and became the majority. This is obvious from reading the Epistle to the Romans. The Roman pagans, disillusioned by the superstitious nature of their former faith, often became proselytes after coming into contact with Judaism, and this ameliorated their conversion to Christianity, because it satisfied their spirit more than Judaism. The Roman philosopher Seneca was reputed to have said that the defeated gave the law of faith to the conquerors, and Juvenal mocked the Roman proselytes, especially Gentile women who converted to Judaism. According to Suetonius, the Jews were exiled from Rome by Claudius because of disturbances caused by Jews who were antagonistic to Christians. The Gentile converts to Christianity were unaffected, because the persecution concerned only the Jews and not for their faith, but for disturbing the peace.

Thus, this community of former Gentiles began to grow and develop independently of the exiled Jewish Christians. When the Jewish Christians returned to Rome, they easily mingled with the former pagans, creating a single unit by firmly separating themselves from Judaism. This separation of the Roman community from any Judaizing tendency was vividly evident when Paul arrived in Rome, because the faithful came out to meet him many miles outside Rome on the Appian Way, whereas the Jews of Rome did not come to Paul until he invited them to visit himself.

THE PURPOSE OF THE EPISTLE TO THE ROMANS

There is no reason to believe, based on the epistle, that the Romans gave Paul any specific reason to write to them. The epistle has a general nature and indicates no specific aspects of the Roman community's everyday life. It is not true that some division or argument in the community was the reason for Paul's epistle (some cite Rom 16:17 as proof), for even this reference is a general one, as are all of Paul's exhortations to the Romans.

The purpose for writing to the Romans was simply Paul's own desire. Ever since he had heard of the conversion of the Romans, he had cherished a long-lived desire to visit them and to make sure that everything was as it should be in the life of the community. After all, he was the "apostle to the nations," and it was natural for him to care for the success of the Christian mission in the cultural capital of the civilized world. Because he planned to visit them, he sent the letter ahead of him to prepare the local community for his arrival. In his letter, he gave a summary of Christian teaching in general and warned the Romans against the infection of Judaizing tendencies.

The most immediate reason for writing this epistle was the intended trip, from Corinth to Rome, of a certain respected deaconess of the Church in Cenchrea named Phoebe. This deaconess did substantial work to spread the faith of Christ and was a personal helper of Apostle Paul (Rom 16:1–2). She had some business in Rome, and St Paul, knowing her merits, considered it his duty to recommend her to the Roman Christians.

THE PLACE AND TIME OF THE WRITING OF THE EPISTLE

Based on the letter itself, we can exactly determine that it was written in Corinth. This is obvious from St Paul's words that he greets the Romans on behalf of Gaius (with whom he then lived) and Erastus, the treasurer of the city (Rom 16:23). From other epistles (1 Cor 1:14, 2 Tim 4:20), we know that Gaius and Erastus resided in Corinth. The same is true of Phoebe, who carried the letter to Rome. She was a deaconess in Cenchrea, which was the name of Corinth's Aegean harbor.

St Paul was in Corinth several times, and so a question arises: which visit coincided with the writing of Romans? The letter itself gives the answer. The apostle told the Romans that he planned to travel to Jerusalem with aid collected in

Macedonia and Achaia, and from Jerusalem he intended to continue to Rome and then to Spain (Rom 15:25-28). Comparing these words with Acts (19:21, 20:3), we can determine that the Epistle to the Romans was written during the third missionary journey, when St Paul spent three months in Greece, that is, in the spring of A.D. 59.

THE AUTHENTICITY OF THE EPISTLE

Even the most scrupulous criticism could not cast doubt on the authenticity of this letter. St Clement of Rome, St Polycarp of Smyrna, St Irenaeus of Lyons, Tertullian, Clement of Alexandria, and all later writers and even heresiarchs knew of this epistle and cited it. Only Marcion rejected the last two chapters, beginning with verse 24 of chapter 14. More recent criticism has followed Marcion in this, considering these sections to be later additions. However, Origen condemns Marcion for his incorrect view on the subject, and the existence of these two chapters in the most ancient of manuscripts, as well as their content itself (which in no way contradicts the spirit, teaching, and circumstances of St Paul's life) are enough proof of the indubitable authenticity of the letter as a whole.

THE STRUCTURE AND CONTENT OF THE EPISTLE

The epistle has sixteen chapters. The major theme is that salvation is only possible—both for the Jew and the pagan—in the Lord Jesus Christ. The majority of the letter (eleven chapters) is dedicated to this theme. Added to this (from 12:1 to 15:12) is general moral instruction concerning the Christian life. The epistle begins with the usual introduction, including a general greeting, and it ends with an epilogue and personal greetings to various individuals.

EXEGETICAL ANALYSIS OF THE EPISTLE TO THE ROMANS

The Epistle to the Romans begins with a general greeting: "Paul, a bondservant of Jesus Christ, called to be an apostle, separated to the gospel of God" (1:1). Calling himself humbly a slave of Christ, St Paul indicates that he takes the Romans into his personal care, based on his apostolic calling by the Lord Jesus Christ Himself, who committed Paul to preach "to the faith among all nations for His name" (1:5), including the Romans themselves. Then the apostle wishes them the customary "grace … and peace" (1:7).

Then, as incitement to enter communion with the Romans, St Paul indicates that "your faith is spoken of throughout the whole world" (1:8), that is, it would be especially pleasant for the apostle to meet such worthy followers of Christ and to raise their faith to an even higher level: "that I may impart to you some spiritual gift" (1:11) and "that I may be encouraged together with you by the mutual faith both of you and me" (1:12). The apostle says that he intended several times to visit them, but was every time hindered. This obstacle was his desire for the faith of Christ to succeed in all places where he had already established communities.

From verse 16, the dogmatic part of the letter begins, in which the apostle proves that before God all are sinful and without excuse (both pagans and Jews) and that only living faith in the Lord Jesus Christ has the capacity to save anyone: "the just shall live by his faith" (Hab 2:4). First of all, the apostle speaks of the sins of the pagans, who did not care to come to know the true God through His natural revelation: "For since the creation of the world His invisible attributes are clearly seen, being understood by the things that are made, even His eternal power and Godhead, so that they are without excuse" (Rom 1:20). The result of this ignorance of the true God led many to idolatry, and the worship of idols led to all manner of lewdness and an immoral, lustful manner of life.

In the second chapter, the holy apostle turns his attention to the Jews. He says that along with the pagans, they are marked for God's judgment, for although they had the revealed Law, they were at times no better than the pagans. While they judged the pagans for their iniquity, they did the same. However, the first sixteen verses of this chapter, as St Theophan the Recluse notes (based on the exegesis of St John Chrysostom), refer not only to the Jews but to mankind in general, to anyone who, while judging others, himself does not abstain from sinning. This is especially true of those in power, rulers of nations, and those with the authority to judge others. Such people must know that "there is no partiality with God" (2:11), and every sinner, no matter who he may be, will be punished justly. Note here that the pagans, who did not have God's revealed Law, will be judged by God according to the law of their conscience, written on their hearts:

> For when Gentiles, who do not have the law, by nature do the things in the law, these, although not having the law, are a law to themselves, who show the work of the law written in their hearts, their conscience also bearing witness, and between themselves their thoughts accusing or else excusing them in the day when God will judge the secrets of men by Jesus Christ. (2:14–16)

From verse 17 to 29, the apostle speaks exclusively of the Jews, that they trust in vain in their circumcision and in the Law, for their circumcision and the Law of God will serve for their greater condemnation if they who boast in the Law dishonor God by their disregard of the Law.

In the third chapter, the holy apostle shows that the Jews have no advantage over the pagans, "for we have previously charged both Jews and Greeks that they are all under sin" (3:9) and "for all have sinned and fall short of the glory of God" (3:23). Therefore, man can receive justification only by faith, "by His grace through the redemption that is in Christ Jesus" (3:24). Nevertheless, the Jews still have some advantage, for "to them were committed the oracles of God" (3:2), containing the most exalted promises for the coming of the Messiah. Despite the Jews' unfaithfulness in keeping this great gift of God, God by His nature will always fulfill His promises. The Law, given to the Jews, makes their responsibility and culpability all the more grievous. And since God is not only the God of the Jews, but of the pagans as well, then there is one common path to salvation for both—by faith. This does not destroy the importance of the Law, but rather confirms it, for the grace of God gave people the opportunity to fulfill the requirements of the Law.

In the fourth chapter, the apostle remembers the Old Testament saints, Abraham and David, showing through them that it is not merely the formal fulfillment of the Law's tenets that gives man justification before God, but faith in God's omnipotent grace, given to man by the mercy of God: "Abraham believed God, and it was accounted to him for righteousness" (4:3).

In the fifth chapter, the apostle describes the foundational truth of the Christian faith concerning sin and salvation. Since from Adam, the natural head of all mankind, sin spread to all of mankind—"just as through one man sin entered the world, and death through sin, and thus death spread to all men, because all sinned" (5:12)—so also Christ, the new spiritual head of all mankind, by His redemptive passion gives salvation to all mankind. Chapter 5, verses 12 to 21, are especially profound in their dogmatic content. The proof of Adam's sin spreading truly to all his descendants is the reality of human mortality, which resulted from Adam's sin, or the so-called ancestral sin. St Paul makes an important point: before Moses there was no Law; consequently, people could not be held accountable for their sins, for "sin is not imputed when there is no law" (5:13). However, people still died before Moses. Thus, the natural conclusion is that humanity was punished with death not for its own sins, but for the ancestral sin, which passed onto it from the forefather Adam.

When the Law was given, and the people did not cease to sin, their culpability before God became even greater (5:20). When sin thus multiplied, grace was also given in abundance through the redemptive suffering of Christ: "But where sin abounded, grace abounded much more" (5:20). Here the word "where" is better translated as "from the moment that" or "when." Christ's redemptive suffering not only washed away the ancestral sin of Adam, but the personal sins of all mankind (5:16).

In the sixth chapter, Paul anticipates an incorrect interpretation of his own words. If it was the increase of sinfulness that caused the abundance of grace, should it not be better to remain sinful, so that the mercy of God will flow more abundantly? Paul immediately insists that Christians must lead a holy and virtuous life. From the moment of baptism, a Christian dies to sin and is reborn for a new, holy life, just as Christ our Saviour, having suffered and died on the Cross, rose from the dead and lives eternally "to God. Likewise you also, reckon yourselves to be dead indeed to sin, but alive to God in Christ Jesus our Lord" (6:10–11).

This section of Romans (6:3–11) is read at the Divine Liturgy on Great and Holy Saturday, when we remember the death and burial of Christ, and His presence in the tomb. "Our old man" must be crucified with Christ, "that the body of sin might be done away with, that we should no longer be slaves of sin" (6:6). Deliverance from slavery to sin makes a Christian truly free. If a Christian can even be called a slave, he is a slave to righteousness.

However, this slavery to righteousness is only an appearance of slavery. It only appears as slavery to the weak, who have not yet fully been freed from slavery to sin, because in the beginning of service to righteousness, one must force oneself to battle against sinful inclinations. But the fruit of this slavery to righteousness is holiness and eternal life, while the consequence of slavery to sin is death. "What fruit did you have then in the things of which you are now ashamed? For the end of those things is death" (6:21).

In the seventh chapter, the apostle explains that because a Christian is freed from slavery to sin, he is free also of the requirement to follow the Law of Moses. "The Law has dominion over a man as long as he lives" (7:1). Thus, the death of a husband frees a wife from the lawful duties of marriage, and she can marry another. "Therefore, my brethren, you also have become dead to the law through the body of Christ, that you may be married to another—to Him who was raised from the dead, that we should bear fruit to God" (7:4). The Law of Moses had its temporary significance: to reveal the full power of sin and to bring man to the thought that salvation is impossible without God's extraordinary, gracious help. The Law merely uncovered the sores of sin, but it did not give healing. It gave man only the bitter knowledge of his powerlessness to accomplish all the ritual requirements of the Law and to receive justification before God through it.

Thus, now we Christians "have been delivered from the law ... so that we should serve in the newness of the Spirit and not in the oldness of the letter" (7:6), that is, the external and formal requirements of the Law of Moses. Again, Paul immediately anticipates another false conclusion, as though the Law itself were the source of sin, and if there were no Law, there would be no sin. No, the source of sin is within man himself. The Law, taken in itself, is holy; its commandments are holy, fair, and directed to the good. The Law only reveals sin that is rooted deeply within human nature, perverted by ancestral sin.

In the second half of chapter 7 (verses 13–25), the apostle explicates the seeming irregularity in the seeming increase of sinfulness after the institution of the Law of Moses. Consequently, an extraordinary deliverance of grace was needed to save mankind: the redemptive sacrifice of the only begotten Son of God. This is one of several places in the New Testament where the perversion of the moral nature of man is painted in profoundly stark colors: "For what I will to do, that I do not practice; but what I hate, that I do" (7:15). Man is not capable of battling the sin nesting within him with his own strength, without the grace of God: "For the good that I will to do, I do not do; but the evil I will not to do, that I practice. Now if I do what I will not to do, it is no longer I who do it, but sin that dwells in me" (7:19–20).

Thus, the apostle vividly describes the cleavage that sin causes in our very nature. "For I delight in the law of God according to the inward man. But I see another law in my members, warring against the law of my mind, and bringing me into captivity to the law of sin which is in my members. O wretched man that I am! Who will deliver me from this body of death?" (7:22–24). Having described this dark reality of man's slavery to sin, St Paul then reveals the all-powerful help of our Redeemer: "I thank God—through Jesus Christ our Lord!" (7:25). The Lord Redeemer, in spite of our accursedness, can make us victors over the sin living within us. The next chapter speaks of this in more detail.

Having described the power of sin and the greatness of the redemptive sacrifice of Christ the Saviour Who freed us from the authority of sin and gave us the possibility of living by the spirit, not the flesh, St Paul (in the eighth chapter) exhorts us to battle sin, for we can no longer excuse our avoidance of this struggle. With us is the omnipotent Spirit of Christ, Who helps us live by the spirit, not by the flesh, and "if anyone does not have the Spirit of Christ, he is not His" (8:9). Led by the Spirit of God, we are the children of God (8:14–16), and "if children, then heirs—heirs of God and joint heirs with Christ, if indeed we suffer with Him, that we may also be glorified together" (8:17).

The striving to live a spiritual life of struggle with sin is fraught with suffering, but Christians must not fear these sufferings, for they are nothing compared to the glory that awaits us in the future life: "For I consider that the sufferings of this present time are not worthy to be compared with the glory which shall be revealed in us" (8:18). This future glory is awaited by us and all of creation, for even the cosmos will be freed from slavery to the law of death and corruption, which were the consequences, even in the world of nature, of man's fall into sin. The Holy Spirit aids our struggle against sin, for He "also helps us in our weaknesses. For we do not know what we should pray for as we ought, but the Spirit Himself makes intercession for us with groanings which cannot be uttered" (8:26). God's pre-eternal predestination for salvation, and our hope in this salvation, also support us in this struggle: "For whom He foreknew, He also predestined to be conformed to the image of His Son, that He might be the firstborn among many brethren. Moreover whom He predestined, these He also called; whom He called, these He also justified; and whom He justified, these He also glorified" (8:29–30).

To correctly understand what St Paul means by "divine predestination," we must keep in mind that the apostle speaks not of "unconditional election" (as the Calvinists teach), but of predestination that is founded on God's foreknowledge. This does not mean that God, in spite of man's free will, chooses some to be saved, while others he consigns to suffer eternally. No, rather God, as the Omniscient One, knows which people will use their free will for good, and who will choose evil. Depending on this knowledge, God predestines the eternal fate of each.

In conclusion, St Paul exhorts all to be firm in their faith in salvation: "Who shall separate us from the love of Christ?" (8:35). He triumphantly confesses his own love and faithfulness to Christ the Saviour, calling all faithful to do the same.

In the next three chapters (9–11), Apostle Paul expresses his great sorrow and "continual grief in [his] heart" (9:2) at the stubborn unbelief of the Jews in Christ the Saviour, and at their rejection by God from the Church of Christ. He then proves that Israel is guilty of its own rejection, because it sought justification not in faith in the Messiah, but in the fulfillment of the external ritual aspects of the Law of Moses. In addition, Paul expresses his conviction that this rejection does not extend to all Jews, because there are believers among them—"there is a remnant" (11:5)—and he is sure that this rejection will not be eternal for the chosen nation. In the proper time, the Jews will convert *en masse* to Christ and will enter His Church. In this temporary rejection of the Jews, completely deserved by them, the holy apostle sees a special revelation of God's wisdom concerning the salvation of all mankind. The fanaticism of the Jews, who stubbornly refused to believe in Christ as the Messiah, forced Paul himself to turn his preaching to the Gentiles. Thus, the hardness of the hearts of the Jews had as its consequence the conversion to Christ of the entire pagan world.

The success of the mission among the pagans and those spiritual gifts that they received will eventually inspire the Jews to convert, and "all Israel will be saved" (11:26). Therefore, Paul exhorts the believers among the pagans not to boast of their salvation before the Jews. Comparing the Jewish people with a domesticated olive tree whose branches had been broken off (by unbelief), he still insists that the root is whole and holy. Paul compares the Gentiles to a wild olive tree that has been grafted to the trunk of the living domesticated tree: "if ... you, being a wild olive tree, were grafted in among them, and with them became a partaker of the root and fatness of the olive tree, do not boast against the branches. But if you do boast, remember that you do not support the root, but the root supports you" (11:17–18).

Moreover, the fallen branches can also be grafted back to the tree, for "God is able to graft them in again. For if you were cut out of the olive tree which is wild by nature, and were grafted contrary to nature into a cultivated olive tree, how much more will these, who are natural branches, be grafted into their own olive tree?" (11:23–24).

The greatness of God's providence, wisely leading all nations to salvation by invisibly guiding their historical destinies, inspires Paul's exalted exclamation: "Oh, the depth of the riches both of the wisdom and knowledge of God! How unsearchable are His judgments and His ways past finding out! For who has known the mind of the Lord? ... to Whom be glory forever. Amen" (11:33–36). This concludes the dogmatic part of the Epistle to the Romans.

Chapters 12, 13, 14, and 15 (until verse 13) consist of moral instruction. The holy apostle delineates the ideal Christian moral life. In chapter 12, he speaks of the duties required of every Christian as a member of the Church, with reference to God (12:1–2) and one's fellow man (12:3–5). Then he describes the many different supernatural gifts, callings, and dispositions of a Christian (12:8–21).

In chapter 13, St Paul speaks of the duties of a Christian as a citizen and member of society. Especially important is his instruction concerning submission to lawful authority: "Let every soul be subject to the governing authorities" (13:1). To properly understand this instruction, we must consider the thought contained in the following verses (13:3–4). Only that authority is "from God," which encourages good and punishes evil. St Isidore of Pelusium (d. c. A.D. 450) reflects on this issue, saying

> thus it is right to say that this matter, by which I mean the authority, that is, the power and the kingship, were established by God, lest the world may fall into disorder. But if some villain lawlessly seizes this authority, we certainly do not say that it was so ordained by God, but rather by God it was allowed (to happen), either so that this man may disgorge his own evil, as the Pharaoh did, and thus to receive the ultimate judgment, or in order to chasten those deserving cruel discipline, as [Nebuchadnezzar] the Babylonian king did to the Jews.[1]

In chapter 14 and in the first thirteen verses of chapter 15, the apostle gives instructions concerning those weak in faith, having in mind certain disagreements that had arisen within the Roman Church. The majority of the Roman Christians from among the Jews boasted in their freedom, so much so that they ate all kinds of food, for the Christian faith does not consider any food to be forbidden, nor does it honor some days over others (14:5). However, some Christians from among the Jews continued to consider certain foods to be unclean and were afraid of defiling themselves by eating them; similarly, they considered the celebration of some Old Testament holidays to be compulsory for all. Paul exhorts the Roman Christians to stop arguing about these things, because they must have compassion for those who are still weak in faith. Personal opinions and convictions must be left to the conscience of every person. The most important thing is not to judge or rebuke each other or to become a temptation for anyone else. Everything is pure for a Christian, yes, but if your brother is tempted by your behavior, it is better to abstain from meat and wine entirely, lest your brother be tempted (14:1–21).

The passages 13:12–14 and 14:1–4 are read during the liturgy of Cheesefare Week, before the beginning of Lent, because it gives us a clear indication of the correct disposition every Christian must have during the days of compulsory fasting.

In conclusion to this letter (from 15:14 to chapter 16), St Paul explains his reasons for writing to the Romans, recommending the deaconess of the Church in Cenchrea, Phoebe, to them (she was the one who brought the epistle to the Roman Christians). Then he gives a series of personal greetings to Christians living in Rome with whom he is already acquainted.

CHAPTER 2

The First Epistle of the Holy Apostle Paul to the Corinthians

THE ESTABLISHMENT OF THE CHURCH IN CORINTH

Corinth lies on the isthmus connecting Greece with the Peloponnesus. It was built more than 1,500 years before the birth of Christ. IN 44 B.C., Julius Caesar had it rebuilt, and it became the first city of the Roman province of Achaia, the residence of the proconsul. It became known for its achievements in science, the fine arts, and for its "party atmosphere," which attracted many people to move there. It was also known for the Isthmian Games and its temple to Aphrodite. One can easily say that during the time of the apostolic preaching, Corinth was the very center of Greek frivolity, levity, and sensuality.

The Church in Corinth was established by Apostle Paul during his second missionary journey (c. A.D. 53), after he had preached in Philippi, Thessalonica, Berea, and Athens. After leaving his disciples Silas and Timothy in Macedonia to help strengthen the faithful, St Paul traveled to Greece, and he arrived in Corinth after a short stay in Athens (Acts 18:11). In Corinth, the holy apostle met the kind and hospitable Aquila and Priscilla, Jews from Pontus who had formerly lived in Rome but had moved to Corinth after Claudius's expulsion of all Jews from Rome. Aquila was a maker of tents by trade, and because Paul also practiced this trade, he moved in with them. If Aquila and Priscilla were not initially Christians, we can assume that they soon were converted by Paul, were baptized, and became helpers in his mission.

Every Sabbath day, Paul preached in the local synagogue, arguing that there was no other salvation outside of the Lord Jesus Christ. When Silas and Timothy arrived from Macedonia, St Paul had an opportunity to strengthen and widen his missionary activity, and he began to teach not only on Sabbath days, but on other days of the week as well. However, the mission among the Jews was of limited success. The Jews opposed Paul, mocking him and the path of the Lord. Then St Paul left the synagogue with an instructive action and word for the Jews. He shook the dust off his clothes, and said, "Your blood be upon your own heads; I am clean. From now on I will go to the Gentiles" (Acts 18:6).

The meaning of these words is that the Jews were responsible for their own spiritual perdition, for Paul showed them the path to salvation, but they refused to accept his words. All subsequent Christian assemblies were held not far from the synagogue, in the house of a certain Justus, who honored God. Pagans gathered here as well, and the mission began to have more success; many believed and were baptized. Among those who believed was the leader of the synagogue, a certain Crispus, with his entire house. However, the overall success of the Corinthian mission was not great, and Paul was ready to abandon corrupt Corinth entirely, especially because some were plotting to kill him (2 Thess 3:2). The Lord Himself appeared to Paul and encouraged him to continue his service in Corinth (Acts 18:9–10). Strengthened by the vision of the Lord, Paul remained in Corinth for a year and a half, and during this time, his preaching began to bring great fruits, so that the Church in Corinth became famous and well known for its abundance of spiritual gifts (1 Cor 1:5–7).

Once the Church in Corinth was firmly established, St Paul had to continue his travels. His leaving Corinth was precipitated also by a tragic event. Irritated by Paul's successful mission, the Jews seized him and brought him before the judgment of the proconsul, Gallio, with a complaint that he "persuades men to worship God contrary to the law" (Acts 18:13). The essence of the accusation was that Paul had founded some new sect that was not legally sanctioned by the Roman authority. Gallio was the brother of the famous Roman philosopher Seneca and the uncle of the poet Lucan, an educated and noble man. He refused to hear the case against Paul, because it had nothing to do with his competency as governor, and he threw the Jews out of the judgment seat. The Greeks, who despised the Jews, took advantage of Gallio's decision to attack the Jews, and they took the leader of the insurrection—the new ruler of the synagogue, named Sosthenes—and "beat him before the judgment seat. But Gallio took no notice of these things" (Acts 18:17). It is possible that this Sosthenes later converted to Christ, and if so, it is this Sosthenes who Paul mentions in 1 Corinthians 1:1.

Doubtless by a special providence of God, the man most responsible for continuing Paul's work in Corinth was a certain Jew named Apollos. He was born and raised in Alexandria, from where he traveled first to Ephesus, and then to Corinth. According to St Luke, he was a man of special eloquence and knowledge of the Scriptures (Acts 18:24). After leaving Corinth, St Paul spent some time in Ephesus, where he left Aquila and Priscilla, and then traveled to Jerusalem and Antioch, from where he began his third missionary journey. After Paul left Ephesus,

Apollos arrived, already a baptized Christian with an ardent spirit, although he had only the baptism of John. Immediately, he began to preach boldly in the synagogue in Ephesus. "When Aquila and Priscilla heard him, they took him aside and explained to him the way of God more accurately" (Acts 18:26). When Apollos had to travel to Greece, the Ephesian Christians gave him a letter of recommendation to present to the local community. Having arrived in Corinth, Apollos helped the local community greatly, openly opposing the Jews and "showing from the Scriptures that Jesus is the Christ" (Acts 18:28).

The significance of Apollos's preaching for the confirmation of Christianity in Corinth was so great that Paul called him the gardener of his own seeds of Christ's faith: "I planted, Apollos watered, but God gave the increase" (1 Cor 3:6). It is unclear how long Apollos remained in Corinth, but when Paul wrote the first Epistle to the Corinthians, Apollos was together with Paul in Ephesus (1 Cor 16:12).

THE PURPOSE OF THE FIRST EPISTLE TO THE CORINTHIANS

While Apollos was preaching in Corinth, St Paul, having visited Jerusalem for the Passover, began his third missionary journey from Antioch and "went over the region of Galatia and Phrygia in order" (Acts 18:23), and then arrived in Ephesus (19:1). In Ephesus, he began to hear various troubling rumors concerning the Corinthian church. He wanted to go himself to Corinth from Ephesus by sea (2 Cor 1:15–16), but he decided to remain in Ephesus and sent Timothy to Corinth in his stead, telling him to travel through Macedonia and pay attention to everything that was occurring in Corinth. In the meantime, the rumors continued and increased. Apparently, one of the Corinthian Christians had allowed himself to sin in a way that was shameful even for the pagans (1 Cor 5:1).

Finally, the members of the household of a certain Christian woman named Chloe came to Ephesus and confirmed the rumors, informing Paul of many disorders in the community in Corinth. What especially grieved Paul was their report concerning religious arguments (1 Cor 1:11–12). It seemed that a schism was brewing in Corinth. The arrival of Stephanas, Fortunatus, and Achaicus from Corinth calmed Paul a little, but they still confirmed many of the rumors. They also informed Paul of other problems: Christians suing each other in civil court, disorder during the agape meals, women refusing to cover their heads during worship, and even the unbelief of some in the resurrection of the dead. Paul was also brought specific questions from the community in the form of a letter—questions concerning marriage and virginity, eating food offered to idols, the gift of tongues, and others. As a result, Paul decided to send his first epistle to the Corinthian Church to help heal all the wounds in the community and to answer all their questions. He also promised to visit them himself (1 Cor 4:19–21).

Another reason for writing this epistle, as seen in 16:1–4, was Paul's desire to gather aid for Palestinian communities.

The Place and Time of the Writing of the Epistle

As we see from the letter itself, it was written in Ephesus: "I hope to stay a while with you, if the Lord permits. But I will tarry in Ephesus until Pentecost" (1 Cor 16:7–8). In the letter, St Paul wrote that he sent Timothy to Corinth (1 Cor 16:10), and in Acts, we find that he sent Timothy from Ephesus before he himself had decided to leave Ephesus (Acts 19:21–22). This was around A.D. 58 or 59.

The Structure and Content of the Epistle

The content is varied, as dictated by the needs of the community, which were many. The letter refers to many issues, giving complete answers to the questions asked by the Corinthians themselves. The letter has sixteen chapters. As with Romans, it begins with a general introduction and ends with greetings to specific individuals.

Exegetical Analysis of the First Epistle to the Corinthians

This letter differs from St Paul's other epistles in the extraordinary variety of issues that he examines. It differs from Romans specifically because it does not deal with the Judaizers, but rather with problems arising from the Greek cultural milieu, that is, Hellenism, with its typical sensuality and its tendency to lean on philosophy. This letter is remarkable in its tendency to deeply delve into the spiritual and moral aspects of life.

The letter begins with the usual introduction and greeting. St Paul includes a greeting from himself and from "Sosthenes, our brother." Blessed Theodoret[2] and St Dimitry of Rostov[3] believe that this Sosthenes was the same ruler of the synagogue in Corinth who was beaten after bringing an unsuccessful petition to the local governor to have Paul imprisoned and judged as a criminal (Acts 18). St Theophan the Recluse is of the same opinion, adding also that the beating he received probably had something to do with his conversion.[4]

The rest of the epistle can be divided into two parts. The first part includes the first six chapters and consists primarily of rebukes. The second part (chapters 7–15) is filled with moral instructions, and chapter 16 is the conclusion, in which the holy apostle speaks of his desire to gather financial aid for the Church in Palestine and his travels on the way to Corinth. Paul also uses this last chapter to pass on personal greetings.

In the first four chapters, Paul accuses the Corinthians of fomenting internal dissent within the community. At first, he praises their faith, expressing his conviction that the Lord will confirm them in their faith "to the end, that you may be blameless in the day of our Lord Jesus Christ" (1:8). From 1:10 onward, he begins his invective. After St Paul left Corinth, his preaching was continued by Apollos; more Christians who knew Paul personally began to move to Corinth, as well as some Palestinian Christians who had heard Christ speak. Inclined to divide along party lines, and evidently keeping to a pagan understanding of the teachers of Christianity being something like philosophers, each of whom established his own school, the Corinthians began to divide into factions, each named after one of the famous preachers of the Gospel: "Now I say this, that each of you says, 'I am of Paul,' or 'I am of Apollos,' or 'I am of Cephas,' or 'I am of Christ'" (1:12).

Initially, of course, the source of this division was a positive attachment to one or another preacher, but subsequently, this division could have led to dangerous consequences for the purity of the faith itself. In a moral sense, this division had led already to many negative phenomena within the Corinthian Christian community, all of which Paul proceeds to attack in his letter. Because this division became the inciting moment for the subsequent moral laxity and inner disorder of the community, the apostle spends nearly four chapters attacking it with exceptional energy and power.

Because the leaders of each faction, following the example of pagan philosophers, influenced the people with their oratory and philosophical reasoning, Paul uses the first chapter to characterize the qualities of true evangelical preaching, as compared with earthly wisdom or philosophy. The preaching of the Cross seems too simple or even foolish to the pagans, who are proud of their education, whereas for those who have believed, the word of the Cross is the power of God that gives salvation. Philosophy—which is cut off from the source of wisdom, God—found itself powerless to order human life, but the preaching of the Gospel, which seems to be madness to those who do not believe, gives people truly everything that is necessary both for earthly life and for eternal salvation. "For Jews request a sign, and Greeks seek after wisdom; but we preach Christ crucified, to the Jews a stumbling block and to the Greeks foolishness, but to those who are called, both Jews and Greeks, Christ the power of God and the wisdom of God" (1:22–24).

It is important to note that "the wisdom of God" (i.e., "Sophia"), in agreement with many other places of the Holy Scriptures, refers to none other than Christ, the Second Person of the Holy Trinity. Then Paul says, "the foolishness of God is wiser than men, and the weakness of God is stronger than men," because "God has chosen the foolish things of the world to put to shame the wise, and God has chosen the weak things of the world to put to shame the things which are mighty" (1:25, 27). This was vividly evident in the poor, ignorant, and illiterate fishermen (as were the apostles and many of the first Christians, who were mostly of low social standing and little education) who shamed all the pagan wisdom of the learned and the philosophers with the power of their faith and preaching, and who brought the whole world to the feet of the Cross of Christ.

"The God of all," says Blessed Theodoret, "by the unlearned conquered the learned, by the poor he conquered the rich, and caught the world with the fishermen's net."[5] Why was this necessary? "That no flesh should glory in His presence" (1:29). So that every pride and arrogance should be humbled, to show that we cannot save ourselves, because Christianity is the path of salvation through humility.

The preaching of the Gospel is simple, foreign to the delusion of purely external, flowery beauty of speech and the external wisdom of pagan philosophers. Instead, it is strong only because of the truth contained within it. To prove this, the holy apostle recalls in the second chapter how he came to Corinth in humble fashion, with a simple word about the Crucified One, so that the believers would not depend on human wisdom, but only on God: "And my speech and my preaching were not with persuasive words of human wisdom, but in demonstration of the Spirit and of power" (2:4), so that their faith would not be founded on philosophical reason, but "in the power of God" (2:5).

For those more firm in the faith, the knowledge of the true wisdom of God is revealed gradually. This wisdom surpasses all human knowledge and is inconceivable to the wise of this world. "But we speak the wisdom of God in a mystery, the hidden wisdom which God ordained before the ages for our glory" (2:7). This is the image of the founding of our salvation in the Lord Jesus Christ, from its source to all its wondrous ends in all aspects of created existence. "Eye has not seen, nor ear heard, nor have entered into the heart of man the things which God has prepared for those who love Him" (2:9).

And for us, true Christians, God revealed all this by His Spirit, for the Spirit "searches all things, yes, the deep things of God" (2:10). Preaching this supremely wise mystery of the salvation of mankind, the apostles had the "mind of Christ," and so only spiritual people could accept their teaching in its fullness. By spiritual, Paul means those who are established in a spiritual and moral life, who have been reborn spiritually, and who accept the truth not only with their minds, but also with their hearts and wills, that is, in the full manifestation of their powers and capabilities. "The natural man," that is, the one who has yet to purify his soul of all passionate attachments, who does not live by the Spirit, but through the lower aspects of the soul, "does not receive the things of the Spirit of God, for they are foolishness to him; nor can he know them, because they are spiritually discerned" (2:14).

The third chapter gives us reason to assume that in Paul's absence from Corinth, his adversaries tried to turn the Christians against him by disparaging his teaching. Apparently, they argued that other preachers of the Gospel, such as Apostle Peter and Apollos, spoke more profoundly and revealed the truths of Christ's faith more eloquently. And so, Paul counters, "I, brethren, could not speak to you as to spiritual people but as to carnal, as to babes in Christ. I fed you with milk and not with solid food; for until now you were not able to receive it, and even now you are still not able; for you are still carnal" (3:1–3). As proof of this, Paul reminds them of the "envy, strife, and divisions among you" (3:3), because of the different factions in Corinth.

St Paul then explains the proper way of looking at the apostles. The apostles are merely the slaves of God: "ministers through whom you believed," while the foundation of salvation lies in Jesus Christ Himself, for "no other foundation can anyone lay than that which is laid, which is Jesus Christ" (3:11). "I planted, Apollos watered, but God gave the increase. So then neither he who plants is anything, nor he who waters, but God who gives the increase. Now he who plants and he who waters are one, and each one will receive his own reward according to his own labor. For we are God's fellow workers; you are God's field, you are God's build-ing" (3:6–9). The worth of the work of every builder-preacher will be determined at the Final Judgment.

There is only one foundation, Jesus Christ, but on this foundation one can build with materials of different worth and durability—from gold, silver, precious stones (the pure, healthy preaching of the word of God), or from wood, straw, hay (teaching tainted with the reasoning of human wisdom or empty eloquence). On the day of the Final Judgment "the fire will test each one's work, of what sort it is. If anyone's work which he has built on it endures, he will receive a reward. If anyone's work is burned, he will suffer loss, but he himself will be saved, yet so as through fire" (3:13–15).

This passage, according to St Augustine, is one of those that St Peter calls "hard to understand" (2 Pet 3:16).[6] The cryptic nature of these words gave Roman Catholic theologians reason to use this passage as proof for their dogma of purgatory, where the purifying fire allegedly cleanses a sinner after death. However, it would be more correct to see the image used here—a house on fire—as a symbol. St Theophan writes the following:

> There is fire all around, and you must run through it. It will be thus for those whose houses (deeds) will be burned down in the final Judgment. Some will go into the fire, while others will receive other degrees of punishment, while still others will be delivered. For even though all are guilty that they built of materials that were not durable, their guilt will also be of varying degrees. Yet another can be guilty even without fault, for he worked on a house that was not durable because he knew no other manner of building. Or perhaps circumstances prevented him from using bet-ter materials, or perhaps there was another reason that will exonerate him.[7]

Perhaps the flock itself is at fault that it provided the pastor with rotten materi-als. Then the pastor will avoid condemnation after a strict review of his life at the impartial judgment of God (thus, he is saved, "as through fire").

Thus, teachers and preachers must build the Church of Christ with great care and deliberation, remembering that every Christian is the temple of God, because the Spirit of God lives within him, accepted by each person through the sacra-ments. "Do you not know that you are the temple of God and that the Spirit of God dwells in you?" (3:16). Vain human wisdom can destroy this temple, because "the wisdom of this world is foolishness with God" (3:19). "You are Christ's," that is, as soon as you believed in Christ and became members of His Church, you came to belong exclusively to Him, and so is it proper for you to divide into factions because of Paul, Apollos, Cephas, or any other preacher?

In the fourth chapter, the holy apostle shows that by weighing the relative merits of various apostles—becoming, effectively, their judges—the Corinthians revealed their lack of the most important Christian virtue, humility. By being proud of their spiritual discernment, the Corinthians forgot that if they have anything precious, it was given to them by the apostles, who can be judged only by the degree of faithfulness to their calling to preach, not according to some external qualities that depend on natural gifts (such spurious judgment was typical of those who followed various philosophical schools).

To bring the Corinthians to their senses and to inspire in them a proper sense of gratitude to all apostles equally (because all apostles work for their benefit), Paul compares their situation with his own. It is as if he is saying that the Corinthians had barely begun to taste the fruits of faith, and "You are already full! You are already rich! You have reigned as kings without us" (1 Cor 4:8). According to Theodoret of Cyrus, "We are still in peril, we still suffer for our preaching, but you are already enjoying the fruits of the kingdom."[8] You are acting as though the kingdom of glory has already arrived, the crowns have been distributed, and the time for blessed rejoicing has come. But how can this be without us, the apostles? "We labor, we endure all manner of deprivation, but you seem to have already entered the kingdom!"[9]

Then Paul describes in painful detail all the sorrows and deprivations that await true preachers of the Gospel: "For I think that God has displayed us, the apostles, last, as men condemned to death; for we have been made a spectacle to the world, both to angels and to men. We are fools for Christ's sake, but you are wise in Christ! We are weak, but you are strong! You are distinguished, but we are dishonored!" (4:9–10).

Of course, these juxtapositions are meant to be bitterly ironic. St Theophan the Recluse, however, offers a different interpretation: the labors and deprivations of the apostles serve to increase the glory and honor and confirmation of faith for those who have believed in their preaching. St Paul then concludes his accusations with the reassurance that he does "not write these things to shame you, but as my beloved children I warn you. For though you might have ten thousand instructors in Christ, yet you do not have many fathers; for in Christ Jesus I have begotten you through the gospel. Therefore, I urge you, imitate me" (4:14–16).

This is a profoundly important passage! The holy apostle says that even though the Corinthians may have thousands of teachers, they have only a few fathers. He, Paul, gave birth to them through his preaching, that is, he is their *spiritual father*. Apostle Paul calls himself the father of those he converted to Christianity. In the meantime, various Protestants insist that no priest has the right to call himself a "father," incorrectly citing the words of the Lord in Matthew 23:9, which referred only to the apostles.

For the enlightenment of the Corinthians, St Paul sent them his beloved disciple Timothy and promised to soon come in person. Evidently, the adversaries of St Paul were spreading rumors that his four-year absence from Corinth was a result of his fear of encountering his adversaries, who were allegedly more eloquent than he. Apostle Paul promises that when he comes to Corinth he "will know, not the word of those who are puffed up, but the power" (4:19), that is, he will test their lives and deeds, not their empty words (4:17–20).

Chapters 5 and 6 contain denunciations of moral failings of the Corinthians.

All of chapter 5 is a condemnation of a certain immoral member of the community who took to wife "his father's wife," that is, his stepmother. St Paul excoriates the Corinthians for their pride: "you are puffed up, and have not rather mourned" (5:2). In other words, it is useless for the Corinthians to think so highly of themselves if such immorality is possible in their ranks. To avoid further temptation, Paul commands them in no uncertain terms, even before his arrival, to "deliver such a one to Satan for the destruction of the flesh, that his spirit may be saved in the day of the Lord Jesus" (5:5).

This is not merely excommunication from the Church, outside of which is the "realm of Satan," so to speak, but this was a specific punishment, according to St John Chrysostom, similar to what occurred to Job, "but not upon the same ground. For in that case, it was for brighter crowns, but here for loosing of sins, that [Satan] might scourge him with a grievous sore or some other disease."[10]

St Theophan the Recluse adds the following: "Carnal sin is punished in the body, for the weakened flesh will also weaken the bonds of sin and will give the spirit room for repentance."[11]

"Do you not know that a little leaven leavens the whole lump?" (5:6). Such a severe punishment was necessary to prevent the evil example from becoming contagious for others. Christians in general must be the "new lump," in which there can be no trace of the "old leaven," that is, sinful passion. "You truly are unleavened. For indeed Christ, our Passover, was sacrificed for us" (5:7). In other words, just as before the face of the avenging angel in Egypt no leavened bread was allowed in any Israelite house, so now before the face of our Paschal Angel, Christ, there can be nothing sinful or passionate. These two verses, together with chapter 3, verses 13–14, from the Epistle to the Galatians, are the epistle reading on matins of Great and Holy Saturday.

In addition to casting out this one immoral member from the assembly, Paul counsels the Corinthians to avoid keeping company with those who call themselves Christians, but who continue a sinful way of life—"not even to eat with such a person" (5:11). "Put away from yourselves the evil person" is a reference to Deuteronomy 17:7, and thus Paul indicates that the expulsion of a sinner from the community for fear of infection by sin was commanded even in the Old Testament.

The first half of chapter 6 accuses the Corinthians of suing each other in Gentile courts (6:1–8), and the second half contains condemnation of immorality in general and gluttony and lust in particular. St John Chrysostom notes that Paul's command to expel the immoral member of the community inspired him to remind the Christians that all the community's issues must be resolved internally, never allowing the possibility of civil courts before the Gentiles.[12] After this, the apostle again returns to his previous subject—the condemnation of an immoral and carnal lifestyle. "Do you not know that the saints will judge the world?" (6:2). Paul speaks of this as something generally known, that Christians will judge the world, and so it is unworthy of Christians to turn to pagan courts. "Judge" in this sense means "condemn," as it does in these passages from Matthew: "The queen of the South will rise up in the judgment with this generation and condemn it" (Matt 12:42) and "The men of Nineveh will rise up in the judgment with this generation and condemn it" (Matt 12:41). So, too, will the twelve apostles judge the twelve tribes of Israel (Matt 19:28). This means that those who believed and became Christians will serve as a condemnation for those who did not believe.

"Do you not know that we shall judge angels?" (6:3). Of course, Paul means the fallen angels, the demons. Again, "judge" in this context means "condemn." Furthermore, St Paul indicates that any sort of court proceedings is unfit for Christians who are supposed to live as brothers (6:7). Especially culpable are such lawsuits if they are brought with sinful motives, with the intention of dishonoring a brother or of taking away his belongings.

Then Paul begins to condemn different kinds of sins that should never have a place in the Church, as it is the community of saints (6:8–11). Then the apostle again returns to condemnation of sexual immorality. These verses (6:12–20) are read during the Sunday commemorating the Prodigal Son. "All things are lawful for me, but all things are not helpful. All things are lawful for me, but I will not be brought under the power of any" (6:12). Judging by the fact that the next verses have to do with food, verse 6:12 can be assumed to refer primarily to the lack of dietary restrictions in Christianity. There are, however, two restrictions to this freedom granted to a Christian. First, our eating must be based on what is healthy and useful for us. Second, we must never allow ourselves to become dependent on any kind of food, thereby losing true freedom—the freedom from any passionate attachment or sin—in the name of merely delusory freedom.

Thus, a Christian must guard himself from becoming a slave of sensuality, which includes gluttony and sexual immorality. The reason lust is a sin is that it defiles both the soul and the body, and it is in effect sacrilege, for both our soul and body are members of Christ and belong to God alone. Someone who sins carnally destroys his union with God and defiles his body, which is the temple of the Holy Spirit dwelling in us. "Therefore glorify God in your body and in your spirit, which are God's" (6:20).

Chapter 7 is the beginning of the second part of the epistle, containing general instruction in Christian moral life. After condemning carnal sin, St Paul now gives instruction concerning marriage and virginity. The main theme of this section is that virginity is greater than marriage, and so it should be preferred by Christians; however, if anyone feels incapable of leading a strict life of abstinence, it is better for that person to marry than to "burn," that is, belabor his soul with carnal lust and subject himself to the constant danger of sinning. Thus, the first moral purpose of marriage is the avoidance of sexual immorality (7:1–2). A wife and husband belong to each other completely, and do not have authority even over their own selves. This means that abstinence from marital relations is allowed only in cases of mutual agreement (7:3–6). Desiring good for all, St Paul presents his own virginity as the best possible state (7:7–8). However, those who cannot bear such a struggle must enter the marriage state, but should preserve marital fidelity and not divorce, even in cases of infidelity, for the will of the Lord is that everyone should remain in that calling in which he or she was called to Christianity (7:10–24).

"The unbelieving husband is sanctified by the wife, and the unbelieving wife is sanctified by the husband; otherwise your children would be unclean, but now they are holy" (7:14). The meaning of this somewhat-confusing expression is the following: a marriage should not be ended if one of the partners becomes a believer while the other remains a pagan. In other words, according to St Theophan the Recluse, "Your marriage with an unbeliever, O believing wife, will not be considered unlawful cohabitation simply due to your new faith; on the contrary, your new faith has sanctified this marriage, and your husband, in the marital union."[13] Equally, the children from such a marriage should not be somehow considered "impure" in the sense of bastardy.

St Paul's purpose is to prevent the destruction of families, which would be problematic and would have a negative effect on the work of his mission. Conversely, there is always the chance that a believing wife will be the reason her husband converts (7:16).

In chapter 7, verses 25–40, St Paul vividly makes the case for virginity. Virgins are freed from "the present distress," meaning the sorrows and troubles connected with marital life, which are many and varied. The short duration of the earthly life, and the imminence of the second coming, should inspire Christians to such an inner disposition in which "those who have wives should be as though they had none" (7:29). ... "He who is unmarried cares for the things of the Lord—how he may please the Lord. But he who is married cares about the things of the world—how he may please his wife" (7:32–33). Married life has many cares that hinder one from completely pleasing the Lord and even distract from service to God. Therefore, it is better to remain a virgin, although if someone does get married, they have not committed sin (7:35–40).

In chapter 8, the holy apostle gives instruction concerning Christian freedom with reference to food offered to idols. Christian freedom does not mean that one is allowed to do everything one wishes, guided by one's own discernment of the truth, because human reason is fallible. Rather, Christian freedom means limiting oneself for the sake of love. Considering idols to be nothing, the Corinthians freely entered into the pagan temples and participated in the feasts there, eating food offered first to idols. By doing so, they were tempting some of their brethren, who had not yet reached a proper understanding of idols as nothing. According to some of weak faith, eating food offered to idols meant a kind of sacramental union with the idols (this is what Paul means by the phrase "consciousness of the idol" in 8:7). Seeing other Christians eating food offered to idols, these Christians of weak conscience were "defiled."

By itself, "food does not commend us to God; for neither if we eat are we the better, nor if we do not eat are we the worse" (8:8). However, one must not forget that man is not merely an animal, but a reasoning, free creature, and so every action, including eating and drinking, has a moral dimension as well as a merely physiological one. Consequently, it is not always morally neutral to eat or abstain from certain kinds of food, such as that offered to idols, or meat during the fasting periods prescribed by the Church. Therefore, St Paul concludes decisively, "if food makes my brother stumble, I will never again eat meat, lest I make my brother stumble" (8:13).

In chapter 9, the holy apostle continues to expand on the same theme of the wise use of Christian freedom, especially the necessity to limit personal freedom for the sake of higher goals. He speaks of his apostolic right to receive financial support from those whom he converted, basing his proof on the ancient command: "those who minister the holy things eat of the things of the temple, and those who serve at the altar partake of the offerings of the altar" (9:13). However, he willingly rejects this lawful right "lest we hinder the gospel of Christ" (9:12).

Paul had always served everyone without avarice, contenting himself with the condition of those around him and denying himself many essentials, all for the sake of the success of the preaching of the Gospel (9:15–23):

> And to the Jews I became as a Jew, that I might win Jews; to those who are under the law, as under the law, that I might win those who are under the law; to those who are without the law, as without law (not being without law toward God, but under law toward Christ), that I might win those who are without law; to the weak I became as weak, that I might win the weak. I have become all things to all men, that I might by all means save some. (9:20–22)

This is a model for a true pastoral approach, widely used by St Paul, who always condescended to the weaknesses of all people, regardless of social class or circumstance, so that he could save at least a few. All that the holy apostle writes to the Corinthians, he writes in the form of commands. Having indicated himself as a model of restraint from personal desires and needs for the sake of others, Paul wants to incline the Corinthians to do the same.

Therefore, he uses a well-known image of a runner in a race (Corinth was well known for its Isthmian Games) and a boxer, both of whom are "temperate in all things" that could make their bodies fat and weak, for the sake of winning merely perishable crowns. "Run in such a way that you may obtain it [the prize]," exhorts the apostle (9:24). Again, St Paul uses himself as an example, saying that he runs the race not as one uncertain, neither does he as a boxer merely "beat the air." In other words, he does not throw his fists around without purpose, as do boxers in training, "who beat the air instead of an adversary to properly train their hands" (Blessed Theodoret). Instead, Paul lands real blows against his enemy, the devil. To achieve this goal, "I discipline my body and bring it into subjection, lest, when I have preached to others, I myself should become disqualified" (9:27). This is the foundation of Christian asceticism: it is impossible to uproot one's sinful passions or succeed in the spiritual life without limiting the needs of the body.

Chapter 10 is directed against eating food offered to idols. The most important thought of the chapter is that those who eat meat sacrificed to idols are, in essence, partaking of a demonic feast. At first, the holy apostle tries to frighten the Corinthians with examples of God's terrifying punishments for the sin of idol worship in the Old Testament. The parallel between Israel and the Church is important: "our fathers were under the cloud, all passed through the sea, all were baptized into Moses in the cloud and in the sea" (10:1–2). In other words, the passage through the Red Sea was a foreshadowing of baptism, and Moses was a foreshadowing of Christ: "all ate the same spiritual food, and all drank the same spiritual drink. For they drank of that spiritual Rock that followed them, and that Rock was Christ" (10:3–4).

The spiritual food was manna, foreshadowing the Eucharist, and the spiritual drink was the water that flowed miraculously from the rock, foreshadowing the blood of the Lord. The main idea here is that the Provider of good gifts to men, both in the Old and the New Testaments, was One and the same Christ. This passage is read on Theophany and during the great blessing of waters.

Having listed a series of examples of Israel's apostasy and God's punishment for it, St Paul warns the Corinthians of the danger of falling back into pagan worship if they continue to eat at feasts in the pagan temples: "Therefore let him who thinks he stands take heed lest he fall" (10:12).

In 10:15–22, the apostle insists that any participation in the sacramental worship of demons is communion with demons, for "the things which the Gentiles sacrifice they sacrifice to demons and not to God, and I do not want you to have fellowship with demons" (10:20). Then the apostle gives more concrete instructions on how a Christian must eat. First, he repeats his thought from chapter 6: "All things are lawful for me, but not all things are helpful" (6:12), reminding the Corinthians that their first care should not be for the free exercise of their Christian freedom but for the conscience of their fellow Christians. Paul insists that no food is unclean, and a Christian can eat everything sold at market and offered at the homes of unbelievers without fear. However, "if anyone says to you, 'This was offered to idols,' do not eat it for the sake of the one who told you, and for conscience' sake" (10:28). All of these recommendations are covered by the rule: "Whether you eat or drink, or whatever you do, do all to the glory of God" (10:31). For us, the glory of God is the most precious of all, and we must always keep it in mind, no matter what the circumstance.

Chapter 11 continues Paul's condemnation and correction of certain disorders in the community, namely (1) women not covering their heads in church (11:1–7), and (2) disorder during the agape or Eucharistic meals (11:17–34).

The essence of the first instruction is that women must attend assemblies of worship with heads covered, and men with heads uncovered. St John Chrysostom explains that in Corinth "[t]heir women used both to pray and prophesy unveiled and with their head bare, but the men went so far as to wear long hair as having spent their time in philosophy, and covered their heads when praying and prophesying, each of which was a Grecian custom."[14]

St Paul found this to be improper for Christians and required that women keep their heads covered as a sign of their subordinate state relative to their husbands. In addition, certain women went into pagan temples with heads uncovered for impure reasons, and so an uncovered head in a worship space was generally considered a sign of shamelessness. Loose women were punished by having their hair cut off, which is why the apostle says, "For if a woman is not covered, let her also be shorn" (11:6).

St Theophan the Recluse says, "At first it was the man, created in God's image, and then the wife was created, but as though in man's image. Therefore, she is an image of an image, or the reflection of the glory of the man."[15]

"For this reason the woman ought to have a symbol of authority on her head, because of the angels" (11:10). St John Chrysostom explains this passage thus: "For although thou despise thine husband … yet reverence the angels."[16] This head covering is then a sign of her modesty, submissiveness, and subordination to her husband. But lest the man consider himself greater than his wife and abuse his position, Apostle Paul reminds the Corinthians: "Nevertheless, neither is man independent of woman, nor woman independent of man, in the Lord. For as woman came from man, even so man also comes through woman; but all things are from God" (11:11–12).

"Does not even nature itself teach you that if a man has long hair, it is a dishonor to him?" (11:14). This sentence is a favorite of the Protestants, who like to use it against Orthodox priests who traditionally wear their hair long. However, Paul is not speaking of priests, but of laypeople, and he is speaking not of a general principle, but the universal local custom of that time for men to wear their hair short, and women growing their hair long. The Protestants forget that God Himself commanded men who give the Nazirite oath to grow their hair long (Num 6:5). One of the reasons that priests and monks grow their hair long is that this practice recalls this Old Testament oath, a consecration of oneself to God.

In the rest of the chapter, Paul rebukes the disorders occurring at the agape meals. As in the first Christian community in Jerusalem, everything in Corinth was shared in common, and all the faithful gathered to eat at a common table.

Following the celebration of the Eucharist and the partaking of the Holy Mysteries, everyone participated in a common meal.[17] The rich brought the food, and the poor, who had nothing, were invited to partake together with the rest of the community. This was the so-called feast of love. The apostle accuses the Corinthians of separating into cliques (either based on family or friendship) and forgetting the poor, which ruined the very purpose of the "feast of love."

To inspire them to the proper reverence during the feasts, the apostle teaches the Corinthians concerning the tradition of the institution of the Eucharist. This passage is read in the Orthodox Church at the Divine Liturgy on Great and Holy Thursday when the institution of the Eucharist and the Mystical Supper are commemorated. For our purposes, the following words are especially important: "Therefore whoever eats this bread or drinks this cup of the Lord in an unworthy manner will be guilty of the body and blood of the Lord" (11:27). These words are significant for their dogmatic importance, for the bread is truly the Body of Christ, and the wine is truly the Blood of Christ. They are not merely symbols, as some extreme Protestants teach. This is why Paul continues thus: "But let a man examine himself, and so let him eat of the bread and drink of the cup" (11:28). In other words, the one who desires to partake of these mysteries must prepare himself, examining his conscience and removing the obstacles to a worthy communion. This is why the Orthodox Church considers it necessary to observe the discipline of prayer, repentance, and fasting before the reception of Holy Communion. This is absolutely essential, for "he who eats and drinks in an unworthy manner eats and drinks judgment to himself, not discerning the Lord's body" (11:29).

In conclusion, in 11:33–34, the apostle tells them to "wait for one another" when coming together for the feasts of love, that is, let them eat with reverence, not hurrying to swallow up all the food selfishly before everyone else. "And the rest I will set in order when I come" (11:34). This is important. Everything comes from the apostles—the order of the Church is established by them, even if not everything is written down specifically in the Scriptures.

Chapter 12 speaks of spiritual gifts in the Church. The extraordinary profusion of the grace of God, manifested as concrete spiritual gifts among the faithful, was a unique aspect of the life of the Church of Christ in the apostolic age. St Paul lists the following spiritual gifts: wisdom, knowledge, faith, healing, working miracles, prophecy, discernment of spirits, speaking in tongues, and interpretation of tongues. These gifts were intended to help promote the success of the preaching of the Gospel. Among the Corinthians, however, many began to grow vain and arrogant over their "personal" spiritual gifts. Attempting to assimilate yet greater and more astounding gifts, some even fell into self-delusion. Not having any gifts at all, they simply made a loud ruckus, uttering incomprehensible babble. Sometimes, in the darkness of their deluded minds and hearts, they even screamed out blasphemy, such as curses against Jesus.

This occurred as a result of the influence of pagan oracles, such as the Oracle of Delphi and the Sibyl. In a paroxysm of self-induced ecstasy, foaming at the mouth, with hair unbound, such people would scream out double entendres or complete nonsense. These performances impressed some people greatly, and many sought answers from these false prophets. In this they were not that different from today's Pentecostals.

The apostle warns Christians against any kind of pagan interpretation of, or relation to, the gifts of the Spirit. He explains that all the spiritual gifts in the Church are the work of the One Spirit of God (12:3–11). Therefore, just as no one inspired by the Holy Spirit can ever utter blasphemies against God, so too should there never be any competition among those in possession of different gifts of the Spirit. Just as a human body has different members—and every member has its own unique designation, with no competition possible among them—so also in the Church there can be no rivalries among Christians, as they are the One Body of Christ, in which every member has his own unique calling. Some have the apostolic calling, some the prophetic; some are teachers, some are healers, some are miracle workers. In the Church, we have "helps, administrations, varieties of tongues" (12:28). Paul exhorts the Corinthians to "earnestly desire the best gifts" (12:31). But the greatest gift of the Spirit is the gift of love. Therefore, the next chapter is dedicated to love.

Chapter 13 is called by some a "wondrous hymn to Christian love." Love alone gives true meaning and purpose to all other spiritual gifts and ascetical struggles. Without love, a person can speak in all the languages of men and even angels, but his words will be like a "sounding brass or a clanging cymbal" (13:1). Without love, a person is nothing, even if he has the gift of prophecy and knows all the mysteries of the world and has all knowledge and faith that would move mountains. Without love, even such great ascetic labors as distributing all one's money or even giving one's body to be burned have no significance.

The qualities of love are such that love truly is the fulfillment of the Law in its entirety, to use St Paul's own expression from Romans 13:10. "Love suffers long and is kind; love does not envy; love does not parade itself, is not puffed up; does not behave rudely, does not seek its own, is not provoked, thinks no evil; does not rejoice in iniquity, but rejoices in the truth; bears all things, believes all things, hopes all things, endures all things" (1 Cor 13:4–7).

Prophecy, the gift of tongues and knowledge—no more than the words, thoughts, and reasoning of a child—have only temporary necessity, whereas love—the attribute of a grown adult—remains forever, it "never fails" (13:8). A person who loves will see God, not as through murky glass, not in guessing, but face to face. "Now I know in part, but then I shall know just as I also am known. And now abide faith, hope, love, these three; but the greatest of these is love" (13:12–13). These three are the greatest gifts, but love is highest of them all, because, according to St John Chrysostom, "faith indeed and hope, when the good things believed and hoped for are come, cease" (i.e., in the age to come).[18] Blessed Theodoret adds, "In the life to come, faith will become obsolete, because the things themselves will be made manifest. Also obsolete will be hope. But love will grow all the stronger when the passions will fade, when our bodies will become incorrupt, when our souls will not choose one thing today, and another tomorrow."[19]

In chapter 14, the holy apostle speaks of the proper use of two spiritual gifts—prophecy and tongues. In the first twenty-five verses, he explains the advantage of the first over the second, and then from verse 26 to verse 38, he gives instructions on how to use both in the Church. Finally, he stresses that everything in the Church must be "done decently and in order" (14:40). The advantage of prophecy over tongues is this: whoever prophesies—that is, utters the will of God understandably concerning not only the future, but also the present and the past—speaks for the edification of all. The one who speaks in a foreign tongue, however, is understood by none except those who know that tongue. For those who do not understand the foreign tongue, it is as if you are "speaking into the air" (14:9). It is no different than the cacophonous sounds of out-of-tune musical instruments.

An excessive preoccupation with the gift of tongues is a kind of immaturity, unworthy of perfected Christians. Therefore, Paul says, "do not be children in understanding; however, in malice be babes, but in understanding be mature" (14:20). The meaning of this instruction is the same as Christ's words: "Be wise as serpents and harmless as doves" (Matt 10:16). In other words, be like children in your lack of anger, but in your minds be adults. Such a childish preoccupation with the gift of tongues is both a disparagement to the faithful (14:22) and an occasion for ridicule on the part of unbelievers (14:23). The general rule for all who possess extraordinary gifts of the Spirit is the following: "Let all things be done for edification" (14:26).

If there are those who speak in a foreign tongue, they should not all speak at the same time, but in turns, and an interpreter must always be present. Prophets should also speak in turn and immediately cease speaking when another receives inspiration, lest there be disorder in church, for "God is not the author of confusion but of peace" (14:33).

"Let your women keep silent in the churches" (14:34): instructing the women in modesty and submission to their husbands, the holy apostle forbids them not only to teach in churches, but even to ask questions, "for it is shameful for women to speak in church" (14:35). In conclusion, the apostle encourages the Corinthians to desire earnestly to prophesy, and not to forbid to speak with tongues (14:39), reminding them that the most important thing in church is that "all things be done decently and in order" (14:40).

The fifteenth chapter is an important dogmatic instruction concerning the resurrection of the dead. We must assume that among the Corinthians there were Christians, influenced by some pagan philosophies, who doubted in the possibility of the general resurrection of the dead. When St Paul began speaking of the resurrection of the dead in Athens (Acts 17:32), some began to mock him. It is possible that a similar philosophy was popular in Corinth. Some, apparently, rejected the resurrection of the dead completely, whereas others said that this resurrection had to be understood allegorically and that it had already occurred in the purification of souls from sin. In his epistle to Timothy (2 Tim 2:17–18), Paul called this wicked teaching a "cancer," calling by name (Hymenaeus and Philetus) the disseminators of the teaching that the resurrection had already occurred. Some merely doubted the manner of the resurrection and what form the risen body would take.

First, Paul proves the truth of the resurrection from the dead of the Lord Jesus Christ, referencing the appearance of the risen Christ to Cephas (Peter), the twelve apostles, the five hundred brethren, Apostle James, all the other disciples of Christ, and, finally, Paul himself (15:1–8). From this truth of the resurrection of Christ, St Paul makes the inescapable conclusion that the general resurrection of all in God's appointed time is an absolute truth, for by His resurrection, Christ laid the foundation for our own resurrection, as the "firstfruits of those who have fallen asleep" (15:20). If one were to even entertain the thought that there will be no general resurrection, then one must reject the truth of Christ's resurrection. But if one does so, one rejects all of Christianity, for "if Christ is not risen, then our preaching is empty and your faith is also empty" (15:14). In addition, the preaching of the apostles was accompanied by such wondrous signs and such extraordinary gifts of the Holy Spirit that no reasonable person would ever call Christianity "empty."

"And if Christ is not risen, your faith is futile; you are still in your sins! Then also those who have fallen asleep in Christ have perished. If in this life only we have hope in Christ, we are of all men the most pitiable" (15:17–20). For what would then be the foundation for faith in the forgiveness of sins? That faith is founded on Christ's redemptive sacrifice and death on the Cross, on the Son's sacrifice being pleasing to the Father, and on the resurrection being proof of that acceptance. If He is not risen, then His sacrifice was not acceptable, and His death was merely a human death, incapable of having any redemptive significance. Then all those who died in the faith and were martyred for it died not for Christ, but only as unfortunate, pitiful people. Then it would be correct to call Christians the most pathetic of all people, for they are deprived of all in this life. They are subjected to persecutions and limit themselves in much, but in the future life, they will receive nothing. Then there would be no sense in guiding one's life by any morality or in battling one's sinful inclinations. Then it would be much more logical to follow the dictates of the Epicureans: "Let us eat and drink, for tomorrow we die!" (15:32). Thus, the rejection of the resurrection of the dead is a disruption of the entire system of Christian morality.

Then, the apostle makes a conclusion about the truth of the general resurrection of the dead from the historical fact of the resurrection of Christ, for Christ is the progenitor of renewed mankind, the New Adam: "For as in Adam all die, even so in Christ all shall be made alive" (15:22). Furthermore, Paul insists that the rejection of the truth of the general resurrection would eventually lead to an admission of the futility of baptism. In other words, all the work and labors of the apostles would then be futile, and all morality would simply be overturned (15:29–32). Desiring to warn the Corinthians against dangerous association with pagans, who, apparently, had infected them with this doubt in the general resurrection, the apostle uses an ancient proverb: "Evil company corrupts good habits" (15:33). He says this to shame them in their not having "the knowledge of God," that is, in their pagan manner of imagining God's omnipotence, which is of course strong enough to raise all the dead (15:33–34).

In the passage 15:35–53, Paul speaks of the manner of this general resurrection. At first he answers the question concerning what power will raise the bodies of the dead (15:36–38); then he speaks of the form the new bodies will take (15:39–50); and, finally, he explains how the actual resurrection will occur (15:51–53). The first question is answered by comparing the human body with a seed. Just as a seed, before it can grow into a full plant, has to die, so the corruption of the bodies of the dead cannot be seen as a hindrance to God's power to raise them again. Paul answers the second question by saying that the bodies of the risen will be different from our current, crude bodies. These will be "spiritual" bodies, similar to Christ's body after His resurrection. They will be incorruptible, for "flesh and blood cannot inherit the kingdom of God; nor does corruption inherit incorruption" (15:50). This is because "we shall not all sleep, but we shall all be changed" (15:51). In other words, those who are still alive in the moment of the general resurrection will transform in the blink of an eye, and their bodies will also become spiritual and incorruptible. "For this corruptible must put on incorruption, and this mortal must put on immortality" (15:53).

All these spiritual bodies will be glorious in different degrees, depending on the level of moral perfection achieved by each person (15:39–49). St Paul finishes his thoughts concerning the resurrection of the dead with the triumphant words of Prophet Isaiah: "He will swallow up death forever" (Isa 25:8) and Prophet Hosea: "O Death, I will be your plagues! O Grave, I will be your destruction!" (Hos 13:14). Then he thanks God Who gave us such victory over death, after which Paul exhorts the Corinthians to be firm and steadfast in their Christian faith and life, knowing that "your labor is not in vain in the Lord" (15:58).

In chapter 16, the apostle gives instructions concerning gathering aid for the Christians in Jerusalem, and then he promises the Corinthians that he will himself visit them from Ephesus, traveling through Macedonia. He asks them to he hospitable to Timothy, and he once again encourages them to be firm and courageous in their faith. Then he passes on the greetings of the members of the Asian churches, from Aquila and Priscilla and all the brethren. As for those who do not love the

Lord Jesus Christ, Paul declares them "anathema, Maranatha," which means, "Let them be expelled until the coming of the Lord." This is the Biblical basis for the Rite of Orthodoxy, which includes the proclamation of the anathema, celebrated in many churches on the Sunday of Orthodoxy. Paul concludes his letter with his usual apostolic blessing.

CHAPTER 3

The Second Epistle of the Holy Apostle Paul to the Corinthians

THE PURPOSE OF THE SECOND EPISTLE TO THE CORINTHIANS

Before traveling to Corinth, the Holy Apostle Paul wanted to know what sort of an impression his first epistle had made on the Corinthians. Moreover, he wanted Timothy, whom he had sent ahead, to have time to finish his gathering of financial aid for the Christians in Jerusalem (1 Cor 4:17). At the same time, he intended to stay a while in Ephesus. The disturbance caused by Demetrius the silversmith, however, forced Paul to leave Ephesus earlier than he intended. It was still too early to go to Corinth, for Timothy could not yet have arrived there to gather aid, and, more important, Paul did not know what effect his first epistle had.

Therefore, he sent Titus to Corinth, and he went to Troas, having given Titus a command to return to him immediately with a report about the state of the community in Corinth. Paul's state of tense expectation in Troas was so strong that he had no peace in his spirit (2 Cor 2:12–13), and so he went to Macedonia to meet Titus sooner. The meeting with Titus in Macedonia calmed Paul considerably. Here, he also met Timothy, who was still only planning on leaving for Corinth. Titus gave Paul many joyful tidings of the positive response to his epistle, but a few unpleasant tidings as well. The meeting with Titus was the main reason Paul wrote the second epistle to the Corinthians. This is clear from the epistle itself (7:6–16).

Titus told Paul that the first epistle inspired one to "[sorrow] in a godly manner" (7:11), leading to repentance, a renewed sense of fear of God, and a desire to improve. It also incited their anger against the member of the community who had married his stepmother and renewed their disdain for all that was pagan. However, Titus also informed Paul that his opponents continued vehemently to try to undermine his authority among the Corinthians. Although they had no reason to condemn Paul for anything unlawful, they tried to make an issue out of Paul's prolonged delay in visiting Corinth (2 Cor 1:16). They apparently wanted the Corinthians to think that Paul was fickle and changeable in character; thus, his teaching—the teaching of a frivolous and unserious man—could not be fully trusted. They tried to interpret Paul's humility, his incredible modesty, and his nonacquisitiveness (so evident in his time in Corinth) as further proof of his weakness and faint-heartedness. "'For his letters,' they say, 'are weighty and powerful, but his bodily presence is weak, and his speech contemptible'" (2 Cor 10:10).

This could not fail to upset Paul, for it did not merely insult him personally, but it cast a shadow on the faith that he preached, which is why he considered it necessary to address these allegations directly in his epistle. Titus also told him that not all the Corinthians had tried to improve after receiving his epistle, and some, having become completely hardened by their impurity, sexual immorality, and indecent manner of life, did not even think of improving (2 Cor 12:20–21). It behooved Paul to incite their repentance in an especially forceful way, lest, as Paul himself says, "being present I should use sharpness, according to the authority which the Lord has given me for edification and not for destruction" (13:10).

Moreover, Apostle Paul wanted to soften the hearts of the Corinthians, so that they would give more generous aid to the Palestinian Christians, lest Paul would be ashamed of them before the Macedonians, to whom he had already boasted of Corinth's generosity (9:4).

The Place and Time of the Writing of the Epistle

Taking into account all that had occurred after the writing of the first epistle, and comparing it with the account in Acts, we can assume that the second epistle was also written in A.D. 58 or 59. The place of writing was doubtless Macedonia, most likely Philippi (2 Cor 2:12–13, 7:5–7, 8:1–6, 9:2–4). This second letter was sent with Titus and another brother, "whose praise is in the gospel" (2 Cor 8:18). This was probably St Luke, the writer of Acts.

The Structure and Content of the Epistle

The Second Epistle to the Corinthians consists of thirteen chapters and can be divided into the following sections:

1. Introduction with the usual greetings (1:1–11).
2. A theoretical section, in which the holy apostle lists the reasons for his inability to yet visit Corinth (1:12–2:11). Then Paul writes of the exalted nature of the teaching that he preaches (2:12–7:1). Finally, returning to his previous subject, he expresses joy at the news given him by Titus (7:2–16).
3. A practical section, dedicated to the subject of aid for the Palestinian brethren (8:1–9:15).

4. Paul's defense of his public ministry, preaching, and exalted apostolic calling (10:1–13:10).

5. Conclusion (13:11–13), including an exhortation of peace and unity of spirit, as well as his usual greetings.

EXEGETICAL ANALYSIS OF THE SECOND EPISTLE TO THE CORINTHIANS

The entire epistle is suffused with a sense of sorrow inspired in the apostle's soul by the harsh conditions of the apostolic ministry. This sorrow does not depress Paul, however; leaving nothing for himself, he completely abandons himself to that power of faith and knowledge of the rightness of his work and the holiness of his accomplished goals. This was always a unique characteristic of the Holy Apostle Paul.

The epistle begins with Paul's usual introduction of himself as the author of the epistle. He also includes Timothy in his initial greeting, and gives his apostolic blessing not only to the Corinthians, but to all the Christians in Greece (Achaia). Having said that the purpose of all his sufferings is the consolation and salvation of the Corinthians, Paul then informs them of his fatal danger in Asia, from which the Lord delivered him thanks in part to the prayers of the Corinthian Church (1:11).

Beginning with the twelfth verse of the first chapter, and including all of chapter 2, Paul informs the Corinthians of the persecutions he endured in Asia Minor, which were the reason for his delay in personally visiting Corinth and seeing their repentance with his own eyes. He wishes to express his joy in their first steps toward moral improvement. In verses 17–20, Paul contradicts those slanderers who tried to accuse him of fickleness and to impugn his preaching as changeable, inconsistent, and false.

"But as God is faithful, our word to you was not Yes and No. For the Son of God, Jesus Christ, who was preached among you by us—by me, Silvanus, and Timothy—was not Yes and No, but in Him was Yes … to the glory of God through us" (1:18-20). These words mean that the preaching of the holy apostle is as firm and unchangeable as Christ Himself. "Now He who establishes us with you in Christ and has anointed us is God, who also has sealed us and given us the Spirit in our hearts as a guarantee" (1:21–22). This passage is a direct reference to the sacrament of Chrismation, and the "formula" used in the service of Chrismation—"the seal of the gift of the Holy Spirit"—is taken directly from these words. The meaning of Paul's words is this: the proof of the truth of his teaching is the evident gift of the Holy Spirit, given in Chrismation.

"Moreover I call God as witness against my soul" (1:23). These words show the permissibility of oaths in certain cases. After calling God to be his witness, Paul reveals the full reason for his delay in coming to Corinth. In fact, he did it for *their* sake, to spare them undue sorrow, and to avoid acting as though he had "dominion over [their] faith" (1:24). In other words, he did not want to act as though he had direct authority over all aspects of their spiritual life. Instead, he wanted them to improve of their volition, so that their meeting with the apostle would be joyful, with no mutual recriminations.

St Paul continues in this manner in the second chapter. He did not want to come to the Corinthians "in sorrow," and so he left it to their discretion to judge the man who had sinned in incest. Because the sinner had repented, Paul allows the Corinthians to be lenient and forgive him, "lest perhaps such a one be swallowed up with too much sorrow," in which case Satan would triumph (2:1–11).

From 2:12 to 7:1, St Paul discourses on the exaltedness of the Christian revelation, that is, the truth of the Gospel, and the manner of that truth's manifestation on earth. It seems that Paul was suddenly inspired to write on this topic, having been reminded of the change in his plans to travel to Corinth, and how he met Titus in Macedonia and was given great joy by his news concerning the positive effect of his first epistle (2:12–13). Paul thanks God, "who always leads us in triumph in Christ, and through us diffuses the fragrance of His knowledge in every place" (2:14). The first quality and action of the divine revelation is that it does not need external proofs; for it makes itself known like a sweet smell that spreads everywhere: "For we are to God the fragrance of Christ" (2:15), although this sweet fragrance does not have equal effect on all people, depending on every person's inner disposition. For some, this fragrance gives life, whereas to others, it brings death. If some are brought to death by this fragrance, it is not the fault of the apostles, for they merely preach the pure and uncorrupted teaching of Christ (2:14–17).

In chapters 3 and 4, Paul speaks of the advantage of the New Testament over the Old, and he indicates the qualities of a true preacher (and proper manner of preaching) of the Gospel.

As we see from chapter 3, Paul's opponents—the leaders of the Judaizing heresy—boasted before the Corinthians that they had letters of recommendation from Jerusalem. They probably implied that Paul's preaching, which they claimed disparaged the Old Testament Law, was not looked upon favorably by the Christians in Jerusalem. In answer to this accusation, St Paul insists that the New Testament revelation does not need any external endorsement. It speaks for itself, and the best recommendation for its truth is the faith and virtuous life of those who have accepted it. "You are our epistle written in our hearts, known and read by all men; clearly you are an epistle of Christ, ministered by us, written not with ink but by the Spirit of the living God, not on tablets of stone but on tablets of flesh, that is, of the heart" (3:2–3).

Christian revelation does not depend on the worthiness or abilities of its preachers, but it in itself glorifies its preachers. If service to the letter—the Old Testament Law that could not justify mankind—gave such glory to those who served it that people could not look at Moses's face without a veil because of the brilliance of the light streaming from it, then how much more glory will illumine the servers of the Spirit, the New Covenant that justifies sinful man before God!

What does the expression "the letter kills, but the Spirit gives life" (3:6) mean? And why does the holy apostle call the Old Testament Law the "ministry of death"? St John Chrysostom explains this beautifully:

> The Law, if it lay hold on a murderer, puts him to death; the Gospel, if it lay hold on a murderer, enlightens and gives him life. And why do I instance a murderer? The Law laid hold on one that gathered sticks on a Sabbath day, and stoned him (Num 15:32, 36). This is the meaning of "the letter kills." The Gospel takes hold on thousands of homicides and robbers, and baptizing delivers them from their former vices. This is the meaning of "the Spirit gives life."[20]

As servants of the Spirit, the holy apostles act with great boldness and do not cover the great mysteries of God's divine economy with a veil (metaphors or parables), for Christ removed the veil that obstructed the Old Covenant. Only for the Jews and Judaizers who are blindly attached to the Old Testament "the same veil remains unlifted in the reading of the Old Testament … But even to this day, when Moses is read, a veil lies on their heart. … Nevertheless when one turns to the Lord, the veil is taken away" (3:14–16).

"Now the Lord is the Spirit; and where the Spirit of the Lord is, there is liberty" (3:17). This expression is a bit vague, and so has different interpretations. Some understand the "Spirit" here to be the Third Person of the Holy Trinity, whereas others understand the "Spirit" to be a general term denoting God as a Spiritual Being. In either case, the meaning of the phrase is the following: if in the Old Testament the great difficulty of the many ritual laws limited one's liberty to act, in the New Testament, the grace of the Holy Spirit gave us the possibility to freely approach the very Lord Jesus Christ, to gaze at His glory, and to become transformed ourselves "into the same image from glory to glory" (3:18).

In chapter 4, Paul lists the qualities of a true preacher of the Gospel, who, despite all the difficulties of this calling, never despairs, for "we do not preach ourselves, but Christ Jesus the Lord" (4:5). These preachers of the Gospel, illumined from on high and enlightened by the "knowledge of the glory of God in the face of Jesus Christ" (4:6), are only weak people, if taken by themselves. However, the power of God clearly manifests itself in these fragile potter's vessels that by all human reckoning should easily break, for despite all attacks that they endure during their service, they remain indomitable. "We are hard-pressed on every side, yet not crushed; we are perplexed, but not in despair; persecuted, but not forsaken; struck down, but not destroyed—always carrying about in the body the dying of the Lord Jesus, that the life of Jesus also may be manifested in our body" (4:8–10). Just as the Lord Himself suffered, so suffer the preachers of His faith, but just as life triumphed over His death, so this life-giving power lives and acts within the apostles, and through them it is passed on to all the faithful.

The constant threat of death, in which the apostles found themselves during their ministry, never frightened them, for they were inspired by their hope in the resurrection of all the dead (4:11–15). Moreover, these physical sufferings bring great benefit to the soul, for "though our outward man is perishing, yet the inward man is being renewed day by day" (4:16–18).

In chapter 5, St Paul continues his previous discussion, saying that death does not frighten true preachers of the Gospel, because with the destruction of the "earthly house," they have a home from God, "a house not made with hands, eternal in the heavens" (5:1). Paul even says that the apostles themselves "groan, earnestly desiring to be clothed with our habitation which is from heaven" (5:2), that is, the spiritual body after the resurrection, incorrupt and full of light (St John Chrysostom). "If indeed, having been clothed, we shall not be found naked" (5:3), that is, deprived of good deeds and the glory of God. Paul further explains in what sense it is desirable to throw off this body: "For we who are in this tent groan, being burdened" (5:4). Of course, this refers to bodily weakness and the passions of the flesh. It would be incorrect to think that the apostle says that he wishes to completely be freed from any kind of body: "not because we want to be unclothed, but further clothed, that mortality may be swallowed up by life. Now He who has prepared us for this very thing is God, who also has given us the Spirit as a guarantee" (5:4–5).

Then the Apostle explains that he is describing his ministry, so full of deprivation and suffering, not to praise himself, but to give the Corinthians the necessary weapon against Paul's adversaries, so that they could "have an answer for those who boast in appearance and not in heart" (5:12). Some of Paul's adversaries in Corinth proved their credibility by saying that they knew Christ in the flesh and heard His teaching with their own ears. Keeping this in mind, Paul insists that what is important is not knowing Christ in the flesh, but living by the spirit of His teaching. Christ died for all, and all must die for their previous sinful life and become "a new creation" in Christ. "Therefore, if anyone is in Christ, he is a new creation; old things have passed away; behold, all things have become new" (5:17). The essence of Christianity is this complete renewal of life through the reconciliation of mankind with God through Jesus Christ. The apostles are "ambassadors for Christ" (5:20) who in Christ's name call for man's reconciliation with God (5:18–19), Who made Christ, "who knew no sin to be sin for us, that we might become the righteousness of God in Him" (5:21).

In the sixth chapter, Paul gives a fiery rebuff to those slanderers who tried to impress upon the Corinthians that the reason for Paul's deprivations and persecutions was his own personal weaknesses. Basically, they tried to paint him as a vacillating, unsteady person who did not command the respect and love of the people to whom he preached. They even suggested that he hindered the work of the Gospel. Preaching that now had come the "acceptable time" for reconciliation with God and salvation, "we give no offense in anything, that our ministry may not be blamed. But in all things, we commend ourselves as ministers of God" (6:2–4). Having said this, Paul then paints a vivid picture of the discrepancy between the difficulty of his position and the greatness of the labors undertaken by him, lest he give anyone reason to doubt him. In these verses (6:1–13), he describes the exalted ideal of Christian service and duty, even to complete self-abnegation, a difficult and unflinching service that tests man's determination and conviction among persecutions and deprivations, supported by the hope in God's almighty help.

Having laid his entire heart bare before the Corinthians, Paul calls them to reciprocal love and trust in him: "Now in return for the same (I speak as to children), you also be open" (6:13). In other words, because I love you so, become enlarged also in love for me as your spiritual father, and accept this teaching that I offer to you with complete trust. To do this, you must completely reject all association with pagans: "what communion has light with darkness? And what accord has Christ with Belial?" (6:14–15). "Therefore, 'Come out from among them and be separate, says the Lord. Do not touch what is unclean, and I will receive you'" (6:17).

In chapter 7, continuing the same sermon, the holy apostle says, "Let us cleanse ourselves from all filthiness of the flesh and spirit, perfecting holiness in the fear of God" (7:1). Then he expresses his joy and consolation at hearing Titus's good news about all that he had seen and encountered in Corinth. Paul's joy in the moral improvement of the Corinthians is so great that he is ready to forget all his previous sorrows (7:4–17). He does not regret that he grieved them with his first epistle, for godly sorrow brings great spiritual benefits, as it leads to repentance: "For godly sorrow produces repentance leading to salvation, not to be regretted; but the sorrow of the world produces death" (7:10). The sorrow incited by Paul's trenchant epistle caused a positive moral transformation in the Corinthians, who desired to correct all the moral laxity in their community. The apostle rejoices that the Corinthians proved worthy of his trust and did not shame their teacher, and he says, "I have confidence in you in everything" (7:16).

Chapters 8 and 9 comprise the purely practical part of the letter. In them, the holy apostle encourages the Corinthians to collect alms for the impoverished Christians in Jerusalem. He incites them to greater generosity by the following:

1. The example of the Macedonian churches, who were not rich, but showed great generosity (8:1–8).
2. Christ's own example: "Though He was rich, yet for your sakes He became poor, that you through His poverty might become rich" (8:9).
3. A reminder that the Corinthians themselves had an earnest desire, only a year ago, to help their poor brethren (8:10–12).
4. The thought of the great benefit of such mutual giving, and a reminder that donations should be commensurate only with their own resources—let each give as much as he can—in the spirit of that equality evident in the gathering

of manna in the desert (8:13–15). St Paul is saying that he had already praised the Corinthians for their generosity, and now they need to justify his praise, lest it be uttered in vain. In addition, the apostle ensures the Corinthians that they can fully trust Titus and the other brother to pass on all of their aid (8:16–24, 9:1–5).

In the second half of chapter 9, the apostle encourages the Corinthians to give without sorrow, cheerfully and generously, for the measure of their cheerful generosity is the measure of God's blessing: "He who sows sparingly will also reap sparingly, and he who sows bountifully will also reap bountifully … for God loves a cheerful giver" (9:6–7). God generously rewards those who help their poor neighbors; moreover, Christian almsgiving animates the entire religious life of all participating Christian communities and does much to bring glory to the Church (9:8–15).

Chapters 10, 11, 12, and 13 (13:1–10) make up St Paul's defense against the slander of his opponents, who were spreading false rumors about him in Corinth, trying to undermine his authority. These chapters differ sharply in tone from the rest of the epistle. It is possible that these chapters were written after the apostle had new tidings of the lies his adversaries were spreading. The tone of forceful authority and a sense of anger tempered with love give these chapters unique power and expression.

Paul takes the following events as the point of departure for his defense. As St Theophan the Recluse explains,

> St Paul was not impressive in appearance, and his health was poor. His personal speech was remarkable for its gentleness and quiet conviction. He begged his new listeners to believe in the Crucified One, and never presented Christ's teaching as a heavenly imprimatur that must be believed at the listener's peril. However, the tone of his writings, addressed to those who already believed, was strict and authoritative. This difference in manner provided a starting point for the attacks of his adversaries. They said that in person he was weak, but out of earshot he was brazen: "his bodily presence is weak, and his speech contemptible" (10:10).[21]

This would not be quite so disturbing to Paul, except that his adversaries interpreted this difference in manner to mean that Paul was one who walked "according to the flesh" (Rom 8:1) and this threatened to undermine the authority of the Gospel. This is why Apostle Paul considered it his duty to firmly defend his apostolic authority.

In chapter 10, St Paul says that he can be as strict as his letters, even in person, if necessary, and he asks the Corinthians not to force him to use this strictness in person when he comes to them (10:1–11). His very apostolic calling empowers him to use such strictness to defend his ministry. Paul proves this by indicating that God Himself called him to preach: "For not he who commends himself is approved, but whom the Lord commends" (10:18). Paul's adversaries praise themselves, imagining themselves to be the most important preachers in Corinth, although they only tilled the field that Paul had planted. Paul, in the meantime, praises the Lord, that is, he does not boast about himself, but rather in God's power and God's gift that inspires him to go and preach.

In chapter 11, the holy apostle, using many disclaimers and noting that he speaks thus only for the benefit of his listeners and not to praise himself, lists everything that could be used to praise him and free him from the slanderous insinuations of his adversaries. Thus, he underlines first of all his complete nonacquisitiveness, that he preached to the Corinthians "free of charge" (11:7), never making himself a nuisance to anyone. Always, he tried to avoid being a burden for anyone. Paul explains that he did not want to use the Corinthians financially, not because he lacked love for then, but to avoid being like those "false apostles" who rip them off. Paul calls such people "deceitful workers, transforming themselves into apostles of Christ" (7:13). In fact, they are not truly apostles, which is not surprising: "For Satan himself transforms himself into an angel of light" (7:14).

In vain, they boast in their physical advantages over Paul, for Paul exceeds them in this as well. Paul then lists all the labors and sorrows that he endured for the sake of Christ's Gospel, only some of which were described in the Book of Acts. Although he lists all these persecutions and sufferings, he ascribes his endurance to God's grace. To himself he ascribes only weakness: "If I must boast, I will boast in the things which concern my infirmity" (11:30).

In chapter 12, St Paul defends his apostolic calling (although he never saw Christ in the flesh), and proves his calling by indicating his exaltation to the third heaven, where he encountered a blessed state and heard unutterable words that no person can relate. Paul speaks of himself as though he were describing someone else's experience: "I know such a man" (12:3). St John Chrysostom explains that St Paul speaks thus "to show by this also that he resorts to the thing unwillingly,"[22] that is, that he says these things only because he is duty bound to defend the exalted character of his apostolic dignity against the slander of his opponents.

Blessed Theodoret interprets the third heaven to be paradise: this was "fourteen years ago." If the epistle was written in A.D. 58, then this vision can be dated to c. A.D. 44, when Paul and Barnabas were bringing aid to Jerusalem and were then sent by the Holy Spirit to their great work of bringing the Gospel to the Gentiles (Acts 13:2–3). Paul immediately adds that "lest I should be exalted above measure by the abundance of the revelations, a thorn in the flesh was given to me, a messenger of Satan to buffet me" (12:7). As St Theophan the Recluse comments,

It was usually assumed that the thorn in the flesh was something that disturbed Paul in his own body, some sort of physical ailment. Some of the newer interpreters have decided that St Paul was speaking of lust. But what is so unusual about lust?

Everyone experiences it, not only those who are virgins, but the married as well. But St Paul expresses himself in a way that indicates that this thorn was something unusual, not typical of all sinners. In addition, the word "to buffet," *kolaphizei* in Greek, means "to beat across the face," mercilessly, cruelly, and openly, while the passions of the flesh are sly and cunning enemies. Therefore, we cannot accept such an interpretation. Orthodox commentators believe that St Paul is speaking, as he was before, of external circumstances and of the hatred from the enemies of the Gospel who were the instruments of Satan.[23]

St John Chrysostom notes that the words of the apostle have the following meaning: "God would not permit the preaching to progress, in order to check our high thoughts, but permitted the adversaries to set upon us." From such attacks of enemies did the apostle beg God to be delivered "three times," that is, "oftentimes."[24]

However, Paul heard this answer: "My grace is sufficient for you, for My strength is made perfect in weakness" (12:9). St John Chrysostom explains these words thus:

> [I]t is sufficient for you [i.e., St Paul] that you raise the dead, that you cure the blind, that you cleanse lepers, that you work those other miracles. But are you pained and dejected lest it should seem to be owing to My weakness, that there are many who plot against and beat you, harass and scourge you? Why this very thing shows My power. "For My power," He says, "is made perfect in weakness," when being persecuted you overcome your persecutors; when being harassed you get the better of them that harass you; when being put in bonds you convert them that put you in bonds.[25]

This is why St Paul continues, "Therefore I take pleasure in infirmities, in reproaches, in needs, in persecutions, in distresses, for Christ's sake. For when I am weak, then I am strong" (12:10), for in such times, the grace of the Holy Spirit is most obvious. Finally, Paul proves his own apostolic dignity by citing all the miracles he performed in Corinth (12:11–13). In concluding this section, St Paul again repeats that when he next visits the Corinthians, he again will not burden them financially, just as Titus did not rely on them for personal funds. His most important desire is the moral correction of the Corinthians. He also fears to find them unrepentant when he returns (12:14–21).

In chapter 13, the apostle warns the Corinthians that if he finds them unchanged upon his return, then he "will not spare" (13:2) them, "since you seek a proof of Christ speaking in me, who is not weak toward you, but mighty in you" (13:3). According to St Theophan the Recluse,

It is as if the apostle says to them, "You yourselves asked for this, and if you do not improve, I must not spare you, but reveal to you the fullness of the apostolic authority and power of Christ that acts within me. Among you some have begun to say that I am weak in body and in speech, impugning thus my very teaching, as though it were not Christ's. Since some among you speak thus, it almost seems as though I must show you the full strength of my strictness, lest you also begin to think as they do! This will harm the work of the Gospel and your own salvation in the extreme. Thus, it has to be one of two choices: either you improve, or I have no choice but to punish you and forcefully excommunicate the insubordinate from the Church or even strike them down with some evident punishment, as I punished the magician Elymas in Cyprus with blindness. And then you will see vividly that within me Christ Himself speaks and acts."[26]

The apostle further says that even Christ Himself seemed physically weak, having no strength when He was crucified, but at the same time, He destroyed the power of death and left Hades in ruins, and rose again in glory. In the same way, when we are persecuted and when enemies amass against us, we will not suffer defeat, but "we shall live with Him by the power of God" (13:4). We will be indomitable "toward you," that is, all this suffering is for your spiritual benefit and salvation (13:4). The holy apostle then exhorts the Corinthians to examine themselves to see whether they are "in the faith … But I trust that you will know that we are not disqualified" (13:5–6). To these strict words, Paul immediately adds words full of love and warmth: "Now I pray to God that you do no evil … Therefore I write these things being absent, lest being present I should use sharpness, according to the authority which the Lord has given me for edification and not for destruction" (13:7, 10).

The last three verses of this chapter are the conclusion of the epistle. The Holy Apostle Paul desires that his Corinthian children rejoice, "Become complete, be of good comfort, be of one mind, live in peace" (13:11). If they do this, they will attract the God of love and peace. Then he calls on them to "greet one another with a holy kiss" (13:12), that is, a pure and sincere kiss that expresses genuine Christian filial love. Finally, he gives a general greeting from all the Christians ("saints"), among whom he now resides. Paul concludes with his customary blessing, which we now always hear spoken by priests and bishops at the conclusion of the Divine Liturgy: "The grace of the Lord Jesus Christ, and the love of God, and the communion of the Holy Spirit be with you all. Amen" (13:14).

 CHAPTER 4

The Epistle of the Holy Apostle Paul to the Galatians

CONCERNING GALATIA

Galatia was a region in Asia Minor located nearly at the center of the peninsula, surrounded on the north by Bithynia, Paphlagonia, and Pontus, and bordering Phrygia, Lycaonia, and Cappadocia on the south. This country was initially settled by Greeks, but in the third century B.C., ancient Gauls (a Celtic tribe) settled there after invading Macedonia and Greece through Thrace. They then gave the region its name (also sometimes called "Gallo-Graecia"). In 189 B.C., the Roman consul Manlius defeated the Gauls in the Galatian War, subjugating the region to Roman rule and becoming its first governor. In A.D. 26, Augustus officially made Galatia a Roman province.

Having moved to this area, the war-like Gauls became peaceful settlers of this fruitful area. Soon they intermarried with the local Greeks and adopted their customs and language. The rich Galatian region began to attract Jews, who from the time of Alexander of Macedon were forced to move out of Palestine into many other areas. Emperor Augustus gave his special patronage to the Jews that moved to Galatia, something explicitly mentioned by Josephus.

THE ESTABLISHMENT OF CHRISTIAN COMMUNITIES IN GALATIA

The first mention of the conversion of the Galatians is found in Acts, during the account of the second missionary journey of the Holy Apostle Paul. Having recounted the quarrel that separated Paul and Barnabas after the Apostolic Council and that caused Paul to take Silas with him through Syria and Cilicia, the writer of Acts tells of how another fellow traveler, Timothy, joined them: "And as they went through the cities, they delivered to them the decrees to keep, which were determined by the apostles and elders at Jerusalem.

So the churches were strengthened in the faith, and increased in number daily. Now when they had gone through Phrygia and the region of Galatia, they were forbidden by the Holy Spirit to preach the word in Asia" (Acts 16:4–6).

Doubtless, it was during this time that Apostle Paul established communities in the most important cities of Galatia—Ancyra, Pessina, Tavia, and Gordium. The Epistle to the Galatians makes it clear that Paul established the Church in Galatia (1:6–9, 4:13, and others). No details are given in Acts, but during the description of the third missionary journey, the writer of Acts mentioned that Apostle Paul "went over the region of Galatia and Phrygia in order, strengthening all the disciples" (Acts 18:23). Of course, one can only strengthen the faith of those who have already been converted to the faith.

Even though the Book of Acts does not give specific details about the establishment of communities in Galatia, we can glean some information from the epistle itself. As we see in Galatians 4:13–15, the Holy Apostle Paul was subject to some physical infirmity when he visited Galatia. Probably this illness forced Paul to remain there for a longer time than he had planned, and this was for the benefit of the Galatians, for it gave Paul the opportunity to preach the name of Christ the Lord so vividly, that they could almost see the Crucified Christ before their very eyes (Gal 3:1). This led to their especially ardent conversion and their extraordinary zeal. They accepted the apostle as an angel of God and loved him so much that they were ready to pluck out their own eyes and give them to Paul (Gal 4:14–15)

THE PURPOSE OF THE EPISTLE TO THE GALATIANS

The reason for writing this epistle was the arrival in Galatia of the Judaizing heretics, who began to insist on the necessity of circumcision (and other rites of the Mosaic Law) for salvation. Continuing his third missionary journey, Paul had arrived in Ephesus from Galatia (Acts 19:1). Rumors of disturbances caused by the Judaizers in Galatia reached him in Ephesus. These heretics probably came from Palestine, because the local Jews, having lived a long time among pagans, could hardly keep to such fanatical and nationalistic Jewish notions. These Judaizers interpreted Paul's laxity concerning the Old Testament Law as his desire to curry favor with pagans, and they also belittled his ministry by suggesting that he was not called to be an apostle by the Lord Jesus Christ Himself and was not a living witness of His work, nor was he a hearer of Christ's teaching from His own lips.

To the great sorrow and wonder of Apostle Paul, many Galatians fell prey to this corrupted preaching, "turning away so soon from Him who called you in the grace of Christ, to a different Gospel" (Gal 1:6). Astounded by such unexpected frivolity and foolishness (Gal 3:1), Apostle Paul immediately decided to write to them to uncover the delusion of their enticers. It is interesting that Paul wrote the epistle in his own hand (Gal 6:11), lest he lose any time having it transcribed. This way, there also could be no doubt that the letter came from him directly.

THE PLACE AND TIME OF THE WRITING OF THE EPISTLE

Paul mentions two previous visits to Galatia in the letter (Gal 4:13). Since he makes a point of expressing his amazement at how quickly the Galatians were turned from his teaching, we can assume that he wrote it soon after his second visit to Galatia. After this visit, he spent nearly three years in Ephesus. Using Acts to anchor our chronology, we can guess to a great degree of accuracy that Paul wrote this epistle around A.D. 56.

THE STRUCTURE AND CONTENT OF THE EPISTLE

This epistle consists of six chapters. In its subject matter, it has much in common with the Epistle to the Romans. From beginning to end, it has a forceful, inspired tone, ardent with zeal for Christ and love for the Galatians. Proofs for the rational mind constantly alternate with encouragement intended to soften the heart. The main idea of this letter is that all people, not the Jews alone, are called by the Lord into His Church, and they are saved in the Church not by the fulfillment of external rites of the Mosaic Law, but rather by faith in the Lord Jesus Christ, expressed in acts of love. The letter is divided into the following sections:

1. Prologue, containing a greeting and an introduction in which Paul expresses his main theme (1:1–10).
2. A defense of Paul's apostolic dignity, which had been brought into question by the Judaizing false teachers (1:11 to 2:1–21).
3. A dogmatic section, in which Paul powerfully and completely reveals the main theme of his epistle—the reference of the Old Testament to the New, and the end of the importance of the Law of Moses after the coming of Christ the Saviour (3:1–29 and 4:1–31).
4. A moral-instructive section, in which the foundation of the Christian life, independent of the Old Testament Law, is described (5:1–26 to 6:1–10).
5. A conclusion, in which concrete instructions are given concerning circumcision and reverence due to the Cross of Christ (6:11–18).

EXEGETICAL ANALYSIS OF THE EPISTLE TO THE GALATIANS

The first chapter begins with an introduction, in which Paul immediately starts with a short summary of his main theme—the defense of his apostolic dignity and an explanation of what comprises salvation. "Paul, an apostle (not from men nor through man, but through Jesus Christ and God the Father who raised Him from the dead)" (1:1). Immediately, Paul underlines the fact of his having been chosen for the apostolic calling by God Himself. This obviously is directed against those Judaizing slanderers who tried to impugn his right to preach.

Characteristic of Paul's style also is the form of the apostolic greeting: "Grace to you and peace from God the Father and our Lord Jesus Christ, who gave Himself for our sins, that He might deliver us from this present evil age" (1:3–4). Paul here indicates the source of our salvation—Christ, not the Old Testament ritual law. Immediately after this greeting, the apostle expresses his amazement at the quick falling away of the Galatians from the true teaching, and he declares a firm anathema against anyone who would dare to preach any Gospel other than the one that Paul brought them, even if that Gospel were offered by an "angel from heaven" (1:8). This is another Biblical basis for the Church officially anathematizing heretics.

In 1:10, St Paul defends himself against the accusation that he, not being a true apostle, frees all pagans from the necessity of following the ritual Law of Moses only to gain their sympathy. "If I still pleased men, I would not be a bondservant of Christ" (1:10).

From 1:11, Paul begins his defense. The false teachers who belittled Paul said that he had never seen the Lord Jesus Christ in the flesh and that he learned the Gospel from other apostles. Furthermore, they said that he deviated from pure apostolic teaching, adding his own teaching about the insignificance of the Law of Moses. To hide this perversion of true teaching, they said, he talked and acted like the other apostles while in their company, so that he would not appear to teach a different faith.

Defending his apostolic dignity, Paul initially reveals the divine nature of his preaching of the Gospel, insisting that he learned the Gospel directly "through the revelation of Jesus Christ" (1:12). In other words, the Lord Himself taught Paul directly by appearing to him. As proof of this, Paul offers the Galatians the indubitable hand of God in Paul's drastic conversion. He tells them how he had been the cruelest of persecutors of the Church of God, but then he became a preacher of the Christian faith that he previously had persecuted (1:11–24).

In this autobiographical account, the following words are especially important: "I did not immediately confer with flesh and blood" (1:16), that is, with other people, especially the apostles, "nor did I go up to Jerusalem to those who were apostles before me; but I went to Arabia" (1:17), where, evidently St Paul was taught all the mysteries of the Christian faith directly by the Lord Himself in many visions (see also Eph 3:3). Only three years later did Paul go to Jerusalem "to see Peter," that is, only to become acquainted with the famous apostle, not to study under him. Paul spent only fifteen days in Jerusalem, during which time he saw no other apostle "except James, the Lord's brother" (1:19).

Paul makes a point to underline these details to show that he did not learn the Gospel from the other apostles, but from the Lord Himself. "Now concerning the things which I write to you, indeed, before God, I do not lie" (1:20). In these words, we see another example of Paul lawfully taking an oath, permissible in certain situations. Then Paul says that "afterward [he] went into the regions of Syria and Cilicia" (1:21), to reiterate that he did not see any of the apostles, who were all preaching in Palestine. In fact, he was not personally known to any of the churches in Judea. Oecumenius, the tenth-century Byzantine bishop and exegete, interprets St Paul's words thus: "See how [St Paul] is saying: 'I did not learn from Peter, but only remained with him. I saw none of the other apostles.' How can one learn from these people, without even having seen them?"[27]

The second chapter continues the defense. In the first ten verses, Paul recounts how he, "by revelation," traveled to the Apostolic Council in Jerusalem, the very council that declared that the ritual observance of the Mosaic Law was not necessary for Christians. St Paul came together with his disciple, the baptized and uncircumcised Titus, whom he presented to the apostles, and whom they did not require to be circumcised. Paul's Gospel received the sanction of all the elder apostles at this council. The eldest of the apostles acknowledged that Apostle Paul's unique calling was to preach to the uncircumcised, just as Peter's preaching was intended primarily for the Jews. As a sign of their complete agreement with his preaching, James, Cephas, and John, "who seemed to be pillars … gave me and Barnabas the right hand of fellowship, that we should go to the Gentiles and they to the circumcised" (2:9).

St John Chrysostom explains, "In the work of the ministry (says St Paul), we divided the world between us, I took the Gentiles and they the Jews, according to the divine decree; but to the sustenance of the poor among the Jews I also contributed my share."[28] Among the Jewish believers there were many poor, they lacked what the Gentiles had, and were persecuted by the unbelievers. We already have seen countless examples of Paul's care for gathering aid in the churches of the Gentiles for these poor Christians (2:1–10).

Then the apostle stresses the firmness and immutability of his convictions, while even some of the other apostles (Peter and Barnabas), condescending to the Judaizers, made certain concessions to them, even including avoiding the company of pagans and not eating with them. In 2:11–21, Paul describes how he actually had the boldness to contradict Peter and publicly rebuke him. This is a wonderful example of the equality of the apostles Peter and Paul, and it is a Biblical argument against the Roman Catholic dogma of Peter's alleged primacy over the apostles. If Peter were the vicar of Christ, Paul of course would not have dared to publicly condemn him of anything. Having then described the nature of his accusation against Peter, St Paul seamlessly moves to the main theme of his epistle: "A man is not justified by the works of the law but by faith in Jesus Christ … for by the works of the law no flesh shall be justified" (2:16).

These words are especially beloved by the Protestants, who see in them a rejection of the necessity of good deeds for salvation. It is entirely obvious, however, that Paul is not speaking of deeds of virtue, but of the works of the Law of Moses, that is, the ritual observances of the Old Testament Law, which lost their importance with the coming of Christ, something that was finally codified by the Apostolic Council in Jerusalem in A.D. 51. In the next verses, the holy apostle says that to require the full observance of the Old Testament Law of Christians means to indirectly accuse the Lord Himself of sin. "Is Christ therefore a minister of sin?"

(2:17). In other words, did Christ lead us to sin by the teaching He proclaimed to the world? Of course not. If the Law of Moses justified man, there would have been no need for the suffering and crucifixion of the Saviour: for "then Christ died in vain" (2:21). In 2:19–20, the apostle insists that all must leave behind the Old Testament Law to attach themselves to Christ with the whole being, to be co-crucified with him in order to live only for Him and in Him: "For I through the law died to the law that I might live to God. I have been crucified with Christ; it is no longer I who live, but Christ lives in me; and the life which I now live in the flesh I live by faith in the Son of God, who loved me and gave Himself for me" (2:19–20).

From the third chapter, Paul begins his dogmatic section of the epistle. It continues through chapter 4 and ends with the twelfth verse of chapter 5. A general point to be made about this entire section is given by St John Chrysostom: "In the former chapters, [St Paul] had shown himself not to be an apostle of men, nor by men, nor in want of apostolic instruction. Now, having established his authority as a teacher, he proceeds to discourse more confidently, and draws a comparison between faith and the Law."[29] Thus, the main subject that Paul examines here is the irrelevance of the Law to the Galatians, because they are Gentiles.

In the third chapter, St Paul first speaks of the irrelevance of the Law for the Galatians. The first proof of this is the experience of the Galatians themselves, who were already filled with the Holy Spirit and the gracious gifts of working miracles (3:1–5). The second proof is the example of Abraham: "Abraham 'believed God and it was accounted to him for righteousness'" (3:6). This makes it clear that "those who are of faith are blessed with believing Abraham" (3:9). Why is this? Paul explains with a citation of Deuteronomy 27:26: "Cursed is the one who does not confirm all the words of this law by observing them." This makes it clear that even in the very beginning, the Law had no power to justify man before God. This is further made clear by another citation from the Old Testament: "the just shall live by his faith" (Hab 2:4). Therefore, if righteousness was possible in the Old Testament, it was possible only through faith in the coming Redeemer of mankind and His redemptive sacrifice, to which the Law led its followers by using types and foreshadowing.

Only Christ freed from the curse all those who could not fulfill the Law to the letter: "Christ has redeemed us from the curse of the law, having become a curse for us (for it is written, 'Cursed is everyone who hangs on a tree' [Deut 21:23])" (3:13). These words are read as part of the epistle reading at the end of Matins of Great and Holy Saturday, because they explain the meaning and importance of the Lord's redemptive sacrifice. Blessed Jerome explains, "In the Old Testament, it was not the hanging on a tree that was accursed, but the grievous sin that led to the hanging."[30] St Theophan the Recluse further explains, "As everything in the Old Testament is a foreshadowing of things to come, so even this legislation about hanging criminals and removing them before evening to be buried was the prefiguration of Christ's death upon the Cross. For He also was hanged on a tree and taken down before evening."[31] Christ accepted the curse that burdened humanity, although he was innocent, and destroyed that curse, "just as someone who was not convicted, but decided to die in place of the criminal condemned to death, saved that criminal from death."[32] This Christ did "that the blessing of Abraham might come upon the Gentiles in Christ Jesus, that we might receive the promise of the Spirit through faith" (3:14).

The second half of chapter 3 refutes the objections concerning faith as the only thing needed for the Gentiles apart from the Law (3:15–29). The apostle disperses all doubts that could arise among the Christians of Jewish extraction, including the following: "Did not the Law cancel the promises given to Abraham for the sake of his faith? Why was the Law given in the first place?" Paul explains that the Law "was added because of transgressions" (3:19). As St Theophan comments, it was given later, because of the sins of the Jewish people, "in order to rein in their criminality, to keep the people in godly fear, lest they give themselves entirely to sin. It was intended to inspire them to live righteously and to prepare them to be worthy of revealing the Promised One in their ranks."[33]

The Law was given to the Jews instead of a rein, lest they live with no fear and reach extremes of iniquity. The Law was given as a teacher to humble and withhold them from breaking at least some of the laws, if not the entire Law. Thus, there was no small benefit from the Law. The Law was given "till the Seed should come" (3:19). Thus, the Law is temporary and passing in importance.

"If the Law was given only until the coming of the Christ," says St John Chrysostom on behalf of St Paul, "then why do you protract it beyond its natural period?"[34] The meaning of the Law is that it "was our tutor to bring us to Christ, that we might be justified by faith. But after faith has come, we are no longer under a tutor" (3:24–25). With the coming of the faith that has the power to justify, the Law became irrelevant. "For you are all sons of God through faith in Christ Jesus. For as many of you as were baptized into Christ have put on Christ" (3:26–27). The faith of Christ returns people to that wondrous time of sinless childhood, during which they could freely fulfill the will of their Father in Heaven and had no need to be humbled by strict discipline.

This is the essence of sonship to God, and in this sonship lies the reason for the irrelevance of the Law as a restraining force. Christians, as sons of God, are free of all formal rules and requirements, for they are all "one in Christ Jesus"; they have "put on Christ" and have no need of compulsion, as "There is neither Jew nor Greek, there is neither slave nor free, there is neither male nor female; for you are all one in Christ Jesus" (3:27–28). As spiritual children of Christ, the descendant of Abraham, Christians are true descendants of Abraham, and so they also inherit that justification and blessing promised to Abraham (3:29).

The fourth chapter contains admonishments to the Galatians to accept this proved truth of the irrelevance of the Law and of binding themselves by the ritualism of the

Old Testament. These admonishments are directed primarily to their minds (4:1–10), their hearts (4:11–20), and their wills (4:21–5:12). As St Theophan says, "Nothing so inspires the mind to reject its own thoughts as the revelation that our thoughts are utterly ridiculous."[35] This is exactly what St Paul does in this chapter. He shows how foolish it is for a grown son to live under the protection and guidance of his parents. This is how Israel was under the law until the proper time. But the end of that period has now come: "but when the fullness of the time had come, God sent forth His Son" (4:4) and through Him led us into the full rights of adult children. How foolish it is to labor like a slave under the law when you are "no longer a slave but a son, and if a son, then an heir of God through Christ" (4:7). The passage 4:4–7 constitutes the epistle reading for the liturgy of the Nativity of Christ.

Initially admonishing the Jews (4:1–7), Paul turns to the Gentiles. As St Theophan writes,

> [The Christians from the Gentiles] could have said, "Why, in previous times, were we converted to Judaism, and why did the chosen only approach us when we completely submitted to the whole Law?" "It was a different time then," answers the apostle. "Then Judaism was the only truth faith on earth, and you did well to accept it. Now, when God Himself has grafted you to Himself without the Law, your turning to the weak forces of the Law makes absolutely no sense."[36]

Because the heart can often be at cross purposes with the mind, Paul then finds it necessary to turn his admonishment to the hearts of the Galatians. These verses (4:11–20) are the most moving in the entire epistle. The apostle reminds the Galatians with what fire they accepted his preaching, with what love their hearts were filled. Was then his preaching all in vain? Blessed Theodoret says, "This is a fatherly voice, proper to the one who remembers his labors, and yet does not groan under them." Gently rebuking the Galatians for the fickleness of their feelings and relationship to him, the apostle calls them to realize the source of their fickleness. Then he indicates the source to be the new false teachers who "zealously court you, but for no good" (4:17), only for the sake of their vanity.

We see the highest degree of Paul's fatherly love for the Galatians in the most moving exclamation of the entire epistle: "My little children, for whom I labor in birth again until Christ is formed in you" (4:19). By turning back to Judaism, the Galatians darkened the image of Christ in their own hearts, and Paul with vivid fatherly love desires to restore this image. St John Chrysostom says, "Do you see the fatherly love and the sorrow, so worthy of an apostle? Do you hear the groaning, far more bitter than the cry of a woman in labor?"[37] Meanwhile, the phrase "I would like to be present with you now and to change my tone" (4:20) is interpreted by St Theophan the Recluse to mean "to change [the tone] in application to what he would see with his own eyes" or "to change it to the lamenting tone and to shed tears and make you all to weep" (St John Chrysostom).[38]

St Theophan explains, "The mind and the heart, once they have turned back to the way of truth, force the will to follow … However, the will can be slow to heed, delaying its decision-making."[39] This is why St Paul then tries to influence the will of the Galatians directly, showing how wonderful it is to remain free of the Law. He reveals this using Hagar and Sarah as metaphors for the two covenants. "For it is written that Abraham had two sons: the one by a bondwoman, the other by a freewoman" (4:22). This he then uses as an allegory of the two covenants. Hagar symbolizes the Old Testament with the Law of Moses, which did not give freedom from sin fully and held mankind in slavery to sin, whereas Sarah symbolizes the New Covenant that gives us complete justification and freedom from sin. "But, as he who was born according to the flesh [Ishmael] then persecuted him who was born according to the Spirit [Isaac]" (4:29), so now the zealots of the Law persecute the Christians. But the Scriptures say, "Cast out this bondwoman and her son; for the son of the bondwoman shall not be heir with my son, namely with Isaac" (Gen 21:10). Thus, we must now abandon the Old Testament Law to inherit our promised blessings, for we are Christians, children not of the slave woman, but of the freewoman (4:25–31).

In the fifth chapter, St Paul calls Christians to firmly hold to the freedom given them by Christ and not to subject themselves again to the slavery of the Law of Moses, "for in Christ Jesus neither circumcision nor uncircumcision avails anything, but faith working through love" (5:6). This chapter begins the moral-instructive part of the epistle, ending in 6:10. The main theme of this section is connected with his teaching concerning Christian freedom, contained in 5:13–14: "For you, brethren, have been called to liberty; only do not use liberty as an opportunity for the flesh, but through love serve one another. For all the law is fulfilled in one word, even in this: 'You shall love your neighbor as yourself.'"

Why does Paul not first mention love of God as the first and greatest commandment (see Matt 22:36–38)? Evidently because his intention is primarily to heal the lessening of mutual love among the Galatians, and true love for one's neighbor is always predicated on the presence of love for God in the person. To live as one free in spirit means to avoid sins and the works of the flesh—adultery, sexual immorality, strife, envy, hatred, murder, drunkenness, and so on—and instead to cultivate the works of the spirit—love, joy, peace, longsuffering, goodness, mercy, faith, meekness, and self-control. The apostle underlines that the moral life of a Christian is not easy; it is a constant fight to the death. It is nothing short of a self-crucifixion, a thought that is vividly expressed by Paul: "And those who are Christ's have crucified the flesh with its passions and desires" (5:24). This crucifixion of the flesh is absolutely necessary for anyone who desires to live a spiritual life, for "the flesh lusts against the Spirit, and the Spirit against the flesh; and these are contrary to one another, so that you do not do the things that you wish" (5:17). Therefore, if we decide to "live in the Spirit, let us also walk in the Spirit" (5:25).

In chapter 6, the holy apostle gives instructions of a moral nature to the perfected and, we can assume, to primates of churches. He commands them to correct those who sin in "a spirit of gentleness," never growing vain or proud, considering themselves to be someone important. Instead, they should be careful lest they also are tempted to sin, because God often permits those who are proud and unmerciful to fall into sin for their humility (6:1–3). "Bear one another's burdens, and so fulfill the law of Christ" (6:2). This is the essence of Christian love. Paul indicates the need for forcefully living a life of virtue by reminding all of God's omniscience: "Do not be deceived, God is not mocked" (6:7). In that final settling of accounts that awaits each of us at the end of the earthly life, "whatever a man sows, that he will also reap" (6:7). However, we must not despair, doing good, but instead hurry to do it, "as we have opportunity" (6:10), while we have the time, before death claims us.

In the conclusion to the epistle, St Paul expresses his special care for the Galatians, telling them that he wrote the letter with his own hand (usually he dictated his epistles to scribes, as in Rom 16:22). Then he opposes the purity of his motives to the motives of the false teachers who force the Galatians to be circumcised only to prevent them from being persecuted for the sake of Christ's Cross, and "that they may boast in your flesh" (6:13), or, in other words, that they may boast of the number of visible signs of circumcision they have won for themselves (Paul is being ironic here).

"But God forbid that I should boast except in the cross of our Lord Jesus Christ, by whom the world has been crucified to me, and I to the world" (6:14). To boast in the Cross of Christ means to believe that only the Cross gives salvation. Through such faith, says the apostle, I have become as a dead man for all the vain things of the world, and I do not care either for the glory or the persecution of this world. The essence of Christianity, the apostle again repeats, is to become a "new creation," and only to this should all Christians strive, for whoever lives thus, to him will "peace and mercy be upon them, and upon the Israel of God" (6:16), that is, the true Israel—all those who follow the teaching of grace.

Paul concludes with the exclamation: "From now on let no one trouble me" (6:17) for he has already explained and interpreted everything. To ask him further questions and to doubt his words now would be only to gratify a spirit of contentiousness—a pointless waste of time. The answer to all possible doubts is "the marks of the Lord Jesus" (6:17) that Paul bears in his body. Let these marks be the witnesses to the truth of Paul's preaching. St John Chrysostom explains these somewhat cryptic words (which some Roman Catholics incorrectly interpret as meaning that Paul had the stigmata): "If anyone sees a bloodied and wounded soldier, will he begin to accuse him of cowardice and treachery, when the solider carries proof of his bravery on his very body? Judge likewise with me, says Paul."

Paul finishes with an apostolic blessing: "The grace of our Lord Jesus Christ be with your spirit. Amen" (6:18).

 CHAPTER 5

The Epistle of the Holy Apostle Paul to the Ephesians

THE ESTABLISHMENT OF THE EPHESIAN CHURCH

Ephesus was a coastal city in Asia Minor on the Cayster River. It was known as a center of trade, arts, and knowledge, and it was the capital of the Roman province of Asia. It was also a great center of the pagan cults. It had a famous temple of Artemis of Ephesus, and the city itself was considered consecrated to the goddess. It was also a center of pagan magic centered on the mysteries of Artemis. People wore scrolls around their necks with esoteric writing as amulets, and small figurines of the temple and the goddess's statue were widely sold (and were a lucrative source of trade). Many Jews also lived in Ephesus, and there was a local synagogue.

The founder of the Church in Ephesus was Apostle Paul, who, as we see in Acts 18:19–21, first visited Ephesus around A.D. 54 during his return journey to Jerusalem, as part of his second missionary journey. Hurrying from Corinth to Jerusalem for the feast of Pentecost, Apostle Paul remained in Ephesus only a short time, but "he himself entered the synagogue and reasoned with the Jews. When they asked him to stay a longer time with them, he did not consent, but took leave of them, saying, 'I must by all means keep this coming feast in Jerusalem; but I will return again to you, God willing.' And he sailed from Ephesus."

This was the first catechization of the Ephesians into the Christian faith, from the mouth of Paul and his helpers Aquila and Priscilla. Evidently, even this introduction had its success, as Paul was asked to remain longer. Soon Apollos, a learned Jew from Alexandria, came to help Aquila and Priscilla in the mission. Initially, he only knew John's baptism, but Aquila and Priscilla instructed him more fully in the faith (Acts 18:24–28). Apollos, "an eloquent man and mighty in the Scriptures" (Acts 18:24), helped much in the establishment of Christianity in Ephesus. However, soon he had to leave to Achaia (Greece), and he traveled to Corinth without waiting for Paul's return to Ephesus.

Paul's most important work in Ephesus occurred during his third missionary journey, to which the nineteenth chapter of Acts is dedicated. After Apollos left Ephesus, the Holy Apostle Paul, having been in Jerusalem and Antioch and having traveled through Phrygia and Galatia, arrived in Ephesus as promised. There he found nearly twelve disciples who, like Apollos, knew and had accepted only the baptism of John. St Paul completed their instruction in the faith, convinced them to accept Christian baptism, and gave them the gift of the Holy Spirit by the laying on of hands (Acts 19:1–7). After this, St Paul began to preach in Ephesus. First, according to his usual custom, he began with the Jews, preaching in the local synagogue. He preached for three months, but "when some were hardened and did not believe, but spoke evil of the Way before the multitude, he departed from them and withdrew the disciples, reasoning daily in the school of Tyrannus" (Acts 19:9). This Tyrannus was perhaps a philosopher with his own "school," as sometimes happened in Greek cities (Acts 19:8-9).

"This continued for two years, so that all who dwelt in Asia heard the word of the Lord Jesus, both Jews and Greeks" (Acts 19:10). St Paul's preaching was accompanied by many wondrous signs and miracles (19:11–20). Paul preached there for two years, and the Church of God put down deep roots. Unfortunately, a riot incited by Demetrius, a local silversmith, forced Paul to leave Ephesus before he had intended. After the end of the riot, Paul visited the Macedonian Churches, remained three months in Greece, and then decided to go to Syria through Macedonia. The road to Syria went through Ephesus; however, because Paul wanted to hurry to Jerusalem for Pentecost, he, fearing to be delayed in Ephesus, bypassed it by sea, instead stopping in Miletus, a little south of Ephesus.

Paul then invited the presbyters of Ephesus and other local churches to meet with him for the last time. This parting was remarkably moving:

> You know, from the first day that I came to Asia, in what manner I always lived among you, serving the Lord with all humility, with many tears and trials which happened to me by the plotting of the Jews; how I kept back nothing that was helpful, but proclaimed it to you, and taught you publicly and from house to house, testifying to Jews, and also to Greeks, repentance toward God and faith toward our Lord Jesus Christ. And see, now I go bound in the spirit to Jerusalem, not knowing the things that will happen to me there, except that the Holy Spirit testifies in every city, saying that chains and tribulations await me. But none of these things move me; nor do I count my life dear to myself, so that I may finish my race with joy, and the ministry which I received from the Lord Jesus, to testify to the gospel of the grace of God. And indeed, now I know that you all, among whom I have gone preaching the kingdom of God, will see my face no more. Therefore I testify to you this day that

I *am* innocent of the blood of all *men*. For I have not shunned to declare to you the whole counsel of God. Therefore take heed to yourselves and to all the flock, among which the Holy Spirit has made you overseers, to shepherd the church of God which He purchased with His own blood. For I know this, that after my departure savage wolves will come in among you, not sparing the flock. Also from among yourselves men will rise up, speaking perverse things, to draw away the disciples after themselves. Therefore watch, and remember that for three years I did not cease to warn everyone night and day with tears. (Acts 20:18–31)

After praying, the presbyters accompanied Paul to the ship and said their final goodbyes. This was the last personal encounter of the Ephesians with Paul, but he did not cease to care for them, as proved by his epistle.

Later, Paul's disciple Timothy occupied the bishopric of Ephesus until his death. After him, the beloved disciple of Christ, John the Theologian, ruled the churches of Asia Minor from Ephesus. In 431, Ephesus was the site of the Third Ecumenical Council.

THE PURPOSE OF THE EPISTLE TO THE EPHESIANS

This epistle does not suggest any specific inciting incident. As seen from several places in the epistle itself, Paul wrote it while imprisoned in Rome (Eph 3:1, 4:1, and others). Judging by the inspiration and the exalted tone of the entire epistle, it is likely that St Paul was inspired to write to them because of his desire to inform his beloved Ephesians of revelations given to him by the Holy Spirit during his imprisonment, in accordance with the interpretation of St Theophan the Recluse. Another reason could have been St Paul's desire to comfort the Ephesians, who were sorrowful at the plight of their beloved spiritual father and teacher (Eph 3:13). Finally, a third reason could have been his fear for the Ephesians, and his desire to warn them against the Judaizers and other false teachers. It is evident that the apostle wanted to reveal to the Ephesians the "mystery of salvation," given to him in a divine revelation, concerning the calling of both Gentiles and Jews to salvation in the Kingdom of Heaven (Eph 3:6–9).

THE PLACE AND TIME OF THE WRITING OF THE EPISTLE

Not all commentators agree on the place or time of the writing. The only fact no one questions is that this epistle was written by St Paul from imprisonment, for he mentions his bonds several times. It is known that St Paul was imprisoned in Caesarea of Palestine, where he remained in the care of the governor Felix for two years until he appealed directly to Caesar, after which he was sent to Rome (Acts 23:35, 24:27, 25:10–11). Then he was imprisoned in Rome (Acts 28:16). There were two distinct Roman imprisonments, between which was a well-known period of time. Ancient commentators ascribe the writing of Ephesians to the time of St Paul's Roman captivity; however, because St Paul does not mention anything about his impending martyrdom in the epistle, as he does in his later Epistle to Timothy (2 Tim 4:6), which was written from Rome as well, and he even boldly expresses his hope to continue preaching (Eph 6:19–20), we can assume that Paul wrote the epistle during his first imprisonment in Rome.

St Theophan the Recluse believed that the epistle was written from Caesarea of Palestine, because it makes no mention of any changes in the Church of Ephesus—positive or negative—which suggests it was written soon after his last visit. Furthermore, Paul explicitly asks the Ephesians to pray that he be given the word, that his mouth be opened to boldly proclaim the mystery of the Gospel. These details suggest the earlier Caesarean imprisonment, for in Rome Paul had greater freedom to accept visitors and preach "with all confidence, no one forbidding him" (Acts 28:31), while in Caesarea, he was more closely guarded and only a few people were allowed to visit him. Furthermore, St Theophan considered that such an active apostle could not remain two years in Caesarea without writing anything of significance, and so he probably took the opportunity to write to those whom he converted to Christianity, teaching and instructing them in the faith. If we are to accept this reasoning, then Ephesians was written in Caesarea in A.D. 60 or 61.

Other commentators, comparing the Epistle to the Ephesians with other epistles and finding that it was written at the same time as Colossians and Philemon and soon after Philippians (compare Eph 6:21 and Col 4:7–8), believe that the Epistle to the Ephesians was written in Rome in A.D. 62 or 63. Paul sent this epistle (together with Colossians) with Tychicus, whom he commissioned to inform the churches concerning his circumstances.

THE AUTHENTICITY OF THE EPISTLE

Tertullian, in his polemic against Marcion, writes that the Marcionites believed this epistle to have been written not to the Church of Ephesus, but to the Church of Laodicea. In some ancient manuscripts, the phrase "in Ephesus" (*en Ephesô*) in verse 1 is omitted, whereas in others, it is found only in the margins. At the same time, in the Epistle to the Colossians, which according to its content and the time of sending indicates it was written at the same time as Ephesians (see Eph 6:21, Col 4:7), Paul speaks about a letter he wrote to the Church of Laodicea, but such an epistle has not survived. Finally, this epistle lacks the personal greetings so typical of Paul, especially considering the three years he spent in Ephesus. All this gives some of the new commentators reasons to doubt this letter's authenticity.

However, St Ignatius of Antioch, who also wrote an epistle to the Ephesians, witnessed the existence of an epistle similar to his own, written by St Paul.[40] All the aforementioned doubts can be easily resolved if we imagine that the Epistle to the Ephesians was a more general epistle, not intended merely for the Church in Ephesus, but for the other churches in Asia as well, including the Church in Laodicea, which could be considered as belonging to the metropolis of Ephesus. Additional early witnesses to the authenticity of Ephesians include St Polycarp of Smyrna, St Irenaeus of Lyons, and Clement of Alexandria, all of whom quote it directly.

THE STRUCTURE AND CONTENT OF THE EPISTLE

Ephesians consists of six chapters. The main theme of the letter, according to the author himself (Eph 3:2–9), is the mystery of divine economy and the moral demands pertaining to salvation. The epistle is easily divided into two parts:

1. A dogmatic section (1:1–22 to 3:1–21).
2. A section dealing with instruction in morals (4:1–31 to 6:1–24).

The dogmatic section is a short summary of the essential doctrinal points of Christianity, primarily the idea of the Church as the Body of Christ. The moral-instructive section teaches the unity of faith and the need for unity in moral activity, which arms one for spiritual struggle. In general, this epistle is incredibly important, because it is a brilliant apology for Christianity. St John Chrysostom and St Athanasius of Alexandria called it a "catechesis" of Christian doctrine. Many commentators see it as a kind of summary of Paul's preaching.

EXEGETICAL ANALYSIS OF THE EPISTLE TO THE EPHESIANS

The Epistle to the Ephesians begins with the usual greeting: "Paul, an apostle of Jesus Christ by the will of God, to the saints who are in Ephesus, and faithful in Christ Jesus: Grace to you and peace from God our Father and the Lord Jesus Christ" (1:1–2).

After the greeting, the dogmatic portion of the epistle begins. The holy apostle first of all praises and thanks God, the Father of our Lord Jesus Christ, for choosing us for a holy life that was predestined "before the foundation of the world" (1:4) and consists in our becoming sons of God through Jesus Christ, Who, having saved us by His Blood and opened to mankind the mystery of God's good will, became the Head of all in heaven and earth, and made us through Himself the heirs of God (1:3–12).

Then the apostle turns his spiritual gaze to the Ephesians directly, who have believed in Christ, and, consequently, have become participants in the benefits given by Him. He thanks God for them, remembering them in his prayers and asking God that He give them the Spirit of wisdom Who will illumine the eyes of their hearts to better understand the riches of His inheritance and the greatness of His power (1:13–19). Verses 20–23 contain an important teaching about the raising up of the Risen Christ, as the God-man greater than all creation, and of the submission of all creation to Him. We see the exaltation of human nature in the person of our Saviour, proof that the Lord Jesus Christ, even as a man, is King and Lord of heaven and earth, angels and men. "And He put all things under His feet, and gave Him to be head over all things to the Church, which is His body, the fullness of Him who fills all in all" (1:22–23).

This teaching concerning the Lord Jesus Christ as the Head of the Church is immensely important. As our own bodily members, together with our head, comprise our complete body, so all the faithful, together with Christ, also comprise one body, both physical and spiritual. Those who are baptized in Christ have put on Christ, becoming one with Him. Therefore, Christ acts in Christians as a "creative and life-giving power."[41] The organic and mechanical life of the body depend on the head. The head, as the casing for the brain, has psychological importance. It has spiritual importance as well, because it is reckoned to be the source of the spiritual life, its directing principle. Apostle Paul's comparison illustrates the Church's complete dependence on the Lord Jesus Christ, the Church's reliance on His direction of His Church.

The expression "the fullness of Him who fills all in all" is vague, and different interpretations have been offered. The most accurate understanding of these words is the following: the Church is a spiritual organism in which there is no place where the divine power of Christ does not act directly. "It is full of Christ. He fills the Church with Himself completely" (St Theophan).[42] St John Chrysostom explains why the apostle did not merely limit himself to describing the Church as Christ's Body, and Himself as its Head:

> In order then that when you hear of the Head, you may not conceive the notion of supremacy only, but also of consolidation, and that you may behold Him not as a supreme Ruler only, but as Head of a body, "the fulness of Him that filleth all in all," he says. As though this were not sufficient to show the close connection and relationship, what does he add? "The fulness of Christ is the Church."[43]

In the second chapter, Paul speaks of how the greatness of God's economy was evident in the renewal of spiritually moribund mankind, raised by God from the worst debasement. Only the grace of God could do this, independent of any merits on the part of fallen mankind: "For by grace you have been saved through faith, and that not of yourselves; it is the gift of God, not of works, lest anyone should boast" (2:8–9). These words are popular among Protestants, who try to use them to prove their false teaching of the irrelevance of good deeds for salvation. However, it is completely clear that here Paul speaks only of a single moment, of the establishment of salvation by God, not of the assumption of this salvation by individual people. That aspect of salvation—that is, the individual effort of every Christian—is spoken of in the following passage: "For we are His workmanship, created in Christ Jesus for good works, which God prepared beforehand that we should walk in them" (2:10).

The meaning of all these words is that "salvation is prepared for us in advance, and we are called to receive it, not because we have deserved it by our deeds, but only by grace. However, we are not called to do nothing on our part, but rather to cooperate in our salvation, becoming rich in deeds of virtue."[44]

Then the apostle speaks of the great goodness of God that reunited those who have been estranged before this moment—the pagans and Jews—into a single body, united "by the blood of Christ" (2:13). The Lord recreated, as it were, all of mankind (2:11–15), having reconciled both Gentiles and Jews with God by the Cross, "having abolished in His flesh the enmity" (2:15) between God and man, the reason for humanity's separation from God on account of sin. Here St Paul stresses the passing of the Old Testament Law with the words: "having abolished ... the law of commandments contained in ordinances" (2:15) and "has broken down the middle wall of separation" (2:14). In other words, He abolished the Law that, like a wall, separated the Jews from the Gentiles. "And He came and preached peace to you who were afar off and to those who were near" (2:17). The essence of Christ's good news is that the Son of God, having become incarnate and suffered for us on the Cross, reconciled us with God. "Those afar off" are the Gentiles, whereas "those who were near" are the Jews (St Theodoret of Cyrus).[45]

Now Jews and Gentiles, united by Christianity, comprise a single Church, a single building founded on the apostles, prophets, and on the Cornerstone—the Lord Jesus Christ. The mortar holding them all together is the Holy Spirit (note that Christ is the Rock on which the Church is founded, not Apostle Peter, as the Roman Catholics maintain).

In chapter 3, the apostle speaks of the hiddenness of the mystery of the calling of the pagans into the Church of Christ, and how he himself was given the grace to preach this mystery of Christ to the pagans. He has suffered much from the Judaizers for his preaching to the Gentiles, but he does not despair and begs the Ephesians not to grieve for him (3:1–13). The dogmatic section concludes with a prayer for the Ephesians (3:14–21), that they be confirmed in faith and love for Christ and that they will come to know "the love of Christ which passes knowledge; that you may be filled with all the fullness of God" (3:19), that is, "that you will have Him completely dwelling in you," as Blessed Theodoret explains.[46] Having exhorted the Ephesians to achieve the pinnacle of Christian perfection, the holy apostle praises God (3:20–21).

The second half of the epistle, comprising chapters 4–6, is the moral-instructive part of the epistle. Having explained that all Christians comprise a single Body with one Head—Christ—the holy apostle then explains how members of such a Body must live and act, as they have been united and renewed by Christ. At first he describes,

1. the general manner of life characterized primarily by unity in faith (4:1–16);
2. rules that apply to Christians of all walks of life (4:17–5:21); and
3. more particular rules that list the responsibilities of husbands and wives, parents and children, slaves and masters (5:22–6:9).

Paul then calls all to struggle with the world and with sin, describing a life of asceticism (6:10–18).

In chapter 4, the apostle exhorts the Ephesians to be worthy of their calling of Christianity. The foundation of this calling must be humble-mindedness, meekness, longsuffering, and love. The most important goal to which we as Christians must strive is "to keep the unity of the Spirit in the bond of peace" (4:3). As the strongest inducement to such spiritual unity, St Paul reminds Christians that "There is … one Lord, one faith, one baptism; one God and Father of all, who is above all, and through all, and in you all" (4:4–6).

Every one of the faithful, as a separate member of a single organism, is given special grace, a special gift that he must use to serve others for the good of all. This variety of gifts not only does not hinder "unity of spirit," but rather strengthens this unity among Christians, just as the differences between parts of the body do not prevent the body from growing and becoming strong, thanks to the cooperation of its members. To aid the growth of the Body of His Church, "for the equipping of the saints for the work of ministry, for the edifying of the body of Christ" (4:12), Christ "gave some to be apostles, some prophets, some evangelists, and some pastors and teachers" (4:11). Clearly, Paul here confirms the divine establishment of the Church's hierarchy, to the shame of Protestants, who deny the need for a lawful priesthood.

The reason that a hierarchy is necessary in the Church is to help believers reach spiritual perfection: "till we all come to the unity of the faith and of the knowledge of the Son of God, to a perfect man, to the measure of the stature of the fullness of Christ" (4:13). St Theophan the Recluse explains: "This will be when all will rise to a state of complete peace in God and, having made of themselves worthy dwelling places for God, will have Him inhabiting in themselves. This is the 'measure of the stature of the fullness of Christ.'"[47] The most important goal of a moral Christian life is not to remain as children—vacillating and distracted by every new teaching—but, like a healthy organism, to become united with each other in love, to help the Body of Christ's Church flourish, to "grow up in all things into Him who is the head—Christ" (4:15).

In the second half of this chapter, Paul, describing the negative aspects of the pagan manner of living (i.e., the manner of life of the Ephesians before their conversion), exhorts them to "put off … the old man which grows corrupt according to the deceitful lusts … and … put on the new man which was created according to God, in true righteousness and holiness" (4:22–24). This inner renewal must reveal itself first and foremost in truth: "Therefore, putting away lying, 'Let each one of you speak truth with his neighbor'" (4:25). Second, this renewal is reflected in a lack of anger: "'Be angry, and do not sin': do not let the sun go down on your wrath" (4:26). In other words, make peace with those whom you angered before the day is done. Then Paul exhorts the Ephesians not to steal, but to work with their own hands, "that he may have something to give to him who has need" (4:28), to avoid "corrupt words" (foul language), and to be modest and instructive in words, not to offend the Holy Spirit with one's behavior, to avoid all strife, irritation, anger, "clamor, and evil speaking," and instead to be kind to one another, "tenderhearted, forgiving one another, even as God in Christ forgave you" (4:29–32).

Continuing the same moral instruction in the fifth chapter, Paul exhorts the Christians to emulate God in their love, just as children emulate their father, taking him as their example for all things. As an inducement to live a moral life, Paul reminds the Ephesians that sinners will be denied the kingdom of God. Paul especially warns them against sexual sins and drunkenness, as well as "all uncleanness or covetousness." Instead, Christians should "walk as children of light" (5:8), "finding out what is acceptable to the Lord" (5:10). The state of an inveterate sinner is similar to a deep sleep, but even he can wake up from the sleep of sin, and to him the apostle calls out: "Awake, you who sleep, arise from the dead, and Christ will give you light" (5:14). Some commentators believe that these words are a paraphrase of and an allusion to Isaiah 60:1 and 26:9, 19: "Arise, shine; for your light has come! ... Your dead shall live; Together with my dead body they shall arise."

Paul then continues teaching that this temporary life is given to us to prepare for eternity. Keeping in mind the great number of sinful temptations that surround us in this life, St Paul exhorts the Ephesians, "See then that you walk circumspectly, not as fools but as wise, redeeming the time, because the days are evil" (5:15–16). In other words, we are not to waste our precious time, but to use it to prepare ourselves for eternity. For this, first of all, we must not be "unwise, but understand what the will of the Lord is" (5:17). Paul especially warns against drunkenness, saying that it leads to dissipation. Instead of physical pleasures, Christians must seek spiritual joys, being filled with the Spirit and "speaking to one another in psalms and hymns and spiritual songs, singing and making melody in your hearts to the Lord" (5:19).

The second half of chapter 5 is dedicated to instructions concerning married life. The apostle imagines the marital union as a symbol of the mystical union of the Lord Jesus Christ with His Church. For this reason, 5:20–33 is the epistle reading for the wedding service. Apostle Paul requires that husbands have self-rejecting love for their wives, while he requires wives to be submissive to their husbands: "Wives, submit to your own husbands as to the Lord" (5:22). Paul explains why this must be so: "For the husband is head of the wife, as also Christ is head of the church; ... Therefore, just as the church is subject to Christ, so let the wives be to their own husbands in everything" (5:23–24), that is, in everything good. This also makes it clear that the submission of the wife is not a state of slavery or even something compelled, but "as to the Lord," that is, sincere and heartfelt, founded on love.

The husband's "headship" in a Christian marriage must be understood only as a state of precedence, something that is inevitable in any society or union consisting of more than one person. However, it is not lordship over the wife. The husband is the natural head of the family because the weight of the family's responsibilities lies on the husband, not the wife, because of the relative gentleness of her nature and her relative physical weakness. "Husbands, love your wives, just as Christ also loved the church and gave Himself for her" (5:25). Consequently, the love between husband and wife must primarily be spiritual, not physical, for it has a concrete moral purpose: "that He might sanctify and cleanse her with the washing of water by the word, that He might present her to Himself a glorious church … but that she should be holy and without blemish" (5:26–27). Just as Christ, through the laver of baptism, purifies all who enter the Church from sin, so a husband must strive for the moral purity and salvation of the soul of his wife.

At the same time, the husband must express his love in his care for his wife, as though she were his own body, to "nourish and cherish" her "just as the Lord does the Church" (5:29). Again, this stresses the need for spiritual love between husband and wife. The husband must look at his wife not as a tool for the slaking of his physical passions, but as a part of himself. In connection with this, Paul reminds the Ephesians of the Biblical basis for such love: "Therefore, a man shall leave his father and mother and be joined to his wife, and they shall become one flesh" (Gen 2:24). With these words, Paul desires to inspire Christians to maintain strong marital bonds and to show how unnatural and repugnant to God are all disagreements between spouses, not to mention divorce.

"This is a great mystery, but I speak concerning Christ and the church" (5:32). St John Chrysostom offers the best interpretation of these words:

> For indeed, in very deed, a mystery it is, yea, a great mystery, that a man should leave the one that gave him being, the one that begat him, and that brought him up, and her that travailed with him and had sorrow, those that have bestowed upon him so many and great benefits, those with whom he has been in familiar intercourse, and be joined to one who was never even seen by him and who has nothing in common with him, and should honor her before all others … A great mystery indeed, and one that contains some hidden wisdom.[48]

"I speak concerning Christ and the Church." By these words, Paul desires to remind the husband and wife that their intimacy and union in a blessed Christian marriage is so great and contains within itself such a great mystery that the best possible comparison is the unity of Christ with His Church, in which image they also have their prefiguration. It is as if the apostle says that there is already a great mystery in a secular marriage between a man a woman, but a Christian marriage is greater, for it is an image of the union of Christ with the Church. Such a marriage is the greatest of mysteries, for it is a sacrament of the Church. Of what nature is the union of the Church with Christ? It is the most intimate of unions, infused with love, holy and indivisible. This is how united a husband and wife in a Christian marriage must be.

In conclusion, the apostle says, "Let each one of you in particular so love his own wife as himself, and let the wife see that she respects her husband" (5:33). Everything must be mutual in a Christian marriage. In the beginning, the apostle said, "submitting to one another in the fear of God" (5:21). However, the husband is still the head, and so the wife's duty is submission to him. Because women often tend to resent the authority of their husbands, while husbands often take advantage of their position of headship to lord it over their wives, St Paul concludes his teaching on marriage by pointing out those precepts of marital life that are most likely to be broken: he commands love to husbands, and obedience to wives.

The older English translation of Ephesians 5:32, "let the wife see that she fears (*phobêtai*) her husband," must be understood only metaphorically, lest it be interpreted as referring to a wife's slavish fear of her husband, for which there can be no place in Christianity. This "fear" is nothing else than her respect for her husband taking care not to offend him and thus not to diminish the love that they have between themselves.

In the sixth chapter, the holy apostle describes the responsibilities of children toward their parents, and the responsibilities of parents toward their children. Children must listen to their parents, for natural law demands it, as does the fifth commandment of the Decalogue. As for the parents, they must not be severe to their children, they must not lead them into sin, but must wisely raise them in "the training and admonition of the Lord" (6:4). Then the apostle exhorts slaves to show obedience to their masters, and masters to be fair and condescending to slaves. St Paul does not even touch the political or social issue of the legality or abolition of slavery. The Christian Church in general has never set itself the goal to drive forward external political or social revolutions. Instead, Christianity seeks the interior transformation of mankind, which then will naturally entail the external changes in the social or political aspects of the entire life of humanity.

In concluding this moral portion of the letter, St Paul calls all Christians to wage unseen spiritual warfare against the enemy of our salvation, the devil and his servants. This is the foundation of Christian asceticism. The entire life of a Christian must be an endless struggle. The apostle calls Christians to arm themselves with God's armor for this warfare:

> Stand therefore, having girded your waist with truth, having put on the breastplate of righteousness, and having shod your feet with the preparation of the gospel of peace, above all, taking the shield of faith with which you will be able to quench all the fiery darts of the wicked one. And take the helmet of salvation, and the sword of the Spirit, which is the word of God. (6:14–17)

Having thus protected themselves, Christians must lead a stubborn battle against the snares of the devil and against the spirits of evil who constantly lead people to the path of sin and the way contrary to the will of God. This section of the epistle (6:10–17) is read on days commemorating certain monastic saints and during the service of the tonsure into monasticism.

The most important weapon in this unseen warfare must be prayer, and not merely prayer, but constant prayer. The evil spirits are here called "the rulers of the darkness of this age" (6:12), not in the sense that they have power over the world, but in the sense that all that is evil in the world, all evil men, do their will. The expression "in the heavenly places" (6:12) means that the evil spirits inhabit the entire space between heaven and earth, that is, they surround us no matter where we are, just like air, and they constantly attack us "like mosquitos in a bog," as St Theophan the Recluse memorably said. "The whole armor of God" is especially necessary for us, so that we can repel the evil spirits "in the evil day" (6:13). This evil day refers to especially significant moments in our life, such as death and the final judgment, when we will need to give God an account of our earthly life.

All this makes it clear that Christians are warriors of Christ, required to battle constantly against the enemy of God and human salvation—the devil, his servants, all the evil that comes from them. A Christian must be completely irreconcilable with any of the devil's evil; however, he must only use Christian weapons to battle him.

The passage 6:19–24 concludes the epistle. Here, Apostle Paul asks first of all for prayer for himself, teaching that the prayers of the Church are more important and greater than the individual prayer of any single person, no matter how righteous. Second, he tells the Ephesians of the coming of Tychicus, "whom I have sent to you … that you may know our affairs, and that he may comfort your hearts" (6:22).

St Paul ends his letter with an exhortation of peace and love to the brethren and his usual apostolic benediction: "Grace be with all those who love our Lord Jesus Christ in [incorruption]. Amen" (6:24). St John Chrysostom interprets the words "in incorruption" as meaning "in sinlessness."

Chapter 6

The Epistle of the Holy Apostle Paul to the Philippians

THE ESTABLISHMENT OF THE CHURCH IN PHILIPPI

The Church in Philippi was established by St Paul during his second missionary journey. When the great apostle of the nations, together with Silas, Timothy, and Luke, traveled through Galatia and Phrygia and reached the shores of the Aegean Sea, the Holy Spirit did not allow them to go either south to Asia or north to Bithynia. Here, in the coastal town of Troas, St Paul had a vision. Before him stood a certain Macedonian man who asked him to come to Macedonia and help them. Many believe that this was the guardian angel of Macedonia. Having received such a direction, St Paul immediately traveled to Macedonia by sea through Naples and arrived in Philippi, which bordered Thrace.

St Luke says that this was the first city of that part of Macedonia, a "colony." When Rome finally invaded Macedonia under its last king, Perseus, it divided it into four regions, and Augustus moved many Italians into this new territory to cement his control. He then established a Roman garrison there and gave the local population the same rights that Italian residents enjoyed (the so-called *jus italicum*). All this so raised the profile of Philippi that it became more important than the capital of Macedonia, Amphipolis.

St Paul remained in Philippi for several days with his fellow travelers, not attempting yet to preach. On the Sabbath, he traveled outside the city to a local Jewish house of prayer, where he began to preach to some women who had gathered there. One of these women, named Lydia, listened to him attentively. She traded in expensive cloth and most likely was a proselyte. Having come to believe in Christ, she was baptized with her entire household, and she offered St Paul and his fellow travelers the hospitality of her home.

After this, St Paul began to preach among the Gentiles, although he continued to preach to the Jews as well. All went well and successfully, until a certain pagan family, evidently influential in the city, incited a riot against Paul after he exorcized a demon from one of their slave girls, who made money for them by predicting the future. When this unfortunate girl met St Paul and those with him, she walked after them and continually cried out: "These men are the servants of the Most High God, who proclaim to us the way of salvation" (Acts 16:17).

Paul, realizing that such words coming from the mouth of a demon could harm the preaching of the Spirit of Truth, forbade the evil spirit from speaking and cast it out by the name of Jesus Christ. The enemy took this opportunity to raise a storm against Paul. The masters of the slave woman, seeing that she was no longer a source of easy income, seized Paul and Silas and brought them to the magistrates of the city. There they accused them of troubling the city by preaching newfangled rites, "which are not lawful for us, being Romans, to receive or observe" (Acts 16:21). According to the most recent laws of the Roman Empire, new religious sects were indeed forbidden, lest they further weaken Rome's already tottering control over the provinces.

The city magistrates, having torn the clothes off the apostles' backs, "commanded them to be beaten with rods" (Acts 16:22). Then they were cast into prison. The night guardsman cast them into the deepest part of the prison and even put their feet into stocks. By God's providence, however, this imprisonment only served for the greater glorification and success of the mission. Near midnight, when Paul and Silas sang praises to God and the other prisoners listened to them, the earth began to quake so fiercely that the foundation of the prison cracked, all the prison doors opened, and the chains holding all the prisoners simply fell off. The jailer, fearing to be held responsible for the escape of all the prisoners, pulled out his sword and was about to kill himself. Paul consoled him, however, and he, with the help of a torch, could not avoid the conclusion that all that occurred was due to the power of God.

Amazed by this, he fell at the feet of Paul in trepidation, then led Paul and Silas out and asked, "Sirs, what must I do to be saved?" They told him, "Believe on the Lord Jesus Christ, and you will be saved, you and your household" (Acts 16:30–31). Then they preached the word of God to him and all who were in his house. All believed and were baptized in that same hour.

In the meantime, with the coming of day, the city magistrates who had ordered the apostles to be beaten on the previous day—likely this was done not so much because they were convinced of their guilt as to calm the rioting masses—ordered that the apostle be released. However, St Paul, doubtless to protect the good name of the ministry, required that the magistrates offer an official apology, as Paul was a Roman citizen. The magistrates were afraid when they heard this, because it meant that they had unlawfully subjected Romans to corporal punishment, and without a trial to boot. They personally came to the apostles and apologized, asking them merely to leave the city quietly.

The apostles, however, did not leave immediately, but first came to the house of Lydia to strengthen the faith of the newly established community in Philippi. Merely taking care of the essentials, so that the community would be able to survive on its own, the apostles continued on their way (this was in A.D. 51 or 52). Although Paul left Philippi, he left Timothy and Luke behind for a short while to help with the transition.

Paul's relationship with the Philippians did not end there. The Church in Philippi became the most ardent and faithful in its love for its founder and was especially remarkable for its Christian almsgiving and charity. No matter where Paul was, the Philippians followed his progress with a filial gaze and constantly sent him financial and moral support in his difficult and sorrowful life. The apostle loved them with equal ardency. "My beloved and longed-for brethren, my joy and crown" is how Paul addressed them in his epistle (Phil 4:1). They sent him aid to Thessalonica several times (Phil 4:16) and probably also sent aid to Corinth (2 Cor 11:8–9). When the apostle was sent to Rome to await Caesar's judgment, the Philippians sent Epaphroditus, their eldest presbyter, to Rome with money for Paul.

St Paul never missed an opportunity to visit Philippi in person, whenever it was possible. During his third missionary journey, having spent three years in Ephesus and deciding to continue from there to Greece, Paul traveled through Macedonia and visited Philippi twice (Acts 19:21, 20:3–6).

THE PURPOSE OF THE EPISTLE TO THE PHILIPPIANS

After his third missionary journey, the Holy Apostle Paul traveled to Jerusalem, where he was subjected to a vicious attack by the Jews and was put in bonds, eventually appealing to Caesar, after which he was sent to Rome. All this time, the Philippians tried to support Paul financially, something that Paul himself implicitly mentions in the epistle (Phil 4:10), but circumstances hindered them. When the apostle finally arrived in Rome, the Philippians took the opportunity to gather a large sum of money and sent it directly to Rome with Epaphroditus, whom the holy apostle calls his brother, fellow laborer, and ascetic (Phil 2:25).

Having accepted their money from Epaphroditus as "a sweet-smelling aroma, an acceptable sacrifice, well pleasing to God" (Phil 4:18), Paul found out that the Philippians, in addition to sorrowing for his suffering, were divided by opinions concerning the future of the persecuted faith of Christ. Some were afraid for the future, and there was no unity in the struggle against the enemies of the Church. Furthermore, some members of the Philippian community had grown proud and arrogant, and as a consequence, there was no peace in the community. It is possible also that the Judaizers had made inroads there, as they did in so many other places.

Finally, Epaphroditus told the apostle about some people who were a great temptation in the community.

All this together motivated the Holy Apostle Paul to write an epistle to the Philippians. Epaphroditus's arrival soon turned to sorrow for the apostle, however, because his fellow laborer fell grievously ill and was at death's doorstep. News of this reached Philippi. Finally, God had mercy on him, and not only on him, but "on me also, lest I should have sorrow upon sorrow" (Phil 2:27). When Epaphroditus was well enough to undertake the difficulties of travel, the holy apostle sent him back to his community with the epistle in hand.

As is natural to assume, the main theme of the epistle was his expression of love and gratitude to the Philippians. He praises their sincere and unhypocritical faithfulness to the Church. No epistle of the great apostle could avoid instructions in the faith, but in this case, the instructions are given without his usual logical sequence. This letter lacks Paul's usual division into dogmatic and ethical parts: it is a private, not an official letter. It is reminiscent more of a father's cheerful letter and is filled with meek and gentle emotion, typical of the relationship between Paul and the Philippians. We see no strict accusations, no categorical commands, and no authoritative apostolic orders. Especially interesting is the complete lack of any rebukes.

THE PLACE AND TIME OF THE WRITING OF THE EPISTLE

In the letter itself, Paul expresses the hope that he will soon be delivered from his bonds and be able to visit Philippi (Phil 1:25–26, 2:24). He also mentioned that the faith he preached had even reached the house of Caesar (Phil 4:22). There is also a reference to the "palace guard," the Praetorians (Phil 1:13). Paul was obviously in Rome. That this was the first imprisonment, not the second, can be concluded from Paul's greeting to the Philippians, in which he mentions Timothy's presence with him in Rome. Timothy was not with Paul during his second imprisonment in Rome (see 2 Tim 4:9–10). Thus, the epistle was written from Rome in late A.D. 63 or early A.D. 64.

THE STRUCTURE AND CONTENT OF THE EPISTLE

The Epistle to the Philippians consists of four chapters. Although it has no definite thematic plan, as in other epistles, it still can be divided into the following sections:

1. The usual introduction with a greeting (1:1–12).
2. News concerning himself, especially concerning his successful preaching and his hopes for quick release (1:12–26) and instruction on how best to live as a preacher of the Gospel (1:27–2:18).
3. His intentions to send Timothy to Philippi (Phil 2:19–24) and to return Epaphroditus to them (2:25–30).

4. Warnings against the Judaizers (3:1–3); Paul offers himself as a model for emulation (3:4–16).

5. In conclusion, the apostle instructs several people and gives a general instruction as well concerning how to live a Christian life (4:2–9). In his customary epilogue, the apostle remembers their generous financial support and gives them his apostolic benediction (4:10–23).

EXEGETICAL ANALYSIS OF THE EPISTLE TO THE PHILIPPIANS

The epistle begins with the greeting: "Paul and Timothy, bondservants of Jesus Christ, to all the saints in Christ Jesus who are in Philippi, with the bishops and deacons" (1:1). Timothy is here mentioned probably because he was involved with Paul in the establishment of the community in Philippi, and he was close to them. In utter humility, Paul calls himself and Timothy merely slaves of Christ, not underlining his apostolic dignity as he does in other, more official, epistles, in which it was necessary to establish his authority to those who had begun to doubt it. With respect to the expression "with the bishops and deacons," St John Chrysostom asks a relevant question: "Can it be that in a single city there were several bishops? No. The apostle here speaks of the presbyters. For then, the titles of bishop and presbyter were still interchangeable." At that time, all the faithful were called "saints," because they were sanctified by the grace of the Holy Spirit. The apostle, as was his custom, bestows upon the readers the wishes of "grace to you and peace" (1:1–2).

In chapter 1, Paul expresses his gratitude to God for that zeal with which the Philippians take part in the preaching of Christ, through their generous financial support. He prays that this love "may abound still more and more in knowledge and all discernment," and that they may be "sincere and without offense till the day of Christ, being filled with the fruits of righteousness" (1:9–11). Paul stresses that they do not give *him* their charity, but to God directly, and he prays to God that the Philippians, succeeding ever more in virtue, will prepare themselves properly for the day of Christ, that is, the second coming and final judgment.

St Paul assuages the Philippians' worry concerning his fate in Rome by saying that his imprisonment in Rome greatly facilitated his preaching of Christ. Soon all of Rome knew of Paul's imprisonment, and the greater part of Roman Christians, emboldened by the bonds of the apostle, began to preach the word of God without fear. They saw that Paul's preaching, even in bonds, not only did not cause him any harm, but only made him more famous among the elites of Rome and even in the imperial court. True, some preached Christ "not sincerely" (1:16) but "from envy and strife" (1:15), that is, out of an impure love for arguments, or even "supposing to add affliction to my chains" (1:16), but Paul only rejoices that Christ is being preached in the world, no matter in what way. It is possible that these petty people were envious of Paul's glory and wanted to take advantage of his imprisonment to become famous, to assume his glory as a preacher of Christ's teaching to themselves. Some probably acted openly against Paul, contrary to his wishes, but in any case, they were not heretics.

For himself, Paul has no fear. He is not even afraid of death: "For to me, to live is Christ, and to die is gain" (1:21). The apostle even seems to be at a loss what to choose—death or life? "For I am hard-pressed between the two, having a desire to depart and be with Christ, which is far better. Nevertheless to remain in the flesh is more needful for you" (1:23).

Then Paul expresses his confidence that he will soon be released, upon which he wants to visit Philippi (as it happened, Paul's desire did come true). The apostle tells the Philippians to live "worthy of the gospel of Christ." The most important quality of such a life is immediately indicated: "that you stand fast in one spirit, with one mind striving together for the faith of the gospel" (1:27). This firm standing in the truth, unity of spirit, and fearless confession of the faith that Paul desires to see in his beloved Philippian disciples is the first and most important quality that should be characteristic of every true Christian. The Church of Christ in an antagonistic world is and must be a Church militant, and its followers must always be fighters and confessors, ready to suffer for the truth.

In chapter 2, the holy apostle impresses on the Philippians the need for complete spiritual unity and mutual love, to which another quality must be added, characteristic of a true Christian life—humble-mindedness. The highest example of this humble-mindedness, an example worthy of emulation for all Christians, is Christ Himself, who humbled Himself even to death on the Cross:

> Let this mind be in you which was also in Christ Jesus, who, being in the form of God, did not consider it robbery to be equal with God, but made Himself of no reputation, taking the form of a bondservant, and coming in the likeness of men. And being found in appearance as a man, He humbled Himself and became obedient to the point of death, even the death of the cross. (2:5–8)

This is a soul-piercing image of divine self-abnegation, self-diminution, and divine kenosis for the sake of mankind. This is also an inspiring example for emulation. If the only begotten Son of God so humbled himself, then how can we, accursed sinners, not humble ourselves? This is a natural impetus to humility for all true followers of Christ. And because in these words Paul speaks of the incarnation of the Son of God, of His coming into the world as a Man, this very passage, together with the verses 9–11 that follow, is appointed by the Church as the epistle reading at the Divine Liturgy on the most important feasts of the Theotokos (e.g., Dormition, Nativity).

This humility of the Son of God, paradoxically, served to glorify Him: "Therefore God also has highly exalted Him, and given Him the name which is above every name" (2:9). Of course, Paul here speaks of the exaltation of the human nature of Christ. In other words, because of His humility, even the humanity that He assumed is exalted to the level of the divine, led into the glory and power of the Godhead. A consequence of this exalting humility of the Son of God must be that "at the name of Jesus every knee should bow, of those in heaven, and of those on earth, and of those under the earth" (2:10). All of creation—the angels in heaven and people on earth and the dead buried under the earth—bows before Christ. "[E]very tongue should confess that Jesus Christ is Lord, to the glory of God the Father" (2:11). It is clear that the Son is equal in glory to the Father.

After this, having praised the Philippians for their obedience, the Holy Apostle Paul gives them a series of moral instructions, inspiring them to "work out your own salvation with fear and trembling" (2:13; compare with Psalm 2:11) and exhorts them to do everything without complaining or doubting, so that they might become blameless and pure children of God in the midst of "a crooked and perverse generation" (2:15). These words are especially illuminating: "for it is God who works in you both to will and to do for His good pleasure" (2:13). Of course, this does not mean that man has no free will; rather, Paul shows that true righteousness is a gift of God, given only to the humble. However, God can only give inspiration to strive toward virtue, but the virtue itself depends on the person, whether or not he will answer God's call with his own free will. The grace of God cooperates with a person, helping him in his good deeds, but it never acts in compulsion, moving a person as though he were a puppet. This, according to St Macarius of Egypt, is how the grace of God cooperates in our deeds of virtue.

In the rest of chapter 2, the Apostle Paul informs the Philippians of his intentions for the future. Aware of how much the Philippians worried for him, he promised to send them his faithful fellow laborer Timothy as soon as Caesar's judgment will be known (2:19–23). Another reason to send Timothy was to receive trustworthy news about the state of the Philippian church, to calm his own worries about them. "Oh, what longing had he toward Macedonia!" said St John Chrysostom, "[This] is a proof of excessive care: for when he could not himself be with them, he sent his disciples, as he could not endure, even for a little time, in ignorance of their state."[49]

St Paul sent Timothy because he was his most trustworthy disciple (2:20–22). Knowing by the Spirit's inspiration that he would soon be released, Paul promises also that he will come to them soon. In the meantime, he intends to send back Epaphroditus with the epistle, keeping in mind that Epaphroditus was seriously ill in Rome, and the Philippians, not knowing how the disease progressed, were worried for him. Paul praises Epaphroditus's great labors, especially that he undertook the 1,000-kilometer journey to Rome and even fell ill because of it. Calling him a brother, "fellow worker, and fellow soldier," the holy apostle asks the Philippians to "receive him therefore in the Lord with all gladness, and hold such men in esteem" (2:29).

In chapter 3, the holy apostle, exhorting the Philippians to rejoice in the Lord, warns them against the Judaizers. Apparently, Judaizers disdainfully called all Gentiles—and any Jews who associated with them—"dogs." The apostle finds it more fair to apply the nickname to the Judaizers themselves, as to those who have an inclination to the things of the flesh. "Beware of dogs, beware of evil workers, beware of the mutilation" (3:2). Note the irony of St Paul who compares the rite of circumcision, formerly the seal of the chosen people, to the self-inflicted mutilation of some pagan cults or to a simple and meaningless cutting of the flesh. Those who are truly circumcised are those "who worship God in the Spirit, rejoice in Christ Jesus, and have no confidence in the flesh" (3:3).

St Paul continues by saying that he could have boasted in the physical advantages of the Jews no less than anyone else, and perhaps even more than others, but he had abandoned all of that for the sake of Christ. "But what things were gain to me, these have I counted loss for Christ. ... I have suffered the loss of all things, and count them as rubbish, that I may gain Christ" (3:7–8). Not only was he a Jew by ethnicity, but he was even raised in the best Pharisaical school and was the most ardent persecutor of Christianity. From the perspective of Old Testament righteousness, he could consider himself "blameless" (3:6), but all this he now considers not an advantage, but rubbish. The only thing he now seeks is knowledge of Christ the Lord, a participation in His sufferings, and the attainment of the resurrection from the dead (3:9–11).

In no way, however, does the humble apostle consider himself to have reached perfection: "Not that I have already attained, or am already perfected, but I press on, that I may lay hold of that for which Christ Jesus has also laid hold of me" (3:12). St Paul expresses his conversion to Christ as though Christ Himself were following him and has finally caught him. "Forgetting those things which are behind and reaching forward to those things which are ahead, I press toward the goal for the prize of the upward call of God in Christ Jesus" (3:13–14). Nothing makes our virtue so futile, nothing so puffs us up as remembrance of our good deeds. Therefore, Paul tells the Philippians that he always forgets all the good that he has done, striving at all times to move forward toward the heights of Christian perfection.

It behooves us to pay special attention to Paul's words in verses 15 and 16, for many mystical sects that reject the ecclesiastical hierarchy like to cite them, thinking that St Paul stresses the supremacy of inner illumination and the direct revelation of the Holy Spirit in the heart: "Therefore, let us, as many as are mature, have this mind; and if in anything you think otherwise, God will reveal even this to you" (3:15). This does not mean that every person has the right to discern and teach as he wills or that God will reveal the truth to him. If taken in context, the meaning is quite different. When Paul says, "let us have this mind," he is continuing his previous discourse about the need for total humility and "lowness of mind" when considering one's good deeds, especially when we compare our virtues with the goodness of Christ the Saviour. Such a humble manner of thinking ("I do not count myself to have apprehended" [3:13]) is required for all Christians who are firm in the faith.

This is how St John Chrysostom interprets it: "These words were spoken not concerning doctrines, but concerning perfection of life, and our not considering ourselves to be perfect."[50] As St Paul implies, "if in anything you think otherwise" (3:15), I am sure that God will reveal to you the incorrectness of your thoughts and will direct you to the properly humble manner of thinking, for, as St John explains further, "he who considers that he has apprehended all, has nothing."[51]

"Nevertheless, to the degree that we have already attained, let us walk by the same rule, let us be of the same mind" (3:16). This passage can be understood thus: in all things we should follow our conscience. Whatever conscience considers true and necessary, that we must do. As far as our manner of thinking and the rules of life, we must continue in the way we walk, as long as it agrees with our conscience. Oecumenius has the following explanation: "Until God reveals more to us, let us stand in that measure to which we have already attained, lest we lose what we have already achieved."[52]

St Paul continues by exhorting the Philippians to follow his example and to fear emulating those who walk as enemies of the Cross of Christ: "whose end is destruction, whose god is their belly, and whose glory is in their shame—who set their mind on earthly things" (3:19). St Paul speaks of those people who are completely committed to their carnal lifestyle, to physical joys and pleasures, who walk the wide and easy path, not desiring to crucify themselves to the Cross of Christ, as true Christians must. Paul is telling them to follow him along the straight and narrow path, the way of the Cross, for it is not proper for Christians to become attached to the earth, because "our citizenship is in heaven, from which we also eagerly wait for the Saviour, the Lord Jesus Christ, who will transform our lowly body that it may be conformed to His glorious body" (3:20–21). True Christians should strive to think of the heavenly, not the earthly, to train themselves in the rules and laws of the kingdom of heaven.

Chapter 4 contains exhortations of how to "stand fast in the Lord" (4:1). The chapter begins with a moving address to the Philippians that reveals how dear they were to his heart. He calls them "my beloved and longed-for brethren, my joy and crown" (4:1). More specific instructions then follow to two certain women—Euodia and Syntyche—"to be of the same mind in the Lord." They were probably influential women and their private doubts concerning certain truths of Christianity could have been stumbling blocks for other members of the community.

In 4:3, Paul addresses a certain "true companion," whose name is left out, with a request to help instruct those aforementioned women, because they "labored with me in the gospel." The "Clement" mentioned in this same verse is usually assumed to be St Clement, future bishop of Rome after Linus and Anacletus. In conclusion, the apostle gives general instructions to all. He tells the Philippians to rejoice in the Lord, to be meek, not to waste time in various earthly cares, but to reveal all requests in prayer to God. All of these are characteristic traits of a life in Christ.

If one lives such a life, "the peace of God, which surpasses all understanding, will guard your hearts and minds through Christ Jesus" (4:7) from all disorder stemming from the passions. The apostle does not wish to continue enumerating the responsibilities of true Christians, but instead teaches the Philippians to meditate on the virtues: "Whatever things are true, whatever things are noble, whatever things are just" (4:8). Then he says, "The God of peace will be with you" (4:9).

In the last part of the chapter, the holy apostle remembers the financial assistance they offered him, and he expresses his joy at their solicitude. Although he truly lacks nothing, their care is pleasant and precious to him. In this, the Philippians excel among all the churches, for not only once did they help Paul thus. This last offering, brought by Epaphroditus, Paul accepts as "a sweet-smelling aroma, an acceptable sacrifice, well pleasing to God" (4:18). Finally, St Paul tells them to greet "every saint in Christ Jesus," that is, every Christian, and then gives his usual benediction (4:21–23).

 CHAPTER 7

The Epistle of the Holy Apostle Paul to the Colossians

THE ESTABLISHMENT OF THE CHURCH IN COLOSSAE

Colossae is located in Phrygia, a region of Asia Minor, on the banks of the Lycus River, a tributary of the Meander. In ancient times, it was a large and prosperous city. In the Book of Acts, Colossae is not mentioned, and we have no exact information concerning the founding of the Church in Colossae. We can only guess that the local community was established either by St Paul during one of his journeys, or by one of his disciples. In Acts, we read that Apostle Paul twice traveled through Phrygia: during his second missionary journey on the way to Europe (Acts 16:6) and during his third missionary journey on the way to Ephesus (Acts 18:23). Colossae was a constant trade partner of Ephesus, where St Paul lived for two and a half years during his third journey. Perhaps, if Paul himself was not in Colossae, the community was established by Epaphras and Philemon, whom Paul had converted in Ephesus.

Paul calls Epaphras his beloved fellow laborer and in the Epistle to the Colossians he directly says that they "heard and knew the grace of God in truth; as ... learned from Epaphras, our dear fellow servant, who is a faithful minister of Christ on your behalf" (Col 1:6–7). From 4:12–13 it is evident that Epaphras had the spiritual care of the Christians both in Colossae and in two neighboring cities—Laodicea, the most important city of the region, and Hierapolis. Philemon is called Paul's beloved "fellow laborer," and his son Archippus is called Paul's "fellow soldier" (Phil 1:1–2). In the Epistle to the Colossians, he asks to have a message relayed to Archippus: "Take heed to the ministry which you have received in the Lord, that you may fulfill it" (Col 4:17).

Certain passages of this Epistle to the Colossians, such as 1:4 and 2:1, suggest that St Paul had not been in Colossae in person. However, neither do these passages prove this to be the case absolutely. St Theophan the Recluse preferred to say that St Paul was probably not in Colossae, but perhaps he was. In any case, Christianity in Colossae was founded by him, even if indirectly.

THE PURPOSE OF THE EPISTLE TO THE COLOSSIANS

The epistle makes it clear that the reason it was written was the appearance in Phrygia of false teachers who threatened the purity of the Christian faith. Paul desired to warn the Colossians from becoming enamored of these false teachers. From the words that Paul himself used to characterize these teachers (see Col 2:4, 8, 16, 20–23), it is clear that the heretics did not have any kind of strict theological system and were not particularly clear in their theology, but rather had some strange mix of pagan philosophy, proto-Gnosticism, and Judaism, as they continued to hold fast to prohibitions concerning food, the Old Testament feasts, and circumcision (Col 2:11–15). St Paul, imprisoned in Rome, was informed about these false teachers by Epaphras, who then asked St Paul to write the Epistle to the Colossians.

The purpose of the epistle was to warn the Colossians against being deluded by the cajoling words of the false teachers, who suggested that one can trust in someone or something other than Christ the Lord. He also tried to convince them to hold to that teaching that Epaphras had given them, as he was a true servant of Christ.

THE PLACE AND TIME OF THE WRITING OF THE EPISTLE

In this epistle, Apostle Paul twice mentions that he is in bondage (Col 4:3, 18). This was the first Roman imprisonment, as we know Timothy was with him (Col 1:1), and Timothy was not with Paul during the second imprisonment. It was written earlier than the Epistle to the Philippians and at the same time as the Epistle to Philemon. Consequently, it was written in Rome probably around A.D. 61 or 62. Tychicus and Onesimus took the epistle back to Colossae, while Onesimus also bore a special letter to Philemon, his former master (Col 4:7–9).

THE STRUCTURE AND CONTENT OF THE EPISTLE

The epistle has four chapters. The main theme of the epistle is the refutation of the false teachers who attempted to prove that one can approach God and be saved without the Lord Jesus Christ. The epistle can be divided into the following sections:

1. Introduction (1:1–11)
2. Dogmatic section (1:12–2:23)
3. Moral-instructive section (3:1–4:6)
4. Conclusion (4:7–18)

EXEGETICAL ANALYSIS OF THE EPISTLE TO THE COLOSSIANS

As usual, the epistle begins with a greeting from "Paul, an apostle of Jesus Christ by the will of God, and Timothy our brother" (1:1). Having given them grace and peace, the holy apostle says that from the moment that he heard from Epaphras of their faith and love for all the saints, that is, all Christians, he has not ceased to pray for them so that they will spiritually become more and more perfect.

The purpose of his letter is to warn the Colossians against false teachers. Therefore, in the dogmatic section of the letter, Paul first of all describes the divine economy concerning the salvation of mankind. To do this, he begins by thanking God for delivering Christianity from the power of darkness and leading the faithful into the kingdom of His beloved Son (1:12–14). After this, Paul begins his discussion of the person of the Divine Saviour, Who is "the image of the invisible God, the firstborn over all creation" (1:15). According to St Theophan the Recluse, "The image indicates the oneness in essence with the Father. Why? Because He is begotten. Since He is begotten, he is one in essence. Since he is one in essence, he is the image."[53]

"The firstborn over all creation"—this means that the Son of God is begotten of the Father, but is not the creation of God the Father. "For by Him all things were created that are in heaven and that are on earth, visible and invisible, whether thrones or dominions or principalities or powers. All things were created through Him and for Him" (1:16). This sentence contains an important dogmatic truth concerning the Son as Creator of all that exists. Because He created everything, He cannot Himself be created. At the same time, this does not mean that the Father and the Spirit did not participate in the creation of the world. Paul, setting as his goal the refutation of these specific false teachers who rejected the divinity of Jesus Christ, limited his remarks to the confirmation of Christ's divinity. The dogmatic importance of this passage is also found in the indication of the existence of ranks in the angelic world: "whether thrones or dominions or principalities or powers" … "And He is before all things, and in Him all things consist" (1:16–17). As St John Chrysostom notes, "[St Paul] repeats these expressions in close sequence; with their close succession, as it were with rapid strokes, tearing up the deadly doctrine by the roots. 'And he is before all things,' he says. This is befitting God."[54] Thus, the Son of God, who became incarnate in the person of Jesus Christ, "not only is the Fashioner of all things, but He also provides for everything He created and He governs creation, and creation stands by His wisdom and power," according to Blessed Theodoret of Cyrus.[55] The order of the world is not held together by spirits that mediate between God and the world, not by aeons, as the gnostics taught, not by angels, but rather by that same Son of God Who created all things, including the angels. These words of the apostle rebuke all deists who refuse to consider God's providence for the world. The world does not stand by itself, directed by soulless laws of nature like a wound-up clock, but by the direct involvement of the Creator in its life. As St John Chrysostom says, "Not only did He Himself bring them out of nothing into being, but Himself sustains them now, so that were they dissevered from His providence, they were at once undone and destroyed."[56]

Having explained that the Lord Jesus Christ is God, the apostle then proceeds to explain Who He is in the economy of our salvation. Two important dogmatic truths are expressed: the exaltedness of the God-man Who became the Head of the Church and His most important work—the reconciliation of mankind with God. "And He is the head of the body, the church, who is the beginning, the firstborn from the dead, that in all things He may have the preeminence" (1:18). As Chrysostom again explains, "[H]aving spoken of His dignity, he afterwards speaks of His love to man also … out of a wish to show His great friendliness to us, in that He who is thus above, and above all, united Himself with those below," like a head with a body.[57] Christ is the "beginning" in the sense that he became the progenitor of a new mankind, renewed by Him.

Chrysostom interprets the phrase "the Firstborn from the dead" thus: "He was the first to rise again, and all others will follow after Him,"[58] because He is the foundation and source of the general resurrection, as Blessed Theodoret also shows.[59] "That in all things He may have the preeminence" (1:18). As St Theophan the Recluse comments, this is said "to refute the false teachers who introduced the idea of many powers (aeons) and by this the idea of multiple spiritual authorities."[60]

"For it pleased the Father that in Him all the fullness should dwell" (1:19). In other words, the Son contains all perfection, "everything that is necessary for anyone, at all times and in eternity" (St Theophan).[61] This thought is also directed against the early gnostics. The gnostics taught that the fullness, or *pleroma*, of being is composed of many layers of beings who have various degrees of perfection, but the apostle insists that all perfection is contained in the one Son of God (1:19).

"And by Him to reconcile all things to Himself, by Him, whether things on earth or things in heaven" (1:20). St Paul indicates the most important work of the God-man— to reconcile all with God. Human sin introduced enmity between God and creation; the crucifixion of the Son of God brought peace, having taken from man his culpability and having reconciled him with God. This, in its turn, also reconciled angels with men. The angels, as faithful servants of God, could not help but be antagonistic toward sinful man. "The angels became enemies to men," says St John Chrysostom, "through seeing the Lord insulted."[62] Now, after the work of redemption fulfilled by Christ, the angels are like our elder brothers, even as spirits sent to serve those who will inherit salvation (Heb 1:14). This is what is meant by "things in heaven."

Having outlined the essence of the economy of our salvation, the Holy Apostle Paul applies his teaching first to the Colossians (1:21–23) and then to himself and his apostolic calling (1:24–29). He says that the Colossians also can receive the fruits of the redemptive work of Christ if only they remain firm and unshakable in their faith, and not fall from the teaching of Christ given to them by Paul. Concerning himself, the apostle says that he rejoices in his sufferings for the sake of the Colossians and the entire body of the Church, for he suffers, by God's providence, as a servant of the word of God and a preacher of that mystery of salvation, which he had just explained to the Colossians.

Chapter 2 is directed against the false teachers who are trying to delude the Colossians. St Paul begins his accusation with a reference to his labors, desiring the Colossians to heed him. At first he praises the Colossians, and with them the inhabitants of Laodicea and Hierapolis, that their hearts strive to understand all the mysteries of God the Father and Christ, "in whom are hidden all the treasures of wisdom and knowledge" (2:3). The first thought is that the Lord Jesus Christ, as the Son of God and God, Himself knows everything, and if this is so, then, as St John Chrysostom puts it, "you ought to ask all things from Him; He himself gives wisdom and knowledge."[63] However, these words also have another meaning, as shown by St Theophan: "Whoever comes to acknowledge Him as the Saviour will in this very act of acknowledgement acquire all wisdom and all knowledge."[64]

It is as if Paul is telling them that if someone comes to them, pretending to be wise, and begins to offer them a wisdom that does not agree with the knowledge of the mysteries of God concerning Christ Jesus, they must not listen to him, for it is not wisdom that he teaches, but ignorance (Ambrosiaster and St Theophan the Recluse).[65] St Paul is warning them, lest anyone deceive them with cunning words: "Beware lest anyone cheat you through philosophy and empty deceit, according to the tradition of men, according to the basic principles of the world, and not according to Christ" (2:8). Evidently, the false teaching that threatened the purity of the Colossians' faith had a philosophical character. It was of purely human provenance and, apparently, tried to use natural magic to communicate with the spiritual world, something typical of various mystical sects of that time (and also theosophist and spiritualist movements in Russia and other places).

"For in Him dwells all the fullness of the Godhead bodily" (2:9), that is, incarnate and perceptible to the senses, not only symbolically or metaphorically, just as the soul dwells in the body. "But do not imagine," Oecumenius explains, "that He is enclosed in a body, limited or encompassed, for He is uncircumscribed according to divinity."[66]

"And you are complete in Him, who is the head of all principality and power" (2:10). In other words, you do not need false teachers, because you already have Christ. In Christ you have all fullness, and you should refer to no one else for your salvation. He is the head of all the angelic powers—an important point, because the false teachers apparently taught that angels were more powerful than Christ Himself.

"In Him you were also circumcised with the circumcision made without hands ... buried with Him in baptism ..." These words are clearly directed against the Judaizers who required circumcision of the Gentile converts. The circumcision made without hands signifies "putting off the body of the sins of the flesh" and purification in the sacrament of baptism (2:11–12). In this passage, we encounter an important concept about the replacement of Old Testament circumcision with New Testament baptism. It is interesting to note that the apostle compares baptism with burial; thus, the correct form of baptism is full immersion, not sprinkling, as has become the normative practice in the West since the Middle Ages.

"Having disarmed principalities and powers, He made a public spectacle of them, triumphing over them in it" (2:15). St John Chrysostom explains these words thus: "[The apostle] here means the diabolical powers, because human nature had arrayed itself in these."[67] This makes it clear also that the demons have their own hierarchy, as do the angels. With these words, Paul again warns the Colossians against worship of angels—good angels can offer no exalted knowledge compared with that knowledge that is revealed by the Lord Jesus Christ, while the evil spirits have been defeated by Him and can no longer harm the faithful, those who follow the teachings of Christ. Thus, one should not curse them or enter into any sort of relation with them.

In 2:16–23, St Paul gives three warnings against specific errors. The first warning refers to Judaic rituals that are no longer necessary for Christians: "So let no one judge you in food or in drink, or regarding a festival or new moon or sabbaths, which are a shadow of things to come, but the substance is of Christ" (2:16–17). The second warning exhorts them not to be deceived by the false humility of heretics or their worship of angels. These false teachers taught that union with God was achieved not through Christ, but through communion with angels. This communion was achieved by various mystical rites, including, interestingly enough, fasting. Like the later gnostics, they sought an exalted, esoteric knowledge, and considered Christians to be beneath their notice, although in appearance, they were humble.

This false teaching did put down roots, so much so that the local Council of Laodicea (A.D. 365) considered it necessary formally to prohibit the "Phrygian worship of angels" (Canon 35). St Theophan the Recluse writes, "Was not this something similar to our own theosophy and Spiritism, with their mystical rites and actions? The spirit was the same in both."[68]

The third warning was not to become enamored of human reasoning concerning the necessity of abstaining from certain things— "Do not touch, do not taste, do not handle" (2:21). Evidently, these prohibitions did not concern proper fasting or abstinence in the ascetic sense (which has always existed in the practice of the Christian Church), but some superstitious fears of certain kinds of food. Interestingly enough, followers of theosophy and other such movements also taught that certain types of foods can harm a person spiritually, and so one should avoid them entirely. "Which all concern things which perish with the using—according to the commandment and doctrines of men" (2:22). In other words, you should not give food any kind of spiritual significance, for all things that we eat end up in the same place, so to speak. How can one give it any mystical significance?

"These things indeed have an appearance of wisdom in self-imposed religion, false humility, and neglect of the body, but are of no value against the indulgence of the flesh" (2:23). In other words, these prohibitions "are only seemingly wise, but are actually nothing but empty words" (Oecumenius).[69] "Self-imposed religion" refers to the fact that these false teachers made up their own worship rituals, similar to nothing that preceded them, perhaps of an ecstatic or mystical nature (like the Russian Khlysty sect). St Theophan imagines the appearance of these false teachers as follows:

Rags for clothing, quiet speech, averted gaze, tousled hair—there is your humble-mindedness! This is exactly how the Turkish dervishes are. No matter how unimportant such external details are in actual fact, they have always attracted people, and not only the simple. It is somehow difficult to free oneself from the thought that such people are of some special, exalted spirit. And thus they have always been respected and obeyed.[70]

"Neglect of the body" is also an aspect of these teachers that differs from true Christian asceticism. Possibly, like the Manicheans, they considered the body to be evil.

From the third chapter, St Paul begins his moral instruction. The holy apostle at first represents the Christian life as it should be (3:1–17), then indicates how general rules can be applied to specific situations and states (3:18–4:6). He begins thus: "Seek those things which are above ... set your mind on things above, not on things on the earth. For you died, and your life is hidden with Christ in God" (3:1–3). In the sacrament of baptism, Christians die to sin and rise again with Christ to a new, God-pleasing life. Therefore, they must think not of earthly things, but of the heavenly, and their life must be completely enclosed in God. This is the inner life, the spiritual life, hidden from others. The fruits of this life hidden in God will be revealed to everyone "when Christ who is our life appears" (3:4), after the second coming and during the general resurrection.

Remembering the glory awaiting the righteous, Christians must avoid all kinds of evil, some of which the apostle lists in verses 5–9. The calling of a Christian is "put off the old man with his deeds, and ... put on the new man who is renewed in knowledge according to the image of Him who created Him" (3:9–10). St Theophan the Recluse explains, "We must throw aside our self-pleasing selfishness with all our passions, and aspire to live in self-rejection, pleasing only God. This decision, encompassing the entire being of the person who approaches the Lord with faith and who is baptized, makes man new."[71]

"There is neither Greek nor Jew, circumcised nor uncircumcised, barbarian, Scythian, slave, nor free, but Christ is all and in all" (3:11). St Theophan says, "The grace of God in Christ Jesus unites all, making of diverse peoples a single body ... Therefore, in Christ Jesus all natural distinctions disappear."[72] Having disrobed a Christian of his passions, the apostle then vests him in virtues, listing them in 3:12–17 as things necessary for every Christian. He especially stresses "love, which is the bond of perfection" (3:14). It is the "combination and abundance of all things that comprise excellence, the root of perfection" (St Theophan).[73] St Paul offers specific means to succeed in a moral Christian life—the enriching of the mind by knowledge of divine truth, prayer, and doing everything in the name of God.

In the second half of chapter 3, verses 18–25, the holy apostle gives specific moral instruction to Christians depending on their unique situations: to wives, to husbands, to children, to parents, and to slaves.

In 4:1–6, these specific instructions continue. Paul commands that masters be just to their slaves, and then once again Paul returns to general instructions for all Christians, regardless of their social status, telling them all to pray constantly and be spiritually vigilant with gratitude for all things. In conclusion, the apostle asks them to pray for him and his fellow laborers, "that God would open to us a door for the word, to speak the mystery of Christ" (4:3). Paul commands wise interaction with those "who are outside," that is, unbelievers, and exhorts them, "let your speech always be with grace, seasoned with salt," that is, sincere, coming from the heart and full of benevolence, but at the same time wise and moderate, which is what "seasoned with salt" means (4:5–6).

In the rest of the epistle, the apostle tells the Colossians that he will send this epistle with Tychicus, "a beloved brother, faithful minister, and fellow servant in the Lord" (4:7–8). With him, he will send Onesimus, the former slave of Philemon. In conclusion, St Paul sends greetings from specific people with him in Rome and commands the epistle to be read aloud in the church in Laodicea. He finishes with his usual apostolic benediction.

 CHAPTER 8

The First Epistle of the Holy Apostle Paul to the Thessalonians

THE ESTABLISHMENT OF THE CHURCH IN THESSALONICA

Thessalonica was built on the slope of a mountain in the northwestern corner of the Thermaic Gulf of the Aegean Sea. In apostolic times, it was the capital of the second region of the province of Macedonia, the residence of the Roman praetor. Its geographical placement helped it blossom into a rich, densely populated center of trade. In connection with this, it was well known for its luxurious and immoral manner of living. The majority of the population was Greek, but there was also a large Italian contingent, as well as a significant Jewish minority, most of whom were merchants. Thessalonica did not simply have a house of prayer, as in Philippi, but a synagogue (Acts 17:1).

Acts 17 speaks in detail concerning the establishment of the Church in Thessalonica. This church was established by St Paul during his second missionary journey. Having preached in Philippi, the Apostle Paul, together with Silas and Timothy, traveled through Amphipolis and Apollonia, arriving in Thessalonica, although it is possible that Timothy remained in Philippi for a while to help with the new community, rejoining Paul a little later in Berea. According to his usual custom, St Paul began preaching in the local synagogue.

Citing the Old Testament prophecies, he described to the local Jews an image of the Messiah Who "had to suffer and rise again from the dead" (Acts 17:3). His preaching had great success, as St Luke explicitly writes that "a great multitude of the devout Greeks, and not a few of the leading women, joined Paul and Silas" (Acts 17:4). Of course, Paul did not limit his preaching to the synagogue, but preached everywhere in the streets and squares of Thessalonica, as is evident from his epistle to the Thessalonians, in which he remembers his work in the city (1 Thess 2:9–12). However, some refused to believe, and these people soon incited a riot against Paul and Silas. We can assume that a majority of those who believed were proselytes, while most of the ethnic Jews were not. These people were irritated by the apostles' success among the pagans:

> But the Jews who were not persuaded, becoming envious, took some of the evil men from the marketplace, and gathering a mob, set all the city in an uproar and attacked the house of Jason [whom St Paul calls his relative in Rom 16:21], and sought to bring them out to the people. But when they did not find them, they dragged Jason and some brethren to the rulers of the city, crying out, "These who have turned the world upside down have come here too. Jason has harbored them, and these are all acting contrary to the decrees of Caesar, saying there is another king—Jesus." (Acts 17:5–7)

This was the usual Jewish method of battling the preaching of Christ. The slander against the apostles first disturbed the magistrates, but then, having seen whom the crowd brought and "when they had taken security from Jason and the rest, they let them go" (Acts 17:9), because they understood that the Jews had set them up. Despite the positive resolution to this riot, the brethren considered it best to send Paul and Silas into Berea (a small town south of Thessalonica). Paul's preaching in Thessalonica, as we see from his own words, brought a rich spiritual harvest. The Thessalonians accepted his words "not as the word of men, but as it is in truth, the word of God" (1 Thess 2:13). In a short time—three weeks—St Paul managed to assemble a large, spiritually sound, and ardent community of Christians that would become the model for all who believed in Macedonia and Greece, something that Paul stresses in 1 Thessalonians 1:17.

THE PURPOSE OF THE EPISTLE TO THE THESSALONIANS

St Paul left Thessalonica sorrowful, and he did not cease to think constantly of the fate of his newly converted brethren. His preaching in Berea was also successful, but the Jews followed him there as well, inciting the locals. Then he, accompanied by some faithful for the purpose of protecting him on the way, traveled farther south to Athens. Paul asked these brethren to call Silas and Timothy to him in Athens in the hopes of learning about the state of the Thessalonian community (Acts 17:15). Because Timothy could say nothing (for he did not go through Thessalonica, but directly to Berea), Paul sent him back to Thessalonica (1 Thess 3:1–5). By this time, St Paul had arrived in Corinth, where he did finally hear some comforting news about the Thessalonians from Timothy (Acts 18:1–5).

It turned out that the word of God, preached by Paul, did not weaken in the hearts of the Thessalonians, and they desired to see him again, as he did them. This news encouraged the apostle greatly: "For now we live, if you stand fast in the Lord" (1 Thess 3:8). At the same time, not all of Timothy's news was positive. He told Paul about several members of the community who persisted in the immoral lifestyle of their pagan past, and he also informed Paul that there were certain disagreements in the community that affected everyone. Not all had yet fully rejected the iniquities of pagan sensuality: some could not yet "posses [their] own vessel in sanctification and honor," while others "[took] advantage of and defraud[ed] [their] brother" (1 Thess 4:4, 6). All those who had believed were also in great doubt about the fate of their departed ones, thinking, incorrectly, that only those who were alive during the second coming would enter the kingdom. They had murky and hopeless ideas about what awaited their departed ones after death, and so death terrified them.

All this gave Paul several reasons to write immediately to the Thessalonians. First of all, he wanted to express his joy that they remained in the faith. Second, he wanted to offer them spiritual medicine against the moral laxity that Timothy noticed. Third, Paul wanted to calm them concerning the fate of the dead, and to offer them a dogmatic teaching concerning the second coming of Christ.

THE PLACE AND TIME OF THE WRITING OF THE EPISTLE

Doubtless, this epistle was written very soon after the conversion of the Thessalonians to Christ. According to St Theophan the Recluse, "The apostle was filled with vivid and recent inspiration after the conversion of the Thessalonians." The epistle and the Book of Acts both give us a clear indication about the place where it was written. In the beginning of chapter 3, Paul writes, "When we could no longer endure it, we thought it good to be left in Athens alone, and sent Timothy, our brother ... to establish you and encourage you concerning your faith" (1 Thess 3:1–2). "But now that Timothy has come to us from you, and brought us good news of your faith and love ... we were comforted concerning you by your faith" (1 Thess 3:6–7). This makes it clear that St Paul wrote the epistle as soon as Timothy returned.

From Acts, it is clear that Timothy and Silas both returned to Paul not in Athens, but in Corinth. Thus, the Epistle to the Thessalonians was written in Corinth.

Certain other details in Acts help us determine a specific time of writing. Having arrived in Corinth, Paul settled in the house of Aquila and Priscilla, Jews who were exiled from Rome by Claudius. The edict concerning the expulsion of all Jews from Rome dates, according to Suetonius and Tacitus, to A.D. 52. We can add to this time the approximate year it would take for Aquila and Priscilla to find a new home in Corinth and become settled. Therefore, we can guess that Paul wrote his epistle to the Thessalonians in A.D. 53 or 54. This is Paul's earliest epistle.

THE STRUCTURE AND CONTENT OF THE EPISTLE

The epistle consists of five chapters that are clearly divided into two sections: a historical one and a moral-dogmatic one. In the beginning, as usual, Paul writes an introduction with a greeting, and in the end, he includes personal greetings, specific good wishes, and an apostolic blessing.

EXEGETICAL ANALYSIS OF THE FIRST EPISTLE TO THE THESSALONIANS

The epistle begins with a blessing offered to the Church in Thessalonica on behalf of Paul, Silas, and Timothy. The latter two are mentioned as fellow laborers of Paul, whom the Thessalonians know personally. Paul also mentions them probably because their recent news provided the most immediate motivation to the writing of this letter. St Theophan the Recluse writes, "All three, as with one mouth, gave the Thessalonians the saving teaching of the Gospel."[74] St Paul, interestingly, does not mention his apostolic dignity in this introduction, either because the Thessalonians "were newly instructed, and had not yet had any experience of him," as St John Chrysostom suggests,[75] or, on the contrary, because he already commanded their respect. In any case, this is an expression of his humility, and in general, St Paul only mentioned his apostolic status in situations in which it was absolutely necessary for the benefit of his missionary work.

The first chapter, a short one (just 10 verses), is of purely historical character. The apostle expresses the illumined, gracious, Christian state of the Thessalonians. He thanks God for the success of his preaching among them, and he praises them for their firmness in the faith, saying that they "have become examples to all in Macedonia and Achaia who believe" (1:7). This historical section continues in chapters 2 and 3.

In chapter 2, the apostle describes his time in Thessalonica, underlining two specific moments—the characteristic aspects of his preaching (2:1–12) and the faith and brave abiding in the faith of the Thessalonians (2:13–16). By doing this, he wanted to confirm and inflame their faith and inspire them to stand fast during the inevitable persecutions (St Theophan).[76] For this same reason, he vividly describes the difficulties that he and his fellow laborers endured (2:9). However, Paul speaks of himself and the purity of his convictions also because he wants to prevent any slander from the Jews from having any effect (he did the same in his epistles to the Galatians and Corinthians).

The love of St Paul for the Thessalonians has become so sincere and profound that no slanderous words should shake their faith in his love for them. "But we, brethren, having been taken away from you for a short time in presence, not in heart, endeavored more eagerly to see your face with great desire. Therefore we wanted to come to you—even I, Paul, time and again—but Satan hindered us" (2:17–18). Ambrosiaster writes, "Satan put obstacles in Paul's way to prevent him from spreading the light of truth among the people. He then pushed the unbelievers to prevent the apostles with beatings and imprisonment, lest they speak the word of God."[77] Evidently, in this case, Paul speaks of the antagonism of the Thessalonian Jews who were not converted and tried to kill him. Their especially virulent hatred of Paul is evident in their seeking him out in Berea to continue their persecution.

In chapter 3, the holy apostle remembers how he sent Timothy to them, from whom he then heard consoling good news. In verses 6–10, Paul expresses the full depth of his joy in the strength of their faith with these words: "For now we live, if you stand fast in the Lord" (3:8). In other words, the apostle wants to say that a weight fell from his shoulders when he heard the good news of their faithfulness, and he feels himself as though brought back to life from moribund sorrow for their sakes, which was pressing down on his heart like a stone. Paul finishes this chapter with prayerful good wishes. He prays God to help him come to them, and for them to grow in Christian holiness and to be found blameless during the second coming of Christ.

In chapter 4, Paul begins his moral and dogmatic instruction. This chapter, as well as the next, contains moral lessons (inspired by Timothy's report concerning certain moral issues in the community) among which we find inserted incredibly important dogmatic teachings concerning the second coming of Christ and the general resurrection. The first and most important lesson is the following: "For this is the will of God, your sanctification … For God did not call us to uncleanness, but in holiness" (4:3, 7). The holy apostle indicates the primary calling of a Christian—the ideal of sanctity. In connection with this, Paul exhorts the Thessalonians to refrain from sexual immorality, because apparently this sin persisted, a leftover of their pagan lives (pagans did not consider sexual dissipation to be a sin). Each of the Thessalonians must "possess his own vessel in sanctification and honor … that no one should take advantage of and defraud his brother in this matter, because the Lord is the avenger of all such" (4:4–6). According to the interpretation of the Church Fathers, St Paul is speaking about adultery. In the words of St John Chrysostom,

> Here he speaks concerning adultery, but above also concerning "all fornication." For since he was about to say, "That no man transgress and wrong his brother," Do not think, he says, that I say this only in the case of brethren; you must not have the wives of others at all, nor even women that have no husbands, and that are common. You must abstain from "all fornication"; "Because," he says, "the Lord is an avenger in all these things."[78]

St Theophan the Recluse adds: "God avenges all iniquity, but especially sexual sins, because through them man demeans the image of God in which he was created more than through any other sin."[79]

The apostle insistently reminds them that the commandment concerning purity is given by God Himself; therefore, whoever rejects this commandment "does not reject man, but God, who has also given us His Holy Spirit" (4:8). Then St Paul, as though in passing, reminds them of the need for brotherly love. He praises them for their brotherly love, but he exhorts them to love one another even more, "that you also aspire to lead a quiet life, to mind your own business, and to work with your own hands, as we commanded you, that you may walk properly toward those who are outside," that is, the pagans (4:11–12).

From chapter 4, verse 13, St Paul begins his dogmatic instruction concerning the second coming of Christ, which continues until chapter 5, verse 11. For Paul, this dogmatic teaching is intimately connected with the life in Christ. The passages 4:13–17 are the apostolic reading during the burial of the dead as well as on Saturdays when the dead are commemorated.

"But I do not want you to be ignorant, brethren, concerning those who have fallen asleep, lest you sorrow as others who have no hope" (4:13). The meaning of these words is as follows: "I would like to give you an exact understanding concerning the state of the departed, so that you would be at peace."[80] Among those "others who have no hope" were the Sadducees, who rejected the resurrection from the dead, and all Greeks and Romans, who, although not completely lacking in belief in the immortality of the soul, still understood life after death as dim and joyless, either seeing it as some kind of sleep or even a painful existence. "While there's life, there's hope," wrote the Greek bucolic poet Theocritus (d. c. 270 B.C.), "while the dead have none."[81] And the Roman poet Catullus (d. A.D. 130) reflected:

> Suns set only to rise again tomorrow.
> We, when sets in a little hour the brief light,
> Sleep one infinite age, a night forever.[82]

For a Christian, however, death should not be something dark, for "if we believe that Jesus died and rose again, even so God will bring with Him those who sleep in Jesus" (4:14). Not only here, but also in many other places (Rom 8:11; 1 Cor 15:12–23, 6:14; 2 Cor 4:14), St Paul makes our resurrection contingent on the resurrection of Christ. His resurrection is the pledge of the resurrection of all mankind. Christ, having become man, became the Head of all the faithful, becoming one Body with them. If the Head of the Body rose from the dead, then it is not possible that the members of the body remain dead; therefore, they will arise as well. As St John of Damascus writes, "He raised all men through His own flesh, and therefore He is called the 'Firstborn from the dead' (Col 1:18)."[83]

"For this we say to you by the word of the Lord, that we who are alive and remain until the coming of the Lord will by no means precede those who are asleep" (4:15). With complete conviction (based on the direct revelation of God), the holy apostle assures the Thessalonians that those who will still be alive when Christ comes again will not go before the dead to meet the Lord Who comes with glory to give joy in the eternal life of the coming age. All will be equal.

"For the Lord Himself will descend from heaven with a shout, with the voice of an archangel, and with the trumpet of God. And the dead in Christ will rise first" (4:16). Here Paul contrasts the second coming with Christ's incarnation. The first was quiet and unnoticed, whereas the second will be glorious and majestic, evident for the whole universe to see. The shout that accompanies Christ's coming will be a command that ends time and announces the moment of the resurrection of the dead and the renewal of the world. This divine command will be announced by the first of the angels, Michael, the protector of God's chosen people—Israel in the Old Testament, and the Church of Christ, the New Israel, in the New Testament—and the trumpets of heaven will inform all the ends of the earth of God's command.

"And what is 'at the last trumpet?'" asks St John Chrysostom, and then explains: "Here [the apostle] implies that there are many trumpets, and that at the last one the Judge descends."[84] This trumpet will awake the dead and gather them together with the living, for even in the Old Testament a trumpet called together God's people in assembly to hear the will of God (Lev 25:9; Num 10:2, 31:6). Some believe that the "trumpets" are symbols of calamitous and loud cataclysms in nature (see 2 Pet 3:10) that will occur at the end of the world (see also Matt 24:31).

"And the dead in Christ will rise first." First does not mean, as some heretics believe, that believing Christians will rise first, and only one thousand years later will the unbelievers arise. All this means is that the dead will rise first, and then those still living will join them after their bodies will have been changed in an instant to greet the coming Lord. "Then we who are alive and remain shall be caught up together with them in the clouds to meet the Lord in the air. And thus we shall always be with the Lord" (4:17). The dead will rise with new bodies, and the living will change in an instant. They will receive incorrupt spiritual bodies instead of their crude material bodies, as Paul describes in a different epistle (1 Cor 15:51–52): "Behold, I tell you a mystery: We shall not all sleep, but we shall all be changed—in a moment, in the twinkling of an eye, at the last trumpet. For the trumpet will sound, and the dead will be raised incorruptible, and we shall be changed."

After the resurrection of the dead and the transformation of the living, the judgment and the separation of the good from the evil will commence. St Paul does not speak about this directly in this epistle, but only consoles the Thessalonians that the faithful "shall always be with the Lord," communicants of His glory and blessedness in the same place where He sits at the right hand of the Father. St Theophan writes: "Where exactly is hidden, but in any case, it will be in blessed, eternal communion with Him. This is the highest hope that inspires Christians."[85] St Paul also does not speak here about those who will be raised for eternal damnation, because his purpose here is consolation. Therefore, he finishes with these words: "comfort one another with these words" (4:18).

The first eleven verses of chapter 5 contain a moral component that is a logical conclusion of the dogma of the second coming of Christ. The apostle reminds the Thessalonians that, according to the words of the Saviour Himself, the day of the second coming—"the day of the Lord"—will come unexpectedly, "as a thief in the night" (5:1–2). However, this "day of the Lord," as the fathers teach, can also refer to the day of our death, a day that is also unknown, although inescapable, and leads to our temporal judgment before God.

"If the Lord's long tarrying weakens your conviction that He will come at any moment, then nothing will so strongly reawaken that conviction as the knowledge that death can come at any moment," teaches St Theophan the Recluse.[86] On the other hand, St John Chrysostom writes: "Is not the end of his own life the consummation to every individual? Why are you curious, and travail about the general end? ... For if you make your own a good end, you will suffer no harm from the other, be it far off, or be it near."[87]

"For when they [the frivolous who do not fear the coming of Christ] say, 'Peace and safety!' then sudden destruction comes upon them, as labor pain upon a pregnant woman. And they shall not escape" (5:3). St John Chrysostom interprets this passage thus: "[The apostle] has not only glanced here at the uncertainty, but also at the bitterness of pain. For as [a pregnant woman], while sporting, laughing, not looking for anything at all, being suddenly seized with unspeakable pains, is pierced through with the pangs of labor—so will it be with those souls, when the Day comes upon them."[88]

"The Lord will come unexpectedly not because he wants to find His enemies unprepared," says St Theophan the Recluse, "but rather it is the frivolity of the people themselves that causes their lack of preparedness" (see Matt 24:37–39).[89] This sudden second coming is fearful only for the sons of the night. The sons of the light should not fear this suddenness, for they, constantly vigilant, are already ready to meet the Lord (5:4–7). Therefore, the apostle exhorts them not to lose their vigilance, but to be sober and watchful, "putting on the breastplate of faith and love, and as a helmet the hope of salvation. For God did not appoint us to wrath, but to obtain salvation through our Lord Jesus Christ" (5:9). We must constantly prepare ourselves to receive this salvation.

There are further moral lessons to be gleaned from this teaching on the second coming (5:12–22). The apostle explains the virtues that must be the foundation of the order, firmness, and prosperity of Christian communities. He exhorts the faithful to have a tense bond of love with their pastors (5:12–13) and with each other (5:14–15). He indicates the characteristic elements of a truly Christian life—a Christian must instruct those who are "unruly," to comfort those with weak faith, to support the weak, to be longsuffering, never to answer evil with evil, but always to wish good for all. A Christian must always rejoice, constantly pray, give thanks for everything, never "quench the Spirit" or despise prophesies. "Test all things; hold fast what is good. Abstain from every form of evil" (5:14–23).

In 5:23–24, Paul reminds his readers of the goal toward which every Christian must strive: "May your whole spirit, soul, and body be preserved blameless at the coming of our Lord Jesus Christ." Here we find the divinely inspired teaching concerning the tripartite nature of the human person. The spirit is the highest aspect of the soul and the soul is the life force of a person that animates the body.

The epistle ends with a request for prayer and the usual greetings and blessing.

 CHAPTER 9

The Second Epistle of the Holy Apostle Paul to the Thessalonians

THE REASON FOR WRITING THE SECOND EPISTLE
St Paul heard a rumor that the Thessalonians, having been profoundly affected by the unexpectedness and suddenness of the second coming of Christ, began to be "shaken in mind or troubled, either by spirit or by word or by letter, as if from us, as though the day of Christ had come" (2 Thess 2:2). In other words, some Thessalonians believed the day to be coming very soon. This conviction was aided only by the persecutions and sorrows suffered by the Thessalonians (2 Thess 1:4–5). Paul's words, "We who are alive and remain until the coming of the Lord will by no means precede those who are asleep" (1 Thess 4:15), were interpreted by some to mean that Paul himself hoped to see the second coming; consequently, it was very near.

Such thoughts caused disorder in the normal flow of life in the Thessalonian community. Some began to abandon all care for earthly things, and having abandoned all their duties, dedicated themselves to a wasteful life full of reverie. Others were filled with worry, unable to calmly work and live. Such dangerous moods were apparently not helped by false teachers who passed around a letter attributed falsely to Paul (2 Thess 3:17–18), encouraging such frivolous behavior. Having received news from one of the members of the Thessalonian community who came to visit him, St Paul hurried to heal these new wounds with a new epistle.

THE TIME, PLACE, AND PURPOSE OF THE EPISTLE
The content of the epistle clearly shows that it was written not long after the first, for it is an elucidation of the thoughts of the first, especially those concerning the second coming of Christ. Evidently, no new problem, except for this particular issue, had arisen among the Thessalonians, and so it is safe to assume that this second epistle was

also written in Corinth in the same year as the first (A.D. 54). This is further sup-ported by the fact that this second letter was also signed by Paul, Silas, and Timo-thy, and the latter two were only together with Paul in Corinth. It was written, probably, at the end of Paul's sojourn in Corinth, because he asks them to pray for God's deliverance from some evil and cunning people, hinting, probably, at the riot incited against him in Corinth, as the Book of Acts describes (18:13–18).

The purpose of the second epistle is the same as the first—to impart the divinely inspired teaching concerning the second coming of Christ and the events that must precede it, and in part to calm the Thessalonians, lest they make incorrect deduc-tions from his first epistle and be disturbed by the crooked words of false teachers.

THE STRUCTURE AND CONTENT OF THE EPISTLE

This second epistle contains only three chapters. It can be divided into four parts:

1. The usual introduction and greeting (1:1–2).
2. An inspired summary of the positive aspects of the life of the Thessalonian com-munity, in which Paul praises their faith and endurance in sufferings (1:3–12).
3. A dogmatic section in which St Paul dispels incorrect ideas concerning the sec-ond coming of Christ (2:1–16).
4. A section of moral exhortation, in which the holy apostle rebukes those who sow discord and exhorts them to correct themselves (3:1–18). This chapter also includes the usual greetings and blessing.

EXEGETICAL ANALYSIS OF THE SECOND EPISTLE TO THE THESSALONIANS

The Epistle begins with an introduction similar to the first epistle: "Paul, Silvanus [i.e., Silas], and Timothy, to the church of the Thessalonians in God our Father and the Lord Jesus Christ," after which Paul offers his usual apostolic blessing: "Grace to you and peace … "(1:1–2). The entire first chapter is dedicated to the summary of the praiseworthy qualities of the members of the Church in Thessalonica. St Paul praises the faith and endurance of the Thessalonians, expressed especially during times of persecutions and suffering. He thanks God that their faith and love grow ever stronger, and he encourages them with the coming judgment, during which all those unfaithful who persecute them will be shamed and condemned to eternal suf-ferings, while the faithful will be glorified and receive great joy. At the end of this section, St Paul prays that God will grant the Thessalonians endurance to the end, "that our God would count you worthy of this calling" [i.e., Christianity] and "that the name of our Lord Jesus Christ may be glorified in you, and you in Him" (1:11–12).

In the second chapter, the holy apostle dispels the Thessalonians' incorrect assumptions concerning the second coming of Christ. He explains that the day of the Lord is not as near as they assume, for before it comes, "the man of sin … the son of perdition" must appear (2:3)—that is, the antichrist, and there will also be signs to precede his coming, which have not yet occurred.

"We ask you not to be soon shaken in mind or troubled, either by spirit or by word or by letter, as if from us, as though the day of Christ had come" (2:1–2). The apostle indicates three sources for their incorrect understanding of the coming of the day of the Lord—the spirit, the word, and the letter. By this "spirit," the Holy Fathers understand Paul to mean the spirit of prophecy that came down on certain Christians during their assemblies of prayer, when they began to speak out in inspiration on different subjects, including the future. However, not every inspired speech is from the Holy Spirit. Natural inspiration is also possible. St Paul warns the Thessalonians not to believe all speeches concerning the nearness of the second coming, even in cases when the warning comes from reliable prophets in the church. This warning is similar to a warning he gave to the Galatians concerning angelic words that contradict the Gospel (Gal 1:8).

The "word" Paul speaks of here is of course not the word of the Lord Himself, but words that were falsely attributed to Paul. The same is true of the "epistle" here mentioned—Paul references some kind of false epistle attributed to his hand: "as if from us" (2:2). The sin of the Thessalonians is not that they awaited the day of the Lord, for every Christian must await His coming, as commanded by the Lord Himself (see Luke 12:35–46). Rather, they were engaging in useless calculations regarding the actual date and time of His coming. However, no one knows when He will come again, except God alone (Matt 24:36, 25:13).

"Let no one deceive you by any means; for that Day will not come unless the falling away comes first, and the man of sin is revealed, the son of perdition" (2:3). Until there is a general falling away from Christ and the antichrist is already revealed, the day of the Lord will not come. The "falling away" is something that the Lord Jesus Christ Himself foretold (Matt 24:4–5, 11–15, 23–24), a great general apostasy from the faith and an extreme level of debauchery, in spite of the spread of the Gospel to all nations. St Paul speaks further of this general apostasy in his First Epistle to Timothy (4:1): "Now the Spirit expressly says that in latter times some will depart from the faith, giving heed to deceiving spirits and doctrines of demons." He also speaks of it in 2 Timothy 3:1–8, and Apostle Jude speaks of it in verses 18–19 of his epistle.

The Lord Himself wondered whether he would find any faithful when He came again (Luke 18:8). St Theophan the Recluse vividly paints a picture of this falling away in his commentary on 2 Thessalonians:

> The Gospel will be known in the whole world. However, one part of humanity will remain unbelieving, while another, the majority, will persist in heresy, not following the teachings revealed by God, but instead through their own thinking establishing their own faith, though seemingly based on the words of Scripture. These self-invented faiths will be countless. The one who laid the groundwork for these heresies was the Pope, followed by Luther and Calvin, whose foundational principle of personal interpretation of the Scriptures gave a firm push to the invention of new faiths. Even now, there is a great multitude of such faiths, but there will be even

more. Every new kingdom will have its own new faith, and eventually every region, then every city, and in the end, maybe, there will be one's own confession in each and every head.

Whenever they construe their own faith, rather than receive what was handed down by God, no other eventuality is possible. And many of these will assume for themselves the name of Christians. There will also be a minority that holds to the faith as it was handed down by the holy apostles and preserved in the Orthodox Church; however, many of these will be right-believing in the name only, while their hearts will not have the foundation required by faith, for they will love this age more than Christ. This is how great will be the general apostasy. Though the name of Christians will be heard everywhere, and everywhere we will see churches and worship, all this will be merely an appearance, while inside there will be genuine apostasy. In this world the Antichrist will be born, and he will grow in the same apparent godliness, but actual inner apostasy. Then, having given himself to Satan, he will openly reject the faith and, armed with the delusive snares of the enemy, he will lead away all those who do not hold to Christianity truly, and they will reject the Lord Christ. Eventually, the Antichrist will force everyone to worship him as god.

The chosen will not be led away, but he will seek to delude them as well, if he can. To prevent this from happening, the evil days will be cut off by God. The Lord will appear and will destroy the Antichrist and all his works by the revelation of His coming. This is what the apostle means by the "falling away."[90]

Thus, this apostasy will not only be internal and held back at last somewhat by the laws of governments (for such apostasy has occurred many times before among freethinkers who lay the foundation for the coming of the antichrist). This apostasy will be evident, obvious to everyone, loud, and incited by the antichrist himself, who will give it, so to speak, the "green light." Because the apostle, in the words here cited, assumed no long period of time between the general apostasy and the coming of the antichrist and seems to conflate these two events into one, some Church Fathers (St John Chrysostom, Blessed Theodoret, Blessed Augustine) believe that the word for "falling away" is synonymous with "the one who falls away," meaning the antichrist himself.[91] However, the apostle clearly separates the antichrist from the apostasy of the world.

In 2:3–10, the holy apostle gives a description of the dark personality of the antichrist. Who will he be? The apostle calls him a man. Therefore, those who believe that before the end of the world Satan himself will come in the form of a man, begotten of a prostitute in a blasphemous mimicry of the incarnation, are clearly mistaken. No, this will not be Satan in human form, but a man in Satan's form, a man who will give himself completely to the devil, in whom Satan will reside, and whom Satan will use as his perfect instrument (St Theophan the Recluse).[92] St John Chrysostom asks, "But who is he? Is it then Satan? By no means, but some man, that admits his fully working in him."[93] Oecumenius says something similar, "It is not Satan who will be the antichrist, but a man possessed by Satan, in whom Satan will act. He will be a Jew skilled in necromancy and alchemy."[94]

How does St Paul characterize this antichrist?

First of all, he will be "the man of sin," the nadir of sinfulness, a man saturated with iniquity. The Holy Fathers teach that even the manner of his birth will be iniquitous, that is, he will be born from a prostitute. St Theophan says, "He will be born unlawfully, he will live unlawfully, living in sin, spreading sinfulness everywhere. He will also die in his sin. He will everywhere actualize sin completely, and there will be nothing in him, except lawlessness."[95] He will not have a single positive quality in his soul.

Second, he will be "the son of perdition," one who gives himself to his perdition willingly, walking toward it consciously, knowing that he will be condemned for eternity. He will not be the only one to perish, but he will lead many others to perish with him. He will delude them to follow his will and teaching, and by this he will destroy them. He will find pleasure in this; all of his care will be to lead as many as possible to the abyss.

Let us recall that Christ the Saviour also called Judas the "son of perdition" (John 17:12). St John the Theologian also calls the antichrist the Beast of the abyss who will "go to perdition" (Rev 17:8).

"Who opposes and exalts himself above all that is called God or that is worshiped, so that he sits as God in the temple of God, showing himself that he is God" (2:4). St Paul describes four characteristics of the antichrist:

1. He will "oppose" God and the Lord Jesus Christ, which is the reason why he is "antichrist." St John the Theologian gives him this actual name in several places (1 John 2:18, 22; 4:3; 2 John 7). St John Chrysostom calls him *antitheos*—"the opponent of God" or "one who puts himself in the place of God."[96] Antichrist can thus mean "the one who opposes Christ" or "the one who puts himself in the place of Christ."

2. He will be an overwhelmingly proud man, rejecting everything that is called God or any holy thing, desiring that he be the only person worshiped in the entire universe.

3. He will be a man of unparalleled and unconcealed insolence, who will not even be afraid to enter the temple of God and to "be seated as god." The temple is interpreted by the Holy Fathers to mean not merely the temple in Jerusalem, but "places of worship" in the general sense. St Theophan writes,

> There will be in some place a center of the Antichrist's power, and of course there will be a specific moment when he will declare himself as such (i.e., as a deity). St Paul specifically has in mind the main "temple" of this place. In this "temple," wherever it is, he will sit as god, and then he will sit in the same way in whatever other temple in whatever other places he visits. Or perhaps he will

place some symbol in the other churches to indicate his "sitting as god." The Book of Revelation speaks of the image of the beast. Perhaps this image will be placed in all temples as an object of worship? Of course this means he will appropriate temples as well as people into his service, for he will initiate the greatest apostasy from Christianity ever seen in human history.[97]

It is unlikely that the antichrist's self-proclamation of divinity will be sincere. This will be only blasphemous brazenness and an endless thirst to direct worship of men toward his person. Different kinds of people will be found among his worshipers. Some will evidently have lost their heads completely, others—superstitious and primitive—will be fooled by his show of power, his false signs and miracles, and come to believe in him truly as a god come to earth. A third group will worship him insincerely and falsely, fearing his cruelty or flattering him for personal advancement, which he will freely shower on his followers. In any case, this worship of antichrist will be a consequence of a total loss of fear of God among mankind.

4. The antichrist will receive from the devil the ability to perform false signs and miracles, and by this he will awe people's imaginations. St Theophan continues,

> He will surround himself with such luxury in the temple, he will give himself such a reputation thanks to his delusive signs, that all who approach him will see in this phenomenon something divine, just as Herod, dressed in his kingly robes and sitting on the judgment seat before the people, seemed to them extraordinary, someone no longer human, but divine. (Acts 12:21–22)

In the words of St John Chrysostom, "he will order men to worship him instead of God … for he will perform great works, and will show wonderful signs."[98] According to Oecumenius, "he will use all means necessary—deeds, signs, miracles—to make it seem that he is a god."[99] In other words, he will be something like a magician or a sorcerer.

"Do you not remember that when I was still with you I told you these things?" (2:5). It is clear, then, that this teaching concerning the antichrist was a central dogmatic truth preached by the apostles. Interestingly, despite his short stay in Thessalonica, St Paul still considered this teaching necessary enough to be taught fully, not dismissed as secondary, and now, in his second epistle, he mentions this teaching only in passing. Therefore, it is sinful to dismiss the teaching about the antichrist frivolously, avoiding even talking about him, as is often done in our time. Is this not a sign of his imminent coming?

"And now you know what is restraining, that he may be revealed in his own time" (2:6). What is this restraining force that keeps back the coming of the antichrist? Paul's words make it clear that the Thessalonians already know this, but we are left to guess, using the interpretations of the Holy Fathers. St John Chrysostom writes, "Some indeed say [that it is] the grace of the Spirit, but others the Roman Empire."[100] The same thought is expressed by Blessed Theodoret, Oecumenius, and Blessed Theophylact, although others have their own opinions on the subject.[101] Blessed Theodoret of Cyrus writes,

> Some believe the restrainer to be the Roman empire, while some the grace of the Holy Spirit, for they say that [the Antichrist] will not come while the grace of the Spirit restrains [him]. ... God's providence does not allow the coming of the Antichrist ahead of its time. ... Evidently, the divine apostle knew that the Lord had said that first the Gospel must be preached to all nations, and only afterwards will the end come (Matt 24:14), but he also saw that worship of idols still persisted. Thus, following his Master's teaching, he said that first the dominion of superstition must collapse, and everywhere the salvific preaching [of the Gospel] must shine, and only then will the adversary of truth appear.[102]

St Photius (cited by Oecumenius in his commentary) says with respect to this adversary: "It means, that he will not be manifest now, but in his own time, that is, when the time defined and conceded to him by God will come."[103] And Severus (also cited by Oecumenius) opines that "[i]t is the Holy Spirit who restrains and hinders the appearance of the lawless one. When, however ... due to the wickedness of men, the Spirit will be gone and will depart, then the lawless one will take his place, will reveal himself and rise up, with no one hindering him."[104]

Thus, in summary, the antichrist will not come before the Gospel will have been preached to all the nations of the earth and until the wheat and the tares will have been revealed, according to the famous parable of the Lord (Matt 13:24–30, 36–43). Only when the grace of the Holy Spirit will have gathered from all nations those capable of salvation, and the evil among the rest will have reached such a peak of virulence that people will completely forget God and their own consciences, and even lawful government authority will be torn down (i.e., anarchy will rule)—only then will the antichrist come.

Russian Orthodox commentators, citing the Holy Fathers' use of the Roman Empire as the restraining force, interpreted monarchies in general (and in particular, the Russian tsar, the only benefactor and protector of the Orthodox Church in the world at that time) as the "restrainers." St Theophan the Recluse writes,

> While the tsar, having in his authority the possibility to hold back popular movements, holds himself to Christian principles, he will not allow the people to turn away from them. He will hold the people back. As Antichrist will consider it his most important work to distract everyone from Christ, he will not appear while there is an Orthodox Tsar on the throne. The Tsarist power will not allow him

to succeed; it will hinder his actions in its spirit. This is, in essence, 'he who now restrains.' When the Tsarist power falls and every nation in the world will choose self-government (republics and democracies), then it will be easy for the Antichrist to work. It is easy for Satan to prepare people to reject Christ, as we see clearly from the French Revolution. There will be no one left to 'veto' the Antichrist. No one will even listen to the humble expression of Christian faith. Thus, when everywhere in the world such disorder will make the strivings of the Antichrist possible, then he will appear. He will wait and be restrained until that moment.[105]

St John of Kronstadt writes the following on the subject:

The Lord cares for the good of earthly kingdoms (and especially the good of His Church) through the mediation of earthly authorities that do not allow the spread of godless or heretical teachings and schisms. The greatest villain in the history of the world, who will appear in the end times, the Antichrist, cannot appear among us yet, for we are ruled by the autocracy that holds back the disorderly conduct and ignorant teachings of the atheists.[106]

" ... [T]hat he may be revealed in his own time" also means that the antichrist will not choose his own time for coming, but rather his coming will be allowed by divine providence. He will come, but it will not be contrary to God's will. He is also part of God's plan for the world. This is not because God wants to do evil to mankind, but because people themselves will have led themselves to such a state. God is holding back this time until the last possible moment, waiting to see if there are still those willing to turn to Him and serve Him. When that waiting will be futile, then the Lord will remove His restraining hand, evil will flow forth, and the antichrist will appear (St Theophan).[107]

"For the mystery of lawlessness is already at work" (2:7). It is opposed to the "mystery of godliness" (1 Tim 3:16) that is, the incarnation of the Son of God, and we can conclude that the apostle here speaks of the hidden and cunning efforts of Satan to weaken and darken people's faith in the divine Redeemer, our Lord Jesus Christ, through his encouragement everywhere of unbelief, which will lead mankind to complete moral perversion. St John the Evangelist says, "you have heard that the Antichrist is coming, even now many antichrists have come" (1 John 2:18). St John makes a distinction between the antichrist and "antichrists." The first will come before the second coming of Christ, whereas the second, as his forerunners, have already begun appearing, even during apostolic times, and they will continue to reveal themselves in all times that Christianity exists as representatives of anti-Christian spirit and striving. This includes all kinds of false teachers who have always appeared and will continue to appear in the Church and outside it, in whom, as it were, the anti-Christian spirit is incarnate.[108]

Blessed Theodoret writes,

> I think that the apostle here speaks of nascent heresies, because through them the devil leads many to depart from the truth and makes preparations for destroying them by deception. The apostle called them the "mystery of lawlessness" because within them is hidden the snare of lawlessness. Therefore, the apostle called the coming of Antichrist a "revelation." For what he always prepared in secret, then he will proclaim openly and manifestly.[109]

St John of Damascus says something similar: "The apostle calls the heretical teachings and their false dogmas the 'mystery of lawlessness,' for they come before him (Antichrist), laying down his path and preparing the time of deception."[110] How many heretics do we see in our days, how may sects, false philosophies, anarchists, all of whom undermine the authority of lawful government! Their destructive work among men becomes the "mystery of lawlessness," which must prepare the stage for the revelation of the antichrist. "He who now restrains will do so until he is taken out of the way"—this does not mean that the restrainer will be destroyed, but rather he will cease his restraining influence. The "now" refers not only to the apostolic age, but also to all times, "while it is called 'Today'" (Heb 3:13), while the restrainer still restrains.

"And then the lawless one will be revealed, whom the Lord will consume with the breath of His mouth" (2:8). When there will no longer be "one who restrains," the lawless antichrist will appear, the new lord of the earth, to whom all will bow down in worship. The words "consume with the breath of His mouth" indicate the speed and ease of the Lord's victory over the antichrist. The Lord will only breathe, and all the seemingly unconquerable might of the antichrist will disappear like smoke, like wax melted by fire. Isaiah foresaw this, saying, "a Rod from the stem of Jesse [i.e., the Messiah-Christ] ... with the breath of His lips He shall slay the wicked" (Isa 11:1, 4). Therefore, the Lord Jesus, called the Son of God, is depicted in the Apocalypse as having a sharp sword coming from his mouth (Rev 19:15–20).

"The Lord will ... destroy [the antichrist] with the brightness of His coming" (2:8). In these words, according to the Fathers, we see the all-purifying power of the second coming of the Lord. Not only the antichrist, but also all his works will be destroyed in an instant. As light banishes the darkness, so the Lord's coming will immediately put an end to all sin and lawlessness. The tares will be separated from the wheat, and a new heaven and earth will be revealed, where only righteousness and holiness will reign and live forever (2 Pet 3:13).

In 2:9–12, Paul describes the snares of the antichrist and explains whom they will ensnare. By doing so, Paul also makes it clear that those who will avoid the delusion of antichrist are those who firmly hold to the truth. "The coming of the lawless one is according to the working of Satan, with all power, signs, and lying wonders" (2:9). This means that the antichrist will have the power of Satan himself. This is evident from the Apocalypse as well, where it says that the ancient serpent (the dragon) "gave him his power, his throne, and great authority" (Rev 13:2). By these signs and miracles, the antichrist will attempt to emulate the Lord and the apostles, but his miracles will be delusive, not real—nothing more than a magician's tricks. The Apocalypse further says that "he even makes fire come down from heaven on the earth in the sight of men," that he will make an image of the beast and give it life, so that it will begin to speak (Rev 13:13–15). All this will be nothing more than an illusion meant to fool human senses.

"And with all unrighteous deception among those who perish, because they did not receive the love of the truth, that they might be saved" (2:10). In addition to the false miracles, the antichrist will have great power of speech, intended to ensnare more serious people such as the educated and scientifically minded. They will be fooled by his apparent erudition and by his enticing scientific theories. "Those who perish" describes all who follow the antichrist, all the people of one spirit with the antichrist, who will not accept the love of truth, evidently because their hearts have no sense of the existence of absolute Truth. Such people, according to St Theophan, are like stone, completely lacking in feeling.[111] The theories of antichrist, which will be cunning and wise on the surface, will be closer to their hearts than the wisdom of divine truth, which will seem to them too simple and primitive. The cunning words of the antichrist, in addition, will be flattering to debauched hearts, because he will justify their immoral way of life.

"And for this reason God will send them strong delusion, that they should believe the lie" (2:11). This will be a frightful moral punishment meted out by God. Of course, we must not understand these words literally, but only in the sense that God will allow these people to be deluded by the antichrist as a punishment for their obstinacy. This is precisely how Blessed Theophylact of Ochrid explains this: "[The apostle writes] 'Will send,' instead of 'will allow to be sent.' But see that at first they rejected the truth, then God abandoned them, and the lie prevailed over them."[112]

"That they all may be condemned who did not believe the truth but had pleasure in unrighteousness" (2:12). As St Theophan explains, "God will allow these people to reveal fully the depth of their moral and religious evil, and they will be ripe for the judgment."[113] They will be punished for the moral corruption that led them to lose a sense of the truth and to strive toward lies, merely because these lies flatter the crude and low instincts of their fallen human natures.

In the last verses of chapter 2, the apostle thanks God for the positive religious and moral state of the Thessalonians, whom he had called to the true faith. He exhorts them, "Therefore, brethren, stand fast and hold the traditions which you were taught, whether by word or our epistle" (2:15). These words are incredibly important, for they clearly accuse those who reject Holy Tradition, that is, the

Protestants and many other sectarians. St John Chrysostom says, "Hence it is manifest, that [the apostles] did not deliver all things by Epistle, but many things also unwritten, and in like manner both the one and the other are worthy of credit."[114] Therefore, we must recognize that the tradition of the Church is equally worthy of respect and trust. "It is a tradition, seek no farther."[115]

St Theophan the Recluse adds:

> Much from what the apostles taught was passed on orally and instituted by them personally, and all this later was written down in the writing of their disciples, and it was kept in the hearts or the practices of the Christians. Some things were purposely kept out of the written epistles, such as the order of performing sacraments (according to St Cyril of Jerusalem), because the unbelievers were not worthy to hear or read about the mysteries until they themselves believed. This in itself makes it clear how groundless is the rejection by the heterodox of the teachings and rites of the Orthodox Church that are not explicitly described in Scripture.[116]

Chapter 3 contains instructions of a moral nature. The first five verses serve as a kind of introduction. In them, the holy apostle asks the Thessalonians to pray for the success of his ministry, in spite of all the snares of disorderly and evil people that surrounded St Paul, hoping to hinder the spread of the Gospel message both in Corinth and in other places.

The actual instructions begin in 3:6: "But we command you, brethren, in the name of our Lord Jesus Christ, that you withdraw from every brother who walks disorderly and not according to the tradition which he receives from us." This is a general rule: Christians must in all situations be guided by the apostolic traditions and not associate with those who reject or violate these traditions. However, this passage also hints at a specific case that Paul brings to light in verse 11: "We hear that there are some who walk among you in a disorderly manner, not working at all, but are busybodies." To shame such lazy busybodies, Paul reminds them of his own behavior while he was with the Thessalonians: "For you yourselves know how you ought to follow us, for we were not disorderly among you; nor did we eat anyone's bread free of charge, but worked with labor and toil night and day" (3:7–8). So pure was the apostle's conscience that he could boldly offer himself as an example for the Thessalonians.

This does not mean that the apostle considered himself unworthy of receiving material aid from the Thessalonians. According to the commandment of the Lord Himself, "the laborer is worthy of his wages" (Luke 10:7). St Paul had a right to expect money from the Thessalonians, but because he was extremely tactful and nurtured a gentle, fatherly love for them, he did not want to burden them even the slightest bit. Perhaps, knowing their tendency to be lazy and not work hard, he found it necessary to show them a special example of love for work and nonacquisitiveness. Therefore, he says, "Not because we do not have authority [i.e., to accept pay from the Thessalonians], but to make ourselves an example of how you should follow us" (3:9). In this case, the Holy Apostle Paul gives an eternal example to all pastors of the Church of the care and wisdom necessary to approach the question of financial support from a parish.

Wonderful are these immortal words: "If anyone will not work, neither shall he eat." These words were misused by Socialists and Communists to subject anyone they considered to be social parasites to systematic annihilation. Of course, such an interpretation is extremely incorrect. The meaning of these words is that work is necessary for every human being, because it is part of God's judgment after the Fall (see Gen 3:19). There can be, of course, many different forms of work—physical, intellectual, and spiritual. The apostle's thought is that if someone eats at the expense of another's work, then he sins. It is not the apostle's intention to prevent charity, but to awaken the sleeping consciences of parasitic drones.

In verses 11–12, the holy apostle openly and directly accuses such lazy busybodies, calling them those who "walk among you in a disorderly manner." He exhorts them to "work in quietness and eat their own bread." As St Theophan the Recluse explains, "St Paul commands a humble, isolated, work-loving life as a remedy for idly wasting time."[117]

In the conclusion of the epistle, the Apostle Paul tells the Thessalonians to separate the disorderly from their company for their instruction and correction. Then he sends them the usual greetings. He also mentions that he had written the letter by hand, to differentiate it from the false epistle ascribed to him that was circulating in the community.

PART II

The Pastoral Epistles of the Holy Apostle Paul

The last five (chronologically speaking) epistles written by St Paul are called the Pastoral Epistles. Two were written to Timothy, one to Titus, one to Philemon and one to the Hebrews. They are called pastoral because in them the Holy Apostle Paul gives instructions that are relevant first of all for pastors of the Church, because they refer to the pastoral ministry. At the same time, there is much that is deeply instructive for Christians in general.

 CHAPTER 10

The First Epistle of the Holy Apostle Paul to Timothy

WHO WAS ST TIMOTHY?

St Timothy was the favorite disciple, the untiring fellow laborer of St Paul (see Rom 16:21). In many epistles, St Paul praised him effusively. He was born in Lystra, a city of Lycaonia in Asia Minor. The Book of Acts tells of how he came to be associated with St Paul. St Paul visited Lystra during his first missionary journey. There, he and Barnabas healed a man lame from birth, and the local pagans, amazed by the miracle, believed Paul to be an incarnation of Mercury (Hermes), and Barnabas an incarnation of Zeus. They even prepared to offer them sacrifices. The apostles tried to explain to them that they were not gods, but rather the messengers of the one True God Who had sent them to lead the people away from false religion to the true faith. When they had preached the true faith, many of the pagans turned to Christ.

According to tradition, among those who believed was the grandmother of Timothy, Lois, and his mother, Eunice. It is likely that they were Jewesses who tried to raise Timothy in a spirit of fear of God and to teach him the Old Testament Law of God, even before their conversion to Christ. This is evident from St Paul's own words in 2 Timothy 3:15: "from childhood you have known the Holy Scriptures, which are able to make you wise for salvation through faith which is in Christ Jesus." Paul also wrote that the ardent faith of the pious Lois and Eunice was passed on to Timothy (2 Tim 1:5).

When the Holy Apostle Paul once again came to Lystra during his second missionary journey, the brethren in Lystra and neighboring Iconium recommended Timothy to him (Acts 16:1–2), and the holy apostle, seeing in the young man a zealous fellow laborer in the faith, decided to take him on the remainder of the journey. Because his father was an uncircumcised Greek, St Paul, keeping to his rule of being everything for everyone (1 Cor 9:20–22), circumcised Timothy before leaving Lystra, "because of the Jews who were in that region, for they all knew that his father was Greek" (Acts 16:3). This was necessary to allow Timothy to preach freely among the Jews, who would not associate with the uncircumcised and would not have listened to Timothy's preaching. He would not have been given access to the synagogues, where St Paul usually began his ministry.

Acts, however, does not give us specific details of Timothy's work. His story is parallel to the history of Paul's missionary work. Wherever Apostle Paul was, Timothy was almost always with him, helping him or going on errands to other cities and Christian communities. From the greetings of several of Paul's epistles, we know that Timothy was with him in Rome during his first imprisonment. Soon after this, the Holy Apostle Paul consecrated Timothy as bishop of Ephesus. Then he wrote to Timothy twice, instructing him in his new pastoral calling. The second of these letters was written during Paul's second Roman imprisonment, which ended with Paul's martyrdom. Having visited the apostle in Rome as he requested, St Timothy returned to Ephesus and presided over the church there until his own martyrdom. While in Ephesus, he learned much from St John the Theologian, who also lived in Ephesus and presided over all the churches in Asia from there. During the imprisonment of St John the Theologian on the island of Patmos, St Timothy presided over the Asian churches in his place.

THE PURPOSE, PLACE, AND TIME OF THE WRITING OF THE FIRST EPISTLE TO TIMOTHY

St Timothy was consecrated bishop during St Paul's fourth missionary journey in Ephesus. While imprisoned the first time in Rome, St Paul strove with heart and soul to see all his spiritual children from the many communities he had established (Phil 2:19, 23–24). Therefore, when he was freed, he set aside his initial plan to visit Spain (Rom 15:24) and traveled to Asia Minor (2 Tim 4:13–20). Then, in A.D. 65, faced with the rise of Gnosticism (which he had predicted when he first parted with the Ephesian presbyters, see Acts 20:20–30), St Paul begged his fellow traveler Timothy to remain in Ephesus, telling him to "charge some that they teach no other doctrine, nor give heed to fables and endless genealogies" (1 Tim 1:3–4). Desiring to more firmly connect Timothy with Ephesus, a city in which he spent three intense years of work (Acts 19:1–10), St Paul ordained him as bishop of Ephesus despite his relative youth (he was between thirty and thirty-five years old). St Paul traveled on to Macedonia, where his fatherly heart impelled him to go.

When he was in Macedonia, St Paul heard some tragic rumors about an increase of heresies in Ephesus. St Timothy, up to this point, had never been far from St Paul, and even when he was sent on an errand to a different city, he always acted under the strict supervision and guidance of St Paul. Now he was alone and independent in a very important position. St Paul, who loved him like a father, could not help but see how difficult it was for him to battle against the "ravening wolves" attacking his flock. Therefore, he hurried to help him by sending him the first epistle, which he dispatched from Macedonia (Philippi to be exact), where he had promised to go and where he intended to stay for a while longer. He wrote the epistle between his first and second imprisonment in Rome, in c. A.D. 63 or 64.

More specifically, St Paul's intention in writing the epistle is made evident in the following words: "These things I write to you, though I hope to come to you shortly; but if I am delayed, I write so that you may know how you ought to conduct yourself in the house of God, which is the church of the living God, the pillar and ground of the truth" (1 Tim 3:14–15). Having left Timothy in Ephesus, St Paul could have told him everything he needed, but perhaps he did not have the opportunity or time to do this fully. Therefore, fearing that some might lose respect for him on account of his youth (1 Tim 4:12), he wrote to him what basically amounts to a handbook of pastoral work: "This charge I commit to you, son Timothy, according to the prophecies previously made concerning you, that by them you may wage the good warfare" (1 Tim 1:18).

THE STRUCTURE AND CONTENT OF THE EPISTLE

The first Epistle to Timothy has six chapters, divided thematically as follows:

1. Instructions to Timothy as a warden of the faith (1:1–20).
2. Instructions to Timothy as a primate of the Church—
   a. concerning assemblies of the church (2:1–15), and
   b. concerning members of the clergy (3:1–13).
3. General instructions concerning the exalted calling of the episcopacy—
   a. concerning the essential truth of the Christian faith (3:14–16), and
   b. concerning rules about how to teach the flock with word and life (4:1–16).
4. Instructions concerning the teaching and direction of his flock, depending on their different social classes (5–6:19).
5. A parting exhortation to Timothy (6:20–21).

EXEGETICAL ANALYSIS OF THE FIRST EPISTLE TO TIMOTHY

The epistle begins with a general introduction: "Paul, an apostle of Jesus Christ, by the commandment of God our Saviour and the Lord Jesus Christ, our hope" (1 Tim 1:1). Paul here calls himself a "messenger," or "apostle," desiring to establish his full authority and right to send a letter to Timothy, his true child in the faith, whom he raised spiritually. With these words, he raises Timothy by association with himself.

Chapter 1 consists of instructions to Timothy as a warden of the faith. St Paul teaches Timothy to exhort the Christians not to spend their time with questions and arguments concerning the faith, which only lead to idle talk (1:3–7). He must interpret the meaning of the Law of God, which was instituted not for the righteous but for the lawless and insubordinate, and he must reveal to them that true righteousness is gained only by faith in Christ Jesus, who came into the world to save sinners, of whom he (St Paul) considers himself the worst, because he was previously a blasphemer and persecutor of the Christ's faith. Now, however, he is an example of the mercy and justification of sinners who repent (1:8–17).

The phrase "the law is not made for a righteous person" (1:9) means this: a righteous man, that is, one who has received forgiveness of sins and a renewal of life by grace, no longer needs the directives of the Law, for the grace of the Holy Spirit guides him directly. St John Chrysostom reflects on these words thus:

> What then with respect to the righteous? "The law is not made," [the apostle] says, "for a righteous man." Wherefore? Because he is exempted from its punishment, and waits not to learn from it what is his duty, since he has the grace of the Spirit within to direct him. For the law was given that men might be chastened by fear of its threatenings. But the tractable horse needs not the curb, nor the man that can dispense with instruction the schoolmaster.[118]

"Of whom I am chief" (1:15). As Blessed Theodoret writes in his commentary, "For the Only-begotten became man for the sinners' sake and He Himself has taught in the sacred Gospels: 'For I did not come to call the righteous, but sinners, to repentance' (Matt 9:13). But [the apostle], calling himself the first of all sinners, goes beyond the limits of humility."[119]

St Theophan the Recluse adds: "In this, the apostle reveals a true model for all who repent."[120] This is why these words were incorporated into the prayer before Holy Communion recited during the Divine Liturgy.[121] Such a humble acknowledgment of one's extreme sinfulness is a distinctive quality of every true Christian. In conclusion, St Paul, having rendered praise to God (1:17), exhorts Timothy not to be indifferent to questions of faith, but to be zealous and to fight the good fight, a warrior armed against enemies of the faith, inspired by his own faith and pure conscience. "The most important thing in both the pastor and the sheep is faith and a good conscience," says St Theophan the Recluse.[122]

As a contrary example of the fearful treachery against the faith and conscience, St Paul offers the examples of Hymenaeus and Alexander, whom Paul "delivered to Satan that they may learn not to blaspheme" (1:20). This was not the first time that St Paul had used such a dire punishment. In Corinth, the same punishment awaited the man who had committed incest (1 Cor 6:5). According to St John Chrysostom, this punishment was the excommunication of the sinner from the assembly of the faithful, after which he found himself in the power of Satan.[123] We may assume that, at this point, the guilty party would be struck with some visible suffering—either physical or mental illness.

Chapter 2 of the epistle contains St Paul's instructions to Timothy regarding the latter's ministry as the one who presides over the local church. These instructions concern the church assemblies. The apostle teaches that at the assemblies of the church, that is, at the divine services, "supplications, prayers, intercessions, and giving of thanks be made for all men, for kings and all who are in authority, that we may lead a quiet and peaceable life in all godliness and reverence" (2:1–2). According to St John Chrysostom, "The priest is the common father, as it were, of all the world; it is proper therefore that he should care for all, even as God Whom he serves."[124] This is why St Paul exhorts Timothy to pray for all men without exception, not only for those who belong to the Church, but to those outside it. Especially important is the prayer for the king and the civil authorities, so that God might guide them to act for the benefit—both external and internal—of their subjects: "all godliness and reverence" (2:2).

"For this is good and acceptable in the sight of God our Saviour, who desires all men to be saved and to come to the knowledge of the truth" (2:3–4). Clearly, prayer in the church must be a prayer for the salvation of all mankind; such prayer is pleasing to God, for He desires the salvation of all. The dogmatic significance of these words is the following: they refute the false and joyless teaching of Calvinism, which preaches unconditional predestination for all mankind, regardless of free will. For why should the church pray for those who have been condemned eternally already? "For there is one God and one Mediator between God and men, the Man Christ Jesus, who gave Himself a ransom for all" (2:5–6). This is said as proof that all mankind, without exception, is called to salvation, for the sake of the redemptive sacrifice of "the one Mediator Jesus Christ." Christ is called a Man only to underline that He became a Mediator by means of His incarnation, by becoming the one who is truly man.

However, St Paul's words do not negate the mediatory prayer of saints on our behalf, as some Protestants insist, citing these words. Christ is called the "one Mediator" in the sense that only He could bring Himself as a redemptive sacrifice on the Cross for our sake. This in no way diminishes the effect of the intercessory prayer of those people who have been saved and who desire to help us achieve the same salvation by their prayers. "To be testified in due time"— the testimony here includes all prophecies in the Old Testament concerning the suffering Messiah—"for which I was appointed a preacher and an apostle" (2:6–7).

Then the apostle discusses who should celebrate the divine services, where should these be celebrated, and the manner in which the services should be performed: "I desire therefore that the men pray everywhere, lifting up holy hands, without wrath and doubting" (2:8). In other words, church services must be celebrated by men who were ordained as bishops or presbyters of the churches, whereas women should neither celebrate the services, nor address the liturgical assembly with the word of teaching. St Paul had previously written the same thing to the Corinthians: "Let your women keep silent in the churches … for it is shameful for women to speak in church" (1 Cor 14:34–35).

As we see in Acts 14:23, the Apostle Paul established the clergy for all the communities he founded by ordaining presbyters for them. In 1 Corinthians 14:40, he commands that everything in church be done with the proper order and reverence. Therefore, there is no doubt that the "men" mentioned in 2 Timothy are not merely male members of the church, but those appointed to preside in the churches. These prayers or liturgical worship may be performed "everywhere," meaning not in the temple of Jerusalem alone as it was in the Old Testament. Thus, the prophetic words of the Lord to the Samaritan woman were fulfilled: "the hour is coming when you will neither on this mountain, nor in Jerusalem, worship the Father" (John 4:21). In other words, Christian worship will not be limited to a single place, as Prophet Malachi also foretold: "In every place incense shall be offered to My name, and a pure offering" (Mal 1:11).

How should these prayers, this Christian worship, be performed? By "lifting up holy hands"—that is, prayerful raising of hands must be accompanied by the appropriately reverent disposition of the heart. This holiness is purity of conscience and freedom from "wrath and doubting," that is, evil thoughts and feelings against one's neighbor and all doubts or vacillations in the faith.

Then, St Paul gives instructions to women about how they should behave in church: "in like manner also, that the women adorn themselves in modest apparel, with propriety and moderation, not with braided hair or gold or pearls or costly clothing, but, which is proper for women professing godliness, with good works" (2:9–10). In other words, women must appear in church in modest, chaste clothing and not think about external adornments, but focus instead on the inner adornment of the soul with good works.

"Let a woman learn in silence with all submission. And I do not permit a woman to teach or to have authority over a man, but to be in silence" (2:11–12). Here, St Paul forbids women from teaching in churches or publicly preaching at liturgical assemblies, for such preaching would be tantamount to having authority over men, while the word of God commands a wife to submit herself to her husband. This, of course, does not prohibit a woman from teaching outside of ecclesial assemblies. So Blessed Theophylact of Ochrid comments: "Note that [the apostle] does not prohibit a woman from teaching altogether, but merely in church. It is not forbidden for her to teach in private, since also Priscilla instructed Apollos in the faith, and a believing wife instructs her (unbelieving) husband."[125] "Women are even commanded to instruct their own children," according to Oecumenius.[126]

St Paul's position that the woman must be in a subordinate position and not have pretentions to primacy is based on the Biblical account of the Fall. Adam was created first, and then Eve; Eve sinned first, and then Adam. In addition, in Genesis 2:18, 2:20, and 2:22, we read that the wife was created as a helper for her husband, and naturally a helper takes a subordinate position to the one she is assigned to help. From Eve's first sin, St Paul extrapolates that women are more likely to sin, and so they are not capable of a position of primacy. At the same time, we must keep in mind that the apostle does not mean all men and women individually (there are always exceptions to the rule), but humanity as a whole.

"Nevertheless, she will be saved in childbearing if they continue in faith, love, and holiness, with self-control" (2:15). Naturally, St Paul does not mean that the physical process of giving birth is salvific for the women, but rather that salvation for a woman—and, consequently, her most important calling—is to be a mother and to raise her children to salvation. "By these means they will have no small reward on their account," says St John Chrysostom, "because they have trained up warriors for the service of Christ."[127] Blessed Theophylact writes in the same vein: "She must not merely give birth to children, but raise them as well. This is true birth-giving; otherwise, it is not the child-bearing, but the corruption of children."[128] This is the way a woman may obtain salvation—through her raising of children, she will help spread and confirm the kingdom of Christ on earth, raising true children and warriors for Christ.

Chapter 3 of this epistle speaks of people chosen to be members of the clergy, while its last verses summarize the essential truth of the Christian faith. "If a man desires the position of a bishop [this includes both the office of bishop and presbyter as we now understand them], he desires a good work. A bishop then must be blameless, the husband of one wife, temperate, sober-minded, of good behavior, hospitable, able to teach" (3:1–2). Interestingly, St Paul, after listing the qualifications of a bishop, immediately begins speaking of the qualifications of deacons, without saying anything about the presbyters. We also know that in apostolic times, these two offices of bishop and presbyter were not yet firmly differentiated, and so the designation of "bishops" or "overseers" (*episkopoi*)—who by the duty of their office had to watch over their flock—also was applied to the presbyters (see Acts 20:17–28, Phlm 1:1).

Whom does St Paul have in mind here—presbyters or bishops? According to Blessed Theodoret, "By the title 'bishop' here he means a presbyter .... At that time, bishops and presbyters were called by the same name ... However, it is clear that bishops must follow these rules first of all, since they have the higher honor."[129] Why does someone who want to be a bishop "desire a good work"? Naturally, St Paul is not speaking of ambition for the high honor associated with the position, but rather a zealous desire to serve the Church for the good of all, to labor for the salvation of others. As for the requirement that a bishop be the husband of one wife, this does not mean that "a candidate for bishop should not be a bigamist, for this is forbidden for all Christians. Rather, it means that he cannot have been married twice. Whoever is married to a second wife should not be chosen for the episcopate" (St Theophan the Recluse).[130]

Even though from ancient times the Christian Church has allowed second marriage, it has always considered it to be a lesser of two evils, preferring honorable widowhood to second marriage. This is why Ambrosiaster writes, "Even though it is not forbidden to marry a second time, a man worthy of the episcopate must abstain from what is allowed to others because of the greatness of his calling. Whoever desires this calling must be incomparably higher than the rest."[131] Blessed Theophylact says, "Saying this, the apostle does not make it a requirement for the bishop to be married. How could he do that, if he said, 'I wish that all men were even as I myself' (1 Cor 7:7)?"[132]

In our time, when bishops can no longer be married, this apostolic rule is still valid.

A person may be ordained as a presbyter if he is in his first marriage, whereas bishops can only be celibate or widowers after a first marriage. In apostolic times and in the first centuries of Christianity, celibacy for bishops was not an absolute requirement, because (according to Blessed Theodoret) during that time it was difficult to find, among converted Jews or Greeks, any person who already lived a strictly celibate life. "Greeks did not practice virginity," he comments, "nor did the Jews pursue it, since they considered procreation to be a blessing."[133] But as the Christian Church grew and developed, more and more people were willing to live a virginal life for the sake of the Kingdom of Heaven (in accordance with Matt 19:11–12). Soon bishops began to be chosen primarily from among the celibate men. This rule was finally affirmed by the twelfth canon of the Sixth Ecumenical Council (A.D. 681).

The next requirement for a candidate for the episcopacy is that he must be an exceptionally virtuous man, both in his inner life—"temperate, sober-minded, of good behavior, hospitable"—and in his external behavior—"not given to wine, not violent, not greedy for money." He must also have strong intellectual abilities—"able to teach." He must show his capability of leading the Church by first ensuring good order in his own household. He also must not be a new convert, "lest being puffed up with pride he fall into the same condemnation as the devil" (3:6). Finally, "he must have a good testimony among those who are outside, lest he fall into reproach" and besmirch the good name of the Church of Christ (3:7).

The requirements for candidates for the diaconate are similar to the requirements for bishops and priests: "Likewise deacons must be reverent, not double-tongued, not given to much wine, not greedy for money" (3:8). Interestingly, among the qualifications for deacons, St Paul does not list the ability to teach well; however, he adds that they must "[hold] the mystery of the faith with a pure conscience" (3:9). According to Blessed Theophylact, this means that "together with keeping to the correct dogmas of the faith, they must also hold to a blameless way of life. For a pure conscience is the proof of a life not open to condemnation."[134]

The apostle also requires that candidates first be tested, and those who serve well should then be advanced to higher stations. In his words about the diaconate, the holy apostle says a few words about deacons' wives: "Likewise, their wives must be reverent, not slanderers, temperate, faithful in all things" (3:11). Although some recent commentators insist that this refers only to the wives of deacons, all ancient commentators of Scriptures, including St John Chrysostom, Blessed Theodoret, Oecumenius, Theophylact, and even, more recently, St Theophan the Recluse, believe (with good reason) that these words refer to the order of the deaconesses (women deacons), which existed in the early Church. In other words, St Paul speaks not merely of "deacons' wives" but of "women serving the church," that is, deaconesses, whose responsibilities were enumerated in the fourteenth canon of the Sixth Ecumenical Council (A.D. 681).

At the end of chapter 3, St Paul expresses two incredibly important dogmatic truths:

1. "The house of God ... is the church of the living God, the pillar and ground of the truth" (3:15). In other words, the only teacher of the truth, in essence, is the Church.
2. "Great is the mystery of godliness: God was manifested in the flesh" (3:16). This is the first and most essential truth of Christianity, which is necessary to proclaim for a teacher of truth.

The first dogmatic truth contains the essential teaching about the infallibility of the Church, for the Church is not only the visible assembly of people who believe in Christ, but at the same time it is the invisible spirit, faith, oneness of mind, and doctrine that unites all its members with each other and with their Head, Christ the Lord. Individual people, members of the Church, are all fallible; however, the entire Church as a whole can never be fallible or waver from the truth. This truth is found in the dogmas received by the Church, in the apostolic and patristic tradition of the Church that has remained in her unchanged from the beginning, in the sacraments, in the liturgy, and in all that makes up the spirit of the Church, which is continuously passed on from ancient times to the present day.

This Orthodox teaching concerning the infallibility of the Church has been distorted in different ways by the Roman Catholics and the Protestants. Roman Catholics have chosen to ascribe the infallibility of the Church to one man—the pope of Rome. The Protestants, on the other hand, reject holy tradition outright, and so also have rejected the belief in the infallibility of the Church. Therefore, they interpret these words of Paul differently. After "the church of the living God" they place a period, not a comma, and the words that follow—"the pillar and ground of the truth"—they then apply not to the Church, but instead to the "great ... mystery of godliness." Thus, in the Protestant reading, Paul's words sounds like this: "The pillar and ground of the truth and the great mystery of godliness are found in this: God was manifested in the flesh." This reading contradicts the original Greek text, and such an interpretation is found in not a single ancient commentary. All the Fathers of the church understood the words "pillar and ground of the truth" to refer to the Church.

"And without controversy great is the mystery of godliness: God was manifested in the flesh / Justified in the Spirit / Seen by angels / Preached among the Gentiles / Believed on in the world / Received up in glory" (3:16). In these words, St Paul shows his disciple Timothy which essential truth of the Christian faith he should place as the foundation of his preaching. As St Theophan the Recluse writes,

> The Church proclaims and confirms this truth by its very existence. For the Church is the building whose foundation is Christ the Lord (see 1 Cor 3:11); the Church is the Body whose Head is the Word of God made flesh. Whoever sees a living body knows by its being alive that it has a head. Whoever sees a durable building knows that it is built on a good foundation. In the same way, whoever sees the Church knows that "God was truly manifested in the flesh."[135]

St Paul offers St Timothy to measure every teaching by this truth. Everything that does not agree with this truth must be rejected as that which is contrary to Christian teaching.

"Justified in the Spirit" means that the Spirit of God who remained in Christ Jesus (see Matt 3:16) witnessed that He is the incarnate Son of God. The signs and miracles that He performed by the Power of the Spirit of God are eloquent proof of this (Matt 12:28), as well as the life-giving teaching that He preached, being anointed by the Holy Spirit and filled with His grace (Luke 9:18, John 7:17). "Seen by angels" means that the angels together with us saw the Son of God, Whom they before could not see, for they cannot see the Divine Essence as He is, but only in His manifestation.

"O mystery!" exclaims Blessed Theophylact,

> For with us did the angels see the Son of God, whom they have not seen before. For the Gospel says, "Behold, angels came and ministered to Him" (Matt 4:11). And not merely in this moment, but from His birth to His ascension they served Him. At the time of His birth, the angels hymned Him and proclaimed the good news to the shepherds, and at the time of His ascension they ministered to Him.[136]

When Jesus Christ ascended, the angels saw Him, both God and man, in His full heavenly glory (Heb 1:6, 1 Pet 3:22).

Why is the manifestation of God in the flesh called a "mystery"? Because it is inconceivable to the human mind. The *great mystery* is that he was "preached among the Gentiles, believed on in the world," for the preaching of an incarnate, crucified God naturally would seem to be a stumbling block for Jews and madness for the Greeks, and still this proclamation conquered and transfigured the whole world. As for the "glory" in which the incarnate God "ascended,"[137] St Theophan writes the following: "We must assume that the ascension of the Lord was accompanied by a special glory invisible to people, but seen by the angels and praised by them in song."[138] St Theophan continues,

This is the great mystery of godliness and the power of the economy of God that is proclaimed, confessed, and is miraculously at work in every corner of the world. This mystery is the foundation of the Church that, by the power of this mystery entrusted to it, is the pillar and foundation of the truth. This mystery is the foundation of the salvation of every faithful … The faithful should remember this mystery more often than they take a breath.[139]

In the fourth chapter of the epistle, Apostle Paul gives Timothy some rules concerning pastoral instruction by word and action. He warns Timothy first of all about the possibility of heretics, apostates from the Christian faith. "Now the Spirit expressly says that in latter times some will depart from the faith, giving heed to deceiving spirits and doctrines of demons" (4:1). The latter times are not meant here in the narrow sense of "end of the world," but in the more general sense of the phrase (also found in many other places in Scripture)—the "last age of the world," that is, the epoch that began with the incarnation of the Saviour of the world and His redemption and salvation of mankind (see also 1 Cor 10:11).

St Paul had already warned the Ephesian presbyters about these false teachers in his parting conversation (Acts 20:29–30). The "doctrines of demons" he mentions here are all false teachings, because the source of all heresy is the devil (2 Cor 11:13–15). (However, there were some "demonic doctrines," in the proper sense, in Ephesus as well, as we see in Acts 19:13, 19.) What makes all such false teachers obvious is their hypocrisy; they assume the appearance of somebody "set apart," somebody who has acquired all possible wisdom. In a word, they wear a mask of holiness. Their most characteristic trait is the following: "having their own conscience seared with a hot iron" (4:2). Blessed Theodoret comments, "The apostle called their consciences 'seared' to indicate how unprincipled they are, because a place that is cauterized with an iron dies and loses its former ability to feel."[140]

These false teachers have truly reached such a state that is seems they no longer have a conscience at all, or at least that they have become deaf to its cries. The Greek word used here, which means "to brand a sign onto something," also suggests a second interpretation. As animals are branded to indicate their belonging to a certain owner, so runaway slaves and criminals used to be branded with special signs on the shoulder and on the forehead. In the same way, these false teachers bear the signs of their iniquitous life on their souls.

Then the apostle indicates two aspects of the Ephesian heresy, probably because they were the most obvious: "forbidding to marry, and commanding to abstain from food which God created to be received with thanksgiving by those who believe and know the truth" (4:3). St Paul is not speaking of ascetical labors and the celibate life, but of a certain kind of incorrect attitude toward the body and its needs. Doubtless, these Ephesian heretics were the same as the ones St Paul rebuked in his epistle to the Colossians (2:21–23). These were forerunners of Gnosticism, which flourished in the second century, a dualistic heresy that considered matter and the body to be intrinsically evil, in fact, the source of evil in man. This false teaching is especially dangerous because it casts doubt on the dogma of the incarnation of the Son of God. If the body is evil and a creation of the devil (as, for example, the Encratites and Manicheans taught), then the Son of God could not have assumed a true human body, only a phantasmal body, in which case the entire significance of the redemptive sufferings of the Son of God would be lost.

Contrary to these false teachers, St Paul says, "Every creature of God is good, and nothing is to be refused if it is received with thanksgiving; for it is sanctified by the word of God and prayer" (4:4–5). There is nothing essentially impure; we can eat anything. A Christian should not refuse to eat certain foods because they are impure, for everything that God created is "very good" (Gen 1:31). Turning to God in prayer and calling His name before eating sanctifies any and all food (4:5).

"If you instruct the brethren in these things, you will be a good minister of Jesus Christ" (4:6), because the calling of a pastor is founded by the Chief Shepherd, Jesus Christ. Here Timothy, a bishop, is called in Greek *diakonos*, meaning "servant, minister," another example of how the specific terms to designate the orders of priesthood were not yet firmly in use at that time. "Nourished in the words of faith and of the good doctrine which you have carefully followed" (4:6). Paul indicates an important responsibility of a good pastor—that is, to teach his flock and to learn the truths of the holy faith himself, helping himself and others become stronger in the Christian moral life. The power of the apostolic words here is in the word "nourished." St John Chrysostom advises his audience:

> Suggest these things as matter of advice, and so enter into discourses with them concerning the faith, "being nourished up," he says, meaning to imply constancy in application to these things. For as we set before us day by day this bodily nourishment, so he means, let us be continually receiving discourses concerning the faith, and ever be nourished with them. What is this, "being nourished up"? Ruminating upon them; attending ever to the same things, and practicing ever the same, for it is no common nourishment that they supply ... for by the expression, "nourished up in the words of faith and sound doctrine," is implied that he should not only recommend these things to others, but himself practice them.[141]

"But reject profane and old wives' fables" (4:7). We can assume that these fables were an amalgamation of Greek mythology and Jewish ritual law that was adapted by the proto-gnostics into a strange cosmology. "Exercise yourself toward godliness. For bodily exercise profits a little, but godliness is profitable for all things" (4:7–8). The word used here—"exercise"—is intentional, and the Greek original reminds one of gymnastic exercises that give a person flexibility, agility, and strength. St Paul makes an effective analogy—in the spiritual life, one must exercise as well. If people sometimes spend countless hours and effort on physical exercise, how much more time should they exercise their spirit in labors of godliness! It is for this that we all labor, says St Paul, and endure vilification, and this is what every pastor should teach his flock (4:8–11).

The additional instructions offered to Timothy are applicable generally to all pastors. St Paul desires that no one ignore these instructions, even if he be as young as Timothy. "Let no one despise your youth, but be an example to the believers in word, in conduct, in love, in spirit, in faith, in purity" (4:12). All this refers to the pastor's general responsibility to be a model of behavior for his flock. He must be a model "in word"—that is, he must be a model teacher and preacher and even take care that his speech in private always be instructive, reverent, and appropriate; "in conduct"—he must be able to relate to all kinds of people and be tactful in all situations; "in love"—he must have the same sincere fatherly love for all; "in spirit"— the faithful must see and sense that their pastor is a spiritual man, not a worldly one, not easily distracted and secular; "in faith"—the pastor must be an example of correct, unyielding faith; and "in purity"—that is, in chastity and blamelessness, not only physically speaking, but in the inner life of the thoughts and the heart.

"Till I come, give attention to reading, to exhortation, to doctrine" (4:13). St John Chrysostom exhorts, "Let us then be instructed not to neglect the study of the sacred writings ... 'Till I come,' [the apostle] says, give attendance to reading the divine writings, to exhortation of one another, to teaching of all."[142] Here, specifically, St Paul means the Scriptures of the Old Testament, as the New Testament canon had yet to be assembled and had yet to find universal acceptance in the Church. During apostolic times, readings of Scripture at services were accompanied with interpretations of prophecies and by other exhortations. St Paul offers Timothy such means of exhortation for his flock until Paul should return and give him more detailed instructions in person.

"Do not neglect the gift that is in you, which was given to you by prophecy with the laying on of the hands of the eldership" (4:14). This passage is a clear refutation of the false teaching of the Protestants, who reject the ecclesiastical hierarchy and the sacrament of holy orders. The Holy Apostle Paul convincingly shows that priesthood is a special gift of God (see 2 Tim 1:6) that does not abide in all Christians, but only in some, the chosen few to whom it has been passed down by a special symbolic action—the laying on of the hands of the hierarchy (see also 2 Tim 5:22). The "prophecy" that Paul mentions could have been a special sign from above that Timothy would become bishop, or perhaps St Paul refers to the sacrament of holy orders itself, as well as to the prayer that accompanied the laying on of hands. Why does the passage speak about the "eldership" (i.e. presbyterate), if we know that already in the apostolic period a bishop (who St Timothy certainly was) was ordained by other bishops, and not by presbyters (i.e., elders)? This passage does not refer exclusively to presbyters, but rather to those endowed with the priestly dignity in general. We have learned that in the apostolic period the titles of specific hierarchical offices were not yet firmly established, and the terms "bishops" and "presbyters" often were used interchangeably. Moreover, there is no possibility that St Timothy was ordained as a bishop by presbyters, because it clearly follows from 2 Timothy 1:6 that Timothy was ordained by St Paul himself.

Chapter 5 of the epistle contains instructions concerning the teaching and direction of the flock based on their specific social status. There should not be one general rule of conduct for all people, and the wise pastor knows that the particular situation of each person—his age, his position in the Church and society, his relative wealth— warrants a particular and unique approach. First, the apostle instructs Timothy regarding the young and the old: "Do not rebuke an older man, but exhort him as a father" (5:1)—that is, treat him as though he were your own father who has sinned. The same is true of an old woman, whom the priest should treat like his own mother. As for the young, the pastor should be approachable and gentle, as though they were his own brothers and sisters, for "compliments can more quickly achieve that which authority cannot accomplish," as Ambrosiaster notes.[143]

St Paul does make one qualification concerning young women: "younger women as sisters, with all purity" (5:2). In other words, whenever speaking to a young woman or associating with her in any situation, the pastor must take care to be chaste, lest he give rise to doubts about his purity, or lest his own heart be inclined toward sinful attraction.

In 5:3–16, St Paul speaks of widows. "Honor widows who are really widows" (5:3). First of all, "honor" would be better translated as "help," that is, take them under the church's financial support. In other words, Timothy should sponsor all widows of virtuous character who are in need of charity and care. The meaning of 5:4[144] is that widows who have close relatives of means should not burden the Church, but rather their children or grandchildren must show respect to their mother or grandmother by taking care of them, feeding them, and doing good to them (Oecumenius).[145]

Verse 5 suggests that not only old widows, but even younger widows also can be taken into the Church's care if only they have recommended themselves by a virtuous life, rejected a second marriage, and intend to live chastely, putting their trust in God's help alone. Such pious widows are contrasted in verse 6 with those who "live in pleasure" and are consequently "dead while [they live]." These widows should be commanded to live blamelessly (5:7). "But if anyone does not provide for his own, and especially for those of his household, he has denied the faith and is worse than an unbeliever" (5:8). This rebuke is probably directed at those who try to pass off the financial care of their elderly to the Church because they cannot be bothered to care for their own.

In 5:9–16, the apostle explains that the Church should accept widows into its care only if they are older than sixty, married once, and known for their good deeds. They should not be young, because young widows are more likely to be lured away and desire a second marriage. Some interpreters consider this section to be a list of qualifications for deaconesses, because these qualifications are similar to the qualifications for the diaconate. Others believe, however, this is simply a continuation of the instruction concerning widows who are being considered for the Church's financial aid.

To widows who feel themselves incapable of remaining chaste and celibate, St Paul recommends a second marriage for the sake of their virtue, for Paul is aware of cases in which widows have deviated from the path of righteousness, unable to restrain their physical desires: "For some have already turned aside after Satan" (5:15), that is, fell into carnal sin, according to St John Chrysostom.[146] In 5:16, the holy apostle again repeats that the faithful themselves should care for their relatives who are widows and not burden the Church.

In the second half of the chapter, Paul teaches Timothy how a bishop should relate to his presbyters, or "elders." "Let the elders [*presbyteroi*] who rule well be counted worthy of double honor, especially those who labor in the word and doctrine" (5:17). This "honor," according to St John Chrysostom, is equivalent to "care" and provision of the presbyters with everything necessary for their living.[147] The Church should take care of all the daily necessities of its presbyters, as is confirmed in the next verse: "For the Scripture says, 'You shall not muzzle an ox while it treads out the grain,' and, 'the laborer is worthy of his wages'" (5:18).

"Do not receive an accusation against an elder except from two or three witnesses" (5:19). This is important because presbyters are chosen from among the most worthy people, and so any accusation against them should be subject to doubt. In addition, the very manner and character of the pastoral work, which must instruct sinners and accuse sin, places presbyters at the mercy of slanderers and false accusations. Two or three witnesses in such cases are a well-known requirement from the Old Testament (Deut 19:15). "Those who are sinning rebuke in the presence of all, that the rest also may fear" (5:20). This is said of those same presbyters who have been found guilty of the accusations brought against them. St John Chrysostom asks: "What then? is it not a greater scandal, that one should be rebuked before all?" And he continues:

> How so? For it is a much greater scandal, that the offense should be known, and not the punishment. For as when sinners go unpunished, many commit crimes; so when they are punished, many are made better. God Himself acted in this manner. He brought forth Pharaoh, and punished him openly. And Nebuchadnezzar too, and many others, both cities and individuals, we see visited with punishment. Paul therefore would have all stand in awe of their bishop, and sets him over all.[148]

Then the apostle warns Timothy of the difficulties of choosing the right candidates for the holy orders. "I charge you before God and the Lord Jesus Christ and the elect angels" [it is as though St Paul places Timothy at his own side during the

Final Judgment] "that you do these things [i.e., everything to do with the ordination for the service of the Church] without prejudice, doing nothing with partiality. Do not lay hands on anyone hastily" (5:21–22). Some interpreters believe that verse 5:21 refers to the previous section, that is, judgment over sinful priests, but others suggest that this is a new topic concerning ordination. In any case, ordaining and judging priests alike requires impartiality and a careful investigation of the matter. "First one must examine the life of the one called to the ordained," says Blessed Theodoret, "and only then one may invoke upon him the grace of the Spirit."[149]

"Nor share in other people's sins" (5:22b), that is, the sins of the one about to be ordained, "by elevating an unworthy person to be a celebrant of the mysteries for the people" (Oecumenius).[150]

"Keep yourself pure" (5:22c). In the course of this discourse, it becomes clear that this purity refers to the purity from the sins of the ones being ordained; however, some interpreters consider this to be a personal commandment for Timothy to strive to remain morally pure: "Paul gives a command of chastity" (Oecumenius),[151] "he tells him to remain pure" (Theophylact).[152] "If taken together with the previous verse, St Paul's command sounds like this: 'As you examine the worthiness of a candidate, see that you also do not lose your own worthiness'" (St Theophan the Recluse).[153]

Then St Paul recalls Timothy's weak health, and as though lessening his strict words about maintaining purity, he allows Timothy to "use a little wine for your stomach's sake" (5:23). In other words, it is as if the apostle is saying, "Yes, I told you to remain pure, but that does not mean that you should jump to perform even greater feats of asceticism. Do not do this. You have weak health, and you need a lessening of your asceticism. And so, from this moment, do not drink only water, but drink some wine as well" (St Theophan the Recluse).[154]

In verses 5:24–25, continuing his previous discourse, St Paul wants to say that not all have obvious sins, and so one must take special care to examine the lives of candidates for ordination. Are they subject to some secret sins that could become revealed in the future? It is also possible that some may have secret virtues, and so it is useful to seek out and ordain such men, for they can serve the Church honorably.

Chapter 6 of the epistle contains important instructions that resolve in the spirit of Christianity an important issue of social inequality, which so energizes the people in modern times. The general meaning of these instructions is that Christianity abhors violent social upheavals. Speaking in more contemporary language, Christianity encourages change in social relations by means of gradual development or *evolution*, by instructing and transforming great masses of mankind in the principles of true Christian love, equality, and brotherhood. Conversely, Christianity condemns the path of *revolution*, for it is a path of hatred, violence, and bloodshed. This is why Paul says, "Let as many bondservants as are under the yoke count their own masters worthy of all honor, so that the name of God and His doctrine may not be blasphemed" (6:1). Christian slaves must be especially careful if their masters are also Christian. "And those who have believing masters, let them not despise them because they are brethren, but rather serve them because those who are benefited are believers and beloved.... If anyone teaches otherwise ... he is proud, knowing nothing, but is obsessed with disputes" (6:2–5).

Knowing that, most of the time, discontent with social status is based on the passions of love of money, avarice, and envy for the rich under the guise of evangelical principles of brotherhood, equality, and freedom, St Paul warns against avarice and exhorts all to be content with little: "And having food and clothing, with these we shall be content" (6:8). External material riches are inherently dangerous, for they often lead to many sins and misfortunes: "For the love of money is a root of all kinds of evil" (6:10). St Paul teaches Timothy to be a model of unselfishness and freedom from possessions, and to exhort the rich to hope not in their riches, but in God. "O Timothy! Guard what was committed to your trust," that is, the tradition. This is how the epistle ends, with an emphasis on the importance of the apostolic tradition for the faith preserved by the Church (6:20).

 CHAPTER 11

The Second Epistle of the Holy Apostle Paul to Timothy

THE PURPOSE OF THE SECOND EPISTLE TO TIMOTHY

This epistle can be seen as a last will and testament of the Holy Apostle Paul, written to his favorite disciple and fellow laborer, Timothy. "For I am already being poured out as a drink offering," St Paul wrote, "and the time of my departure is at hand" (2 Tim 4:6). St Paul lamented his extreme loneliness, for his former disciples had either left him, "having loved this present world" (2 Tim 4:10), or they were sent out on various errands. The apostle asked Timothy to come to him quickly and to bring Mark (4:9, 11), and also to bring him some necessary things: a cloak (*phelonion*) that he left in Troas and "the books, especially the parchments" (2 Tim 4:13). Thus, the main reason that St Paul wrote this epistle was his desire to see his most dedicated disciples, sensing his imminent end, and to give them his last instructions and blessings.

THE PLACE AND TIME OF THE WRITING OF THE EPISTLE

The time and place of this epistle can be deduced from internal evidence. St Paul wrote, "Do not be ashamed of the testimony of our Lord, nor of me His prisoner" (2 Tim 1:8) as well as "for which I suffer trouble as an evildoer, even to the point of chains; but the word of God is not chained" (2 Tim 2:9). Thus, St Paul wrote the letter while imprisoned. It is also evident that he was imprisoned in Rome, for St Paul, praising Onesiphorus for not being ashamed of Paul's imprisonment, said, "When he arrived in Rome, he sought me out very zealously and found me" (1:17). Doubtless this was the second imprisonment, not the first, because in the first imprisonment Paul had relative freedom and could preach and give comforting news about his situation to the churches in Asia Minor (Acts 28:30–31, Eph 6:19–20, Col 4:8). During the first imprisonment, not only did he not expect to be executed, but rather expressed his conviction that he would soon be freed (Phil 2:24), and he even anticipated a home for himself in Philemon's house in Colossae (Phlm 22). Moreover, the imprisonment described in this epistle was of another nature. He was treated as a criminal (2 Tim 2:9), his preaching was hindered (4:17), and he was abandoned by all (4:16). He also felt the nearness of his violent end (4:6), and his sole comfort was that "there is laid up for me the crown of righteousness, which the Lord, the righteous Judge, will give to me on that Day" (2 Tim 4:8).

For all these reasons, both ancient and modern commentators agree that the second epistle to Timothy was the last epistle written by St Paul. It was written in Rome not long before his martyrdom, either in late A.D. 66 or early A.D. 67.

THE PURPOSE OF THE EPISTLE

Although he called his beloved disciple to himself in Rome, St Paul was not sure he would survive to see him. At the same time, he was still worried about the many troubles that faced St Timothy in his pastoral ministry in Ephesus. By this time, more people had accepted teachings contrary to evangelical truth, like the Egyptian magicians who opposed Moses in Pharaoh's court: "having a form of godliness but denying its power ... those who creep into households and make captives of gullible women loaded down with sins, led away by various lusts" (2 Tim 3:5–6). St Paul expected Timothy to face even more difficulties in the future: "But evil men and impostors will grow worse and worse, deceiving and being deceived" (2 Tim 3:13). "For the time will come when they will not endure sound doctrine, but according to their own desires, because they have itching ears, they will heap up for themselves teachers; and they will turn their ears away from the truth, and be turned aside to fables" (2 Tim 4:3–4).

Consequently, St Paul, although intending initially only to write about his private concerns, decided to "add also something concerning good pastorship," as St Theophan the Recluse notes.[155] And because this subject was more important than personal requests, it occupied the majority of the epistle, and the personal requests became as though an afterthought. Thus, the purpose of the letter was to inspire Timothy to unwavering vigilance and bravery in his pastoral calling.

THE STRUCTURE AND CONTENT OF THE EPISTLE

This epistle consists of four chapters. It can be divided into three parts:

1. Introduction with greetings and a summary of the main subject of the epistle (1:1–6)
2. Instructions to Timothy concerning his pastoral calling (1:7–4:8)
3. Conclusion with personal requests and a list of reasons why St Paul wrote the epistle (4:9–22)

EXEGETICAL ANALYSIS OF THE SECOND EPISTLE TO TIMOTHY

This epistle begins with the usual introduction: "Paul, an apostle of Jesus Christ by the will of God, according to the promise of life which is in Christ Jesus" (1:1). Having then expressed his love for "Timothy, a beloved son" (1:2) and having remembered the sincere faith of his grandmother Lois and his mother Eunice, St Paul reminds Timothy "to stir up the gift of God which is in you through the laying on of my hands" (1:6). The teaching is clear that in the mystery of ordination, the candidate receives a special gift of divine grace; therefore, the Protestant and sectarian rejection of the mystery of priesthood is deeply flawed, for thus they deprive themselves of the canonical, grace-filled pastors who take their succession from the Apostles. This gift of grace can be "stirred up" only by the fire of pastoral zeal, which is the conscientious fulfillment of the pastoral calling.

In the first section of chapter 1, a moral instruction, St Paul writes about the fruit most likely to be revealed in Timothy by the "stirring up" of the gracious gift of priesthood. The apostle exhorts Timothy not to be ashamed of "the testimony of our Lord," that is, the preaching of His Cross, which is a stumbling block for the Jews and madness for the Greeks. Instead, he should even be ready to suffer, if necessary, for the preaching of Christ, being ever more inspired by the exaltedness of the work accomplished by Christ our Saviour—the economy of our salvation. Paul also offers the example of himself and Onesiphorus, whom Paul praises for not being ashamed of Paul's imprisonment, "but when he arrived in Rome, he sought me out very zealously and found me" (1:17), even though all of Paul's disciples in Asia had abandoned him.

Chapter 2 contains more specific exhortations concerning courage and self-rejection in the pastoral calling. St Paul compares the pastoral calling with service in the army and exhorts Timothy not to fear the sufferings to which he may be subjected, to be "a good solider of Jesus Christ" (2:3).

"The things that you have heard from me among many witnesses, commit these to faithful men who will be able to teach others also" (2:2). The "faithful men" in this passage, according to both ancient and modern commentators, is a reference to bishops and presbyters. In other words, Timothy should prepare people from among the faithful for ordination to the episcopate or presbyterate, so that he could then pass on to them the entire truth of the divinely inspired teaching, especially (as certain commentators believe) the proper celebration of the Church's mysteries, which was passed over as a secret and oral teaching, as St Basil the Great writes,[156] although always in the presence of witnesses from among the oldest of the faithful, so that the tradition would not become corrupted. As St Photius comments, "This [i.e., "faithful men"] refers to the bishops and presbyters whom Timothy was going to ordain."[157]

Then St Paul inspires Timothy to endure sufferings for the sake of Christ with examples—the good soldier, the athlete, and the hardworking farmer. Finally, he gives Timothy the greatest example of all—the Lord Jesus Christ Himself Who suffered and died on the Cross before His glorious resurrection. "You therefore must endure hardship as a good soldier of Jesus Christ. No one engaged in warfare entangles himself with the affairs of this life, that he may please him who enlisted him as a soldier" (2:3–4). St Paul is not saying that a pastor should completely recuse himself from earthly cares, for he himself said that the pastor should bring his own house in order before he begins setting aright the house of God (see 1 Tim 3:4–5). The canons of the Church only forbid a pastor to engage in those aspects of secular life that distract him from service to the Church. "And also if anyone competes in athletics, he is not crowned unless he competes according to the rules" (2:5). Just as any athlete can only win at his chosen sport if he follows the rules of the sport, so too must the pastor of the church live by all the commandments of the word of God that govern the calling of pastorship. "Competition at the games," says Blessed Theodoret, "has certain rules that bind the athletes. Whoever does not follow the rules cannot win the competition."[158] St Theophan the Recluse writes:

> So the pastor should not lead his flock willy-nilly, but with strict diligence and wise forethought. He must make his actions appropriate to every unique place, person, and event, both external and internal, both secular and spiritual, having only one goal in all of this, which is a victory over the enemies, both visible and invisible, through the coming of the true light, of moral purity and sanctification by grace.[159]

"The hardworking farmer must be first to partake of the crops" (2:6). The pastor is not merely like a soldier or an athlete, but he is like a farmer as well. Just as the farmer expects to receive a bountiful harvest from the ground over which he has toiled, so the pastor naturally hopes for the fruits of his zealous pastoral work. "If you see these fruits," says St Theophan, "you will taste consolation and joy of spirit that will feed your soul more sweetly than honey and the honeycomb."[160] The anticipation of such fruits should inspire a pastor to the proper fulfillment of his pastoral calling, just as a farmer awaits the harvest for his own table.

Then the apostle exhorts Timothy to contemplate the profound meaning of these examples. He also inspires Timothy with the thought of Christ's resurrection and his own sufferings for the sake of the ministry of Christ (2:7–10). Every good pastor must follow the same thorny path of suffering, but every good shepherd ultimately will reign together with Christ and share in Christ's glory (2:11–13). St Paul counsels Timothy not to argue uselessly with the false teachers, for "they will increase to more ungodliness" (2:16). Among these false teachers Paul remembers Hymenaeus and Philetus, "who have strayed concerning the truth, saying that the resurrection is already past" (2:18). These doubtlessly were the early gnostics who would eventually reject the resurrection of the body entirely, understanding the general resurrection in a spiritual sense. They taught that the resurrection to new life meant the soul leaving the darkness of ignorance, falsehood, and sin for the light of truth.

Although he warns Timothy against these false teachers, St Paul insists that they ultimately cannot shake the foundation of the Church: "Nevertheless, the solid foundation of God stands, having this seal: 'The Lord knows those who are His,' and, 'Let everyone who names the name of Christ depart from iniquity'" (2:19). The Church, that divine edifice, has a sign or a seal on its doors, consisting of two parts. The first part, "The Lord knows those who are His," means that those who truly belong to God are known by Him and cannot be shaken in their faith, for the grace of God has so rebuilt their entire inner world that they have become firmly entrenched in the truth, they have become the chosen ones of God, and they do not fear any heretical confusion or snare.

The second part of the mark that shines on the chosen ones of God is "Let everyone who names the name of Christ depart from iniquity." This means that the chosen of God not only confess their allegiance to God with their lips, but also with the deeds of their life. In other words, the two aspects of a truly Christian life are the following: faith and an active life informed by that faith.

"But in a great house there are not only vessels of gold and silver, but also of wood and clay, some for honor and some for dishonor" (2:20). This means that, just as in a large house, in the Church, there are different members, some complete and some incomplete. Paul exhorts Timothy to strive to be a "vessel for honor," fleeing "youthful lusts," including not merely lusts of the flesh, but also all unwise passions peculiar to youth, and to hold to "righteousness, faith, love, peace," avoiding foolish quarrels and instead meekly instructing the opponents of the faith (2:21–22).

In chapter 3 of the epistle, the holy apostle foresees a terrible increase of evil and iniquity on earth. "But know this, that in the last days perilous times will come. For men will be lovers of themselves, lovers of money, boasters, proud" (3:1–2). Although these words refer to the last times of the world and humanity, we may also understand the "last age" to refer to the entire period of time that began with the coming of the Saviour into the world. Therefore, these words of the apostle still refer to the same false teachers as before. One of their characteristic traits is that they will externally appear to be pious, that is, they will be hypocrites (3:5).

"For of this sort are those who creep into households and make captive of gullible women loaded down with sins" (3:6). If we study the history of sects, we find a certain pattern. Many founders of sects find the most success in spreading their false teaching by gaining the sympathy of women who lead a distracted, worldly life, whom Paul calls "gullible." These women, content in their ignorance and preferring to live a manner of life founded on reverie and fantasy, are easily swayed by the flattery of the false teachers. Beginning as mere tools for the slaking of the lusts of these false teachers, they soon also became adept at spreading the same delusion they have been fed. Blessed Jerome has this to say in one of his letters:

It was with the help of the harlot Helena that Simon Magus founded his sect. Bands of women accompanied Nicholas of Antioch that deviser of all uncleanness … Montanus, that mouthpiece of an unclean spirit, used two rich and high born ladies Prisca and Maximilla first to bribe and then to pervert many churches … Arius intent on leading the world astray began by misleading the Emperor's sister. The resources of Lucilla helped Donatus to defile with his polluting baptism many unhappy persons throughout Africa.[161]

"Always learning and never able to come to the knowledge of the truth" (3:7). This is said of the same women—they study merely out of curiosity, constantly seeking something new and "modish." "Their inability to understand the truth," says Blessed Theophylact, "is not a natural failing, but rather a consequence of the incorrect direction of their will."

"Now as Jannes and Jambres resisted Moses, so do these also resist the truth" (3:8). Jannes and Jambres were two Egyptian magicians who opposed Moses. Paul most likely knew these names (not found in Scripture) from Jewish tradition. These names are also found in the Targum of Jonathan on Exodus 7:11 and 20:22, and in certain later Talmudic writings, such as in *Zohar*, a thirteenth-century Jewish Kabbalistic treatise. Ephesus was also known for its magicians, which is why Paul's comparison is so apt. St Paul is warning Timothy of the nature of the opposition facing him and how fiercely he must fight back.

The next verse is an encouragement: "But they will progress no further, for their folly will be manifest to all, as theirs also was" (3:9). "The fog raised by them will dissipate and all the phantoms will fade away" (St Theophan).[162] Then the apostle praises Timothy for following Paul's missionary work in all aspects, suffering the same deprivations and sorrows. He comforts Timothy with the thought that "all who desire to live godly in Christ Jesus will suffer persecution" (3:12). "No person who battles evil can avoid sorrows," as St Theophan comments.[163]

"But evil men and impostors will grow worse and worse" (3:13). St John Chrysostom comments: "Let none of these things, he says, disturb thee, if they are in prosperity, and thou in trials. Such is the nature of the case."[164] However, "evil men and impostors" only seem to be prospering, but in actual fact they are only deluding others as well as themselves. This is a state of catastrophic self-delusion, for they are being helped by the very enemy of the human race.

"But you must continue in the things which you have learned and been assured of, knowing from whom you have learned them" (3:14). Timothy, of course, learned from St Paul, but Paul is not insisting on his personal authority. Rather, he underlines the grace of the Holy Spirit that so clearly guided him in his labors, instructing him and making him wise.

"And that from childhood you have known the Holy Scriptures, which are able to make you wise for salvation through faith which is in Christ Jesus" (3:15). This is a second exhortation for Timothy to firmly preserve the teaching he received in childhood, thanks to his mother and grandmother, concerning the Old Testament Scriptures that so well prepared mankind for the coming of the Messiah. The apostle then continues by stressing the great significance of the Holy Scriptures for every person, especially a spiritual guide of the faithful, a pastor of the Church: "All Scripture is given by inspiration of God, and is profitable for doctrine, for reproof, for correction, for instruction in righteousness, that the man of God may be complete, thoroughly equipped for every good work" (3:16–17). The Holy Scriptures teach us both the dogmas of faith and the laws of a moral life, rebuking falsehood and correcting bad habits. This makes it obvious how important the Scriptures are, especially for a pastor, whose entire work is guiding people to the good, teaching people the truth and good, rebuking their sins and errors, correcting their manner of living and their way of thinking, and strengthening them on the way to holiness. If the Old Testament Scriptures are considered to be so beneficial and important (because, of course, St Paul has the books of the Old Testament in mind when he speaks of "Scripture"), then how much more necessary and important is the New Testament! In it, the will of God is revealed in its fullness. It is also a key for the proper understanding of the Apocalypse contained in the Scriptures of the Old Testament.

In 4:1–8, the Apostle Paul continues to instruct Timothy on his calling as pastor, but then he begins to speak of his own personal affairs, which were the reason he wrote the letter in the first place. St Paul powerfully charges his disciple Timothy, reminding him of God's judgment, not to be lazy in the fulfillment of his pastoral duties. "Preach the word! Be ready in season and out of season. Convince, rebuke, exhort, with all longsuffering and teaching" (4:2). In these words, we read the many aspects of the pastoral calling that only vary depending on the moral level of the flock.

What does it mean to be ready "in season and out of season"? In one of his homilies on this epistle, St John Chrysostom answers: "have not any limited season: let it always be thy season, not only in peace and security, and when sitting in the Church. Whether thou be in danger, in prison, in chains, or going to thy death, at that very time reprove. Withhold not rebuke, for reproof is then most seasonable, when thy rebuke will be most successful, when the reality is proved."[165] The pastor, of course, must be in a sense "timeless," never choosing or waiting for the most appropriate time for his own comfort. For example, it would be strange to wake a tired and exhausted member of the flock to read him a sermon or have an instructive discussion with him. If, however, the pastor is lying down to rest and suddenly is called to fulfill his duties, he must not delay or make excuses. It would be strange for a pastor to force his instruction on listeners completely unwilling to listen or even hear him, but when he is called or when he himself sees that his words can be important or beneficial, he must overcome his own personal discomfort and go to preach wherever his duty requires.

Why must one hurry and try to use every beneficial circumstance for preaching? Because "the time will come when they will not endure sound doctrine, but according to their own desires, because they have itching ears, they will heap up for themselves teachers; and they will turn their ears away from the truth, and be turned aside to fables" (4:3–4). There can be no more expressive word than the Greek *"episôreusousi"* ("heap up for themselves"), because the mental picture conjured is a disorderly crowd of teachers who are chosen and confirmed in their ranks by their own disciples (St John Chrysostom).[166] "Moreover, they will choose teachers not on account of sound reason, but will choose those who will justify their desires, saying and doing only what pleases them" (Blessed Theophylact).[167]

"Itching ears" suggests that these false teachers will be good orators, but their oratory will be turned more to flattery than exhortation. The truth will become a bitter thing for these people, and they will instead turn to "fables," that is, as St Theophan interprets, "various fantastical teachings that will attract the imagination with pleasant fantasies, leaving the conscience alone, not awakening it, not bothering it with requirements to correct the uncorrectable in their worldviews and lives."[168]

Just such a false teaching was the strange fascination that Russians had at the end of the nineteenth and early twentieth century with theosophy, the occult, and various other philosophical and sectarian false teachings that avoided the ascetic realities of true Christianity.

"But you be watchful in all things, endure afflictions, do the work of an evangelist, fulfill your ministry" (4:5). This "watchfulness" characterizes the general character of the inner disposition of a good shepherd. Such a good shepherd will carefully look in all directions to anticipate possible dangers for his flock, and he guides his pastoral ministry along these lines.

"Endure afflictions"—this quality characterizes the external life of a pastor. This phrase "does not refer to personal suffering of persecutions for the sake of the faith, but rather a state of lack of comfort ... Undertake every painful labor required for the benefit of your flock, not sparing or pitying yourself" (St Theophan the Recluse).[169] A distracted or luxurious life, the search for pleasures and diversions are not appropriate for a true pastor, for all this goes contrary to the command: "endure afflictions."

"Do the work of an evangelist" (4:5). This is the most important work of a pastor of the Church, the cornerstone of all his other work. A pastor is not a machine who performs the appointed services and rites. First and foremost, he is a zealous preacher of the good news of salvation. "Fulfill your ministry," that is, "do your work properly," not willy-nilly, not with a lukewarm heart, but with a full, ardent zeal.

St Paul ends his pastoral instructions with a prophecy of his imminent martyrdom. It is as if he wants to say, "Be zealous in your pastoral ministry, Timothy, because my time has come. There is no one more zealous left to carry on my work except you, my most beloved disciple" (St Theophan the Recluse).[170] As though bequeathing some final wisdom to Timothy, St Paul leaves him his own example of zealous apostolic ministry. St John Chrysostom comments:

> Often, when I have taken the Apostle into my hands, and have considered this passage, I have been at a loss to understand why Paul here speaks so loftily [about himself]: "I have fought the good fight." But now by the grace of God I seem to have found it out. For what purpose then does he speak thus? He is desirous to console the despondency of his disciple, and therefore bids him be of good cheer, since he was going to his crown, having finished all his work, and obtained a glorious end. Thou oughtest to rejoice, he says, not to grieve.[171]

From 4:9, Paul begins his epilogue. In it, Paul asks Timothy to come soon, "before winter" (4:21), and he gives him various commissions to perform on his behalf. He also passes on greetings and ends with the usual apostolic blessing. In 4:16–17, the apostle speaks of the first session of his trial, which ended well for the apostle, despite the fact that all had left him, because they were afraid. "Also I was delivered out of the mouth of the lion" (4:17). St John Chrysostom and Blessed Theodoret believe that this lion is the despotic emperor Nero,[172] the persecutor of Christians, whereas others think that there was actual danger of Paul being condemned to be eaten by lions in the Coliseum, as happened so often during the persecutions of Christians.

 CHAPTER 12

The Epistle of the Holy Apostle Paul to Titus

WHO WAS ST TITUS?

We have few historical facts concerning St Titus. The Book of Acts does not mention him at all. All we know comes from the epistles of St Paul and oral tradition. The first mention of him in Scripture is in Galatians (2:3), where he is mentioned as one of those who accompanied Paul to the Apostolic Council in Jerusalem. We also find out in Galatians that he was a Greek, while tradition adds that he was a Cretan, one of the local nobility, a lover of wisdom who stood apart from the surrounding pagan culture in that he was a zealot of piety and a celibate (see Epistle to the Philadelphians of St Ignatius of Antioch).[173] According to tradition, Titus was sent by his uncle, the *anthypatos* (proconsul) of Crete, to Jerusalem during the earthly life of Jesus Christ, and he even spoke with the Lord and the apostles and witnessed some of Christ's miracles (see John 12:20–22). He was also a witness of the crucifixion of the Lord and he was convinced of the truth of His resurrection. He was among those Cretans who heard their own language spoken by the apostles on the day of Pentecost.

All this he relayed to his fellow Cretans upon his return home. From there, he traveled to Antioch and became a loyal disciple and fellow traveler of St Paul. The degree of their intimacy and mutual love is clear from 2 Corinthians 8:23, in which St Paul speaks of Titus as "my partner and fellow worker." It is likely that Titus accompanied Paul on his second missionary journey when the Galatians were converted, for in the Epistle to the Galatians, St Paul speaks of Titus as though the Galatians already knew him (Gal 2:1–3). Titus also accompanied St Paul on the third missionary journey, for St Paul sent him from Ephesus to Corinth with an important commission—to see what an effect the first epistle to the Corinthians had on the local community and to arrange certain affairs of the Corinthian church (2 Cor 7:12–15). After Titus wrote to Paul, the apostle wrote the second epistle, and he sent it with Titus also, having commissioned him to gather aid for the poverty-stricken communities in Palestine (2 Cor 8:6, 16-17). St Paul recommended Titus to the Corinthians as a reliable and faithful man (2 Cor 8:20–23).

From the Epistle to Titus, we find out that Titus accompanied Apostle Paul after the end of his first Roman imprisonment on part of his fourth missionary journey. Paul left him on Crete to help establish the community there and to assign presbyters for the entire island (Titus 1:5). As we see in Titus 3:12, however, Titus once again was called by Paul to continue to share the labors of the fourth missionary journey from Nicopolis of Cilicia to Macedonia, Achaia, Spain, and finally Rome, where Paul was imprisoned a second time and eventually martyred. In 2 Timothy 4:9–10, it is clear that Titus remained with St Paul in Rome and was sent by him to Dalmatia on some errand. We further know from tradition that Titus later became bishop of Crete until his old age, having illumined the entire island with the light of Christ's faith. He died at the age of ninety-four, remaining celibate until his death in emulation of his teacher, in A.D. 110. He is commemorated on August 25.

THE ESTABLISHMENT OF THE CHURCH IN CRETE

The Epistle to Titus, of course, also is intended for all the Christians in Crete, over whom Titus presided as bishop. Crete is known as "queen of the islands" of the Mediterranean for its fruitful soil and large size. Even in ancient times, it was densely populated and was known for its rich trade and model jurisprudence.

After the Greek republics began to fall apart, Crete began to fall into disorder. In 69 B.C., the Roman consul Metellus made Crete into a Roman province. The reinvigorated Roman trade attracted many people of low morality, seeking profit, to Crete. As a result, Cretans became well known as morally degenerate and inclined to lie, so much so that there was a Greek proverb: to "speak Cretan" meant "to lie." Even the ancient poet Epimenides (seventh or sixty century B.C.), a native of Crete, noted this proclivity of his own people, and St Paul confirmed it in his epistle to Titus (1:12–13). Many Jews lived on Crete, attracted by the burgeoning trade.

It is unclear when exactly Christianity appeared on Crete. We know from Acts that Cretans were among those present at Pentecost (2:11). Doubtless, these were the first preachers of Christianity in their homeland. It is possible that Titus was among these. The official establishment of the Church in Crete belongs to St Paul, however, as we see from the epistle. St Paul evidently labored in Crete during the fourth missionary journey that followed his first Roman imprisonment. He established communities in all the cities of Crete, but he did not have time to ordain presbyters for each community, and he appointed Titus to do this (1:5). Among Titus's helpers on Crete was a certain Zenas, a lawyer, and Apollos, well known for his erudition and oratory (3:13).

THE PLACE AND TIME OF THE WRITING OF THE EPISTLE
According to St John Chrysostom, "this epistle seems to have been written before that to Timothy, for that he wrote as near his end and in prison, but here, as free and at liberty."[174] St Paul was freed from his first imprisonment around A.D. 64. He then began his fourth missionary journey, during which he visited Crete. After Crete, he went to Asia Minor to visit the churches for which he suffered so much during his first Roman bonds. During this part of the trip, he quickly felt the need of Titus's help and called him to Nicopolis, where he invited him to spend the winter (Titus 3:12). Thus, we can assume that the epistle to Titus was written in A.D. 64 in one of the Asian cities. St Athanasius of Alexandria and Blessed Jerome believed that the city in question was Nicopolis of Cilicia.

THE PURPOSE OF THE EPISTLE TO TITUS
The Christian community in Crete was diverse. Typically Cretan moral problems—lying, laziness, and avarice—as well as the confusion sowed by the Jews among the Christians, all presented serious pastoral issues. Moreover, Titus himself was a Cretan, and so it was necessary to bolster his authority with those who might know him too well. The epistle was also a necessary written instruction to supplement any oral instruction that St Paul may have given Titus. Having received these written instructions, Titus could act more boldly and decisively, bolstered by the authority of the apostolic epistle.

THE STRUCTURE AND CONTENT OF THE EPISTLE
This epistle has only three chapters. There are four clear parts:

1. Introduction with a greeting (1:1–5).
2. Instructions concerning the choosing of priests for the Church (1:6–16).
3. Instructions concerning the pastor's need to teach (2–3:11).
4. Conclusion with some final commissions, greetings, and a blessing (3:12–15).

EXEGETICAL ANALYSIS OF THE EPISTLE TO TITUS
The Epistle to Titus begins with the usual greeting, which in this case sounds especially triumphant and more expansive than in other epistles, reminding the reader of the introductions to Romans and Galatians. By this expansive introduction, Paul wanted to underline the importance of the subject of the epistle. Paul praises Titus, calling him "a true son in our common faith" (1:4), one who has kept unchanged the holy faith taught by Paul himself. The introduction ends with the assertion that Paul left Titus in Crete "that you should set in order the things that are lacking, and appoint elders in every city as I commanded you" (1:5).

Then, hinting at the fact that on Crete there are many people not fitting for the priesthood, the holy apostle advises Titus to be especially careful in choosing prospective candidates. He lists the qualities he should seek in a future priest: "If a man is blameless, the husband of one wife, having faithful children not accused of dissipation or insubordination" (1:6). "The husband of one wife" means "one who has not married twice." St John Chrysostom interprets this requirement thus:

> Why does he bring forward such an one? To stop the mouths of those heretics, who condemned marriage, showing that it is not an unholy thing in itself, but so far honorable, that a married man might ascend the holy throne; and at the same reproving the wanton, and not permitting their admission into this high office who contracted a second marriage. For he who retains no kind regard for her who is departed, how shall he be a good priest? and what accusation would he not incur? For you all know, that though it is not forbidden by the laws to enter into a second marriage, yet it is a thing liable to many ill constructions. Wishing therefore a ruler to give no handle for reproach to those under his rule, he on this account says, "If any be blameless," that is, if his life be free from reproach, if he has given occasion to no one to assail his character.[175]

"Having faithful children," that is, believing Christians, not pagans or godless, "not accused of dissipation or insubordination." The children of a potential priest must be free of any accusation of immoral behavior. As St John Chrysostom points out, "he who cannot be the instructor of his own children, how should he be the teacher of others?"[176] Blessed Jerome indicates that the sins of children can hinder and undermine the success of their fathers' ministry: "For with what sort of freedom can we accuse others' sons and teach them the right paths when the accused can simply retort, 'Teach your own first!'"[177]

Then the apostle lists the negative qualities that a bishop should never have ("bishop" here can mean both a bishop and a presbyter, because the distinction between the two was still nebulous during the apostolic age). "For a bishop must be blameless, as a steward of God, not self-willed, not quick-tempered, not given to wine, not violent, not greedy for money" (1:7). When speaking of the steward of God, Paul is referencing the Lord's parable concerning the faithful steward (Luke 12:42). "Not self-willed"—a bishop should not want to have his will followed constantly, placing his personal desires and egotistical interests above everything else. "Not quick tempered"—all these negative qualities are inappropriate for a good shepherd and steward, as the Lord also says in His parable (Luke 12:45). "Not greedy for money"—this means not merely avarice, but even the desire to become rich, which is unworthy of a servant of Christ, who must emulate the apostles who never sought any profit, but always were content with mere necessities—food and clothing (1 Tim 6:8).

St Paul then follows with a list of positive qualities desirable in a candidate for priesthood: "hospitable, a lover of what is good, sober-minded, just, holy, self-controlled" (1:8). Hospitality is especially prized in times of persecution.

Theophylact of Ochrid interprets "the lover of what is good" as the one who is "kind, gentle, who is measured in all things and never envious."[178] A priest should be blameless of all physical sins, which are possible even in a lawful marriage. Those who are married must be faithful and moderate in their physical relations; those who are celibate must be pure in thought as well as action. "Just" means having no prejudice in their relations with people; "holy," as well as reverent before the holy presence, having true fear of the Lord; "self-controlled," is said not only in the sense of physical desire, but also as the one free of all passions. "He must not be on fire with anger, nor should he plunge into sorrow, nor should he be carried away either in fear or in excessive joy," according to Blessed Jerome.[179]

St Paul then explains what sort of a teacher a bishop must be. He must "[hold] fast the faithful word as he has been taught, that he may be able, by sound doctrine, both to exhort and convict those who contradict" (1:9). A worthy shepherd must not only know the dogmas of the Christian faith, but also must "[hold] fast" to them, that is, he must cherish them as he cherishes his own life. He must instruct others, teaching them not only to know the essential truths of Christ's faith, but also to love and revere them. There can be no doubt in the mind of a good pastor. He must not only know all the teachings of Christianity, but he must also be able to clearly and understandably explain them to others with conviction, and to be ready always to repel the enemies of the Christian faith, protecting his flock from them.

It is worthy of note that St Paul, in listing the positive qualities of a candidate for priesthood, places teaching as last on the list. This is because teaching includes within itself all the other positive qualities of a good priest, making it his most noticeable characteristic. St John Chrysostom says, "All the other qualities can be also found in the flock, such as blamelessness, proper raising of children in obedience, hospitality, justice, piety; however, the bishop and priest are unique in that they catechize the people with proper teaching."

Additionally, the apostle explains why Titus must be careful when choosing candidates for the priesthood, and he even quotes a humorous characterization of Cretans by their own native poet Epimenides as "always liars, evil beasts, lazy gluttons" (1:12). St Paul even calls Epimenides a "prophet," but he uses the term not in the proper Christian sense, but as a concession to pagan usage. Greeks and Romans often called their poets "prophets," considering their words inspired from heaven.

"Not giving heed to Jewish fables" (1:14)—Blessed Theodoret explained that the apostle here speaks "not of the Law, but of the Jewish interpretations of the Law."[180] We also can assume that Paul speaks here of the Judaizing temptation concerning the necessity of fulfilling all the ritual obligations of the Mosaic Law (such as circumcision, the Sabbath, and rules concerning purity of food), even after Christian baptism. Thus, St Paul continues, "To the pure, all things are pure, but to those who are defiled and unbelieving nothing is pure; but even their mind and conscience are defiled" (1:15).

Christ Himself said, "Not what goes into the mouth defiles a man; but what comes out of the mouth, this defiles a man" (Matt 15:11). The apostle repeats the same thought here, insisting that nothing is impure in and of itself. Only an impure mind and conscience makes everything impure; therefore, we must take care only to keep the soul undefiled. In 1:16, the criticism without doubt is directed at the Jews who boasted that they "know God," but who did not live according to the Law of God.

In chapter 2, St Paul begins his instruction to the pastor concerning teaching. The apostle says that old men must be taught to be moderate and firm in faith, while old women must be taught to dress properly and to keep themselves from slander and drunkenness. They should themselves instruct the young women to love their husbands and children and to be chaste. "Likewise, exhort the young men to be sober-minded," in all things models of behavior, to the shame of the enemies of Christianity (2:6). Paul especially exhorts slaves to be faithful to their masters and to live according to the teachings of Christ. Paul does not neglect to remind the teacher to be an example in actions, not merely in words.

Having listed all this, St Paul explains that the purpose of the divine economy of salvation, accomplished for us by the incarnate Son of God, is to transform the life and activity of man: "For the grace of God that brings salvation has appeared to all men, teaching us that, denying ungodliness and worldly lusts, we should live soberly, righteously, and godly in the present age" (2:11–12). This grace includes all the gracious gifts that are given to us thanks to the redemptive sacrifice of Christ. The purpose of grace is to teach us to reject iniquity and to live holily. These words strongly rebuke the false Protestant teaching concerning justification by faith alone, as though good deeds are not necessary for salvation.

St Paul clearly expresses the thought that the entire purpose of the divine economy of salvation is the rebuilding of human life and activity anew, not merely in the empty consolation of hope in salvation, as though faith in Christ were all that was needed. "Looking for the blessed hope and glorious appearing of our great God and Saviour Jesus Christ" (2:13). This glorious appearance of our great God Jesus Christ is a reference to the second coming of our Lord. The appearance of grace on earth has taught people to await the appearance of the glory to come. Both phenomena are so closely united that whoever has experienced the former already spiritually anticipates the latter. This is why the first Christians lived with an intense anticipation of the imminence of the second coming, and that is why in our own times faith has become so dim in the hearts of modern Christians, because many no longer live in the expectation of the second coming, and some even try to interpret the second coming in some excessively allegorical fashion, rejecting its reality outright.

These words of St Paul are incredibly important because they clearly witness to the divinity of the Lord Jesus Christ. Christ is called our "great God … who gave

Himself for us, that He might redeem us from every lawless deed and purify for Himself His own special people, zealous for good works" (2:13–14). Once again, the necessity of good deeds for salvation, through faith in Jesus Christ, is powerfully evident in these words. The purpose of the redemptive sacrifice of Christ was to make us "zealous for good works," the "special [i.e., chosen] people" of God, a spiritual inheritance of God, akin to the people of Israel in the Old Testament. Thus, it is also clear that faith in Christ *alone* cannot save us. The apostle exhorts Titus to preach this constantly "with all authority" (2:15), lest someone despise him for carelessness when the lawless openly sow discord and are not rebuked by those in spiritual authority.

In chapter 3 of the epistle, continuing the previous instruction, St Paul exhorts Titus to remind the Cretans to conscientiously fulfill all their civic duties, to respect the authorities, and "to be ready for every good work" (3:1). Admitting that a virtuous life was very difficult before the coming of Christ, the apostle inspires the Cretan Christians anew with the thought of the miracle of the divine economy of salvation: "But when the kindness and the love of God our Saviour toward man appeared, not by works of righteousness which we have done, but according to His mercy He saved us, through the washing of regeneration and renewing of the Holy Spirit, whom He poured out on us abundantly through Jesus Christ our Saviour" (3:4–6). This passage does not negate St Paul's previous words concerning the necessity of good works for salvation (as the Protestants believe). Quite the contrary is true. Rather, St Paul insists that, for Christians, it is inexcusable to remain in a sinful state after the Lord has renewed them by the Holy Spirit. Christians are called to a new holy life, as they now have all the necessary means of grace to accomplish it. God worked our salvation through Jesus Christ, without our participation, without any good works or merits accomplished by us. If, however, we wish to make ourselves the partakers of this salvific work, we can do this in no other way than through personal labor, and personal struggle in virtue, with the aid of God's grace given to every one of us.

The "washing of regeneration" refers to baptism, during which a person is born again, while the "renewing of the Holy Spirit" refers to the sacrament of the calling down of the Holy Spirit upon the newly baptized. In apostolic times, the latter was accomplished by the laying on of hands; in our own time, it is accomplished in the mystery of chrismation. "That having been justified by His grace we should become heirs according to the hope of eternal life" (3:7). This does not mean that grace justifies us automatically, without our own personal labors, as some Protestants crookedly interpret. Otherwise, St Paul would not insist so forcefully on the improvement of our life: "This is a faithful saying, and these things I want you to affirm constantly, that those who have believed in God should be careful to maintain good works. These things are good and profitable to men" (3:8). Once again, this passage clearly refutes the Protestant doctrine of *sola fide*, "faith alone."

St Paul then exhorts Titus to avoid "foolish disputes … contentions" (3:9), and only to reject a heretic after two admonitions have had no effect, "knowing that such a person is warped and sinning, being self-condemned" (3:11). The epistle ends with personal commissions, greetings, and a blessing.

 CHAPTER 13

The Epistle of the Holy Apostle Paul to Philemon

Who Was St Philemon?

Philemon was a rich and well-known citizen of Colossae. According to the epistle (verse 19), Philemon was converted by St Paul in Colossae or in Ephesus during Paul's long sojourn there, for Colossae and Ephesus were in constant communication through trade and civil administration. Having believed, Philemon became a model (with his entire family) of faith and the life in Christ. His closest helper in all the labors of the Christian life was a certain Apphia, who, St John Chrysostom believed, was Philemon's "partner in life," that is, his wife.[181] Paul addressed her by name in the epistle, as a "beloved sister," as well as Archippus, probably their son, whom Paul honors with the title "our fellow soldier."

In the opinion of St John Chrysostom, Philemon's house "was altogether a lodging for the saints,"[182] and St Paul witnessed that "the hearts of the saints have been refreshed" (1:7) in Philemon's house. Because Paul explicitly calls the house of Philemon the "church in your house" (verse 2), it is suggested that a church was actually in that house, and that Philemon and Archippus celebrated liturgy there, as ordained clergy. It is likely that Philemon helped Epaphras, the bishop of Colossae, in the administration of the local church, being his replacement when the latter traveled. According to tradition, Philemon was later made bishop of Colossae and was martyred with Apphia and Archippus by a rioting pagan mob. They are commemorated on February 19 and November 22. Another tradition says that Archippus was bishop of Colossae, while Philemon was bishop of Gaza.

The Purpose of the Epistle to Philemon

St Paul wrote this letter on behalf of Philemon's slave Onesimus, who, having committed some offense against his master, fled in fear of being punished and arrived eventually in Rome, where Paul was then imprisoned. Since Paul had much freedom to preach during his first imprisonment (see Acts 28:31), he managed to convert Onesimus along with some others. St Paul came to love Onesimus so dearly that he wanted to keep him by his side, but he considered it more prudent to return him to Philemon, asking that Philemon receive him as "my own heart" (verse 12). This entire epistle is directed at the reconciliation of master and slave. Paul finally asks that Philemon accept Onesimus "no longer as a slave, but more than a slave—a beloved brother" (verse 16).

The Place and Time of the Writing of the Epistle

This epistle, as evident from Colossians 4:7–9, was written and sent at the same time as Colossians in A.D. 61 or 62. The epistle itself makes it clear (verses 1, 10, 23) that Paul was imprisoned at the time. Because he hoped for quick deliverance and even asked Philemon to prepare him a place to stay in Colossae (verse 22), it is clear that this was Paul's first Roman imprisonment.

Exegetical Analysis of the Epistle to Philemon

This epistle is not divided into chapters and has only twenty-five verses. The introduction is found in the first nine verses, in which St Paul, after his usual greeting on behalf of himself and Timothy and after a request for grace and peace on Philemon, Apphia, and Archippus, expresses his joy at the piety of Philemon. He says that he would prefer to ask a favor of Philemon, although he, as an apostle, has the right to command. Paul then asks Philemon to accept Onesimus, whom "I have begotten while in chains, who once was unprofitable to you, but now is profitable to you and to me" (verses 10–11), as Paul's own heart. In verses 13–21, the apostle defends Onesimus as follows:

1. Onesimus has so changed for the better that the apostle wants to keep him at his side for help and service in the ministry. "But without your consent I wanted to do nothing, that your good deed might not be by compulsion, as it were, but voluntary" (verse 14).
2. Paul sees the providence of God in this estrangement of slave and master, for a consequence of Onesimus's flight was his encounter with Paul and subsequent conversion in Rome. Onesimus left for a time so that his master could then take him back forever, not as a salve, but as "a beloved brother" (verses 15–16).
3. Paul has come to love Onesimus so dearly that Philemon, if he cares for Paul at all, must accept Onesimus as though he were Paul himself (verse 17).

4. If Onesimus was responsible for any financial loss to Philemon, then Paul promises to pay it all back, saying that "you [Philemon] owe me even your own self besides" (verse 19), meaning that Paul saved Philemon from paganism. This has led some to believe that Onesimus stole from his master and fled with the stolen goods. St Theophan the Recluse explains:

> If the apostle had simply asked Philemon to forgive Onesimus without offering to pay back what was lost, then those who opposed the Gospel might say that he was using the Gospel and the faith to profit at the expense of others: "He converted Onesimus to the faith, and now he requires that his former master receive him back without the goods he stole!" To prevent people saying such things and impugning the honor of the Gospel and the faith, Paul says to Philemon, "I do not say, since you yourself owe me much, that you should forgive your guilty slave's debt. On the contrary, I offer to pay his debt to you and ask, as a mercy, that you accept him back into your good care."[183]

Furthermore, St Theophan paraphrases a more succinct explanation by St John Chrysostom of why, in his view, St Paul used the expression, "you owe me even your own self besides" (verse 19):

> If Paul had said merely, "I will pay for his sake. Here is a receipt," it could have been unpleasant for Philemon, who might think that Paul did not trust him enough to think he was capable of the virtue of forgiving Onesimus his theft. In order to avoid such a thought, it is as if Paul says to him, "Do not think that I am not sure of you. Do I not know how you feel, that you owe me your very self? I know that I need merely say the word, and you will do everything."[184]

5. The only reward St Paul begs of Philemon is this: "refresh my heart in the Lord" (verse 20). St Paul hopes that Philemon will do much more. As St Theophan further explains,

> By doing so, he suggested to Philemon the following thought: "If you love me, Philemon, you will preserve and care for the comfort of my heart, and you will accept Onesimus. By doing this, you will bring consolation to my heart, for without this I will not be at peace. If you do not want to do this for my sake, do it for the sake of Christ. Show mercy to the Lord, if not to me."[185]

By these words: "I write to you, knowing that you will do even more than I say," the apostle defeated any possible opposition that could arise in Philemon's thoughts (verses 20–21).

The Epistle to Philemon vividly shows us that the Church of Christ, by freeing a man from sin, does not at the same time break existing relationships among people. It does not seek to break social or civil order, preferring instead to patiently await the transformation of the social order from within, influenced by the ideals of Christianity. Not only in this epistle, but in others earlier discussed by us, we see that the Church (which of course can never sympathize with slavery!) did not, at the same time, call for its abolition, even recommending that slaves submit to their masters. Therefore, the path of conversion, which freed Onesimus from sin, did not free him, as a slave, from the authority of his master. Onesimus must return to Philemon, and this despite the fact that Paul has come to love him as a son and was in need of his services while imprisoned in Rome. Paul's respect for civil law is also seen in Paul's refraining from ordering Philemon to free Onesimus, which he was fully authorized to do by his position as apostle. Instead, acknowledging Philemon's right as a slaveowner, he asks him to forgive his repentant slave. The apostle's words— "without your consent I wanted to do nothing" (verse 14)—clearly show that Christianity leads man to personal perfection and the amelioration of the social order on the principles of brotherhood, equality, and freedom, and not by the path of forceful action and revolution, but by the path of peaceful exhortation and moral transformation.

The epistle ends with an epilogue in which the Holy Apostle Paul asks Philemon to prepare a home for him in Colossae, as he hopes for a quick deliverance from his imprisonment. He also passes on a greeting from Epaphras, who voluntarily shared the sorrows of imprisonment with Paul during the first Roman bonds. Paul also greets Philemon on behalf of his "fellow laborers" Mark, Aristarchus, Demas, and Luke. Then the usual blessing follows.

In verse 19, we read that St Paul wrote the letter with his own hand. According to tradition, Philemon freed Onesimus and sent him back to Paul. Afterward, Onesimus became bishop of Berea in Macedonia and was martyred in Rome during Trajan's reign. He is commemorated on February 15.

 CHAPTER 14

The Epistle of the Holy Apostle Paul to the Hebrews

THE AUTHOR OF THE EPISTLE TO THE HEBREWS

The last of St Paul's epistles in the order of the New Testament canon is the Epistle to the Hebrews. It was placed at the end not because of the date of its composition, nor because it is somehow less worthy than the others. Rather, from the early centuries of the Church's histories, doubts have persisted about Paul's authorship of this epistle. The reason for these doubts is that there is no usual Pauline greeting at the beginning of the letter, nor is there a specific name of a Church or individual to whom the letter is addressed. The style of the epistle also differs somewhat from the other epistles. Moreover, many ancient sources—including St Clement of Rome, St Ignatius of Antioch, St Polycarp of Smyrna, St Justin Martyr, and St Irenaeus of Lyons—speak of the ancient apostolic provenance of the epistle, but none of them mention St Paul as the author.

Origen presents various possibilities on who the author was— St Clement of Rome or the Evangelist Luke or others. Still, Origen concludes, "If any church, therefore, holds this epistle as Paul's, let it be commended for this also. For not without reason have the men of old time handed it down as Paul's. But who wrote the epistle, in truth God knows."[186] The Eastern churches have always agreed with Origen in this case, and only the Arians considered the epistle to be a forgery. In the West, on the contrary, doubts persisted about the authorship of this epistle for a long time and only with St Augustine's influence at the Council of Hippo in 393 was it appended to the other thirteen canonical epistles of St Paul.[187] From the time of Luther, negative criticism has again tried to resurrect the ancient doubts about the authorship of the Epistle to the Hebrews.

The most important reason cited by the doubters is the lack of Paul's personal greeting at the beginning, as was usual for his epistles.

There are very good reasons for this, however, offered even so early as the second century by Pantaenus, the head of the renowned Alexandrian school (d. c. A.D. 200). In his view, cited by his successor, Clement, "since the Lord, being the Apostle of the Most High, was sent to the Hebrews, Paul, through modesty, since he has been sent to the Gentiles, does not inscribe himself as an apostle to the Hebrews, both to give due deference to the Lord, and because he wrote to the Hebrews also out of his abundance, being a preacher and apostle of the Gentiles."[188] Thus, St Paul did not consider himself the "apostle to the Jews" (being himself the apostle to the Gentiles), and he ascribed the title in the proper sense to the Lord Jesus Christ alone (Heb 3:1, see also Matt 15:24). The apostle had reason to believe that the Jews simply would not read his epistle if they saw from the introduction that he had written it.

As for claims of divergent style, they are not convincing. No matter which possible author we suggest as an alternative to St Paul, the same problems of difference in style persist.

Moreover, upon closer inspection, one cannot fail but admit that the entire epistle is imbued with the spirit of the Holy Apostle Paul. It has the same teaching on the superiority of the New Covenant compared with the Old, the same thoughts, the same images, even certain typical turns of phrase. An entire series of phrases correspond beautifully with expressions found in other epistles of St Paul (e.g., Heb 10:1 and Col 2:17; Heb 7:18–19 and Rom 8:3; Heb 9:15 and 2 Cor 3:6; Heb 1:3 and Col 1:15 and Phil 2:6; and many others). In Hebrews 10:34 and 13:19, the writer mentions his imprisonment; in 13:23, he calls Timothy a brother; in 13:24, he sends greetings from the brethren in Italy; and, in 13:19, he asks for prayers for his deliverance. At the end of the epistle (13:25), he even gives a typically Pauline blessing: "Grace be with you all," which Paul himself offers the Thessalonians (2 Thess 3:17–18) as proof of his authorship.

It is also necessary to remember that, despite certain doubts concerning the writer himself, the epistle has always been accepted by the Church as canonical, inspired by God. We see this in Apostolic Canon 85, in Canon 60 of the Council of Laodicea, and in the writings of the Fathers of the first centuries of the Church, all of whom cite the epistle as God inspired and authoritative without a doubt. In the Peshitta, the fifth-century Syriac translation of the Bible, the Epistle to the Hebrews is listed as one of the Pauline epistles. St Athanasius the Great, St Cyril of Jerusalem, St Epiphanius of Salamis, St Basil the Great, St Gregory the Theologian, St Gregory of Nyssa, St John Chrysostom, and Blessed Theodoret all consider it Pauline. Also important is the witness of Apostle Peter himself, who wrote to the Jews concerning a letter that his beloved brother Paul also wrote to them.

THE INTENDED AUDIENCE OF THE EPISTLE TO THE HEBREWS
The epistle itself does not mention to whom it was written. The content of the epistle makes it clear, however, that it was written to the Jews. Tradition agrees with this. This begs the question: which Jews in particular were the intended audience?

Christians of Jewish ethnicity or unconverted Jews? Palestinian Jews or Jews of the Diaspora? Judging by the first few chapters, one might think that the epistle is directed at all Jews in general, but from chapter 5 on, there are indications that Paul is speaking to Jews who have already come to believe in Christ; who have long ago converted (5:12); who serve the saints greatly, that is, send aid to poor Christian communities (6:10); and who have suffered much for the faith (10:32–34). The conclusion of the epistle further gives proof of this (13:18 and further).

The majority of both ancient and modern commentators are inclined to think that the epistle was written not to all Christian converts from Judaism, but rather to the Christians of Jewish ethnicity residing in a particular area—Jerusalem and Palestine. Confirmation of this can be found in the fact that St Paul expresses his hope to see them soon (13:23), as well as in Paul's praising them for "joyfully accepting the plundering of your goods" (10:34). This plundering of goods was a result of the fanaticism of the Palestinian Jews who did not convert to Christ. Paul's long passages concerning the temple and Jewish worship, with the clear intention of weakening in his readers a blind attachment to Old Testament ritual piety, also seem to confirm that the epistle was intended for Christian Jews of Jerusalem, who were still markedly attached, because of their proximity, to the triumphant worship of the temple.

The Purpose and Style of the Epistle to the Hebrews

St Paul wrote this epistle because of the widespread apostasy of Christians of Jewish extraction back to Judaism and their separation from Christians in their assemblies of prayer (10:25). This happened because it was difficult for Jewish Christians to fully reject their attachment to the ritual Law of Moses, as well as their false hopes to see the coming of the Messiah as a political revolution, culminating in the enthronement of a new king in Jerusalem. Although the Jewish Christians who lived outside Palestine gradually and consistently merged with the Christians of pagan background, losing the typically Jewish nationalism and its associated false hopes for an earthly Messiah, Palestinian Christians found themselves influenced by the constantly increasing fervor of Jewish nationalism that eventually led to the general rebellion against Roman rule, culminating in the Jewish Wars and the destruction of Jerusalem. Not insignificant were the efforts of the Judaizers, who insisted on the necessity of the Law for salvation.

After St James, the brother of the Lord, was killed during the high priesthood of Ananias, fanatical Judaism in Palestine effectively declared war on Christianity in Judea. The persecution was so fierce that many who were not firm in their faith began to apostatize (10:25).

When St Paul learned of this, he wrote his epistle, intending to show the great supremacy of the New Covenant over the Old, which was only a "shadow of the good things to come" (10:1). He wanted to inspire the Palestinian Christians to patiently endure sorrows and persecutions for the faith, bringing examples of the Old Testament righteous (chapters 11 and 12) and reminding them of the horrifying consequences of apostasy from Christianity (10:28–31). Even though St Paul was the apostle to the Gentiles, not the Hebrews, his ardent love for the Lord and the chosen nation, to whom he himself belonged (see Rom 9:3), inspired him to write this epistle to warn his fellow Jews from the path to perdition.

As for the literary style of the Epistle to the Hebrews, although some Western fathers consider that it was first written in Hebrew and only later translated to Greek, either by St Luke or Clement of Rome (Roman Catholics in particular shared this point of view in the past), no Hebrew original is extant, only the Greek text. It is unlikely that there ever was a Hebrew original, because in the Greek text all of the citations from Scripture are taken from the Septuagint, not the Hebrew text of the Bible. We must also remember that for St Paul, Greek was a native tongue, because he was born in Tarsus of Cilicia, a place known for its Greek education.

The Place and Time of the Writing of the Epistle

From the epistle, it is clear that it was written before the destruction of Jerusalem, for the writer speaks of the temple and its worship as current. If the temple were destroyed, the writer would not have written about its worship in the present tense (this is another, if tangential, proof of St Paul's authorship, because St Paul died before the destruction of the temple). The place of the writing is clear from the epistle: "Those from Italy greet you" (13:24). Consequently, St Paul was in Italy and, as would be natural to assume, in Rome, from where he wrote several other epistles. Paul was in Rome twice, and both times he was imprisoned. In this epistle, he speaks of his imprisonment, but as a past event: "for you had compassion on me in my chains" (10:34). In 13:19, the apostle expresses his hope that he will see them all soon, and in 13:23 he says, "Know that our brother Timothy has been set free, with whom I shall see you if he comes shortly." Thus, we can assume that St Paul wrote this epistle soon after (or just before) his deliverance from his first Roman imprisonment, that is, in A.D. 63 or 64.

The Structure and Content of the Epistle

This epistle has thirteen chapters. Unlike the other epistles, there is no introduction or greeting, and it begins immediately with the exposition of the dogmatic teaching. Like other Pauline epistles, it has two parts:

1. Dogmatic instruction (1–10:28)
2. Moral instruction (10:29–13:17)

Chapter 13, verses 18–25, form a conclusion.

EXEGETICAL ANALYSIS OF THE EPISTLE TO THE HEBREWS

Chapter 1 is dedicated entirely to the explanation of the supremacy of the Lord Jesus Christ, the Mediator of the New Covenant, over the angels. This section is a kind of thematic introduction to the idea of the superiority of the New Covenant over the Old. The Old Testament Law was given to the chosen people through the angels and Moses, whereas the New Testament Law was given by Jesus Christ. Therefore, the holy apostle sets himself the goal to prove to the Jews, on the basis of the Old Testament Scriptures, that Christ is greater than the angels (chapters 1 and 2) and Moses (chapters 3 and 4).

The epistle begins thus: "God, who at various times and various ways spoke in time past to the fathers by the prophets, has in these last days spoken to us by His Son, whom He has appointed heir of all things, through whom also He made the worlds" (1:1–2). As St Theophan the Recluse explains, "Since the issue at hand is one of faith, and only God can teach the true faith by means of His divine revelation, St Paul begins his discourse with this. From ancient times, God has taught us how to believe, and He continues to this day. But then, He taught through the prophets, while now, He teaches through His Son."[189]

This leads to the natural conclusion that the new word of God cannot fail to be in harmony with the old. The prophetic revelations, spoken "at various times and various ways," are by this very criterion incomplete, while the fullness of the true teaching of faith is revealed only by the Son of God, Whom God the Father "has appointed heir of all things," that is, He has given Him everything, making Him Lord of all, not only by divinity (which He already possessed), but even in His humanity, as the Lord Jesus Christ said after His resurrection to the apostles: "All authority has been given to Me in heaven and on earth" (Matt 28:18). As St Theophan explicates further, "Everything is given into the hands of the Lord Saviour so that the purpose of the economy of the incarnation may be fulfilled, so that all the powers of heaven and earth and all creation would be directed to this alone, and so that He would gather to Himself all those who are saved."[190]

"Through whom also He made the worlds" (1:2). This verse speaks of the eternity and preexistence of the Son of God. As Blessed Theodoret writes, "These words demonstrate the divinity [of the Son of God],"[191] for only God can create, and eternity is the proper to God.

"Who being the brightness of His glory and the express image of His person, and upholding all things by the word of His power, when He had by Himself purged our sins, sat down at the right hand of the Majesty on high" (1:2–3). This is an extremely important dogmatic teaching: the Son of God is a most complete and perfect image of the essence and of the Person of God the Father. In other words, He is equal and consubstantial (one in essence) with the Father. Like the Father, He is not only the Creator, but also the Sustainer of the world, for He upholds "all things by the word of His power." He is also the High Priest, who offered Himself as a sacrifice for the sins of mankind. But He is also the One who "sat down at the right hand of the Majesty on high," thereby raising up the human nature, which He had assumed, higher than all creation and deifying it.

In the following verses of the first chapter, Apostle Paul cites the Old Testament, primarily the Psalms, with the purpose of proving the superiority of the Son of God, Who gave us the New Covenant, over the angels. In these citations, the Messiah is called by the following names:

1. Son of God in essence (1:5–6)
2. God, Whose royal throne is forever and ever (1:7–8)
3. The Anointed One of God, greater than all other anointed ones, including kings, priests, and prophets (1:9)
4. The preexisting and changeless Creator of heaven and earth, Who will abide forever (1:10–12)
5. The One Who sits at the right hand of God, at Whose feet all enemies will fall (1:13)

This is the divine dignity of the Founder of the New Covenant. The angels, however, are only "ministering spirits sent forth to minister for those who will inherit salvation" (1:14). The service of angels is like the service of the forces of nature, such as winds and fire (1:7). The Son of God, even in His humanity, now has divine authority over the universe, and angels of God bow down in worship. This we saw in the moment of the Nativity of Christ, when the angels proclaimed, "Glory to God in the Highest," after Jesus's victory over the tempting devil when they came and served Him (Mark 1:13), and when they met Him with exclamations and the sound of trumpets as the Conqueror of death and hell during His ascension into heaven. They will also bow down before Him when they accompany Him, as the King of heaven and earth, to the final Dread Judgment (1:6).

Chapter 2 continues the discussion of the superiority of the Son of God over the angels and, consequently, the superiority of the New Testament over the Old. The apostle says that if the Old Testament Law, given by the angels, had to be strictly followed at the risk of punishment, then the punishment will be all the greater for those who refuse to follow the Law of the New Testament, because it has been given by the Lord Himself (2:4). Incidentally, the Book of Acts also mentions that the Old Testament was received "by the direction of angels" (Acts 7:53, compare with Gal 3:19).

In the Old Testament, however, there are no direct indications that the Law of God was given through the angels. St John Chrysostom believed the angels were present when God gave Moses the stone tablets containing the Ten Commandments, and these angels, who had the care of the chosen nation of God, were responsible for the cloud, fire, and sound of trumpets on Mt Sinai.[192] They also took implicit part in everything that was said and done in the Old Testament. Evidently, this angelic intercession was remembered in the Jewish oral tradition.

"For He has not put the world to come, of which we speak, in subjection to angels" (2:5). This "world to come" in this case refers to the newly revealed kingdom of the Messiah or to the "life to come," according to Blessed Theodoret.[193] In the next verses (2:6–9), the Holy Apostle Paul cites the Psalms to prove the natural superiority of man over the creation that is subject to Him, but he applies the citation more specifically to Jesus, both God and Man, Who in His person raised fallen human nature and exalted man to the heights for which he was created in the beginning. Psalm 8 is a prophetic psalm, for Christ Himself cited it when speaking of the praise coming from the mouths of babes and children during his triumphant entry into Jerusalem (LXX Psalm 8:3, Matt 21:16). "But we see Jesus, who was made a little lower than the angels, for the suffering of death crowned with glory and honor, that He, by the grace of God, might taste death for everyone" (2:9). This "diminishing," self-humiliation (*kenosis*) of Christ refers to the crucifixion and death of Jesus (see also Isa 53:3). It was merely a temporary humiliation ("a little lower") that subsequently led to the glorification of the human nature of the Lord, raised higher than all creation.

The apostle himself interprets this humiliation in the sense that the love of God for mankind led Him to "taste death for everyone." In verse 10, Apostle Paul preemptively answers any temptations that could arise as a result of the death of Jesus Christ: "For it was fitting for Him, for whom are all things and by whom are all things [i.e., God the Father], in bringing many sons to glory, to make the captain of their salvation perfect through sufferings." This means that Christ, the Captain of our salvation, had to walk the dolorous path by which mankind had to walk (in the Old Testament) if he were to lead mankind to the glory for which they were created.

"For both He who sanctifies and those who are being sanctified are all of one, for which reason He is not ashamed to call them brethren" (2:11). This means that the salvation of people through the Redeemer Christ became possible only as a consequence of Christ's assumption of human nature to Himself. This thought—the unity of nature of the Lord Jesus Christ and the people He redeemed—is strengthened with proofs from Psalms 21:23 and Isaiah 8:17–18.

"Inasmuch then as the children have partaken of flesh and blood, He Himself likewise shared in the same, that through death He might destroy him who had the power of death, that is, the devil, and release those who through fear of death were all their lifetime subject to bondage" (2:14–15). The children mentioned here are all those who are saved, that is, all mankind. To defeat the devil, who had subjected mankind to death, and to destroy the fear of death, Christ Himself assumed flesh and blood, our moribund human nature. He shared in our common death, a truth that clearly refutes the Docetist heresy, which claimed that Christ's human nature was only a phantasm and not real.

"For indeed He does not give aid to angels, but He does give aid to the seed of Abraham" (2:16). In other words, the Son of God did not assume angelic nature, but human nature, the same nature as the seed of Abraham. Again, the Son of God is clearly superior to the angels, but now human nature is greater than angelic nature. The kenosis of the Lord was necessitated by the essence of His redemptive work: He came to earth not to save the angels, but to save mankind, and so He took to Himself the lower, human nature, not the nature of angels. But it was this human nature that, after the ascension of Christ, has been raised higher than the angels, for it partakes of the glory of the divinity and sits on the right hand of God the Father. Having become by His nature like us, weak human beings, Christ became our high priest, having experienced in Himself the weakness of human nature. Eventually co-suffering with us in the most complete way possible (His death), He could in the best way fulfill the great purpose of redeeming mankind (2:17–18). Because these verses (2:11–18) concern the incarnation and the redemptive sacrifice of Christ, they are read during certain feasts of the Mother of God (Annunciation and the Synaxis of the Mother of God) and on Holy Friday during the service of the Sixth Hour.

In the third chapter of the epistle, the holy apostle speaks of the superiority of the Lord Jesus Christ over the captain of the Hebrew nation, Moses. The Lord Jesus Christ is greater than Moses first of all because He is the builder of the house in which Moses is but a servant. This "house" (3:1–6) is the Old Testament Church. Furthermore, St Paul remembers (by citing the passage from Psalm 94:7–11) how often the Hebrews murmured against God during their forty-year wandering in the desert, and how the Lord grew angry with them and swore that they would not enter His rest, the Promised Land (3:7–11). Using this negative example from Jewish history, the holy apostle warns Christians to fear a similar hardening of their hearts, for they will come under the same divine wrath as the Hebrews in the desert. They also will lose the promised rest, which in the New Testament means the highest spiritual consolation, for which Canaan and the land flowing with milk and honey were merely shadowy figures. The Israel of the New Testament should follow the example of those firm and strong men of Moses's time who did not lose faith during the wandering and never complained, people such as Joshua and Caleb.

In chapter 4 of the epistle, Paul speaks of this highest spiritual rest that Christians will inherit if they do not waver in their faith and hope. Although the Hebrews of old, despite the promise, did not enter the land of rest because of their faithlessness and their complaining against God, the Israel of the New Testament will enter the promised rest. In the New Testament, God announced a new Sabbath, that is, a new day of rest when Christians will enter into His rest (i.e., His kingdom). The apostle exhorts Christians to strive to enter this spiritual rest and to avoid being disobedient to God.

St Paul supports his warning with a threat for the insubordinate and the complainers that comes from the very mouth of God, and "the word of God is living and powerful, and sharper than any two-edged sword, piercing even to the division of soul and spirit, and of joints and marrow, and is a discerner of the thoughts and intents of the heart. And there is no creature hidden from His sight, but all things are naked and open to the eyes of Him to whom we must give account" (4:12–13). The word of God is not left unfulfilled; it gives what it promises. The terrifying and punishing power of the word of God that reveals the most secret mysteries of our thoughts is compared to a two-edged blade. Also important here is the Pauline division of the human person into spirit, soul, and body (see also 1 Thess 5:23).

Beginning with verse 14, St Paul speaks of the Lord Jesus Christ as a High Priest, thereby showing His superiority over the entire Old Testament priesthood. In the last verses (4:14–16), he offers a summary of his most important dogmatic theme: the High Priesthood of Christ. "Seeing then that we have a great High Priest who has passed through the heavens, Jesus the Son of God, let us hold fast our confession. For we do not have a High Priest who cannot sympathize with our weaknesses, but was in all points tempted as we are, yet without sin." An entire series of extremely important points are found in this passage.

First, Jesus Christ is a *Great* High Priest, the one and only, exalted above all other high priests. Second, He "has passed through the heavens," that is, appeared before the face of God Himself, while the Old Testament high priests could only once a year enter the holy of holies of the temple, which was merely a place of the appearance of the divine glory. Third, Jesus Christ is the Son of God, whereas the other high priests were only mortal men. Fourth, Jesus Christ is the Great High Priest Who, despite His unapproachable majesty, was still able to "sympathize with our weaknesses," because He was also tempted in all things, except sin. Therefore, St Paul concludes, "Let us therefore come boldly to the throne of grace" (4:16) on which the Great High Priest sits, the One Who is so much exalted but Who at the same time is so approachable and capable to share in our suffering.

In chapter 5 of the letter, the holy apostle compares the Old Testament priesthood (the order of Aaron) with Christ's High Priesthood "according to the order of Melchizedek" (5:6). The essential qualities of an Old Testament priest were as follows: he "is appointed for men in things pertaining to God, that he may offer both gifts and sacrifices for sins ... Since he himself is also subject to weakness" (5:1–2), he had to bring sacrifices not only for the people, but for his own sins as well. As for the honor of the high priesthood, he could not receive it from himself, but only from God, as did Aaron (see 5:1–4).

In general, all these same qualities are found in Jesus Christ as well, as He is the true High Priest. He receives His High Priestly calling directly from God Himself, which the apostle proves by the words of the Psalmist, so persuasive for the Hebrews: "Thou art My Son, this day have I begotten Thee" (Psalm 2:7), and also "Thou art a Priest for ever, after the order of Melchizedek" (Psalm 109:4). As for Christ's partaking in our human weakness, St Paul's words show that as well: "who, in the days of His flesh, when He had offered up prayer and supplications, with vehement cries and tears to Him who was able to save Him from death" (5:7). St Paul references the prayer in the garden of Gethsemane, where He asked for the cup of the Passion to be taken away from Him, "and was heard because of His godly fear" (5:7). Heard, not in the sense that He was delivered from crucifixion, for He came to die willingly, but in the sense that the Heavenly Father sent Him an angel to strengthen Him for the coming passion (Luke 22:43).

"Though He was a Son, yet He learned obedience by the things which He suffered" (5:8). These words are an indication of Christ's sacrificial priesthood. The passion of Christ upon the Cross for the sake of mankind became that great and atoning sacrifice, prefigured by the manifold and frequent sacrifices offered by the high priests in the Old Testament. "And having been perfected, He became the author of eternal salvation to all who obey Him" (5:9). Because He attained the highest perfection (in his humanity, of course) through His passion upon the Cross, Christ became the source of the eternal salvation of all people who are obedient to Him, because He is their all-powerful Mediator before the throne of His Father in the heavens.

Thus three characteristic qualities of priesthood came together in the person of the Lord Jesus Christ: divine election, the ability to co-suffer with mankind by sharing their nature, and priestly mediation for men before God (5:5–10). In conclusion of his thought, St Paul notes with reproach that the Jews, stubbornly holding onto their delusions, are incapable of understanding and accepting this important teaching about the High Priesthood of Christ. Because the Jews were chosen by God before all other nations, they should have become the teachers, but instead they remain as children who still need to drink milk (i.e., the initial principles of Christianity), because they cannot stomach "solid food" (5:11–14).

Even though St Paul names the Jews "children" in the faith, incapable of receiving solid food, he does this only reproachfully, considering that they are fully capable of understanding even the most profound of Christian truths. With God's help (6:3), St Paul hopes to overcome the most significant hurdle to this knowledge: nationalistic prejudices of the Jews. Therefore, from chapter 6 on, St Paul begins to explain in detail this most exalted teaching of the Lord Jesus Christ as the High Priesthood according to the order of Melchizedek.

In chapter 6 St Paul first underlines the heaviness of the sin of apostasy after baptism, and the impossibility of renewal through a repetition of the sacrament of baptism: "For it is impossible for those who were once enlightened, and have tasted the heavenly gift, and have become partakers of the Holy Spirit, and have tasked the good word of God and the power of the age to come, if they fall away, to renew them again to repentance, since they crucify again for themselves the Son of God and put Him to an open shame" (6:4–6). In these words, we see St Paul's treatment of the worst of sins, called by the Lord Himself the blasphemy against the Holy

Spirit (Matt 12:31). This is the sin of hardened refusal to repent, stubborn opposition to God. This is the sin of the devil and all the other fallen angels, as well as all the people used by them in their war against God, such as the scribes and Pharisees who, seeing the miracles of Christ, did not see them at all, and hearing the wondrous, exalted teaching of Christ, seemed to understand nothing at all. They even crucified Him, continuing to mock Him even as He hung on the Cross.

In these words of St Paul, we see what happens to those who apostatize after previously having reached the heights of spiritual perfection. For such people, the fall is especially terrible, and reconversion is hopeless. The apostle compares them with soil that has lost its fruitfulness, soil that drinks in rainwater but still only produces thorns and briars. Such land is "rejected and near to being cursed, whose end is to be burned" (6:8). Paul, however, expresses hope that the Jews to whom he writes are not yet in such a state, and he invites them to patiently labor over their own salvation like Abraham, who "after he had patiently endured, he obtained the promise" (6:15).

"For men indeed swear by the greater, and an oath for confirmation is for them an end of all dispute" (6:16). These words are important because they refute the belief of certain false teachers (such as the Quakers, Leo Tolstoy, and others) that the word of God forbids making oaths outright. God Himself used an oath, St Paul says, when He swore to Abraham by Himself. In the same way, God the Father swore to mankind concerning the High Priesthood of His Son to strengthen their faith, as the Psalmist David said, "The Lord hath sworn, and will not repent, Thou art a priest for ever after the order of Melchizedek" (Psalm 109:4).

Chapter 7 is dedicated in its entirety to the further elucidation of the teaching concerning Christ's High Priesthood. The first three verses explain why Christ's Priesthood belongs to the Order of Melchizedek. In Genesis 14:18–20, we read how Abraham, returning after the defeat of the Canaanite kings, was met with bread and wine by Melchizedek, King of Salem, who was also a priest of the Most High God. He blessed Abraham with the name of the Most High God, and Abraham gave him a tithe of his spoils. With the exception of Psalm 109, there are no other references to Melchizedek in the entirety of the canonical Old Testament.

His name and the mysterious character of his appearance and disappearance from the story of Abraham made him a very important figure, almost a supernatural one. This is why David, describing the Messiah in Psalm 109 as an eternal priest, calls Him a priest after the order of Melchizedek. The Holy Apostle Paul underlines the similarities between Melchizedek and the Lord Jesus Christ, presenting the former as a prefiguration of the latter. These similarities are as follows:

1. His very name is Melchizedek, which means "king of righteousness."
2. He was the king of Salem, which literally means the "king of peace."
3 He was a priest of the Most High God.

4. He came out to meet Abraham and blessed him.
5. Finally, Abraham gave him a tithe of his best spoils.

St Paul indicates several other unusual characteristics of Melchizedek that are not mentioned in the Scriptures, especially the unknown and mysterious character of his genealogy: "without father, without mother, without genealogy, having neither beginning of days nor end of life, but made like the Son of God" (7:3). It is important that Melchizedek was the first person in the Holy Scriptures to be called a priest, and moreover a priest of the Most High God. It almost seems as though he received his priesthood directly from God. "Remains a priest continually," not, of course, in his own person, but in the person of the One he foretold: Jesus Christ.

The superiority of the priesthood according to the order of Melchizedek over the priesthood of Aaron's descendant Levi is the subject of the next few verses. First of all, St Paul discusses the tithe that Abraham gave to Melchizedek. A tithe generally is given by a subordinate to an elder. Abraham was a free and independent owner of massive wealth, and he had just defeated five Canaanite kings and had received great promises from God. If this progenitor of God's chosen people was so great, then how much greater must Melchizedek have been, if Abraham humbly brought a tithe of his best spoils to him, as though he were Melchizedek's vassal. In 7:5–6, the holy apostle shows that Melchizedek had no familial tie with Abraham, and so the latter could not have felt an obligation to give him a tithe, as later the Jews would do by Law to the priests of the order of Levi.

Finally, there is this interesting point: "but he whose genealogy is not derived from them received tithes from Abraham and blessed him who had the promises. Now beyond all contradiction the lesser is blessed by the better" (7:6–7). Abraham was himself the recipient of great promises from God and was the progenitor of the chosen nation of God, as well as the Levitical priesthood, and still, it is Melchizedek who blesses Abraham. The natural conclusion is that Melchizedek was greater than Abraham; consequently, his priesthood is greater than the priesthood according to the order of Aaron, the descendant of Abraham.

In 7:8–10, St Paul makes the natural conclusion that in the person of Abraham, Levi and all of his descendants—that is, the Old Testament priesthood—admitted himself to be subservient to Melchizedek, the priest with eternal dignity. The apostle insists that the priesthood according to the order of Melchizedek, actualized in the person of Jesus Christ, is greater than the Old Testament priesthood, and he proceeds to prove this in the following verses.

In 7:11–12, Paul makes the general point that a new priesthood according to the order of Melchizedek was foreshadowed even during the time of the Old Testament priesthood. The latter, as incomplete, will be eventually replaced by the former, because it is more perfect, and so the very Law of the Old Testament, as it was connected with the Aaronic priesthood, will be changed. Then Paul reveals how this substitution of one priesthood with another was accomplished:

1. The Lord Jesus Christ came not from the tribe of priests (Levi), but from the tribe of Judah, just as Melchizedek was not of the family of Abraham (7:13–15).
2. The Lord Jesus Christ is a priest "not according to the law of a fleshly commandment," that is, His priesthood is not received by inheritance, as it was in the tribe of Levi. Rather, He is a "priest forever according to the order of Melchizedek" (7:16–17).
3. The Old Testament Law was insufficient, for it did not lead people to perfection, and so God established, with an oath, "a better hope," the New Covenant, whose founder was Jesus, who also established a better, new priesthood (7:18–22).

In conclusion to this chapter, St Paul explains the superiority of the new priesthood of Christ:

1. Christ's priesthood is a priesthood of only one person, and it will never have another (7:23–25).
2. The High Priest of this priesthood is holy and blameless, Who brought Himself as a sacrifice of atonement for the sins of mankind (7:26–28).

Chapter 8 continues the same discourse, and in the first two verses, we see the third superiority of Christ as High Priest—His service is accomplished not on earth, as it was with the Old Testament priesthood, but in heaven, directly before the altar of God, for He himself sat "at the right hand of the throne of the Majesty" (8:1). These verses (7:26–8:2) are read during commemorations of hierarchs, because every hierarch of the Church of Christ is great in his likeness to the great High Priest, the Lord Jesus Christ, in holiness and blamelessness. The greatness of Christ's service in heaven also includes the bringing of sacrifice. This sacrifice is His constant mediation for us before His Heavenly Father as a consequence of that great sacrifice that He brought for us once and forever on the Cross (8:3).

On earth, He would not have been accepted as a priest for formal reasons; moreover, there is an essential difference between the Old Testament priesthood and Christ's High Priesthood, for the Old Testament priests performed the rites that served merely a symbolic and prefigurative role. All these symbols and types found their fulfillment in Christ, Who established the New Covenant foretold in the prophecy of Jeremiah (31:31–34). Jeremiah's words about the establishment of the New Covenant are cited by Paul in their entirety in 8:8–12, after which he offers his own conclusion: "In that He says, 'A new covenant,' He has made the first obsolete. Now what is becoming obsolete and growing old is ready to vanish away" (8:13).

Chapter 9 is dedicated entirely to the comparison of the two testaments, the Old and the New, to the complete advantage of the New. By describing in the first seven verses the arrangement of the tabernacle, the apostle shows that its very organization and ritual service, with the bringing of animals as sacrifice, already inspired the thought of its insufficiency and temporal character. As he describes the tabernacle, St Paul pays special attention to the inaccessibility of the holy of holies, which was unapproachable not only for the people, but even for the priests, and where only the high priest, once a year (on the Day of Atonement), could enter, "not without blood, which he offered for himself and for the people's sins committed in ignorance" (9:7). This passage from Hebrews (9:1–7) is read during the liturgy of several feasts of the Theotokos, such as the Entry into the Temple (November 21) and the Protection of the Theotokos (October 1), as this tabernacle was a prefiguration of the Mother of God, whose body became the true temple where God Himself came to dwell.

The structure of the tabernacle showed that in the Old Testament the heavens were shut from mankind, and mankind was separated from God. All the Old Testament rites had merely a temporary significance (9:8–10). The superiority of the New Testament is evident in that Christ, "the High Priest of the good things to come" (9:11), serves in the uncreated tabernacle of heaven, not with the blood of goats and calves, but with His own Blood, by which He, once and for all, obtained for us eternal redemption (9:11–14). The great significance of the sacrifice of Jesus Christ upon the Cross is that through the shedding of His Own Blood, He became for us the Mediator of the New Covenant (9:15).

In 9:16–17, the holy apostle explains the necessity of the death of the Mediator of the New Covenant: "For where there is a testament, there must also of necessity be the death of the testator. For a testament is in force after men are dead, since it has no power at all while the testator lives." The apostle deduces the necessity of Christ's death from two circumstances: both of them are indicated by a single Greek word *diathêkê*. This word means both a "covenant" in the proper sense of a union or mutual contract and a "testament" in the sense of the last will of a person before he dies. Christ had to die, because the Old Testament was founded on the blood of sacrificed animals, and so the New Testament could be established only on the blood of the Mediator between God and man. Only by this blood could sin be destroyed, and sin was the reason for the estrangement of God and man.

At the same time, Christ had to die in order to leave mankind His "testament," that is, to make them the heirs of the eternal salvation that was prepared for them. In 9:18–23, St Paul explains that the blood of goats and calves in the Old Testament had only symbolic meaning, and its power depended only on its being a prefiguration of the atoning sacrifice of the Lamb of God, Christ, Who shed His blood for the sins of mankind. The great supremacy of Christ as the High Priest of the New Covenant is also shown in His performing the atoning sacrifice once and for all, not entering the holy of holies as the Old Testament priests did, but entering heaven itself (i.e., the eternal holy of holies) to mediate now for us before the face of God.

"It is appointed for men to die once, but after this the judgment" (9:27). This is an important teaching that refutes the false teaching of the transmigration of souls. Why does St Paul say that "Christ was offered once to bear the sins of many" (9:28), but not the sins of all? As St John Chrysostom explains, "Because not all believed. For He died indeed for all, in order to save all—that is His part, for that death was a counterbalance against the destruction of all men. But He did not bear the sins of all men, because they were not willing."[194]

In chapter 10, the superiority of the New Testament over the Old is further explained. St Paul speaks of the abolishment of the Old Testament sacrifices and the Old Testament priesthood, because they have become obsolete. The apostle says that the Law (the Old Testament) was only "a shadow of the good things to come, and not the very image of the thing" (10:1), that is, its purpose was one of foreshadowing. The Old Testament sacrifices did not give purification from sins, for if they did, they would not have to be constantly repeated. These sacrifices were only a reminder, once a year, of the sins of the people, and thus also, consequently, a reminder and a foreshadowing of that one great sacrifice that Christ would offer once and forever for the purification of the sins of mankind (10:1–4).

St Paul then offers some remarkable Old Testament prophecies. He begins with the Psalmist, whose great Descendant, the Messiah, upon entering the world, expressed His readiness to give His own body for suffering for the sake of man after the Old Testament sacrifices and whole burnt offerings had become useless to the Heavenly Father: "Sacrifice and offering Thou wouldest not, but a body hast Thou made for me; whole-burnt offerings, and sin offerings, hast Thou not required. Then said I, Lo, I come; in the heading of the book it is written of me, That I should long to do Thy will, O my God; yea, Thy Law is within my heart" (LXX Psalm 39:7–9).

In the Hebrew text of the Bible, instead of "a body You have prepared for me" (Septuagint), we read, "You have revealed to me," or, more specifically, "You have pierced my ears." It is unclear how this difference came about, but in both versions, the same thought is expressed: the Messiah is completely obedient to His Heavenly Father. In ancient times, freedmen who wished to remain in the services of their former masters had their ears pierced. This was a symbolic sign of their loyalty (see Exod 21:5–6). St Paul interprets this ancient prophecy to mean that the Old Testament sacrifices have become obsolete, for instead of those, it was the single sacrifice of Jesus Christ upon the Cross that accomplished the salvation of mankind (10:5–10). The oft-repeated sacrifices of the Old Covenant could not destroy sins; Christ, having once and for all brought *Himself* as a sacrifice for sins, forever is seated on the right hand of God and "He has perfected forever those who are being sanctified" (10:14).

The apostle confirms all of this by a citation from Jeremiah concerning the coming of the New Covenant, after which God will forget the sins and iniquities of mankind: "Now where there is remission of these [i.e., sins], there is no longer an offering for sin" (10:18). In other words, after the shedding of the Blood of Christ, the Old Testament, with its symbolic priesthood and powerless sacrifices, must have ended.

From 10:19, St Paul begins his moral instructions. The most important theme of this section is an exhortation to be firm in faith.

In 10:19–39, the apostle exhorts the Jews to keep firmly to their Christian confession of faith, to be filled with love for one another, and not to abandon the Christian assemblies. He reminds them that if those who rejected the Law of Moses were punished by death, then how much more terrible will be the punishment for those who apostatize from the Christian faith! "It is a fearful thing to fall into the hands of the living God" (10:31). The apostle reminds the Hebrews about the great zeal that they had immediately after conversion, how they bravely endured persecutions, and how they even "joyfully accepted the plundering of [their] goods" (10:34). He admonishes them not to lose their Christian hope, but rather to arm themselves with patient endurance, so that, having fulfilled the will of God, they will receive the promised blessings. He consoles them with the promise of the second coming of Christ, when every person will receive a just reward, and he cites a prophecy of Habakkuk: "Behold the proud, His soul is not upright in him; But the just shall live by his faith" (Hab 2: 4).

Chapter 11 is dedicated entirely to the exposition of an important teaching concerning faith. The apostle first gives an incredibly important dogmatic definition of faith itself: "Now faith is the substance of things hoped for, the evidence of things not seen" (11:1). Blessed Theodoret interprets these words in this way: "For through faith we see the things unseen, and it becomes our eyes to see the things we hope for, and so that which has not yet come to pass appears to us as already occurred. When all the dead are still in the tombs, faith paints a vivid picture of the resurrection and teaches us to imagine immortality in the ashes of the bodies."[195]

Those who were righteous in the Old Testament were glorified by having such faith, and so the rest of the chapter is dedicated to describing their faith.

Before beginning this section, however, St Paul gives another definition of the importance of faith: "By faith we understand that the worlds were framed by the word of God, so that the things which are seen were not made of things which are visible" (11:3). Only faith can help us understand how God could create this visible world from nothing and yet within time, for it is much easier for the mind to imagine that matter is eternal and that everything came to be from matter through the natural laws of evolution. This is a favorite teaching of materialist atheists. However, the world was created within time, and time itself only began with the creation of the visible, material world. This is what the apostle means by "the worlds were framed."

The rest of chapter 11 is dedicated to the Old Testament saints, beginning with Abel, who lived with faith in the fulfillment of those promises that God gave to

Adam and Eve, even before they were cast out of paradise. Abel believed in the coming of the promised Redeemer of the world, Whose sufferings were foreshadowed by the Old Testament sacrifices. Having spoken of Abel and Enoch, St Paul underlines the necessity of faith to please God: "But without faith it is impossible to please Him, for he who comes to God must believe that He is, and that He is a rewarder of those who diligently seek Him" (11:6). These words follow his previous words about Enoch, who was taken to heaven while still alive because he had true faith and directed his life completely and exclusively by the will of God (see Gen 5:21–22).

"By faith Noah ... prepared an ark for the saving of his household, by which he condemned the world" (11:7). Only faith in God and in the immutability of His words concerning the coming deluge could inspire Noah to such a seemingly mad labor as building an ark. By this faith, Noah condemned the world, that is, he proved that the world was worthy of punishment, for the world could have believed with Noah and have been saved from the coming flood.

"By faith Abraham obeyed when he was called to go out to the place which he would receive as an inheritance" (11:8). The height and purity of Abraham's faith is seen in his coming to an unknown land, living as a nomad in expectation of the fulfillment of God's promise of receiving the heavenly inheritance. "For he waited for the city which has foundations, whose builder and maker is God." In other words, he waited for the kingdom of heaven, feeling, as did all the Old Testament saints, "strangers and pilgrims on the earth" (11:13).

"By faith Abraham, when he was tested, offered up Isaac ... concluding that God was able to raise him up, even from death, from which he also received him in a figurative sense" (11:17–19). This was also a prophecy of the Heavenly Father bringing His Son as a sacrifice for the sins of the people, Whom He then raised up on the third day. "By faith Jacob, when he was dying ... worshiped, leaning on the top of his staff" (11:21). Jacob prefigured the Cross and the Messiah Himself, who was to come from his seed, when he venerated the top of the staff of Joseph. "By faith Moses, when he was born, was hidden three months by his parents, because they saw he was a beautiful child; and they were not afraid of the king's command" (11:23). St Paul believes that it is not merely parental love that inspired Moses's parents to hide him, but faith first and foremost, because they believed that such a beautiful child could not but be predestined for a great work.

According to St John Chrysostom,

> Thus from the beginning, yea from the very swaddling-clothes, great was the grace that was poured out on that righteous man, this being not the work of nature. For observe, the child immediately on its birth appears fair and not disagreeable to the sight. Whose work was this? Not that of nature, but of the grace of God, which also stirred up and strengthened that barbarian woman, the Egyptian, and took and drew her on.[196]

"By faith Moses, when he became of age, refused to be called the son of Pharaoh's daughter, choosing rather to suffer affliction with the people of God than to enjoy the passing pleasures of sin, esteeming the reproach of Christ greater riches than the treasures in Egypt" (11:24–26). As a type or prefiguration of Christ, Who suffered for mankind, Moses preferred to suffer for his people to deliver them from the bondage of the Egyptians.

"By faith he forsook Egypt, not fearing the wrath of the king" (11:27). St John Chrysostom comments on this passage:

> What dost thou say? That he did not fear? And yet the Scripture says, that when he heard, he "was afraid" (Exod 2:14), and for this cause provided for safety by flight, and stole away, and secretly withdrew himself; and afterwards he was exceedingly afraid. Observe the expressions with care: he said, "not fearing the wrath of the king," with reference to his even presenting himself again. For it would have been [the part] of one who was afraid, not to undertake again his championship, nor to have any hand in the matter. That he did however again undertake it, was [the part] of one who committed all to God: for he did not say, "He is seeking me, and is busy [in the search], and I cannot bear again to engage in this matter." So that even flight was [an act of] faith. Why then did he not remain (you say)? That he might not cast himself into a foreseen danger. For this finally would have been tempting [God]: to leap into the midst of dangers, and say, "Let us see whether God will save me."[197]

"By faith he kept the Passover and the sprinkling of blood, lest he who destroyed the firstborn should touch them" (11:28). Blessed Theodoret in his commentary explains Moses's faith: "Without faith, how could he have believed that death could be stopped merely with the blood of a lamb? But through the type, he foresaw the reality, and imagined the power of the Blood of the Master."[198]

"By faith the walls of Jericho fell down after they were encircled for seven days" (11:30). Where do we see the faith of the Hebrews in this event (Josh 6:1–19)? In their firm obedience to God's command. Behind the walls of Jericho waited strong, well-armed enemies who could have attacked the besiegers at any time, and in the meantime, the Israelites were commanded to walk around the city seven times! Such a procession, judging by human standards, could have exhausted the army completely on the eve of battle. However, they listened to their commander Joshua, evidently hoping not on the strength of their arms, but in the miraculous aid of God. And their faith was not brought to shame. At the sound of the trumpets, the walls of Jericho fell. As St John Chrysostom notes, "assuredly the sound of trumpets is not able to throw down stones, though one blow for ten thousand years; but faith can do all things."[199] "By faith the harlot Rahab did not perish with those who did not believe, when she had received the spies with peace" (11:31). Rahab's story is recounted in the second chapter of the Book of Joshua. Regarding Rahab's labor of faith, it is remarkable that she was a foreigner and did not even know of the true faith before the spies' arrival. Furthermore, her life up to this point was quite sinful. However, the power of her faith accomplished the complete renewal of her heretofore-sinful soul. St John Chrysostom emphasizes that the apostle intentionally included Rahab in his list of Old Testament saints, because "It would then be disgraceful, if you should appear more faithless even than a harlot. Yet she merely heard what the men related, and immediately believed."[200]

Then the holy apostle lists other Old Testament saints who performed wondrous labors and miracles by the power of faith. Some he names, others he does not, contenting himself with their labors. Blessed Theodoret expounds on this passage in detail:

> "Stopped the mouth of lions"—this was Daniel. "Quenched the violence of fire"—this is about Hananiah, Azariah, and Mishael. "Escaped the edge of the sword"—these are those who were victorious in wars. "Out of weakness were made strong"—this is said about those who returned with Zorobabel, having been freed from the Babylonian captivity and defeated the neighbors who rose against them. "Became valiant in battle"—these are those already spoken about, as well as the children of Mattathias, Judah, Jonathan, and Simon. "Women received their dead raised to life again" (11:35)—these are the miracles of Elijah, together with Elisha, the first of whom raised the son of the widow, and the second—the son of the Shunammite woman. "Others were tortured, not accepting deliverance, that they might obtain a better resurrection"—these include, for example those with Eleazar, the seven Maccabees, and their mother. < ... > "They were stoned"—this is spoken about the priest Zechariah, son of Judah. "They were sawn in two"— this is said concerning the suffering of the prophet Isaiah. < ... > "They wandered about in sheepskins and goatskins, being destitute, afflicted, tormented—of whom the world was not worthy. They wandered in deserts and mountains, in dens and caves of the earth" (11:37–38). Such were the great Elijah and the great Elisha, the heir of his gift; such were the great majority of prophets who did not have homes, but cutting trees were making huts for themselves.[201]

"And all these, having obtained a good testimony through faith, did not receive the promise, God having provided something better for us, that they should not be made perfect apart from us" (11:39–40). St John Chrysostom comments on this passage thus:

> They [i.e., the saints of the Old Testament] gained their victory so many ages ago, and have not yet received their reward. And you who are yet in the conflict, are you vexed? < ... > What then shall Abel do, who was victor before all, and is sitting uncrowned? And what Noah? And what, they who lived in those early times, seeing that they wait for thee and those after thee?[202]

In other words, St Paul wants to shame the impatient and fainthearted Palestinian Jews, who, having not yet finished their Christian labors, would prefer already to see the fulfillment of their Christian hope. Paul consoles them by reminding them how long the Old Testament saints waited for the reward for their patience—until the great sacrifice of Christ opened for them the doors of the Kingdom of Heaven.

In chapter 12, the apostle offers the Jews, gazing upon the example of the Old Testament saints, to "run with endurance the race that is set before us, looking unto Jesus the author and finisher of our faith," the highest example for all who labor (12:1–2). The passages from 11:9–10, 17–23, 32–40 are appointed as the epistle reading at the Divine Liturgy on the Sunday before Nativity, the Sunday of the Holy Fathers, when the Church commemorates all the Old Testament saints. With the addition of 12:1–2, this excerpt is read on the Liturgy of the Sunday of All Saints, beginning at 11:33. Beginning with 11:24, this passage is also read on the Sunday of Orthodoxy.

In the rest of chapter 12, the holy apostle explains the importance of suffering as a corrective punishment from God for those people who are His sons, citing Proverbs: "For whom the Lord loves He chastens" (12:6). The rest of chapter 12 and all of chapter 13 are dedicated to moral instruction concerning peace, purity, brotherly love, respect for elders, and good deeds. Chapter 13, verses 18–25, conclude with an expression of St Paul's hope to see them soon, along with his greetings and his apostolic blessing.

PART III

Part III

The General Epistles

WHY ARE SOME EPISTLES CALLED "GENERAL"?

Seven of the apostolic epistles in the New Testament are called "general"—one by St James, two by St Peter, three by St John the Theologian, and one by St Jude. In the Russian Bible, these epistles generally follow Acts, whereas in the English, they follow the epistles of St Paul. The label "general" was not given to these epistles by the writers themselves. They were thus named by the Church at a later time, but still quite early in the history of the Church. In his *Church History*, Eusebius of Caesarea cites the testimony of Apollonius, a second-century Christian writer, who recalls that one Themiso, a Montanist heretic, dared to compose a "general epistle" in imitation of the apostle John, pretending to "instruct those whose faith was better than his."[203]

In what sense then are these epistles "general" (*katholikos* in Greek)?

One of the most prominent early Christian theologians, Clement of Alexandria, calls the official letter sent out by the Apostolic Council in Jerusalem "a general epistle" (see Acts 15). In other words, that epistle was not written to any private individual or even a single community, but rather to all Christian communities in the Church at large. Thus, "general" in this sense means that the letters were "encyclical."

Thus, the epistles of James, Peter, John, and Jude are called general because they are written not for a specific community, as were St Paul's epistles, but rather to all Christians. 1 Peter and 1 John are called "general" epistles in the sense of a "circular letter" by Origen and Dionysius of Alexandria. The first instance in which the entire corpus of these epistles was called "general" is found in Eusebius's *Ecclesiastical History*.[204] Even though 2 John and 3 John were intended for specific individuals and so were not, strictly speaking, "general," they are appended to the first epistle, as they are complementary to it thematically.

As eventually the term "catholic" began to be applied to the Church herself in the meaning of the "true, genuine, Orthodox" Church, so also with respect to these epistles the term "catholic" or "general" came to acquire the meaning of "true, genuine, canonical" containing in themselves the unchangeable rule of a true Christian life. It is in this sense that Origen calls the Epistle of Jude "general," and the same meaning is given by Eusebius to all of them together.[205]

These seven epistles thus were first named "general" or "catholic" by Eusebius to underline both their encyclical nature and their undoubtedly canonical character, as opposed to many other false epistles circulating at the time. Gradually, Eusebius's characterization was accepted by the church at large.

These epistles are different from the epistles of St Paul in the sense that they have more general and foundational instructions, whereas St Paul spoke to specific issues and problems of the local churches to which he wrote. Although St Paul's epistles are thus more specific in their focus, they do not lose their universal significance for all times and places in the life of the Church of Christ. Moreover, the epistles of St Paul are imbued with the force of his personality, often including specific details of his own life and expressions of his own feelings of joy, sorrow, indignation, and so forth. The general epistles, on the contrary, do not reflect the personalities of their authors to the same extent, but rather they offer the set of rules concerning faith and piety that are binding for all Christians.

 CHAPTER 15

The General Epistle of the Holy Apostle James

THE AUTHOR OF THE EPISTLE

The writer calls himself "James, a bondservant of God and of the Lord Jesus Christ" (Jas 1:1). We know of three people with the name "James" in the Gospels: (1) James, the son of Zebedee, one of the Twelve and the brother of John the Theologian; (2) James, the son of Alphaeus, the brother of the Evangelist Matthew, also one of the Twelve; (3) James, the so-called brother of the Lord, who was one of the Seventy and the brother of Joses, Judas, and Simon (Matt 13:55). Subsequently he became the first bishop of Jerusalem and called by the Jews "the Just." He was also called "the Lesser" to distinguish him from the apostles by that name who were among the Twelve.

St James the son of Zebedee ended his life very early as a martyr (around A.D. 44 in Jerusalem, according to Acts 12:2). St James the son of Alphaeus, as we know from tradition, preached among the Gentiles. This epistle, however, is clearly meant for the Jews of the Diaspora (Jas 1:1). Ecclesiastical tradition thus considers this general epistle to have been written by the "third" apostle James, that is, the brother of the Lord, the first bishop of Jerusalem. As bishop of Jerusalem, he could fairly consider himself to have jurisdiction over all Christians from the Jews, no matter where they lived. Moreover, he was greatly respected and commanded authority among all Jews, even those not converted to Christ, because of his virtuous life. He led a strictly ascetic life, was celibate, drank neither wine nor strong drink, never ate meat, wore only linen clothing, and strictly followed the Law, often praying in the temple alone. The Jews, even those unconverted, called him "just," and "the pillar of the people." Considering all this, it is natural that he would turn with his authoritative, forceful word to all those "twelve tribes which are scattered abroad" (Jas 1:1).

We have considerable information about the life of Apostle James. He was the eldest son of Joseph, the betrothed of the Most Pure Virgin, from his first wife. He was also the brother of Simon, Judas, and Joses, all of whom are mentioned in the Gospels (Matt 13:55). For this reason, he is called "brother of the Lord." According to tradition, he accompanied Joseph and Mary with the child Jesus on their flight to Egypt. Nevertheless, he and his brothers did not believe in their brother's Messianic dignity for a long time (see John 7:3–5), which is probably why he was not included in the number of the Twelve. Later, he came to believe with his whole heart, and after the resurrection, the Lord appeared to him in a personal vision (1 Cor 15:7). After the ascension of Christ, he, as designated by the Lord himself, became the first bishop of the Church in Jerusalem. For this reason—as well as the respect of the other apostles—he chaired the Apostolic Council in Jerusalem (Acts 15).

It is safe to assume that his preaching was limited to Palestine and that he did not travel to other countries as did the other apostles. He died a martyr's death (c. A.D. 64) by being cast down from the pinnacle of the temple by the Jewish authorities. Josephus, while listing the reasons for the fall of Jerusalem in the war against the Romans, indicated that the Lord Himself punished the Jews at least partially because they killed James the Just. Tradition ascribes to James the composition of an ancient liturgy, the Liturgy of Apostle James, which is celebrated in Jerusalem on October 23, the day of his memory.[206]

THE AUDIENCE, TIME, AND PLACE OF THE WRITING

As we see from the first verse, St James wrote the epistle to "the twelve tribes which are scattered abroad," that is, the Jews of the Diaspora. Apparently, the epistle was not directed only at Christians of Jewish ethnicity, but to all Jews. This is not unusual, considering that in the first century, the Christians of Jewish extraction did not readily separate themselves from their unconverted brethren, even praying together with them, as we see in the Book of Acts. Apostle James, as we have already mentioned, was universally respected by Jews and Christians alike, and so he could address even the Jews who had not converted with a forceful word of instruction. Note that the expression "twelve tribes which are scattered abroad" does not include the Jews living in Palestine proper.

The time and place of the writing of the epistle are not indicated in the text. Apostle James was martyred c. A.D. 64. Apparently, this epistle was written not long before his death, for the state of the Jewish Christian communities is described in similar terms to the characterization given to those communities by St Paul in the Epistle to the Hebrews. Most commentators broadly date this epistle to A.D. 55–60.

St James probably wrote the epistle in Jerusalem or somewhere else in Palestine, as there is no historical record indicating that James ever left Palestine.

THE PURPOSE OF THE EPISTLE OF JAMES

The cause for the writing of the epistle was probably that the Jewish Christians living in the Diaspora suffered much, both from their unconverted brethren and especially from the Gentiles. These trials were so great that many, not finding enough strength to endure and not understanding how the coming of the Messiah did not immediately result in benefits for the Jewish nation, began to lose heart and grow weak in faith. Some among them even allowed themselves to murmur at God Himself, not having a proper understanding of the source of their trials. At the same time, they persisted in their false belief that salvation depended on only their ancestry from Abraham. They also had incorrect views on prayer; they did not ascribe enough importance to the doing of good deeds; and many of them readily instructed others, thinking themselves to be worthy teachers by virtue of their ancestry alone. In addition, the rich lorded it over the poor. Consequently, many lusted for earthly riches, while brotherly love grew cold.

This behavior gave St James reason to correct his flock through the moral instructions of a general epistle.

THE AUTHENTICITY OF THE EPISTLE OF JAMES

According to Origen and Eusebius of Caesarea, not everyone in the early Church recognized the authenticity of this epistle. This gave Martin Luther, the sixteenth-century German Reformation leader, a reason to doubt its authenticity, because it contains a moral truth so uncomfortable for Protestants: "faith without works is dead" (Jas 2:26). However, none of the most respected and famous Fathers and teachers of the Church ever doubted its genuine attribution. The reason for ancient doubts could only be that not all ancient writers of the Church cite this epistle, as there is little material in it that is useful for the apologetic and polemical writings that characterized the earliest writing of the early Church. Moreover, the greeting says nothing about James's own apostolic authority, as St James humbly remains silent about it. There is, however, reason to believe that such Fathers as St Clement of Rome; Hermas, the author of *The Shepherd*; St Irenaeus of Lyons; Clement of Alexandria; and Tertullian knew of the existence of this epistle. It is also included in the Peshitta, the fifth-century Syriac translation of the Bible. From the time of Eusebius of Caesarea, the doubts concerning its authenticity no longer persist, and the epistle was generally accepted by the Church and included in the list of canonical books of Scripture.

THE STRUCTURE AND CONTENT OF THE EPISTLE

This epistle mostly concerns itself with moral instruction. James's moral instructions are remarkable for their particular power, exalted tone, and ascetical rigor. The exposition of the themes in this epistle is sporadic, and its tone is weighty but at the same time full of love. The epistle has five chapters, divided thematically as follows:

1. Chapter 1: Introduction and greeting (1:1). A teaching concerning temptation (1:2–4), on wisdom and prayer (1:5–8), on the worthlessness of earthly riches (1:9–11). The source of temptations is not God (1:12–18). On the reining in of anger and the tongue. On the fulfillment of the Law (1:19–26). On the essence of true piety (1:27).

2. Chapter 2: An exhortation to love all equally (2:1–13). A teaching concerning the correlation of faith and good works (2:14–26).

3. Chapter 3: A warning against self-proclaimed teachers and giving free rein to the tongue (3:1–14). True and false wisdom (3:15–18).

4. Chapter 4: Accusatory speech against evil desires (4:1–3), against friendship with the world (4:4–10), against speaking evil of others (4:11–12), and against arrogant self-assurance (4:12–17).

5. Chapter 5: A denunciation of the hard-hearted rich (5:1–6). Instruction on patient endurance of sufferings (5:7–13), on the sacrament of unction (5:14–15), on the confession of sins (5:16–18), on the conversion of those who are lost (5:19–20).

EXEGETICAL ANALYSIS OF THE EPISTLE OF THE HOLY APOSTLE JAMES

In the beginning of the epistle, St James, remaining silent about his apostolic dignity, calls himself a "bondservant of God and of the Lord Jesus Christ." The usual ancient greeting— "rejoice!"—has an especially exalted meaning in the mouth of an apostle, signifying the joy in the Lord Jesus as Redeemer. After the greeting, the holy apostle immediately begins speaking about temptations, a term that encapsulates all the trials and misfortunes that Christians must undergo during earthly life. These trials make our faith stronger and raise us higher and higher on the ladder of moral perfection through the labor of endurance. If in the battle with these trials and tribulations a person feels his own weakness, he must not despair or lose courage. He must ask God for the wisdom to overcome the temptation and "it will be given to him" (1:5).

The virtue of a perfect Christian endurance is so great that without the gift of spiritual wisdom given by the Lord God, it is unattainable for us weak mortals. "But let him ask in faith, with no doubting, for he who doubts is like a wave of the sea driven and tossed by the wind. For let not that man suppose that he will receive anything from the Lord; his is a double-minded man, unstable in all his ways" (1:6–8). The most important condition for prayers to be answered is unswerving faith. This is because only such faith can lead a person to moral union with God through which divine grace can be assimilated. Filled with true Christian wisdom, a person will be able to joyfully endure all trials and misfortunes, whether he be rich or poor.

"Let the lowly brother glory in his exaltation" (1:9), that is, let the poor man be consoled by the knowledge of the exalted character of his endurance of the sorrows sent by God. Christians in general must look at sorrows as the work of God's mercy and goodwill. "But the rich in his humiliation, because as a flower of the field he will pass away" (1:10). The rich man can glory or console himself only in the knowledge of his own insignificance, in the perishability of his riches. "Blessed is the man who endures temptation" (1:12), because the endured temptation helps in the spiritual perfection of man and gives him the "crown of life" (1:12). The Lord sends people trials not to lead them into sin, but to strengthen them to oppose sin. If a person falls during his battle with temptation, the fault is in the person himself, because "each one is tempted when he is drawn away by his own desires and enticed" (1:14). The Lord only helps the man do good; He only ever aids man's moral perfection. "Every good gift and every perfect gift is from above, and comes down from the Father of lights, with whom there is no variation or shadow of turning" (1:17).

Then Apostle James speaks of the relation of the Christian to the word of truth (1:18–27). Because we are all born of God by the word of truth, we must assiduously care for our moral development, and for this reason we must be "swift to hear" the word of truth, but slow to speak our own words and slow to grow angry, even if it seems our anger is a righteous defense of that word of truth, "for the wrath of man does not produce the righteousness of God" (1:20). We must be fulfillers of the word, however, not hearers only, lest we become like a person who carefully looks at the mirror but ignores what he sees there, as though it were not reflected. Only the active fulfillment in life of all the moral requirements of the Law of God can make a person truly virtuous; otherwise, his "religion is useless" (1:26).

In chapter 2, the apostle condemns "respect of persons" in man's relation with his neighbor. Such preference is a sign of "useless religion," and it proves that faith alone, without an accompanying life of virtue, has absolutely no significance. Just like a single word of sympathy can do nothing to warm or feed the naked and the poor, "thus also faith by itself, if it does not have works, is dead" (2:17). What saves a person, faith or works? Is this not a contradiction of Paul's words that a person is saved independently of the works of the Law (see Rom 3:28)? We can assume that these words about the necessity for living, active faith were written by St James because many Jews had incorrectly understood the words of Apostle Paul. Apostle Paul insistently preached to the Jews that from the time of the coming of Christ the Saviour, the ritual law of Moses lost its significance, and only faith in Christ was needed for salvation, not the ritual observance of the Law. Many Jews assumed that these words meant the rejection of good deeds in general for salvation and the necessity for faith alone.

Apostle James thus underlines that a mere cold rational faith is not enough for salvation, for "even the demons believe—and tremble" (2:19). The meaning of these words is that true saving faith is intimately united with good deeds. Faith comes first, as the cause, but the works follow, as the consequence. Neither faith, nor deeds, taken separately from each other can save a person, for without each other they are impossible. These are two united, yet distinct sides of the same coin.

"For whoever shall keep the whole law, and yet stumble in one point, he is guilty of all" (2:10). Why is this so? Because the entire Law, with all its many and varied commandments, is a single expression of the one will of the One Law-Giver, God, and transgression against a single commandment is thus disobedience against the will of the One Law-Giver. Consequently, it is a transgression against the Law in its entirety. Blessed Theodoret understands the "whole law" to mean "Christian love," which includes, according to the words of the Lord Himself, "all the Law and the Prophets" (Matt 22:40):

> Whoever loves his neighbor will not commit adultery or murder ... The apostle here is not saying that virtuous men never had shortcomings, but rather that our love must not be conditional; it must not be a respecter of persons, but it must be all-encompassing. The same can be said of other virtues. Whoever is incompletely chaste or incompletely just harms the entire body of virtue by his incomplete fulfillment of virtue. Thus, one must understand the whole law to be the law of love.[207]

Thus, "Mercy triumphs over judgment" (2:13). The judgment in accordance with God's righteousness threatens condemnation for every sinner, and all faithful Christians are also found to be sinners before the righteousness of God. Mercy and charitable love bear within themselves a hope that it can overcome the threatening power of the judgment and can free us sinners from our deserved punishment. St Peter expresses a similar idea in his epistle: "And above all things have fervent love for one another, for 'love will cover a multitude of sins'" (1 Pet 4:8).

This is why the works, especially the works of Christian love and charity toward one's neighbor carry such great significance. St James further indicates that the Old Testament saints such as Abraham and Rahab were saved not only by faith, but by deeds as well, for by their deeds did they reveal their faith. "For as the body without the spirit is dead, so faith without works is dead also" (2:26).

"Useless religion" that never goes farther than empty words often likes to teach others how to live. In chapter 3, St James condemns this urge to teach others. He shows what great importance the word has in human life, and how great is the moral responsibility of a teacher. Therefore, one must approach the moral instruction of others with great care. "My brethren, let not many of you become teachers, knowing that we shall receive a stricter judgment" (3:1). The importance of the tongue, the organ of speech, in human life is compared by St James with a bridle, a rudder, and fire. In the human hands, even a small bridle forces a large and headstrong horse to submit, while a small rudder gives direction to a massive ship, even in contrary winds.

"Even so the tongue is a little member and boasts great things. See how great a forest a little fire kindles! And the tongue is a fire, a world of iniquity. The tongue is so set among our members that it defiles the whole body, and sets on fire the course of nature" (3:5–6). Set afire by Gehenna itself (i.e., the devil, the father of lies), the tongue never submits to be reined it by man's exertions. Only with the help of God's grace can a person bridle his tongue. Calling all Christians to do this, the holy apostle stresses the incongruity of blessing God and cursing people with the same tongue. Considering the two-edged significance of the human word, only one who has bridled his wagging tongue and obtained true wisdom has the right to instruct others. The essence of Christian wisdom is this: it is not merely empty knowledge, but it is life itself.

Whoever has true Christian wisdom is pure in his intentions and dispositions. He is meek, humble in his desires, and obedient to his elders—that is, he subjects himself to authority. He is filled with mercy and good deeds. A contrast to this heavenly wisdom is the earthly, psychological, and demonic wisdom, the source of which is the father of lies, that is, the devil. The characteristic traits of this so-called wisdom are envy and irritability. This "wisdom" leads only to disorder and evils.

In chapter 4, the apostle demonstrates the results that this demonic wisdom has in social life. The preachers of this so-called wisdom pander to the lowest desires of people, urging love for earthly goods and inspiring the proud thought that man himself, by his own efforts, without the help of God, can achieve happiness and prosperity. Bitter reality mercilessly destroys any such self-satisfied and frivolous theory of human happiness. The pervasive spread of this earthly so-called wisdom gives rise only to enmity and dissention in human relations. Excessive attachment to earthly goods and prideful self-confidence is unfaithfulness to God and service to the devil. Therefore, "God resists the proud, but gives grace to the humble" (4:6). The apostle teaches humble compunction in the face of our sins, for only humility can morally raise a person. The apostle then gives further instruction: not to speak evil of one another and not to judge, for judgment belongs to God alone. He also teaches people not to be vainglorious, for vainglory naturally leads to pride.

While calling on all Christians to submit themselves to God and to oppose the enticements of the devil, the apostle in chapter 5 condemns hard-hearted rich people, threatening them with God's punishment, which can turn any earthly riches into nothing. At the same time, he encourages those suffering from the persecution of the rich, as well as all Christians in general who patiently suffer for their faith or endure the hardships of life. This endurance will not be limitless: soon, the Lord will come. This exhortation to patience is strengthened by an analogy with the agricultural life. Just as a farmer patiently waits for the fruit of the harvest, so also the Christian must patiently await the harvest of the fruits of his life, when Christ will appear in His glory and will give to each according to his deeds.

"The coming of the Lord is at hand" (5:8). The apostles often speak of the imminence of the second coming of Christ. It is truly near in its inner moral unity with Christ's first coming, for from the moment of Christ's coming to earth, the last age of the world began, as even the Old Testament prophets predicted (Isa 2:1, 4:2). The second coming of Christ is therefore close, because we know neither the day nor the hour of His coming, and we must be always ready to meet Him. To strengthen this exhortation for the patient endurance of sufferings, Apostle James offers examples from Old Testament history: the prophets, who were persecuted often by the leaders of the people, and the great sufferer Job, who was later greatly rewarded for his sufferings by God.

Then the apostle exhorts his listeners not to misuse oaths, almost in the same words as the Lord used in Matthew 5:33–37. In all circumstances of life, both sorrowful and joyful, we must turn to the Lord with prayer, petition, praise, and thanksgiving. If we are sick, the apostle commands us to run to the healing of the priests through unction with prayer: "Is anyone among you sick? Let him call for the elders of the church, and let them pray over him, anointing him with oil in the name of the Lord. And the prayer of faith will save the sick, and the Lord will raise him up" (5:14–15).

This is a clear indication that the sacrament of holy unction (anointing of the sick) has apostolic origin and was celebrated by several presbyters. The Protestants are mistaken in their interpretation of this anointing as merely physical application of oil for the healing of wounds. Several aspects of this passage make it clear that he does not refer simply to the medicinal use of oil, but to the sacramental rite. First, it were the elders (presbyters) of the church, not lay physicians, who were to be called. Second, these elders (presbyters) were called to perform a prayer over the sick person. Moreover, it was necessary that not one, but several presbyters be called, which would be superfluous if the oil was merely to be used medicinally. Furthermore, it would be strange to use oil as medicine for all diseases, if this anointing was done simply for the purpose of healing. On the contrary, this anointing is clearly a sacrament that uses oil as its material element, and it is not the oil, but the "prayer of faith" that saves the sick man. Finally, it is also clear that after unction, the sick man receives the remission of sins. All this leaves no doubt that the apostle speaks here of a sacrament.

Likewise, the apostle recommends that Christians confess their sins to each other to be healed of spiritual ailments, that is, sins. The connection with the previous section about the anointing of the sick through the use of the conjunction "therefore" (*oun* in Greek) suggests that Apostle James is speaking about confession before the church, that is, of the sacrament of repentance. Even in the contemporary practice of the Orthodox Church, the confession before one's spiritual father may often be offered in conjunction with the sacrament of unction.

"The effective, fervent prayer of a righteous man avails much" (5:16). The "righteous men" in this passage are those people whose prayer is more perfect. Here, of course, the Apostle does not only have in mind the people who are just and righteous, but, again, the presbyters of the Church endowed with a special gift of grace to intercede for people and to perform the sacraments. As an example of such intercessory and effective prayer, Apostle James offers the example of the prophet Elijah, whose prayer stopped the rain and then started it again. However, lest people think that this example is beyond the emulation of ordinary people the apostle says that "Elijah was a man with a nature like ours," that is, he had the same passionate human nature that we do.

In the conclusion of his epistle, the apostle speaks of the greatness of missionary ministry that strives to convert those who have wandered from the way of truth: "if anyone among you wanders from the truth, and someone turns him back, let him know that he who turns a sinner from the error of his ways will save a soul from death and cover a multitude of sins" (5:19–20). Having spoken already of the necessity of works of virtue and mercy for the sake of the body, the holy apostle speaks of far more important good deeds—the works of spiritual mercy are especially precious in the sight of God.

 CHAPTER 16

The First General Epistle
of the Holy Apostle Peter

THE AUTHOR OF THE EPISTLE

Both the witness of ancient tradition and internal evidence give indisputable proof that this epistle was written by Apostle Peter. St Polycarp of Smyrna, a disciple of St John the Theologian, cited it in his writings, as did St Papias of Hierapolis. We also find quotations from this epistle in the writings of St Irenaeus of Lyons, Tertullian, Clement of Alexandria, and Origen. It is included in the Peshitta, the Syriac translation of the Scriptures. The tone of the writing in many places fully corresponds with the fiery temperament of Peter, so often in evidence in the Gospels, and the clarity and exactitude of expression also reflect the authorship of Peter who converted thousands by his word, as witnessed in the Book of Acts.

The Holy Apostle Peter, formerly called Simon, was the son of a fisherman named Jonah from Bethsaida of Galilee (see John 1:42, 45). He was the brother of St Andrew the First-called, who brought Peter to Christ. St Peter was married and owned a house in Capernaum (Matt 8:14). Called to the apostleship by Christ the Saviour while fishing in the Lake of Gennesaret (Luke 5:8), he used every possible opportunity to express his faithfulness and zeal to Christ, for which reason he was especially close to the Lord, along with the sons of Zebedee (Luke 9:28). Strong, fiery of spirit, and decisive, Peter naturally took the first place among the apostles of Christ. He was the first to definitively confess the Lord Jesus as the Christ, that is, the Messiah (Matt 16:16), and for this reason Christ called him Peter or Cephas (i.e., "rock"). On this rock of Peter's faith, the Lord promised to establish His Church, which even the gates of hell would not overcome (Matt 16:18).

Even so, Peter rejected the Lord three times before the Passion. His repentance was heartfelt, however, and he washed away his sin with bitter tears of repentance. Consequently, after the resurrection, the Lord reinstated Peter to the apostolic dignity, and Christ committed His sheep and lambs to Peter's care, also three times, commensurate with the number of times Peter had denied Him (John 21:15–17). Peter was the first to labor in spreading and building up of the Church of Christ after the descent of the Holy Spirit, having preached so powerfully before a crowd at Pentecost that three thousand people converted to Christ. Another fiery speech spoken at the occasion of the healing of a man lame from birth converted five thousand more (Acts 2:4).

The first part of the Acts is dedicated primarily to Peter's apostolic proclamation. However, after his miraculous deliverance from prison by an angel and his subsequent departure to another place (Acts 12:17), Acts mentions him only once during the account of the Apostolic Council in Jerusalem (Acts 15). All other information concerning Peter's life was preserved only by tradition, and it is often contradictory or incomplete. Regardless, we know that he preached the Gospel in Palestine and along the Phoenician and Syrian shores of the Mediterranean Sea. He established the Church in Antioch and consecrated its first bishop, St Evodius. He traveled throughout Asia Minor, preaching to the Jews and proselytes, and then he went to Egypt, where he consecrated St Mark as the first bishop of Alexandria. From there, he went to Achaia (Greece) and preached in Corinth (1 Cor 1:12). According to tradition, St Peter then traveled to Italy and resided in Rome, after which he traveled to Spain, Carthage, and Britain. Toward the end of his life, St Peter once again came to Rome, where he was martyred along with St Paul in A.D. 67, being crucified upside down.

The Purpose of the Epistle of Peter

The motivation for writing the epistle is seen in the epistle itself: St Peter wrote "to the pilgrims of the Dispersion in Pontus, Galatia, Cappadocia, Asia, and Bithynia" (1 Pet 1:1). All these are provinces of Asia Minor. The "pilgrims" mentioned are primarily Christians of Jewish ancestry, as St Peter was primarily the apostle to the circumcised (see Gal 2:7). However, as we see from several places in this epistle (1 Pet 2:10, 4:3–4), Peter also alludes to Gentile converts, who were members of the Christian communities in Asia Minor, as we know from the Acts and the epistles of St Paul.

Why did St Peter write to the Christians of Asia Minor if most of the communities there had been established by St Paul?

One reason was the Lord's command to St Peter to "strengthen your brethren" (Luke 22:32). Another reason was the disorder in some of these communities and especially the persecution at the hands of the enemies of the Cross of Christ (1 Pet 1:6–7; 4:12-13, 19; 5:9). Other than external enemies, more subtle enemies had arisen within the Church itself—false teachers. Taking advantage of St Paul's absence, they began to pervert his teaching concerning Christian freedom and began to promote all sorts of immorality (1 Pet 2:16, see also 2 Pet 1:9, 2:1). There are also reasons to believe that Silas,

Apostle Paul's fellow traveler (who after Paul's imprisonment helped Peter's ministry), personally told Peter of the trials of the communities in Asia Minor.

Thus, the purpose of the epistle was to encourage and console the Christians in Asia Minor and to strengthen their faith. In St Peter's own words, "By Silvanus [i.e., Silas], our faithful brother as I consider him, I have written to you briefly, exhorting and testifying that this is the true grace of God in which you stand" (1 Pet 5:12).

THE PLACE AND TIME OF THE WRITING OF THE EPISTLE

St Peter indicates that he wrote this epistle from Babylon (1 Pet 5:13). Roman Catholics insist that, as Peter was bishop of Rome for twenty-five years, "Babylon" is an allegorical name for Rome. It is strange, however, that such an allegorical name is used in the parting greeting of a letter. It would be more natural to understand the name Babylon literally. It is not possible that this is the Babylon on the Euphrates, for Peter never traveled that far east. However, there was a small town in Egypt on the banks of the Nile built by exiles from Mesopotamia, and it was also called Babylon. We also know of a Christian community in Babylon of Egypt from *The Lives of the Saints*.[208] Because we know that Peter was in Egypt and consecrated St Mark as bishop of Alexandria, it is possible that he could have written it from there, especially because he passes on Mark's greeting in 1 Peter 5:13. At the same time, Clement of Alexandria, as cited by Eusebius, interprets the place name "Babylon" as allegorically indicating the city of Rome.[209]

It is impossible to determine an exact date for this epistle. Any guesses are based on the fact that Peter was accompanied at that time by both Silvanus (Silas) and Mark (5:12–13). Both of these apostles were regular fellow travelers of Apostle Paul and were well-known by the Christians in Asia Minor. It is likely that both of them would have left St Paul's side only after Paul was imprisoned and sent to Rome to face Caesar's judgment (Acts 26–27). It was thus natural for Peter, after Paul's imprisonment, to care for Paul's flock. And since the first epistle was written not long before the second (which was written not long before Peter's martyrdom in A.D. 67), the date usually given is between A.D. 62 and 64.

THE STRUCTURE AND CONTENT OF THE EPISTLE

The First General Epistle of Peter has five chapters, divided thematically as follows:

1. Chapter 1: Introduction and greeting (1:1–2). Glorification of God for the grace of rebirth (1:3–5), for which reason Christians must rejoice in sufferings (1:6–9) and which all the prophecies of the Old Testament foretold (1:10–12). Exhortation to holiness of life (1:13–21) and mutual love (1:22–25).
2. Chapter 2: Instruction on spiritual growth (2:1–3) and foundation (2:4–10), on the virtuous life (2:11–12), on submission to authority (2:13–17), on slaves' submission to their masters (2:18–20). The example of Christ's sufferings (2:21–25).

3. Chapter 3: Moral instruction to wives (3:1–6), husbands (3:7), and all Christians (3:8–17). Christ Who suffered, descended to Hades, rose from the dead, and ascended (3:18–22).

4. Chapter 4: Instruction to Christians concerning different moral qualities and virtues (4:1–11), especially concerning innocent suffering (4:12–19).

5. Chapter 5: Instruction to pastors and their flock (5:1–9). Apostolic blessing (5:10–11). News and greetings (5:12–14).

EXEGETICAL ANALYSIS OF THE FIRST EPISTLE OF PETER

St Peter begins his first general epistle with the words "Peter, an apostle of Jesus Christ" (1:1). It is impossible not to see that the holy apostle intentionally begins with his apostolic dignity, because he did not personally establish the churches he addressed and he may not have had a personal acquaintance with them. Having indicated his intended audience, St Peter tries to use various divinely inspired instructions to strengthen and uplift the moral life of the suffering Christians in Asia Minor. In the first two chapters, he reveals the greatness and glory of salvation in Christ Jesus, and so this section is largely dogmatic in nature. The rest of the chapters consist primarily of moral instruction.

St Peter calls the Christians of Asia Minor "pilgrims" in two senses. First, they live outside of their homeland, Palestine. Second, all Christians consider life on earth as a pilgrimage, for the only proper homeland for a Christian is the life to come, the world of the spirit. The apostle calls them "elect" in the sense that in the New Testament all Christians are a new chosen nation of God, as the Hebrews were in the Old Testament. "Elect according to the foreknowledge of God the Father, in sanctification of the Spirit, for obedience and sprinkling of the blood of Jesus Christ" (1:2)—all three Persons of the Holy Trinity are involved in the salvation of mankind. God the Father, by His foreknowledge, knows which people will use their free will for salvation. God the Son, by His death on the Cross, accomplished the actual work of human redemption. The Holy Spirit, by His grace, sanctifies the elect, appropriating to them the work of salvation wrought by Christ.

From the depth of his heart, filled with gratitude to God for the redemption of the world, the apostle praises God Who gave man "an inheritance incorruptible" (1:4) to counter the crude, earthly inheritance expected by the Jews of the coming Messiah. Explaining that the power of God prepares people for salvation "through faith" (1:5), the apostle exhorts his listeners that this salvation will reveal itself in all its power only in the last times. Now, it is necessary to suffer "for a little while" (1:6), so that faith can be tested by the fires of temptation, becoming more precious than purified gold "at the revelation of Jesus Christ" (1:7), that is, at His second coming. St Paul concludes his doxology by indicating the incredible importance of the divine economy of our salvation, to which all the prophecies of the Old Testament pointed. The mystery of salvation is so profound that even "angels desire to look into" it (1:12).

On the basis of these dogmatic truths, Apostle Peter then offers a series of moral instructions, strengthening them with exalted dogmatic contemplation. The first general instruction concerns complete trust in the grace of Christ, with child-like obedience to God as Father, as well as proper striving to become like Him in holiness of life: "Be holy, for I am holy" (1:16). We also should be inspired to live holily by the thought of the great price of our redemption: "knowing that you were not redeemed with corruptible things, like silver or gold ... but with the precious blood of Christ" (1:18–19). Thus, we must preserve the faith of Christ and hold firm to it, in spite of all trials and tests.

In the second chapter, St Peter exhorts Christians living among antagonistic pagans to show by their holy, virtuous life that they are "a chosen generation, a royal priesthood, a holy nation, His own special people, that you may proclaim the praises of Him who called you out of darkness into His marvelous light" (2:9). Then the Gentiles, seeing the virtuous life of the Christians, will themselves convert and glorify God for what they previously had vilified.

Here, in contrast to the false teaching of the Roman Catholics that the rock on which the Church is built is Apostle Peter himself, it is important to note that St Peter calls the "rock" not himself, but the Lord Jesus Christ (see 2:4). The establishment of the Church, its cornerstone, is Christ Himself, while all the faithful members of the Church are "living stones." They must build of themselves, founded on the Rock, "a spiritual house, a holy priesthood, to offer up spiritual sacrifices acceptable to God through Jesus Christ" (2:5). Just as the Lord in the Old Testament had His temple and priests who served Him by offering sacrifices, so too in the New Testament, the entire Christian community in a spiritual sense must be at the same time a temple of God and its priesthood. Of course, St Peter is speaking figuratively, and in no way is he abolishing priestly hierarchy as a select group of people ordained in the Church to teach, to celebrate the sacraments, and for the work of administration.

All the faithful are called a "royal priesthood" because they must bring "spiritual sacrifices" to God, that is, the sacrifices of good works. Virtues are called "sacrifices" because doing good is always accompanied by the struggle against passions and sinful desires. In 2:6–8, St Peter once again calls the Lord Jesus Christ the "cornerstone" in a citation from Isaiah 28:16 that without doubt prefigured the Messiah. Jesus Christ also applied this prophecy to Himself (see Matt 21:42). In 2:9, the holy apostle calls Christians "a chosen generation, a royal priesthood, a holy nation, His own special people." All of these qualities are taken from the Old Testament names of the chosen Hebrew nation, and are now applied to Christians, because Christianity brings into fulfillment all that was prefigured in the use of these titles in the Old Testament (see Exod 19:5–6). St John the Theologian, in his Apocalypse, also wrote that in a spiritual sense the Lord Jesus Christ made us Christians all kings and priests to His God and Father (Rev 1:6). However, this figurative language cannot be understood as intending to abolish the need for priestly hierarchy in the Church, as some Protestants like to maintain with reference to this passage.

"Who once were not a people but are now the people of God, who had not obtained mercy but now have obtained mercy" (2:10). These words reference Hosea 2:23, in which God, calling the Hebrew nation no longer His people because of their sinfulness, promises that during the time of the Messiah, another people will become worthy of being called God's nation. This promise was fulfilled when the better part of the Jewish nation accepted Christianity.

From 2:11, the apostle begins his practical section of moral instructions concerning the internal and external life of a Christian. He reveals in detail the essence of the royal priesthood, what sort of spiritual sacrifices this priesthood should offer, and how Christians should act, so that pagans, seeing their virtuous life, would come to praise them instead of slandering them.

It is a historical fact that those among the pagans who were most antagonistic to Christianity in its early age were the elites, and Christianity initially spread among slaves. The difficult situations of these slaves only worsened after they accepted Christ, because generally Christians were persecuted. The sense of unfairness arising from this situation could lead those still new to the faith to abandon it altogether. To avoid this, St Peter (2:13–19) teaches submission to all human authorities "for the Lord's sake." This submission and the fact of Christian freedom are not mutually exclusive; on the contrary, true freedom places an obligation on the Christian to be obedient and to do one's duty to those in authority. Christian freedom is a freedom of the spirit, not an external freedom. Its essence is freedom from the bondage to sin, the sinful world, and the devil; however, at the same time, it is obedience to God. Therefore, it has its own responsibilities, required by the word of God. One can easily misuse Christian freedom, reinterpreting it to mean "the freedom to commit any sin one desires," and this is exactly what Christians must avoid. In his warning against such misuse of Christian freedom, the apostle, it is possible, had in mind the early gnostics who had begun to appear at that time. Calling all to a patient endurance of unjust suffering, the apostle shows us the ultimate example— Christ Himself (2:20–25), the "suffering Servant." St Peter exhorts us Christians to "follow His steps" and emulate His patient endurance of suffering.

In the third chapter, the apostle gives specific instructions to wives, husbands, and Christians in general. He commands wives to be submissive to their husbands. Here he especially speaks of Christian wives of pagan husbands. Of course, the lives of such women were especially difficult. They were often subject to a specific temptation—to put themselves under the direct guidance of people already converted to Christ, that is, men who were not their husbands and perhaps even the husbands of other women. This could lead to all manner of disorder in family life. The apostle takes special care to warn these wives against such a temptation, exhorting them to submit to their own husbands, even if they be unfaithful, pointing out the exalted purpose of this submissiveness: "that even if some do not obey the word, they, without a word, may be won by the conduct of their wives" (3:1).

Apostle Peter then explains that the true adornment of a Christian woman is not her external beauty, but the inner beauty of "a gentle and quiet spirit, which is very precious in the sight of God" (3:4). St Peter offers the example of Sarah, who was submissive to her husband Abraham. The difficult situations of wives, both in the ancient pagan and the Old Testament Hebrew worlds, must have inspired the apostle to give further instruction to the husbands concerning their wives, lest his words about a wife's submission lead husbands to abuse their wives. A good husband will treat his wife, the "weaker vessel" (3:7), with gentle care and love.

St Peter goes on to give more general instructions to Christians, telling them to rejoice if they are suffering for the truth, for "Christ also suffered once for sins, the just for the unjust, that He might bring us to God, being put to death in the flesh but made alive by the Spirit, by whom also He went and preached to the spirits in prison" (3:18–19). As the Greek word used here demonstrates, the word "prison" actually refers to hell or Sheol—a place where, as the Jews believed, the souls of all dead people went to await the coming of the Messiah. According to the Jewish reckoning, this place was located literally under the earth or within the earth. This is not hell as Christians understand it, a place of eternal suffering for sinners, although it was still an unpleasant, undesirable place of constraint, as indicated by the word "prison."

Before the coming of Christ, all those who died in the Old Testament went to this place, although it seems there were different degrees within Sheol that depended on the righteousness of a soul during life. It was to this "prison" that the Lord descended after His death to preach salvation to those already dead. He called all those who had died before His coming to enter the kingdom of Christ, and without doubt those who repented and believed were freed from this prison and were led by Christ to paradise, the place of rest for the righteous. According to tradition, this preaching of Christ in Sheol was preceded by St John the Baptist's preaching to the dead, as the Church professes in the troparion to St John the Baptist.[210]

"Who formerly were disobedient" (3:20)—this means that the preaching of Christ the Saviour was directed even to the most recalcitrant sinners, symbolized by those contemporaries of Noah who died during the flood. We can assume that even some of these people were saved by Christ's preaching in hell: "For this reason the gospel was preached also to those who are dead, that they might be judged according to men in the flesh, but live according to God in the spirit" (4:6). Thus, the apostle underlines that the preaching of Christ was directed to all people without exception, even to the most sinful of pagans (3:19–20).

Using the flood and the ark as a springboard, the apostle then discourses on the sacrament of baptism, of which the flood was a symbol. In 3:21, St Peter explains the essence of baptism. It is not "the removal of the filth of the flesh," such as, for example, the various oblation rituals of the Jews that could wash only the body but did not wash away the stain of sin. It is rather "the answer of a good conscience toward God." These words do not mean that baptism does not wash away spiritual stain, for baptism saves "through the resurrection of Jesus Christ." The apostle rather shows us the necessity for the baptized to live a new life according to a good conscience.

Chapter 4 is entirely dedicated to moral instruction, inspired by the sufferings of Christ: "Since Christ suffered for us in the flesh, arm yourselves also with the same mind, for he who has suffered in the flesh has ceased from sin" (4:1). The theme of this chapter is the patient endurance of suffering for the sake of the faith and the necessity to defeat the malicious attitude of the enemies of the faith by living a virtuous life. "He who has suffered in the flesh has ceased from sin"—physical suffering, either by willful ascesis or external persecution, weakens the activity and power of sinfulness in man. This also echoes St Paul's teaching in Romans 6—the one who has crucified himself together with Christ and who has died with Him dies to sin and must consider himself dead to sin, but alive only for God. St Peter urges Christians not to be disturbed that pagans revile them for the cardinal change in their manner of living after conversion, reminding them that the same pagans will have to answer for their dissolute life (4:2–6).

"But the end of all things is at hand" (4:7), for a Christian must always be ready for Christ's coming. A Christian must live a moral life crowned by love, because "love will cover a multitude of sins" (4:8), as St James also taught in his epistle. Chapter 4 ends with instructions for martyrs: "Beloved, do not think it strange concerning the fiery trial which is to try you" (4:12). Christians must confess their faith fearlessly, never worrying about revilement or suffering, instead always praising God for "the extent that you partake of Christ's sufferings" (4:13).

The fifth chapter contains instruction both to the pastors and to their flock, and it concludes with an apostolic blessing and personal greetings. St Peter urges pastors to "shepherd the flock of God ... serving as overseers, not by compulsion but willingly, not for dishonest gain but eagerly; nor as being lords of those entrusted to you, but being examples to the flock" (5:2–3). The flock, on their part, should submit to their pastors and humbly allow themselves to be led by the firm hand of God, but still to be sober and vigilant, "because your adversary the devil walks about like a roaring lion, seeking whom he may devour" (5:8).

St Peter here indicates three essential characteristics of a good pastor:

1. "Shepherd the flock of God which is among you, serving as overseers, not by compulsion but willingly" (5:2). The pastor must be filled with love for his great work. He must feel an internal calling to it, lest he become a hireling instead of a true pastor.

2. "Not for dishonest gain but eagerly" (5:2). Nonacquisitiveness is the second essential characteristic of a good priest. This does not mean that a pastor should expect no financial support from his flock (see 1 Cor 9:7, 13, 14), but only that a pastor dare not place his personal gain and financial profits as the cornerstone of his pastoral activity.

3. "Nor as being lords over those entrusted to you, but being examples to the flock" (5:3). A pastor cannot avoid having authority over his flock, but this power over them cannot be like earthly governments, filled with violence, constraint, and oppression—all of these being signs of self-love. A true pastor must be a good example of virtue to his flock. Then he will easily, without constraint, gather to himself the authority and spiritual influence over his flock.

For such good pastoral service, the holy apostle promises a "crown of glory" from the Chief Shepherd, Christ (5:4). "Likewise you younger people" (5:5), that is, all those who are not elders (presbyters) and are subordinate in the ecclesiastical hierarchy, "submit yourselves to your elders. Yes, all of you be submissive to one another, and be clothed with humility, for God resists the proud, but gives grace to the humble" (5:5). This means that everyone must submit to one's elders and the people in direct authority over them. By doing this, people show their humility, and humility is the only thing that attracts God's grace to man.

Then the apostle calls all to sobriety and spiritual vigilance, explaining that the enemy of our salvation, the devil, "walks about like a roaring lion, seeking whom he may devour" (5:8). Like a hungry beast, the devil is spiritually insatiable and eternally furious at those whom he cannot eat, and so he seeks to frighten them like a lion roaring and even to cause them harm. The best way to oppose the devil is by steadfast faith, for faith unites one with Christ, the defeater of the devil.

St Peter ends his first epistle with his desire that they be firm, unconquerable in faith. Then he passes on greetings from the Church in Babylon (or Rome) and from "Mark my son."[211] He then prays for "peace to you all who are in Christ Jesus" (5:14).

 CHAPTER 17

The Second General Epistle of the Holy Apostle Peter

THE PURPOSE OF THE SECOND EPISTLE OF PETER
As we see from this second epistle (2 Pet 3:1), it was written to the same Christians in Asia Minor that were the intended recipients of the first epistle. In the second epistle, Apostle Peter, with special forcefulness, tries to warn the faithful against the dissolute false teachers whose activity had apparently become even more dangerous than before. These false teachers were similar to those condemned by Apostle Paul in his pastoral epistles to Timothy and Titus. The Epistle of Jude condemns false teachers of a similar nature as well. Both apostles (Peter and Jude) describe the iniquitous heretics in almost the same terms (compare 2 Pet 2 with Jude). These false teachings were rooted in immorality and pagan pride.

THE PLACE AND TIME OF THE WRITING OF THE EPISTLE
We can determine the time of writing from internal evidence: "shortly I must put off my tent, just as our Lord Jesus Christ showed me" (2 Pet 1:14). Consequently, this second epistle was written not long before the martyrdom of St Peter, which occurred in A.D. 67, according to church tradition. And because this second epistle was obviously written after the first, it can be safely dated to A.D. 65–66. During the last years of his life, St Peter, according to tradition, lived in Rome, where he was martyred along with St Paul. Thus, the second epistle was written from Rome, being in a manner of speaking St Peter's last will and testament.

THE AUTHENTICITY OF THE EPISTLE
This second epistle was apparently not as widely circulated as the first epistle in the early Church. Therefore, some have expressed doubt about its authenticity. It was not included in the Syriac

Peshitta. However, we do find indications and hints of its existence in some of the Apostolic Fathers, such as St Clement of Rome; Hermas, the author of *The Shepherd*; Barnabas; and Polycarp. St Justin Martyr, Irenaeus of Lyons, and Theophilus of Alexandria refer to this epistle directly. According to Eusebius, Clement of Alexandria also wrote a commentary on this epistle. Origen cites the epistle, even though he did not hide his doubts about its authenticity. In the fourth century, Eusebius included it in his collection of the "general epistles," although he noted doubts concerning its authenticity. Jerome included it in his canonical collection as authentic.[212] Didymus of Alexandria did not have doubts about its canonicity. From the fourth century, all doubts concerning its authenticity cease.

The greater part of this epistle clearly bears the marks of the vivid personality of Apostle Peter, just like the first. If there are certain differences in voice or style compared with the first epistle, they are not significant and are easily explained by St Peter's lack of formal education. The general character of the epistle is obviously apostolic, and obviously Petrine.

The Structure and Content of the Epistle

The Second General Epistle of Peter has three chapters, divided thematically as follows:

1. Chapter 1: Introduction and greeting (1:1–2). The ladder of virtues (1:3–9). Exhortation to firmness, with a reference to his own death (1:10–15). On the transfiguration of Christ (1:16–18). Old Testament prophecy (1:19–21).
2. Chapter 2: False prophets and false teachers (2:1–3). Examples of divine punishment (2:4–9). A detailed characterization of false teachers (2:10–15). The example of Balaam (2:15–16). Continuation of the characterization (2:17–19). Woe to them (2:20–22).
3. Chapter 3: False teachers and false teachings concerning the second coming of Christ and the end of the world. A new heaven and new earth (3:1–15). Apostle Paul (3:16). Final instructions (3:17–18).

Exegetical Analysis of the Second Epistle of Peter

The first chapter can be called instructional, the second—cautionary, the third—prophetic.

Chapter 1 begins, as usual, with an introduction, in which the author calls himself "Simon Peter, a bondservant and apostle of Jesus Christ" (1:1). He immediately raises the recipients of his letter to a similar dignity with himself as those "who have obtained like precious faith." It is possible that by using this expression Apostle Peter wanted only to underline that Christians from among the Jews are not preferred over Christians from the Gentiles, because the faith of both is equally precious in the sight of God. In verse 2, he expresses his desire that "grace and peace be multiplied to you in the knowledge of God and of Jesus our Lord." By this he means that the abundance of grace and peace depend on the knowledge of God and Jesus Christ. The deeper and greater this knowledge, the more grace we receive.

The apostle then begins to describe a ladder of virtuous ascent to Christian perfection. The base of this ladder of ascent is faith. If one believes, one must strive to prove the truth of faith by an active, virtuous life, which then leads gradually to the height of Christian perfection, to love. Whoever disregards these fruits of true faith "is shortsighted" (1:9). Having offered this ladder of spiritual ascent, the Holy Apostle Peter urges us to ascend it: "Therefore, brethren, be even more diligent to make your call and election sure" (1:10). The apostle worries that his listeners will not walk up this ladder, and so he considers it necessary to repeat his instructions to them while he is still "in this tent … knowing that shortly I must put off my tent" (1:13–14). Peter exhorts them to continue recalling his words even after his death, for his teachings are not without proof. Everything he teaches, he saw himself as an eyewitness of the glory of the Divine Teacher, Jesus Christ. He was even present on Mt Tabor during the Transfiguration of Christ.

If all this is not enough proof, then "we have the prophetic word confirmed" (1:19). The Old Testament prophets foresaw everything that Peter saw and heard in person. The apostle indicates to his listeners that they should be guided by these prophetic words, for they are "as a light that shines" in the darkness of the human heart, still unillumined by the light of Christ's teaching "until the day dawns and the morning star rises in your hearts" (1:19). What a wonderful image of the illumination of a human soul that has risen up from sinful sleep to see the light of Christ's teaching! "No prophecy of Scripture is of any private interpretation, for prophecy never came by the will of man, but holy men of God spoke as they were moved by the Holy Spirit" (1:20–21).

In chapter 2, the apostle warns against false teachers. Just as in previous times false prophets appeared among the people, so they will continue to appear even now. Their characteristic trait is "denying the Lord who bought [redeemed] them" (2:1), that is, they will reject the dogma of the incarnation of the Son of God. However, their condemnation, as those unrepentant, is already prepared by God (2:1–3).

To turn the people away from false teachers, St Peter then offers frightening examples of God's punishment. He reminds them of the fallen angels who, bound by the chains of hellish darkness, await their final judgment. Then, St Peter speaks of the punishment of all sinful mankind in the flood, when only eight people survived. God's judgment also did not spare the inhabitants of Sodom and Gomorrah, and only Lot was saved. St Peter concludes that God knows how to deliver the righteous and how "to reserve the unjust under punishment for the day of judgment" (2:9).

In his characterization of false teachers, St Peter says that they "walk according to the flesh in the lust of uncleanness and despise authority. They are presumptuous, self-willed. They are not afraid to speak evil of dignitaries" (2:10). It is well known that these false teachers despised the apostles of Christ, not to mention presbyters and priests. They, like irrational beasts, were guided in their activity by sensual motivations and desire for profit: "They have forsaken the right way and gone astray, following the way of Balaam the son of Beor, who loved the wages of unrighteousness" (2:15). This Balaam, whose story is told in Numbers 22, was ready to do an evil deed for money—to curse the nation of Israel. But he was rebuked by God through the mouth of his own donkey, who spoke to him in a human voice.

These traits described by Peter correspond to the teaching of certain later gnostic sects, as well as of the forerunners of gnostics, the followers of Simon Magus and Nicholas. As a way of subverting people to their false teaching, these heretics (whom St Peter calls "wells without water" in 2:17) use "great swelling words of emptiness" (2:18) as well as the enticement of lust and the promise of so-called freedom. Flattering words, carnal lust, and a promise of freedom are the usual enticements used by both ancient and modern deluders of mankind. Being in actual fact "slaves of corruption" (2:19) and sin, they only cover their own lasciviousness with a delusion of freedom.

At the end of chapter 2, the apostle mentions a particular iniquity of these heretics: "It would have been better for them not to have known the way of righteousness"—for their ignorance would have mollified their fault, as we see in Luke 12:48—"than having known it, to turn from the holy commandment delivered to them" (2:21). The apostle compares them with dogs that return to their own vomit and pigs that jump into the dirt right after being washed.

In chapter 3, St Peter speaks of "scoffers" who mock the Christian expectation of the second coming of Christ. Then he tells of the fate of the world at its end. Just as the first world was destroyed in the waters of the flood (even though the people of that time believed that the world was eternal and could not be destroyed), so this world will be destroyed by fire. The world created by the Word of God is preserved by the same Word, but only for a time, until the "day of judgment and perdition of ungodly men" (3:7). As for the apparent delay in the Lord's coming, it cannot be ascribed to the One for Whom time does not exist and for Whom "one day is as a thousand years, and a thousand years as one day" (3:8). If God's providence concerning the end of the world has yet to be fulfilled, the reason is God's love for man and His longsuffering. "The Lord is not slack concerning His promise … but is longsuffering toward us, not willing that any should perish but that all should come to repentance" (3:9).

The end of the world will come unexpectedly: no one will know when it will come. Like the Lord, Peter compares it to a thief breaking into a house at night (see Matt 24:43). This image is not accidental, because those who are submerged in the sleep of sin and lack of vigilance will lose everything that they have gained and had, for the end will come and take it all and destroy it. With the coming of this day of the Lord, the world will itself be transfigured: "The heavens will pass away with a great noise, and the elements will melt with fervent heat; both the earth and the works that are in it will be burned up" (3:10, see also Matt 24:35, Rev 20:11). These "elements" are the constituent parts of nature, which the ancients believed to be fire, water, air, and earth. All will fall apart but will not be destroyed. It will all be transformed and renewed, but the earth and all its "works"—that is, nature, art, trees, plants, minerals, animals, cities, houses, weapons, institutions—all this will be destroyed in terrifying fashion by fire (cf. Hab 2:13).

This old world, destroyed by fire, will then be revealed as transfigured and renewed. Just as in the beginning of the world formless chaos was molded in the six days of creation into a beautiful and orderly form, so too during the end, the world will be recreated from the chaos of the inferno by the same creative word of the Creator into a more beautiful and perfect life. "Nevertheless we, according to His promise, look for new heavens and a new earth in which righteousness dwells" (3:13). This prophecy echoes Isaiah, when he was speaking in the name of God: "For behold, I create new heavens and a new earth; and the former shall not be remembered or come to mind" (Isa 65:17). "For as the days of a tree, so shall be the days of My people, And My elect shall long enjoy the work of their hands" (Isa 66:22). St John the Theologian also foresaw this end: "Now I saw a new heaven and a new earth, for the first heaven and the first earth had passed away" (Rev 21:1).

In that new world, righteousness will dwell—the full and complete harmony between the righteousness of men and the righteousness of God. It will be a world of justice that does not exist on this earth. Without doubt, St Peter said this to comfort the faithful who had endured sorrows from human injustice. However, this word "righteousness" can be understood in a broader sense—in the promised land an eternal life of blessedness will begin for the righteous, no longer marred by any manifestation of evil, for there God will be "all in all" (1 Cor 15:28).

Keeping the hope of this coming world alive, St Peter urges the faithful to preserve themselves unspotted and blameless. "And consider that the longsuffering of our Lord is salvation—as also our beloved brother Paul, according to the wisdom given to him, has written to you, as also in all his epistles, speaking in them of these things, in which are some things hard to understand, which untaught and unstable people twist to their own destruction, as they do also the rest of the Scriptures" (3:15–16). Evidently, false teachers misused the epistles of St Paul and falsely insisted that there were disagreements between the teachings of Peter and Paul. Perhaps they had heard of their well-known argument in Antioch (see Gal 2:11) and used this to confuse the faithful. Therefore, St Peter calls St Paul a beloved brother, desiring to affirm his authority.

The difficulty in understanding some of Paul's words that Peter references cannot be understood as a shortcoming in Paul's own teaching. Rather, Paul's teaching is so profound and exalted that it can be inaccessible to people who are newly established in the faith, and thus it can be easily perverted by the wicked. St Paul admitted as much in his epistles (Rom 3:8, 2 Thess 2:2).

In the conclusion to his letter, St Peter urges the faithful to be aware of the false teachers, to be firm in faith, and to grow in grace and knowledge of the Lord Jesus Christ, "to [Whom] be the glory both now and forever. Amen" (3:18).

 Chapter 18

The First General Epistle
of the Holy Apostle John the Theologian

The Author of the Epistle

Although the author never identifies himself by name in the epistle, ancient tradition has always ascribed it to the beloved disciple of Christ, the evangelist St John the Theologian. The very style of the letter vividly reminds the reader of the language of St John's Gospel, as do also many expressions and phrases.

St John the Theologian was the son of a Galilean fisherman named Zebedee and his wife Salome. Tradition says that Salome was a daughter of Joseph the Betrothed from his first marriage. Therefore, she was the Theotokos's stepdaughter, and a stepsister to Christ. This made St John effectively Christ's nephew, in the eyes of the people. He had an older brother, James, who was also one of the Twelve. Both brothers were called "Boanerges" by the Lord, which means "Sons of Thunder," for their powerful spirit and fiery zeal (see Mark 3:17). Submitting to the call of the Lord (Matt 4:21, Luke 5:10), St John left his father's house and became one of Christ's closest disciples, along with Peter and his brother James (Mark 5:37; Matt 17:1, 26:37).

The Lord loved John especially ardently, which was touchingly evident at the Mystical Supper, when John reclined against the breast of his Divine Teacher (John 13:23, 25), and especially at the crucifixion. From the Cross, Christ committed His Most Pure Mother to John's filial care (John 19:26). Gratefully remembering all this, St John never called himself by name in his Gospel, but referred to himself only as "the disciple whom Jesus loved" (John 13:23; 19:26; 20:2; 21:7, 20). He returned Christ's love with a devoted love of his own; if the love of Peter was more active and fiery (John 18:10, 21:15), then the love of John was most profound and loyal. Only John, of all the disciples, did not abandon his Master during His passion, but stood on Golgotha at the foot of the Cross (John 19:26).

After the ascension of the Lord and the descent of the Holy Spirit, St John remained in Jerusalem for fifteen years until the blessed repose of the Mother of God, who had been entrusted to St John's care. Together with Peter and James, St John played an active role in the formation of the Church in Jerusalem, and so together with them he is considered one of its pillars (Gal 2:9). When the newly converted Samaritans were baptized, St John traveled to them together with St Peter to invoke the Holy Spirit upon them (Acts 8:14). Later he preached in the Roman province of Asia Minor, and after the deaths of Peter and Paul, he established his permanent place of residence in Ephesus. From there, he presided over all the churches of Asia Minor as their supreme pastor.

From Ephesus, he was exiled to the island of Patmos during the reign of Domitian, after his life had been miraculously preserved when he was thrown into a vat of boiling oil. During this exile, he composed the Apocalypse concerning the future of the Church and the world. During Nerva's reign, he returned to Ephesus and there, already at the end of the first century, he composed his Gospel and then his three epistles because of the persistent urging of many. He remained a virgin his whole life and died a somewhat-mysterious death at the dawn of the second century, being more than one hundred years of age. He died in Ephesus, which was known during the Ottoman times as *Agios Theologos* (Holy Theologian) in Greek, or *Ayasoluk* in Turkish, in honor of St John.

ATTRIBUTION OF THE FIRST EPISTLE OF JOHN

Even though St John never calls himself by name in the epistle, he does present himself as an eyewitness of the earthly life of the Lord Jesus Christ (1 John 1:1–4). All of Christian antiquity universally accepted St John the Theologian as the author of this epistle. Especially important are the witnesses of St Polycarp and St Papias of Hierapolis, who were disciples of St John, as well as St Irenaeus of Lyons, who was a disciple of St Polycarp. We also find references to St John's authorship in Clement of Alexandria, Tertullian, Origen, Dionysius of Alexandria, and others. This epistle is included in the Muratorian Canon and in the Syriac Peshitta. Eusebius included it among the indisputably canonical books of Scripture.[213] There have never been any doubts concerning the authenticity of this epistle in the early Church.

All internal evidence points to the authorship of the same person who wrote the fourth Gospel. It has the same voice and style, the same spirit and tone of love and heartfelt warmth, united with fatherly gravity, the same depth and power of feeling. Dionysius of Alexandria notes the repetition of words and phrases in the Gospel and the epistle:

> [T]here is indeed a mutual agreement between the Gospel [according to John] and the epistle, and they begin alike … [The author] is consistent with himself and does not depart from what he has proposed, but proceeds throughout under the same

heads and expressions ... But the attentive reader will find frequently in one and the other "the life," "the light," "turning from darkness," continually "the truth," "the grace," "the joy," "the flesh and blood of the Lord," "the judgment," "the forgiveness of sins," "the love of God toward us," the commandment that we should "love one another," that we should "keep all the commandments," the "conviction" of "the world," of the devil, of the Antichrist, the promise of the Holy Spirit, the adoption of the sons of God, the faith that is demanded of us throughout; the "Father" and "the Son": these are to be found everywhere.[214]

THE PLACE AND TIME OF THE WRITING OF THE EPISTLE

The first words of the epistle and its tone and character make it obvious that it was written after the Gospel. The first words refer to another written work of this same author: "That which was from the beginning, which we have heard, which we have seen with our eyes ... we declare to you" (1 John 1:1–3). This is what St John spoke of in his Gospel, and he reminds his readers of that Gospel to strengthen them in the true faith. This is why there is an ancient tradition in the Church that says that this first epistle was written a long time after the Gospel, probably at the end of the first century.

Since the last years of his life were spent in Asia Minor in Ephesus, without doubt this epistle was written there.

THE PURPOSE OF THE FIRST EPISTLE OF JOHN

By its content, we can determine that the first epistle of St John was written for the Christians of the churches in Asia Minor that had long ago been established. By now, these churches were predominantly filled with Christians of pagan background rather than of Jewish extraction (1 John 5:21). By the time of the writing of this epistle, various cunning gnostic heresies had arisen and spread widely, largely replacing the Judaizing heresies and paganism. By this time, Apostles Jude, Peter, and Paul (in his pastoral epistles) had all written against the spread of these dangerous heresies. This danger continued to threaten the churches in Asia Minor, and so Apostle John decided to write his own refutation (1 John 2:19–22; 4:1–3, 5).

These gnostics rejected the divinity of Jesus Christ and His role as the Saviour of the world, and for this reason, they also rejected the reality of His incarnation. They were remarkable for their pride in their so-called wisdom (1 John 2:3, 4, 29; 4:6), they were morally dissolute (1 John 3:4–10), insisting that their exalted knowledge (*gnosis*) gave them the right for complete moral freedom, meaning debauchery, to which they abandoned themselves.

Thus, the character of this epistle is exhortative and accusatory, although it is not openly polemical, just as there is no polemic in John's Gospel. St John's purpose in writing the epistle is the same as in writing the Gospel—to strengthen faith in Jesus Christ as the Son of God, so that all can receive through Him eternal life and abide in truth and love.

THE STRUCTURE AND CONTENT OF THE EPISTLE

The First Epistle of John has five chapters, divided thus:

1. Chapter 1: The indubitable truth of the Gospel of the word of life (1:1–4). God is light (1:5). Communion with God and Christ (1:6–10).
2. Chapter 2: Christ, the propitiation for the sins of the whole world (2:1–2). Knowledge of Christ and communion with Him as with the light of love (2:3–11). The possibility of such communion for everyone (2:12–14). Opposed to this is the love of the world (2:15–16). The last times, the antichrist, and antichrists (2:17–19). The true teaching of Christ, as opposed to false anti-Christian teachings (2:20–29).
3. Chapter 3: Sons of God and children of the devil (3:1–10). Brotherly love for one's neighbor and hatred (3:11–18). The consolation of the heart in God (3:19–22). Faith and love (3:23–24).
4. Chapter 4: The Spirit of God and the spirits of delusion (4:1–6). The love of God and love for God (4:7–10). Love for one's neighbor (4:11–12). Love for God and one's neighbor (4:14–21).
5. Chapter 5: The victory of the faithful and love over the world (5:1–5). Three witnesses in heaven and on earth (5:6–9). The inner witness of a believer (5:14–15). A brother who falls into sin (5:16–19). God is true (5:20–21).

EXEGETICAL ANALYSIS OF THE FIRST EPISTLE OF JOHN

In his first epistle, St John speaks to the faithful as a father to his children, completely without artifice, not following a strict order to his thoughts, often repeating the same expressions. Therefore, it is difficult to arrange the epistle thematically.

The first chapter begins with an authentication of the truth of the Gospel of the Word of Life. John speaks of the purpose of writing the Gospels: "that you also may have fellowship with us; and truly our fellowship is with the Father and with His Son Jesus Christ" (1:3), and also "that your joy may be full" (1:4). As in his Gospel, St John calls the Second Person of the Holy Trinity "the Word." St John witnesses that what he speaks of is not hearsay, rather he was a direct eyewitness of all that he writes about. "That your joy may be full"—this expression is quintessentially Johannine (John 15:11, 17:13).

Then St John describes the conditions and commandments upon which communion with God depends:

1. Walking in the light: "If we say that we have fellowship with Him, and walk in darkness, we lie and do not practice the truth" (1:6).
2. Love of one's neighbor: "If we walk in the light as He is in the light, we have fellowship with one another, and the blood of Jesus Christ His Son cleanses us from all sin" (1:7).

3. Confession of sins: "If we confess our sins," that is, not only acknowledge their existence but repent of them openly before God and witnesses who have the right to bind and loosen (see John 20:22–23), then "He is faithful and just to forgive us our sins and to cleanse us from all unrighteousness" (1:8–9). However, "if we say that we have not sinned, we make Him a liar, and His word is not in us," we reject the entire teaching of Christ about His redemptive sacrifice for the sins of mankind (1:10).

In the second chapter, the apostle says that Christ is "the propitiation for our sins, and not for ours only but also for the whole world" (2:2), not only the people living then, but also those who lived before and who will live until the second coming. This is the essential teaching of Christianity. But how are we to use this propitiation? By fulfilling the commandments: "Now by this we know that we know Him, if we keep His commandments" (2:3). This keeping of the commandments is the only way a person can prove his love for God and fellow man, for the chief commandment of God is the commandment to love. This commandment is both ancient and new. It is ancient, because it existed in the Old Testament, written on the tablets of the Law and the hearts of the pagans, but before the coming of Christ, the world was a kingdom of darkness, and so the natural sense of love for others was dimmed by the contrary inducements of the devil.

When Christ offered Himself as a sacrifice and by His own blood redeemed the ancestral sin of mankind, he destroyed the kingdom of darkness on earth and renewed the ancient commandment of love in the hearts of reborn mankind. And so the ancient commandment became new and truly acquired a renewed, exalted character of purity, nonacquisitiveness, and inspiration, far greater than the love of pagans and Jews. Christian love is established on the exalted idea of the universal redemption accomplished by Christ and the spiritual unity of all mankind in Christ as members of a single spiritual body of Christ. This is why only Christianity insists on love for enemies, an idea that is absurd both for Judaism and paganism.

Therefore, whoever says that "he is in the light, and hates his brother, is in darkness until now" (2:9), that is, he is not yet a Christian. There is only one proof of a truly Christian disposition of soul—love for one's neighbor. Beginning with verse 12, the apostle begins a new instruction, a warning against love for the world directed at Christians of various ages. The thematic connection with the previous section is as follows: just as the unique characteristic of Christian perfection is love for God and man, so the greatest obstacle to achieving this essential commandment of Christianity is love for the world and for what is in the world. Therefore, the apostle warns people of all ages—children, parents, youths, and elders—against such love.

Evidently, St John means not physical age, but relative spiritual growth, although it is not necessary to fully exclude physical age as well, because sometimes (although not always) spiritual maturity corresponds with physical age. The apostle speaks to each age-group separately, exhorting them not to become attached to the world. For children, or those who after baptism have only begun the Christian life, the motivation to avoid love for the world is the forgiveness of sins in the sacrament of baptism. For parents, the motivation is the knowledge of God the Father, which they have already partially obtained as they developed in the moral and Christian life. For youth, whose tendency to become attached to the world is as strong as their inspiration to battle it, the motivation is the success they have already obtained in their victories over the evil one, as well as that knowledge of the all-powerful word of God that they have already gained by their careful study of the Scriptures. For "fathers," that is, men who have reached a high level of moral perfection, the knowledge of the One without beginning and His accomplishment of the great mystery of the salvation of mankind (determined from the beginning by God through His only begotten Son Jesus Christ) is motivation enough to prevent an attachment to the perishable and transient goods of this world.

"Do not love the world or the things in the world" (2:15). Of course, the "world" here is not the beautiful and all-wise creation of God, but everything that is corrupted by sin and everything that feeds sin in this world, that is, everything that has become antagonistic to God. The apostle himself gives a definition of the world that one should not love: "the lust of the flesh, the lust of the eyes, and pride of life" (2:16). According to the Holy Fathers, these are the three children of self-love, or "selfness," and these three in their turn are also the fathers of all other passions that bind a person. These include sensuality, love of money, and love of glory. To prevent people from loving and becoming attached to this world, the apostle explains that "the world is passing away, and the lust of it" (2:17), and only he who does the will of God will abide forever.

"Little children, it is the last hour" (2:18)—that is, the final epoch of God's economy for man has begun, which will end with the second coming of Christ and the end of the world. "And as you have heard that the Antichrist is coming, even now many antichrists have come" (2:18). The teaching about the coming of the antichrist, an actual human person (not a metaphor), can be found in the words of Jesus Christ Himself (John 5:43), as well as in the epistles of St Paul, written much earlier than the epistles of St John (2 Thess 2:3–9). Even though the antichrist has not yet come, his forerunners, the bearers of his spirit, have already appeared. These are doubtless the false teachers, such as Simon Magus, Cerinthus, and other gnostic heresiarchs against whom Apostles Peter and Jude had already written.

"They went out from us," that is, they were once orthodox Christians, but only nominally, while their inner disposition was foreign to the Church (2:19). "But you have an anointing from the Holy One, and you know all things" (2:20). Apostle John does not speak in detail about the "antichrists," for he is sure that Christians are illumined by the Spirit through the sacrament of chrismation. In the beginning of the Church, Christians received the gift of the Holy Spirit through the laying on of apostolic hands, but soon this action was replaced with the anointing of oil, as we see in 2 Corinthians 1:21–22 and Ephesians 4:30. "You know all things"—this means that Christians know all that is necessary for salvation, and so can discern the errors of the heretics.

Still, the most effective sign of recognizing false teachers is this—they either reject or pervert the true significance of Jesus Christ, the incarnate Son of God, as Redeemer of mankind from sin. Such a person "does not have the Father either" (2:23), for only through the Son of God can we come to know and love God the Father (Matt 11:27). If one wishes to attain such close union with the Son and the Father, one must firmly hold to the apostolic confession of faith, that is, all that "you heard from the beginning" (2:24). Only then can one receive eternal life.

Furthermore, the holy apostle again underlines the importance of the great gift of grace that the faithful receive through the sacrament of chrismation: "the anointing which you have received from Him abides in you, and you do not need that anyone teach you" (2:27). Then he exhorts them to hold firmly to the confession of the divinity of Jesus Christ, finishing his exhortation with a reminder of the imminence of the second coming of Christ and a promise of boldness, that is, a conviction that the faithful will be justified in the day of judgment: we will "not be ashamed before Him at His coming" (2:28).

In the third chapter, the apostle, based on his previous thoughts, speaks of the manifestation in this life of communion with God. By their lives, St John divides people into children of God and children of the devil. Because of the sin of Adam, mankind was bound to the devil; however, by the redemption of the Lord Jesus Christ, all people are given the possibility of becoming children of God, having received new life in the sacrament of baptism and being constantly strengthened in the divine life by the other sacraments and their own striving to follow the footsteps of Christ in this world by keeping His commandments.

"Whoever has been born of God does not sin" (3:9), meaning not that a believing Christian never sins (this would contradict John's own words in 1:8–10), but rather that a Christian does not quickly let himself return to the slavery to sin, but fights with all his strength against sin. If he does fall into sin, he hurries to confess it (1:10), not to serve it like an idol. In the same way, the expression "he who sins is of the devil" (3:8) does not refer to someone who hates the sin or evil that he does (see Rom 7:20), but rather this concerns the person who loves to sin and who sins with pleasure. This is one who abandons himself to his sin constantly and without remorse, not one who sins from weakness and, acknowledging the sin, repents of it and tries to wash it away through pure repentance and confession.

A unique characteristic of the children of God, as opposed to children of the devil, is their love for their fellow man and their faith in Jesus Christ as the actual Son of God, not a phantom (as some heretics, such as the Docetists, taught), Who came into the world in the flesh and Who suffered for the sins of the world. An example of the children of the devil is Cain. St John says that not only murderers are like Cain, but "whoever hates his brother" is like Cain, a murderer (3:15). The greatest example of true love for man is the Lord Jesus Christ Himself, Whom we must follow, Who "laid down His life for us" (3:16). True love for one's neighbor is proved with deeds of mercy: "My little children, let us not love in word or in tongue, but in deed and in truth" (3:18). The knowledge of true love for man that comes from the doing of good deeds calms the conscience and makes us bold in our prayers before God, giving us a kind of filial conviction that He will hear us. More-over, the apostle reminds his listeners that the command of God is one, although it consists of two parts: "that we should believe on the name of His Son Jesus Christ and love one another, as He gave us commandment" (3:23). If we fulfill this com-mandment, we will be found worthy of true unity with God, the proof of which is the Spirit of God abiding within us.

In the fourth chapter, the holy apostle exhorts Christians not to believe every spirit, "but test the spirits, whether they are of God" (4:1). The test to be used is the essential dogma of Christianity—the incarnation of the Son of God: "Every spirit that con-fesses that Jesus Christ has come in the flesh is of God, and every spirit that does not confess that Jesus Christ has come in the flesh is not of God" (4:2–3). Here "confesses" does not merely mean "with the lips," for we know from the Gospels that even the demons confessed the divinity of the Lord Jesus Christ through the mouths of the possessed. This confession refers more to the manner of life lived. According to St Irenaeus of Lyons, these words are directly aimed at the Docetists, who falsely taught that the Lord had only a phantasmal body, but He was not really physically incarnate.

This manifestation in the world of the "spirit of the antichrist" through the heretics should still not disturb Christians: "You are of God, little children, and have overcome them" (4:4). The work of God must triumph over all heresies. False teachers are victorious only temporarily, for they are of the world and know how to make their teachings palatable to the tastes and passions of the world, which is why the world listens to them. "We are of God. He who knows God hears us" (4:6). This is how to differentiate between "the spirit of truth and the spirit of error."

Another unique characteristic of the children of God is love for one's neighbor. Such love makes children of God spiritually like God and leads to close commu-nion with Him: "Let us love one another, for love is of God … God is love" (4:7–8). Whoever does not love his fellow man "does not know God." The expression "God is love" is found only in the writings of St John, not anywhere else in the Sacred Scriptures in this exact form, although its meaning is found in other places. This is the best and most complete expression of God's nature.

The most perfect demonstration of God's love for man is this: "that God has sent His only begotten Son into the world, that we might live through Him" (4:9). This is the strongest inducement for us to love both God and our fellow man, for only "he who abides in love abides in God, and God in him" (4:16). This love is so exalted in its perfection that it even attains boldness before the judgment of God, and completely banishes fear from the heart of the believer. Of course, the apostle only speaks here of the fear of the slave, which is incompatible with filial love for God; the fear of sons for their father is not excluded from such love. Calling all Christians to such love for God, the apostle forcefully insists that one can love God only if one actively loves one's fellow man: "If someone says, 'I love God,' and hates his brother, he is a liar" (4:20). It is much more difficult to love the invisible than the visible, and if someone does not love his brother, whom he sees, he cannot love God. More than that, this is the command of God, that he who loves God should love his brother as well (see Matt 22:38–39).

In the fifth chapter, the holy apostle explains that the commandment to love one's fellow man is not difficult for a Christian, for it naturally follows from the commandment to love God: "Everyone who loves Him who begot also loves him who is begotten of Him" (5:1). Love for one's fellow man is an essential consequence of our divine sonship. God is our common loving Father, and all of us are His children. Therefore, all mankind are our brothers. The sign of true love for God is the keeping of His commandments, which is not difficult for one who loves God. The believer also has special power to help him keep the commandments, a power that triumphs over the world with all its temptations. This power is faith in the Son of God: "This is the victory that has overcome the world—our faith" (5:4), because, depending on our faith, we are given gracious help of God to fight temptations. The greatest example of victory over the world is the apostles of Christ, who brought the entire inhabited world, which was initially so opposed to God, to the foot of the Cross.

As proof of the truth of our faith in Jesus Christ as the incarnate Son of God, Who came into the world and Who gave us eternal life and victory over the world with its sinful temptations, St John refers to three witnesses in heaven and three witnesses on earth. The heavenly witnesses are the Father, the Word, and the Holy Spirit, and the earthly witnesses are the Spirit (the same Holy Spirit, not in His hypostasis, but in His energies that bear witness to Christ and make the redemption accomplished by the Redeemer their own for those who believe in Him), water, and blood, which flowed out of the side of Jesus, the true Man. These then became the material elements of the two greatest sacraments—baptism and the Eucharist.

In the Levite worship of the Old Testament, the most important sacred actions that purified sins and reconciled Israel with God were the purification by water and purification by the sacrificial blood (see Num 19:9, Lev 14:5–7). These actions, and indeed the entirety of the ritual law of Moses, had a prefigurative meaning with reference to Christ and the atonement of mankind that he accomplished (see Heb 10:1, 1 Cor 10:1). Christ abolished the types and figures of the Old Covenant and replaced it with the very essence of things or with the truth, but under an image, because for mankind (made up of body and soul), the image is necessary to understand the full truth. Thus, the type or figure is replaced by the antitype (or image). Water is an image of baptism, and blood is the image of the redemption of mankind by the death of Christ the Saviour upon the Cross.

Thus, the coming of Jesus Christ by blood and water (5:6) is the establishment by Him of the sacraments of baptism and communion. "Not only by water, but by water and blood": These words, evidently, are directed against Cerinthus, a heretic who taught that the divinity of Christ descended upon the man Jesus at the moment of his baptism by John, and then departed from Jesus during the Passion, so that it was not the Son of God who suffered and died, but only a man.

Furthermore, a Christian has an inner witness to this truth as well (see 2:20): this is the affirmation or witness in his own spirit which is sealed by the anointing (2:20) or by the seal of the Holy Spirit (see 2 Cor 1:21–22), by which he knows and is sure that he is reconciled with God in Christ and has hope for eternal life. The Lord Himself spoke of this inner witness (see John 7:16, 3:33).

This inner witness is also expressed by boldness in prayer: "If we ask anything according to His will, He hears us" (5:14). Therefore, if we pray for our sinful brother as an expression of love, "He will give him life" (5:16). At the same time, the apostle makes an important qualification: "if anyone sees his brother sinning a sin which does not lead to death" (5:16). This differentiation between a mortal sin and "a sin which does not lead to death" has the same meaning as the Lord's words about every sin being forgiven, except blasphemy against the Holy Spirit (Matt 12:31–32). A sin that does not lead to death is any sin that comes from human weakness, a sin that is purified by sincere repentance and compunction, not leading the sinner to spiritual death. A mortal sin is a grievous sin that so hardens the sinner that he becomes incapable of repentance.

Such sins include stubborn unbelief; apostasy that refuses to listen to any exhortation; and persistence in heretical beliefs or unrepented sins that become, as it were, a second nature for the sinner (and, therefore, impossible to heal). Apparently, St John believed that one cannot be sure of the power of prayer for a sinner who is guilty of mortal sin, for this prayer is actively opposed by the person's unbelief and obduracy.

In the conclusion to his letter (5:18–21), the apostle briefly summarizes the main themes of the epistle: those born of God do not sin, that is, they are not defeated by sin permanently, because they keep within themselves the grace of renewal, and the evil one cannot touch them; Christians are of God, and the world of unbelief lies in evil; and the Son of God gave us a true calling—to keep ourselves from idols, that is, from evil in general.

 CHAPTER 19

The Second General Epistle
of the Holy Apostle John the Theologian

PRELIMINARY REMARKS

Origen, Eusebius, and Blessed Jerome enumerated the Second General Epistle of St John (just as the Third General Epistle of St John) among the books of Scripture that were not universally accepted as canonical or belonging to the apostle. This epistle and the third epistle are absent from the Peshitta, the early fifth-century Syriac translation of the Bible, although this does not mean that the Syriac churches did not accept these epistles as authentic. St Irenaeus of Lyon, a disciple of St Polycarp of Smyrna, who himself was a disciple of St John the Theologian, however, cites the Second General Epistle of St John in his writings. Clement of Alexandria considered the epistle to be authentic, and so did St Dionysius of Alexandria. Clement wrote a commentary on all seven general epistles, including 2 John. The Muratorian Canon mentions "many" epistles of St John. And even though Origen, Eusebius, and Jerome attest to the doubts that existed regarding the authorship of 2 John, they themselves do not seem to question the epistle's authenticity.[215]

There is also internal evidence for the authenticity of this epistle. The spirit, tone, style, and language of the epistle remind the reader both of the first epistle and of the Gospel of John. It is not unusual that this epistle, just as 3 John, was not immediately known throughout the Church, for it is very short; moreover, both were written to private individuals. With time, they gained general acceptance and eventually were included in the canon of the New Testament Scriptures.

We have no firm evidence concerning the original purpose of this epistle outside of what is written in the epistle itself. Who the "elect lady and her children" were is not known. It is only clear that they were Christians. As for the time and place of writing, we can only assume that it was written around the same time as the first epistle, also in Ephesus.

The Second General Epistle of John has only one chapter. In it, the apostle expresses his joy that the elect lady's children walk in the truth. He promises to visit her and insists forcefully that she have no interaction with false teachers.

EXEGETICAL ANALYSIS OF THE SECOND EPISTLE OF JOHN

In the beginning, St John does not call himself by name, instead preferring to refer to himself as "the elder," probably because he was already quite old at the time of writing (around one hundred years old). The "elect lady" to whom the epistle is addressed was probably a Christian woman of means, well known, perhaps of a noble or ruling family. Because St John mentions her children, but not her husband, we may assume she was a widow. The apostle says that he loves her pious family "in truth," with love in Christ, and not only he, but "all those who have known the truth" (verse 1). The reason for this love is the truth, which is a constant first principle for the spiritual life of Christians.

In the first half of this epistle, having bestowed upon her "grace, mercy, and peace," the apostle expresses his joy in the faith and piety of her children "walking in truth," that is, on the correct path of Christian truth, both in the knowledge and in the worship of the true God. He exhorts both the elect lady and her children to be ever more confirmed in love, the foundational Christian commandment (verse 6).

The second half of the letter is dedicated to warnings against the powerful influence of "deceivers … who do not confess Jesus Christ as coming in the flesh," that is, who reject the mystery of the incarnation of the Son of God, "that we do not lose those things we worked for" (verses 7–8), that is, lest our efforts to win eternal salvation come to naught. Having called these false teachers "deceivers and antichrists," the apostle forbids her to accept them into her house or even to greet them, clearly because whoever becomes friendly with a false teacher subjects himself to the danger of being affected by his heresy. This unusual strictness of the "Apostle of love" is striking and so contrary to the modern idea of ecumenism that hopes for closer cooperation with the heterodox for the sake of "mutual understanding."

St John concludes his letter by expressing his hope to see the lady in person soon and passes greetings from the children of her sister ("the children of your elect sister greet you"), who either lived in a different place or had died. The letter closes with "Amen" (verses 12–13).

[Some Christian writers (Hilary of Arles, Oecumenius, Andrew) have suggested, however, that the reference to the "elect lady" in this epistle may refer allegorically to a local Christian church to which St John addresses the letter, in a similar manner as the Church is described symbolically as a Lady in the second-century work *The Shepherd* by St Hermas (Vision 2, 4). In this case, the "elect sister" with her "children" at the conclusion of the epistle refer to the local church community where St John resided at the time. Blessed Theophylact of Ochrid references this opinion, but does not explicitly support it.[216]]

 CHAPTER 20

The Third General Epistle
of the Holy Apostle John the Theologian

PRELIMINARY REMARKS

Both tradition and internal evidence confirm the authenticity of the Third General Epistle of St John. If we compare the tone, spirit, and style of this epistle with the first epistle and John's Gospel, it becomes evident that this third epistle was also composed by the beloved disciple of Christ.

This epistle was written to a certain Gaius. Who this Gaius was is not exactly certain. We know several bearers of this name from apostolic writings and from the church tradition (see Acts 19:29, 20:4; Rom 16:23; 1 Cor 1:14; and others), but it is not possible to determine whether any one of these is the intended recipient of the letter. Apparently, this Gaius was not a priest or bishop, but merely a pious Christian known for his hospitality.

Both the third and second epistles supposedly were written at about the same time, probably in the same city of Ephesus, where St John lived out the final years of his earthly life.

This epistle has only one chapter. In it, the apostle praises Gaius for his virtuous life, firmness in faith, and his walking in the truth. Especially praised is his hospitality to traveling preachers of the word of God. St John also condemns a certain Diotrephes and passes on private news and greetings.

EXEGETICAL ANALYSIS OF THE THIRD EPISTLE OF JOHN

In this epistle, as in the second, the holy apostle does not call himself by name, going by the title "Elder." He calls Gaius "beloved," an address he often uses in the first general epistle. The apostle expresses his desire "that you may prosper in all things and be in health, just as your soul prospers" (verse 2). In other words, St John hopes that his earthly affairs have the same success as his life in the Gospel. This is the greatest of praise that the apostle could give. St John explains that some others have told him that Gaius holds firm to the teaching of the Gospel and "walk[s] in the truth."

"I have no greater joy than to hear that my children walk in truth" (verse 4). This is an important and characteristic thought, showing that in Christianity, it is the *truth*—that is, the uncorrupted, authentic, pure teaching of Christ—that is the most precious treasure. St John praises Gaius for his hospitality to the "brethren," or Christians in general, and especially "for strangers" (verse 5), meaning those who travel from distant places. In particular, the word "strangers" referred to itinerant preachers of the Gospel. They "have borne witness of your love before the church" (verse 6). Evidently, having stayed with Gaius and come to Ephesus, these preachers told of his hospitality to all. "If you send them forward on their journey in a manner worthy of God, you will do well" (verse 7). In other words, if he continues his hospitality by offering them everything necessary for their journey, it will be the right thing to do (see also 1 Cor 16:10–11, Titus 3:13).

The manner in which St John speaks about these "strangers" that "they went forth for His name's sake" (verse 7), makes it clear that these "strangers" were preachers of the Gospel, who were at that time known as "evangelists." These evangelists took nothing from pagans, lest ill-intentioned people consider their preaching to be a source of profit. Therefore, it was the responsibility of other Christians to provide material support to these preachers (verses 5–8).

"I wrote to the Church," St John continues. It is unclear to which church he wrote or why, but apparently it is the one to which Gaius belonged, as well as a certain Diotrephes, mentioned later in the letter. We cannot imagine, however, that this letter did not survive. It would be perhaps more accurate to read this passage as follows: I would have written to your church concerning these traveling preachers, but "Diotrephes, who loves to have the preeminence among them, does not receive us" (verse 9). It is unclear who this Diotrephes was, although he was evidently a proud, ambitious, and self-willed man. St John accuses Diotrephes of lacking brotherly love for the traveling preachers of the Gospel, and he threatens him with a strict and powerful word to cease his disorderly behavior.

St John exhorts Gaius not to follow the example of such evil men, but to continue to do good. He then praises a certain Demetrius who, according to tradition, was the bishop of Philadelphia. He then promises to come himself and passes on greetings from friends.

 CHAPTER 21

The General Epistle
of the Holy Apostle Jude

THE AUTHOR OF THE EPISTLE

The author names himself as "Jude, a bondservant of Jesus Christ, and brother of James" (verse 1). This suggests that this is the same person as Apostle Judas of the Twelve, who was known also as Judas the son of James, Thaddeus, or Lebbaeus (see Matt 10:3, Mark 3:18, Luke 6:16, Acts 1:13, John 14:21). He was a son of Joseph, the betrothed of Mary, from his first wife, and a brother to James, the bishop of Jerusalem, called the Just, as well as to Joses and Simon, who later also became bishop of Jerusalem. According to tradition, his first name was Judas, and the name Thaddeus he received after his baptism from John the Baptist, while the name Lebbaeus he received when he joined the rank of the Twelve, perhaps to differentiate him from Judas Iscariot, who became a traitor.

Some consider that the writer of this epistle had nothing in common with the Judas of the Twelve (in verse 17, he seems to exclude himself from the rank of the apostles). These people consider him to be an apostle only in the general sense, because he was the brother of James and thus "a brother of the Lord." John 7:5 is usually cited to support this, because it says that the brothers of Jesus did not believe in Him during His earthly life, which is why they were not included in the Twelve. Moreover, the adherents of this view believe that Apostle Judas of the Twelve could not have written this epistle, because he preached in Syria and died in Edessa, but the Peshitta, the Syriac translation of the Scriptures, does not include the Epistle of St Jude. This opinion is a plausible one, but due to limited evidence, it is hardly possible to determine the final resolution of this question.

Tradition tells that Judas preached in Judea, Galilee, Samaria, and Idumea after the ascension of the Lord, and later he traveled to

Arabia, Syria, Mesopotamia, Persia, and Armenia. The same tradition tells that he was in Edessa, where Apostle Thaddeus (Addai) of the Seventy had preached a short while before. According to one tradition, St Jude died peacefully in Edessa, whereas another tradition says that he died in Beirut. Yet another tradition tells of his martyrdom in Armenia after being hanged on a tree and pierced with arrows.

THE AUTHENTICITY OF THE EPISTLE OF JUDE

Tertullian and Clement of Alexandria clearly attest to the authenticity of this epistle. Origen praises it as filled with heavenly grace. It is included in the number of the general epistles of the Muratorian Canon, but it is missing from the Syriac Peshitta. Eusebius, Jerome, and Amphilochius mention that not all churches initially accepted the canonicity of this epistle. The reason for their doubts, according to Jerome, was the content of the epistle itself. In verse 14, St Jude cites a prophecy of Enoch that was probably taken from the apocryphal Book of Enoch, and some considered this reference enough reason to discount the canonicity of Jude as well. Moreover, verse 9 speaks of an argument between Archangel Michael and the devil concerning the body of Moses, but this argument is not known in the Old Testament Scriptures, although it is found in the apocryphal "Assumption of Moses" (also known as the "Ascension of Moses"). In the fourth century, all doubts ceased, and the Epistle of St Jude was accepted into the New Testament canon.

THE PURPOSE OF THE EPISTLE OF JUDE

From verse 3, we know that St Jude wanted to write "concerning our common salvation." Another reason was the spread of false, proto-gnostic teachings against which the Apostles James, Peter, and John also struggled, as can be clearly seen in their general epistles. St Jude openly says that he writes because certain evil people have crept into the society of Christians "who turn the grace of our God into lewdness" (verse 4). Doubtless these were early gnostics who preached debauchery under the pretext of "Christian freedom" and, ironically, for the purposes of mortifying the flesh, as they considered matter not to be God's creation, but the creation of lower powers opposed to God. These are all the same heretics who St John condemned in chapters 2 and 3 of the Apocalypse.

The purpose of this epistle was to warn Christians against following these false teachers who enticed the physical senses and passions. The epistle was written to all Christians in general, but we can see from the epistle itself that it was directed at a certain group of people who were under the influence of these false teachers. It can be safely assumed that the same churches in Asia Minor to whom Apostle Peter wrote on the same topic are also the intended audience here.

THE PLACE AND TIME OF THE WRITING OF THE EPISTLE

Doubtless, this epistle was written before the destruction of Jerusalem (A.D. 70), because St Jude, having mentioned in this epistle nearly all extraordinary manifestations of

God's judgment, would not have failed to mention this most frightening example. The similarity of this epistle with St Peter's general epistles suggests that it was written, perhaps, a long time before the destruction of Jerusalem. Because St Peter spoke of the heresies in the future tense, we can assume that the Epistle of Jude was written after Peter's epistle, and St Jude probably used Peter's characterization of the false teachers (word for word in some places). Therefore, the epistle must have been written between A.D. 67 (the year of St Peter's death) and A.D. 70. We have no information about the place where it was written.

THE CONTENT OF THE EPISTLE OF JUDE

There is only one chapter in this epistle, being from the beginning to the end a single unbroken discourse directed against the teachers of false doctrines.

EXEGETICAL ANALYSIS OF THE EPISTLE OF JUDE

In the beginning of the epistle, St Jude gives his name and indicates that he is a brother to James. He does not dare call himself a brother of the Lord, but only "a bondservant of Jesus Christ" (verse 1). Perhaps he mentioned his relationship to James hoping to bring attention to his epistle, because James the Just commanded great respect and authority. After the usual greeting—"Mercy, peace, and love be multiplied to you" (verse 2)—St Jude exhorts Christians to "contend earnestly for the faith which was once for all delivered to the saints" (verse 3). He explains that this is especially important now, with the appearance of "certain men … who long ago were marked out for this condemnation, ungodly men, who turn the grace of our God into lewdness and deny the only Lord God and our Lord Jesus Christ" (verse 4).

Who are these false teachers? St Jude does not give more specific information. Most likely, these were the same early gnostics against whom the Holy Apostles Peter, Paul, and later John wrote epistles of their own. Jude threatens them with divine punishment, reminding his readers of three harrowing examples of divine judgment: the punishment of the Israelites after their deliverance from Egypt, the punishment of the fallen angels, "reserved in everlasting chains under darkness for the judgment of the great day" (verse 6), and the destruction of Sodom and Gomorrah. The same punishment awaits "these dreamers [who] defile the flesh, reject authority, and speak evil of dignitaries" (verse 8), that is, they do not acknowledge the authority of spiritual leaders such as the apostles, the bishop, and presbyters.

What St Peter said concerning angels not daring to pass judgment, Apostle Jude applies to Archangel Michael specifically. He cites an ancient tradition, according to which the devil argued with Archangel Michael over the body of Moses.[217] Michael did not dare calumniate the devil, but only forbade him with the name of God, saying, "The Lord rebuke you!" (verse 9). In the meantime, the false teachers "speak evil of whatever they do not know" (verse 10). St Jude does not spare his words in giving the most negative possible characterization to these false teachers, comparing them to irrational beasts, Cain, Balaam, and Korah, who rebelled against Moses and Aaron.

Then in verses 14–15, St Jude cites a prophecy of Enoch, known from the apocryphal Book of Enoch (dated to the first century B.C.) concerning the coming judgment of God over the ungodly, a prophecy that is probably connected with the sins of Cain's descendants.[218] In conclusion, St Jude exhorts Christians to "keep yourselves in the love of God" (verse 21) and to be compassionate to those who have followed the teachings of the heretics, after which he praises God.

PART IV

The Apocalypse (The Book of Revelation)

This section was translated, edited, and annotated by Hieromonk Seraphim (Rose) and previously published by St Herman Press.[219]

Translator's Note: The text of the Apocalypse used in this book is that of the King James Version of the New Testament. The text of Archbishop Averky did not include the whole text of the Apocalypse which he was interpreting. In this translation, this whole text has been furnished, so that the translation proceeds verse by verse. In some cases, explanatory material from St Andrew's commentary, which Archbishop Averky did not cite, has been added in order to provide a commentary on every verse. The aim of Archbishop Averky, however, and of this translation, has been *not* to make an exhaustive interpretation of the text of the Apocalypse (which would require a book many times longer), but rather to provide a brief and practical understanding of the book for serious Orthodox Christians of these latter times.

The footnotes, which chiefly attempt to give explanatory material from other books of Scripture and from the Holy Fathers, are those of the translator and are so identified.

—Hieromonk Seraphim (Rose) (+1982)

CHAPTER 22

The Book of Revelation
of St John the Theologian
Translated by Hieromonk Seraphim (Rose)

THE SIGNIFICANCE OF AND INTEREST IN THE APOCALYPSE

The Apocalypse or, as it is translated from the Greek, the *Revelation* of St John the Theologian, is the only prophetic book of the New Testament. It is the natural culmination of the whole cycle of the New Testament sacred books.

In the books of the Law, of history, and of instruction, the Christian draws knowledge concerning the foundation and historical growth of the life of the Church of Christ, as well as guidance for his own personal activity in life. In the Apocalypse, however, there are given to the believing mind and heart mystical prophetic indications of the future fate of the Church and of the whole world. The Apocalypse is a mystical book which gives itself to a correct understanding and interpretation only with great difficulty; as a consequence, the Church Typicon does not indicate readings from it during the time of the Divine services.

But at the same time, it is precisely this mystical character of the book that draws to it the gaze both of the believing Christians and of simply curious thinkers. Over the course of the whole New Testament history of humanity, men have striven to decipher the significance and meaning of the puzzling vision described in it. There exists an immense literature about the Apocalypse, including many absurd works which touch on the origin and content of this mystical book. One might indicate, as one of such works in recent times, the book of N. A. Morozov, *The Revelation in Thunder and Storm*. Proceeding from the preconceived idea that the visions described in the Apocalypse depict, with the precision of an astronomical observer, the condition of the sky with its stars at some definite moment of time, Morozov makes astronomical calculations and comes to the conclusion that such precisely was the sky with its stars on September 30, 395. Replacing the persons, actions, and pictures of the Apocalypse with planets, stars, and constellations, Morozov makes broad use of indefinite, vague forms in the clouds, making them take the place of the missing names of stars, planets, and constellations in order to depict the full picture of the sky corresponding to the facts of the Apocalypse. If even the clouds do not help him, with all the softness and the receptivity of this material in capable hands, then Morozov redoes the text of the Apocalypse to fit the meaning which he needs. Such a free and easy attitude toward the text of Sacred Scripture Morozov justifies either by the mistakes and the ignorance of the copyists of the Apocalypse, "who did not understand the astronomical meaning of the picture," or even by the idea that the writer of the Apocalypse himself, "thanks to his preconceived idea," made forced interpretations in describing the picture of the sky with its stars. By such a "scientific" method, N. A. Morozov determines that the writer of the Apocalypse was St John Chrysostom (347–407), Archbishop of Constantinople. To the total historical absurdity of his conclusions, Morozov pays no attention whatsoever.

In our times—the period of the First World War and the Russian Revolution, and then the yet more frightful Second World War when mankind has experienced so many terrible shocks and misfortunes—the attempts to interpret the Apocalypse as applied to the events being experienced have increased yet more. Some of these attempts have been more, some less, successful.

In making such attempts, there is one important and essential thing to remember: in interpreting the Apocalypse, as in general in interpreting any book of Sacred Scripture, it is essential to make use of the facts given in the other sacred books which enter into the composition of our Bible, as well as of the works of interpretation of the Holy Fathers and the teachers of the Church. Among the special patristic works in the interpretation of the Apocalypse, especially valuable is the *Commentary on the Apocalypse* of St Andrew, Archbishop of Caesarea,[i] which gives a summary of the whole understanding of the Apocalypse in the pre-Nicenean period (before the First Ecumenical Council in 325). Likewise very valuable is the *Apology on the Apocalypse* by St Hippolytus of Rome (about c. 230).

In more recent times, there have appeared so many works of commentary on the Apocalypse that there were already ninety of them by the end of the nineteenth century (in the Russian language). Among the Russian works the most valuable are: (1) Alexander Zhdanov, *The Revelation of the Lord Concerning the Seven Churches of Asia* (Moscow, 1891) (an attempt to explain the first three chapters of

---

[i]   Almost nothing is known of St Andrew apart from his authorship of this *Commentary*. He lived apparently in the fifth century or a little later and quotes also fourth-century Fathers, such as St Gregory the Theologian. (S.R.)

the Apocalypse); (2) Bishop Peter (Yekaterinovsky), *Explanation of the Apocalypse of the Holy Apostle John the Theologian* (Tomsk, 1885); (3) N. A. Nikolsky, *The Apocalypse and the False Prophecy Exposed by It* (1879); (4) Nikolay Vinogradov, *Concerning the Final Fate of the World and of Mankind* (Moscow, 1892); and (5) Matvey Barsov, *Collection of Essays for the Interpretation and Edifying Reading of the Apocalypse* (Simbirsk, 1894).

THE AUTHOR OF THE APOCALYPSE

The writer of the Apocalypse calls himself "John" (Rev 1:1, 4:9). In the common belief of the Church, this was the Holy Apostle John, the beloved disciple of Christ, who for the height of his teaching concerning God the Word received the distinctive title of "Theologian." To his inspired pen belongs also the fourth canonical Gospel and three catholic epistles. This belief of the Church is justified both by facts indicated in the Apocalypse itself, and by many inward and outward signs.

1. The writer of the Apocalypse calls himself "John" at the very beginning, saying that to him was given the Revelation of Jesus Christ (1:1). Furthermore, greeting the seven churches of Asia Minor, he again calls himself "John" (1:4). Later he speaks of himself, again calling himself "John" saying that he "was in the isle that is called Patmos, for the word of God, and for the testimony of Jesus Christ" (1:9). From the history of the Apostles it is known that it is precisely St John the Theologian who was subjected to exile on the island of Patmos. And finally, at the end of the Apocalypse, the writer again calls himself "John" (22:8). In the second verse of the first chapter he calls himself an eyewitness of Jesus Christ (compare 1 John 1:3).

   The opinion that the Apocalypse was written by a certain "Presbyter John" is totally without foundation. The very existence of this "Presbyter John" as a person separate from the Apostle John is rather dubious. The only testimony which gives reason to speak about "Presbyter John" is a passage from a work of Papias of Hierapolis which has been preserved by the historian Eusebius. It is extremely indefinite and gives opportunity only for guesses and suppositions, which contradict each other. Likewise, the opinion is totally without foundation that ascribes the writing of the Apocalypse to John Mark, that is, the Evangelist Mark. Even more absurd is the opinion of the Roman presbyter Gaius (third century) that the Apocalypse was written by the heretic Cerinthus.

2. The second proof that the Apocalypse belongs to the Apostle John the Theologian is its similarity to the Gospel and the epistles of John, not only in spirit but also in style, and especially in several characteristic expressions. Thus, for example, the apostolic preaching is called here "testimony" or "witness" (Rev 1:2, 9; 20:4; compare John 1:7, 3:11, 21:24; I John 5:9–10). The Lord Jesus Christ is called "the Word" (Rev. 19:13; compare John 1:1–14, and I John 1:1) as well as "the Lamb" (Rev. 5:6, and 17:14; compare John 1:36). The prophetic words of Zechariah, And they

shall look on Him Whom they pierced (Zech. 12:10), both in the Gospel and the Apocalypse are cited according to the Hebrew text of the Scripture (KJV; Rev. 1:7, and John 19:37).

Some have found that the language of the Apocalypse is supposedly to be distinguished from the language of the other writings of the Holy Apostle John. This difference is easily explained, both by the difference of content and by the conditions in which the writings of the holy apostle had their origin. The Holy Apostle John, even though he knew well the Greek language, still, finding himself in exile far from the living conversational Greek language, naturally placed in the Apocalypse the seal of the powerful influence of the Hebrew language, being himself a native Jew. For the objective reader of the Apocalypse, there is no doubt that on its whole contents there lies the seal of the great spirit of the Apostle of love and contemplation.

3. All the ancient as well as later Patristic testimonies acknowledge as the author of the Apocalypse St. John the Theologian. His disciple, Papias of Hierapolis, calls the writer of the Apocalypse "Elder John," a name which the holy Apostle gives to himself in his own epistles (2 John 1, 3 John 1).

The testimony of St Justin the Martyr is also important. Before his conversion to Christianity he lived for a long time in Ephesus, the city where the great Apostle himself lived for a long time and reposed.

Further, many Holy Fathers cite passages from the Apocalypse as from a divinely inspired book belonging to St John the Theologian. Such quotations are to be found in the works of St Irenaeus of Lyons, the disciple of St Polycarp of Smyrna, who himself was the disciple of St John the Theologian; St Hippolytus, Pope of Rome and disciple of Irenaeus, who even wrote an apology on the Apocalypse; and Clement of Alexandria, Tertullian, and Origen likewise acknowledge the Holy Apostle John as the writer of the Apocalypse. In the same way, Ephrem the Syrian, Epiphanius, Basil the Great, Hilary, Athanasius the Great, Gregory the Theologian, Didymus, Ambrose, Augustine, and Jerome were convinced of this. The thirty-third canon of the Council of Carthage, ascribing the Apocalypse to St John the Theologian, places it in the rank of the other canonical books. The absence of the Apocalypse in the Syriac translation (Peshitta) is explained solely by the fact that this translation was made for reading at Divine services, and the Apocalypse was not read during Divine services. In the sixtieth canon of the Council of Laodicea, the Apocalypse is not mentioned, since the mystical content of the book did not allow it to be recommended to all, and it could give rise to false interpretations.

THE PLACE AND TIME OF THE WRITING OF THE APOCALYPSE

We do not have precise facts concerning the time of the writing of the Apocalypse. However, ancient tradition indicates for this the end of the first century. Thus,

St Irenaeus writes, "The Apocalypse appeared not long before this and almost in our own time, at the end of the reign of Domitian."[220] The church historian Eusebius states that the pagan writers contemporary to him mention also the exile of the Holy Apostle John on the island of Patmos for his testimony of the Divine Word, and they refer to this even in the fifteenth year of the reign of Domitian, A.D. 95 or 96. Clement of Alexandria, Origen, and Blessed Jerome affirm the same thing.

The Church writers of the first three centuries are in agreement also in indicating the place of the writing of the Apocalypse: the island of Patmos, which is referred to by the Apostle himself as the place where he received the revelations (Rev 1:9–10). But after the discovery of the sixth-century Syriac translation of the Apocalypse, where, in a superscription, Nero is named in place of Domitian,[221] many began to refer the writing of the Apocalypse to the time of Nero, that is, in the 60s of the first century. St Hippolytus of Rome likewise ascribes to Nero the exile of St John to the island of Patmos. Such people likewise find that one cannot refer the time of the writing of the Apocalypse to the reign of Domitian because, judging from the first two verses of the eleventh chapter of the Apocalypse, the temple of Jerusalem was not yet destroyed at that time, since in these verses they see a prophecy of the future destruction of the temple—something which under Domitian had already been accomplished. The indication of the Roman emperors which some people find in the tenth verse of the seventeenth chapter fit more than anyone else the successors of Nero. They likewise find that the number of the beast (Rev 13:18) can be found in the name of Nero: Nero Caesar, 666. The very language of the Apocalypse, which is full of Hebraisms, likewise, in the opinion of certain people, indicates an earlier origin compared to the fourth Gospel and the epistles of St John. The full name of Nero was: Claudius Nero Domitius, as a result of which one could also confuse him with the emperor Domitian, who reigned later. According to this opinion, the Apocalypse was written about two years before the destruction of Jerusalem, that is, in the year A.D. 68.

Against this, however, it is objected that the condition of Christian life as it is presented in the Apocalypse speaks for a later date. Each of the seven Asia Minor churches which St John addresses already has its own history and a direction of religious life which in one way or another has already been defined. Christianity in them is already not in its first stage of purity and truth; false Christianity strives to occupy a place in them side by side with true Christianity. All this presupposes that the activity of the Holy Apostle Paul, who preached for a long time in Ephesus, was something that had occurred in the distant past. This point of view, founded upon the testimony of St Irenaeus and Eusebius, refers the time of writing of the Apocalypse to the years A.D. 95–96.

On the other hand, it is quite difficult to accept the opinion of St Epiphanius, who says that St John returned from Patmos under Emperor Claudius (A.D. 41–54). Under Claudius, there was no general persecution of Christians in the provinces, and there was only a banishment from Rome of the Jews, among whose number Christians might also be included. Likewise unbelievable is the supposition that the Apocalypse was written at a yet later time, under the Emperor Trajan (A.D. 98–108), when St John had already ended his life.

Concerning the place of the writing of the Apocalypse, there is another opinion: that it was written in Ephesus, after the return there of the Apostle from banishment. However, the first opinion is much more natural, that the epistle to the churches of Asia Minor, which is contained in the Apocalypse, was sent precisely from Patmos. It is also difficult to suppose that the holy Apostle did not immediately fulfill the command to write down what he had seen (Rev 1:10–11).

The Chief Subject and Purpose of the Writing of the Apocalypse

In the beginning of the Apocalypse, St John himself indicates the chief subject and aim of its writing: to show things which must shortly come to pass (Rev 1:1). Thus, the chief subject of the Apocalypse is a mystical depiction of the future fate of the Church of Christ and of the whole world. From the very beginning of its existence, the Church of Christ had to enter into fierce battle with the errors of Judaism and paganism with the aim of effecting the triumph of the Divine Truth, which had been brought to earth by the Incarnate Son of God, and through this to give to mankind blessedness and eternal life. The aim of the Apocalypse is to depict this battle of the Church and its triumph over all enemies, to show clearly the perdition of the enemies of the Church and the glorification of her faithful children. This was especially important and necessary for believers in those times, when frightful and bloody persecutions had begun against Christians, so as to give them consolation and encouragement in the sorrows and difficult trials which had overtaken them. This vivid picture of the battle of the dark kingdom of Satan with the Church and the final victory of the Church over the "old serpent" (Rev 12:9) is necessary for the believers of all times for precisely the same reason: to console and strengthen them in the battle for the truth of the faith of Christ, a battle which they must always wage against the servants of the dark forces of hell, who strive in their blind malice to annihilate the Church.

The Church's View of the Content of the Apocalypse

All the ancient Fathers of the Church who wrote commentaries on the sacred books of the New Testament unanimously look on the Apocalypse as a prophetic picture of the last times of the world and the events which are to be accomplished before the second coming of Christ on earth and at the opening of the Kingdom of Glory, which is prepared for all truly believing Christians. Despite the darkness under which the mystical meaning of this book is hidden, as a consequence of which many unbelievers have striven in every way to defame it, the deeply enlightened Fathers and divinely wise teachers of the Church have always had great respect for it.

Thus, St Dionysius of Alexandria writes: "The darkness of this book does not prevent one from being astonished at it. And even if I do not understand everything in it, it is only because of my incapability. I cannot be a judge of the truths which are contained in it or measure them with the poverty of my mind; being guided more by faith than by understanding, I find them only surpassing my understanding." Blessed Jerome expresses himself concerning the Apocalypse in a similar spirit: "In it there are as many mysteries as words. But what am I saying? Every praise of this book will be beneath its worth."

Many consider that even Caius, the presbyter of Rome, did not consider the Apocalypse to be the work of the heretic Cerinthus, as some infer from his words; for Caius speaks not of the book called "The Revelation," but of "revelations." Eusebius himself, who quotes these words of Caius, does not say a word about the fact that Cerinthus was the author of the book of the Apocalypse. Blessed Jerome and other Fathers who knew this passage in the works of Caius and acknowledged the authenticity of the Apocalypse, would not have left this without reply if they had considered the words of Caius as referring to the Apocalypse of St John the Theologian.

But at Divine services, the Apocalypse was not read and is not read. One must suppose that this is because in antiquity the reading of Holy Scripture at Divine services was always accompanied by an interpretation of it, and the Apocalypse is too difficult for (an ordinary) interpretation. This also explains its absence in the Syriac translation, the Peshitta, which was intended especially for use in Divine services. As has been shown by researchers, the Apocalypse was originally in the list of the Peshitta and was excluded from it only after the time of St Ephrem the Syrian. We know this because St Ephrem quoted the Apocalypse in his works as a canonical book of the New Testament and uses it widely in his own Divinely inspired writings.

RULES FOR THE INTERPRETATION OF THE APOCALYPSE

As a book of God's decrees concerning the world and the Church, the Apocalypse has always attracted to itself the attention of Christians, and especially in those times when outward persecutions and inward temptations have begun to disturb the faithful especially powerfully, threatening from all sides with all kinds of dangers. In such periods, believers have naturally turned to this book for consolation and encouragement and have tried to use it to decipher the meaning and significance of the events which are occurring. However, the figurativeness and the mystical quality of the book make it extremely difficult to understand. Therefore, for careless interpreters there is always the risk of being drawn beyond the boundaries of truth, and there is thus occasion for fantastic hopes and beliefs.

Thus, for example, a literalistic understanding of the images of this book has given occasion, and even now continues to give occasion, for the false teaching of

"Chiliasm"—the thousand-year reign of Christ on earth. The terrors of the persecutions which were endured by Christians in the first century and which were interpreted in the light of the Apocalypse gave occasion for some people to believe that the last times and the second coming of Christ were already at hand then, in the first century.

In the nineteen centuries which have since elapsed, there have appeared a multitude of commentaries on the Apocalypse, and they have been of the most varied character. One may divide all these commentaries into four groups. Some of them refer to all the visions and symbols of the Apocalypse to the "last times"—that is, the end of the world, the appearance of the antichrist, and the second coming of Christ. Others give to the Apocalypse a purely historical significance, referring all the visions to the historical events of the first century—to the times of the persecutions raised against the Church by the pagan emperors. A third group strives to find the realization of apocalyptic prophecies in the historical events of recent times. In their opinion, for example, the Pope of Rome is the antichrist, and all the apocalyptic misfortunes are announced in particular for the Church of Rome. A fourth group, finally, sees in the Apocalypse only an allegory, considering that the visions described in it have not so much prophetic as a moral meaning, and allegory is introduced only to increase the impression, with the aim of striking the imagination of readers.

The most correct commentary, however, is one that unites all these approaches, keeping in mind that, as the ancient commentators and Fathers of the Church clearly taught, the content of the Apocalypse in its sum is indeed directed to the last part of the history of the world. There can be no doubt, moreover, that in the course of the whole past history of Christianity, many of the prophecies of the Apostle John concerning the future fate of the Church and the world have already been fulfilled. But great caution is required in applying the apocalyptic content to historical events, and one should not misuse this approach. One interpreter has rightly said that the content of the Apocalypse will only gradually become understandable to the degree that the events themselves approach and the prophecies uttered in the book are being fulfilled.

A correct understanding of the Apocalypse, to be sure, is hindered most of all by the departure of people from faith and true Christian life; this always makes people dull, and even leads to a complete loss of the spiritual vision which is essential for the correct understanding and spiritual evaluation of the events which occur in the world. The total devotion of contemporary man to sinful passions which deprive one of purity of heart, and consequently of spiritual vision (Matt 5:8), serves as the cause of the fact that certain contemporary interpreters of the Apocalypse wish to see in it only an allegory and teach that even the second coming of Christ is to be understood allegorically. The historical events and persons of the times we are now experiencing—times which, in all justice, many already call "apocalyptic"—convince us of the fact that to see in the book of the Apocalypse only an allegory truly means to be spiritually blind. Everything now happening in the world does indeed remind one of the frightful images and visions of the Apocalypse.

THE STRUCTURE AND CONTENT OF THE APOCALYPSE

The Apocalypse contains twenty-two chapters. The book can be divided, according to its content, into the following sections:

1. An introductory picture of the Son of God Who appeared to John commanding him to write to the seven churches of Asia Minor (chapter 1).
2. Instructions to the seven churches of Asia Minor: The churches of Ephesus, Smyrna, Pergamos, Thyatira, Sardis, Philadelphia, and Laodicea (chapters 2 and 3).
3. The vision of God sitting on the throne, and the Lamb (chapters 4 and 5).
4. The opening by the Lamb of the seven seals of the mystical book (chapters 6 and 7).
5. The voices of the seven trumpets of the angels declaring various misfortunes to those living on the earth at the taking away of the seventh seal (chapters 8, 9, 10, and 11).
6. The Church of Christ in the image of the woman clothed with the sun who is in the pangs of childbirth (chapter 12).
7. The beast (the antichrist) and his helper, the false prophet (chapter 13).
8. Preparatory events before the general resurrection and the Last Judgment (chapters 14, 15, 16, 17, 18, and 19).
   a. The hymn of praise of the 144,000 righteous ones; and the angels who declare the fate of the world (chapter 14).
   b. The seven angels who have the seven last plagues (chapter 15).
   c. The seven angels who pour out the seven cups of the wrath of God (chapter 16).
   d. The judgment upon the great harlot who sits on the many waters and is seated upon the scarlet beast (chapter 17).
   e. The fall of Babylon, the great harlot (chapter 18).
   f. The battle of the Word of God with the beast and his army, and the destruction of the latter (chapter 19).
9. The general resurrection and the Last Judgment (chapter 20).
10. The revelation of the new heaven and the new earth; the New Jerusalem and the blessedness of its inhabitants (chapters 21 and 22:1–5).
11. Conclusion: Confirmation of the truth of everything said and the testament to preserve the commandments of God; the giving of a blessing (chapter 22:6–21).

EXEGETICAL ANALYSIS OF THE APOCALYPSE

1. THE PURPOSE OF THE APOCALYPSE AND THE MEANS BY WHICH IT WAS GIVEN TO JOHN
  1:1 *The Revelation of Jesus Christ, which God gave unto him, to shew unto his servants things which must shortly come to pass.*

These words clearly define the character and purpose of the Apocalypse as a prophetic book. By this, the Apocalypse is to be essentially distinguished from the other books of the New Testament, the content of which is primarily one of instruction in faith and morals. The importance of the Apocalypse is evident here from the fact that its writing was the result of a direct revelation and a direct command given to the holy Apostle by the Head of the Church Himself, the Lord Jesus Christ. The expression "shortly" indicates that the prophecies of the Apocalypse began to be fulfilled right then, immediately after the book was written, and likewise that in the eyes of God a thousand years are as one day (2 Pet 3:8). The expression of the Apocalypse concerning the revelation of Jesus Christ, "which God gave unto him," one must understand as referring to Christ in His human nature, for He Himself during His earthly life spoke of Himself as of one who did not know everything (Mark 13:32) and as one who receives revelations from the Father (John 5:20).

  1:1–2 *And he sent and signified it by his angel unto his servant John: who bare record of the word of God, and of the testimony of Jesus Christ, and of all things that he saw.*
  1:3 *Blessed is he that readeth, and they that hear the words of this prophecy, and keep those things which are written therein: for the time is at hand.*

  The book of the Apocalypse has, consequently, not only a prophetic but also a moral significance. The meaning of these words is as follows: blessed is he who, reading this book, will prepare himself by his life and deeds of piety for eternity, for the translation to eternity is near for each of us.

  1:4 *John to the seven churches which are in Asia.*

  The number seven is usually taken as an expression of fullness. St John addresses here only the seven churches with which he, as one who lived in Ephesus, was in especially close and frequent contact. But in these seven he addresses, at the same time, the Christian Church as a whole.

  1:4 *Grace be unto you, and peace, from him which is, and which was, and which is to come.*

Grace to you and peace from the Tri-Hypostatical Divinity. The phrase 'which is' signifies the Father, Who said to Moses: I am He that Is (Exod 3:14). The expression 'which was' signifies the Word, Who was in the beginning with God (John 1:2). The phrase 'which is to come' indicates the Comforter, Who always descends upon the Church's children in holy baptism and in all fullness is to descend in the future age (Acts 2). (St Andrew of Caesarea, Commentary on the Apocalypse, chapter 1).[222]

1:4 *And from the seven Spirits which are before his throne.*

By these "seven Spirits," it is most natural to understand the seven chief angels who are spoken of in Tobit 12:15. St Andrew of Caesarea, however, understands them to be the angels who govern the seven churches. Other commentaries, on the other hand, understand by this expression the Holy Spirit Himself, Who manifests Himself in seven chief gifts: the spirit of the fear of God, the spirit of knowledge, the spirit of might, the spirit of light, the spirit of understanding, the spirit of wisdom, the spirit of the Lord or the spirit of piety, and inspiration in the highest degree (compare Isa 11:1–3).

1:5 *And from Jesus Christ, who is the faithful witness, and the first begotten of the dead, and the prince of the kings of the earth.*

The Lord Jesus Christ is called here "the faithful witness" in the sense that He has witnessed His Divinity and the truth of His teaching before men by His death on the Cross.

"As Life and Resurrection, He is the first-born from the dead (Col 1:18, I Cor 15:20), and those over whom He rules will not see death, as did those who died and rose before, but will live eternally.[ii] He is 'prince of kings,' as King of kings and Lord of lords (I Tim 6:15), equal in might to the Father and one in essence with Him" (St Andrew, chapter 1).

1:5–6 *Unto him that loved us, and washed us from our sins in his own blood, and hath made us kings and priests unto God and his Father; to him be glory and dominion forever and ever. Amen.*

"Kings and priests" are to be understood here not in the strict meaning, of course, but in the sense in which God has promised this to His chosen people through the prophets (Exod 19:6); that is, He has made us, the true believers, to be

---

[ii] St Athanasius the Great interprets this passage as follows: "He is said to be 'the First-begotten from the dead,' not that he died before us, for we had died first; but because having undergone death for us and abolished it, He was the first to rise as man, for our sake raising His own Body. Henceforth, He having risen, we too from Him and because of Him rise in due course from the dead" (*Second Discourse Against the Arians* 21, *The Nicene and Post-Nicene Fathers*, series 2, vol. 4, 381). (S.R.)

the best, the holiest people, which is the same thing that a priest and king are with relation to the rest of mankind.[iii]

> 1:7 *Behold, he cometh with clouds; and every eye shall see him, and they also which pierced him: and all kindreds of the earth shall wail because of him.*

Here is depicted the second glorious coming of Christ, in complete agreement with the depiction of this coming in the Gospels (compare Matt 24:30, 25:31; Mark 13:26; Luke 21:27; see also John 19:37). After the greeting (in the first verses of the book), in this verse the holy Apostle immediately speaks of the second coming of Christ and of the Last Judgment in order to signify the chief theme of this book; this is done to prepare readers to accept the great and fearful revelations which he has received about this.

> 1:7–8 *Even so, Amen. I am Alpha and Omega, the beginning and the ending, saith the Lord, which is, and which was, and which is to come, the Almighty.*

To confirm the unchangeableness and inevitability of the second coming and the Last Judgment of God, the holy Apostle adds on his own part: "Even so, Amen," and then testifies to the truth of this by indicating Him Who is the "Alpha and Omega, the beginning and the ending" of everything existing: The Lord Jesus Christ is the One alone Who is without beginning and without end, the cause of everything existing; He is eternal; He is the end and the aim towards which everything strives.[iv]

[iii] St Peter in his First Catholic Epistle also speaks of Christians as a royal priesthood, a holy nation (1 Pet 2:9) in the sense that they have direct access to God, as only priests did—and that imperfectly—in the Old Testament. By this, of course, he does not deny the specific office of priesthood in the New Testament, as modern sectarians do; in this specific sense, only those ordained to the office of priesthood can be ministers of God's grace through the Holy Mysteries. (S.R.)

[iv] In 1:4 above, the words "Which is, and which was, and which is to come" refer to the Three Persons of the Holy Trinity, as explained by St Andrew; this is clear because the same sentence continues (in 1:5), and from Jesus Christ. Here, however, with the addition of the words "the Almighty," the same words refer to One Person of the Holy Trinity, Jesus Christ, and are used by St Gregory the Theologian in his treatise "On the Son" as a proof that Jesus Christ is truly God (*Third Theological Oration* 17; NPNF, series 2, vol. 7, p. 307). St Athanasius the Great, in his *First Discourse Against the Arians*, uses the same quote from the Apocalypse to prove the same thing (4, NPNF, series 2, vol. 4, p. 312). Concerning this St Andrew says in his Commentary (chapter 1), "The divinely splendid words are fitting equally for each of the Persons separately and for All together." (S.R.)

1:9 *I John, who also am your brother, and companion in tribulation, and in the kingdom and patience of Jesus Christ, was in the isle that is called Patmos, for the word of God, and for the testimony of Jesus Christ.*

As for the means by which he was given revelations, St John indicates first of all the place where he was vouchsafed to receive them. This is the island Patmos, one of the Sporades Islands in the Aegean Sea, a desert and precipitous place 40 miles in circumference, located between the island of Icaria and the Cape of Miletus, little inhabited because of the lack of water, the unhealthy climate, and the barrenness of the earth. In a cave in a certain mountain, even now there is indicated the place where St John received the revelations. Here there is a small Greek monastery called the "Monastery of the Apocalypse."

In the same verse there is mentioned also the time when St John received the Apocalypse. This was at the time when St John was in exile on the island of Patmos, in his own expression, "for the word of God and for the testimony of Jesus Christ," that is, for his fervent apostolic preaching of Jesus Christ. The fiercest persecution against Christians in the first century was under Emperor Nero. Tradition says that St John first of all was thrown into a cauldron of boiling oil, out of which he came unharmed and with renewed strength. The expression "in tribulation," according to the meaning of the original Greek expression, signifies here the "suffering" which occurred from persecution and torment—the same thing as "martyrdom."

1:10 *I was in the Spirit on the Lord's day, and heard behind me a great voice, as of a trumpet.*

In this verse, St John gives the very day on which he was vouchsafed the revelations. This was "the Lord's day" (in Greek, *kyriakê hêmera*), which is Sunday.[v] This was the first day of the week, which the Jews called (in Greek) *mia sabbatôn*, that is, "the first day after Saturday"; but the Christians called it "the Lord's day" in honor of the Risen Lord. The very existence of such a name already indicates that the Christians celebrated this day in place of the Old Testament Sabbath.

Having mentioned the place and time, St John indicates likewise his own condition, in which he was vouchsafed the apocalyptic visions. "I was in the Spirit on the Lord's day," he says. In the language of prophets, "to be in the Spirit" is to be in the spiritual condition when a man sees, hears, and feels not with his bodily organs, but with all his inward being. This is not a dream, for such a condition occurs also when one is awake.

In such an extraordinary condition of his spirit, St John heard a loud voice as of a trumpet:

1:11 *Saying, I am Alpha and Omega, the first and the last: and, What thou seest, write in a book, and send it unto the seven churches which are in Asia; unto Ephesus, and unto*

---

[v] The same expression is still used for Sunday in Modern Greek. (S.R.)

Smyrna, and unto Pergamos, and unto Thyatira, and unto Sardis, and unto Philadelphia, and unto Laodicea.

There follows the description of four visions, according to which many divide the contents of the Apocalypse into four chief parts: The first vision is set forth from chapter 1, verse 12, through chapter 3; the second vision, in chapters 4 through 11; the third vision, in chapters 12 through 14; and the fourth vision, in chapters 15 through 22.

The first vision is the apparition to St John of a certain one "like unto the Son of Man" (1:13). The loud voice, like that of a trumpet, which John heard behind him, belonged to Him. He called Himself not in Hebrew, but in Greek: "Alpha and Omega, the first and the last." To the Jews in the Old Testament, He revealed Himself under the holy and unpronounceable name YHWH, which signifies, "He that exists from the beginning," or "He that Is"; but here He calls Himself by the first and last letters of the Greek alphabet, indicating by this that He contains within Himself, like the Father, everything existing in all the manifestations of being from the beginning to the end. It is characteristic that He declares Himself here as it were under a new name, and it is a Greek name, "Alpha and Omega," as if desiring to show that He is the Messiah for all peoples, who at that time spoke everywhere the Greek language and used the Greek written language.

The revelation is given to the seven churches comprising the metropolis of Ephesus, which St John the Theologian then governed, having his permanent dwelling in Ephesus. Of course, in the person of these seven churches, the revelation is given also to the whole Church. The number seven, moreover, has a mystical meaning, signifying completeness. Therefore, it may be placed here as a symbol of the Universal Church, to which as a whole the Apocalypse is addressed.

1:12–13 *And I turned to see the voice that spake with me. And being turned, I saw seven golden candlesticks; and in the midst of the seven candlesticks one like unto the Son of man, clothed with a garment down to the foot, and girt about the paps with a golden girdle.*

Chapter 1, verses 12–16 describe the outward appearance of the One Who appeared to John "like unto the Son of man." He stood in the midst of seven candlesticks, symbolizing the seven churches (as explained in 1:20) and was clothed in a "garment down to the foot"—the ephod, the long garment of the Hebrew high priests (Exod 28:31). He was, like kings, girded about the breast with a golden belt. These features indicate the high-priestly and royal dignity of the One Who appeared.

"The voice which the Apostle heard was not sensory. This he makes clear by the word 'turned': That is, he turned not in order to hear it, but to see it; for spiritual hearing and seeing signify one and the same thing" (St Andrew, chapter 2).

1:14 *His head and his hairs were white like wool, as white as snow; and his eyes were as a flame of fire.*

Whiteness of the hair serves usually as a sign of old age. This sign testifies that the Son of Man Who appeared is one with the Father, that He is the same as the "Ancient of Days" Whom the holy prophet Daniel also beheld in a mystical vision (Dan 7:9–10, 13–14), that He is the same eternal God as is God the Father.[vi] His eyes were like a fiery flame, which signifies His Divine zeal for the salvation of the human race, that before His glance there is nothing hidden or dark, and that He is flaming with anger against every iniquity.

1:15 And his feet like unto fine brass, as if they burned in a furnace.

Brass is a precious metallic mixture with a fiery red or golden yellow sheen (compare Dan 10:5–6).

"The feet are the Apostles, as the support of the church.… The feet of Christ are the Apostles, who have been heated, in emulation of Christ, in the furnace of temptations" (St Andrew, chapter 2).

1:15 And his voice as the sound of many waters.

That is, His voice was like the voice of a threatening judge who strikes with trembling the disturbed souls of condemned men.

1:16 And he had in his right hand seven stars.

According to the explanation given to John by the One Who appears, these seven stars signify the seven representatives of the churches, or bishops, called here

---

[vi] The Orthodox church service for the Meeting of the Lord (February 2) identifies the "Ancient of Days" with God the Son ("The Ancient of Days appears this day as a babe"). Thus, in this interpretation, when Daniel beheld the Ancient of Days and the Son of Man together, it was a vision of the Divine and human natures of Christ. Some Fathers, however, understand the Ancient of Days to be God the Father; in this case, the vision is of Two Persons of the Holy Trinity, and as St John Chrysostom says in his commentary on Daniel, this prophet "was the first and only one (in the Old Testament) to see the Father and the Son, as if in a vision." For the devout student of Scripture, of course, there is no "contradiction" between these two interpretations; in such mystical visions we do not see a "literal picture" of the Godhead (such as to believe that God is really an "old man," but only a hint of Divine mysteries). Thus, in his commentary on the same passage of Daniel, St John Chrysostom adds: "Do not seek clarity in prophecies, where there are shadows and riddles, just as in lightning you do not seek a constant light, but are satisfied that it only flashes momentarily." (S.R.)

the "angels of the churches." By this we are told that the Lord Jesus holds in His right hand the shepherds of the Church.

1:16 *And out of his mouth went a sharp twoedged sword.*

This symbolizes the all-penetrating power of the word which comes from the mouth of God (compare Heb 4:12).

1:16 *And his countenance was as the sun shineth in his strength.*

This is an image of that unutterable glory of God by which the Lord shone on Mt Tabor (Matt 17:2). All these characteristics present to us the whole image of the fearful Judge, Chief Priest and King, as the Lord Jesus Christ will one day appear on earth in His second coming to judge the living and the dead.

1:17 *And when I saw him, I fell at his feet as dead.*

From this one may conclude that the beloved disciple, who had once lain on the breast of Jesus, did not recognize in the One Who had appeared a single familiar feature. And this is not surprising; for if the disciples did not easily recognize their Lord after His Resurrection in His glorified body on earth, all the more difficult would it be to recognize Him in this resplendent heavenly glory.

1:17–18 *And he laid his right hand upon me, saying unto me, Fear not; I am the First and the Last: I am he that liveth, and was dead; and, behold, I am alive for evermore, Amen; and have the keys of hell and of death.*

From these words, St John had to understand that the One Who appeared was none other than the Lord Jesus Christ, and that his appearance could not be fatal for the Apostle, but on the contrary, would be life giving. To have the keys to something signified among the Jews to receive authority over something. Thus, "the keys of hell and of death" signify authority over the death of the body and the soul.[vii]

1:19–20 *Write the things which thou hast seen, and the things which are, and the things which shall be hereafter; The mystery of the seven stars which thou sawest in my right hand,*

[vii] One might add here that Christ has authority over hell and death in that He Himself tasted of death in the body and descended to hell in His soul after death (1 Pet 3:19), but in His Resurrection gained victory over both. The Divine services of the Orthodox Church are full of this teaching; for example, "O Lord our Saviour, Who has taken hell captive and trampled on death...." (*Octoechos*, Tone 5, Sunday Vespers, "Lord I have cried.") (S.R.)

and the seven golden candlesticks. The seven stars are the angels of the seven churches: and the seven candlesticks which thou sawest are the seven churches.

In conclusion, the One Who had appeared commands John to write down that which he has seen and what is to be, explaining that the seven stars are the angels or the representatives of the seven churches, and the seven candlesticks signify these churches themselves.

"Since Christ is *the true Light* (John 1:9), those who have become enriched by His illumination are like candlesticks which illuminate the darkness of the present life" (St Andrew, chapter 2).

2. INSTRUCTIONS TO THE CHURCHES OF ASIA MINOR: EPHESUS, SMYRNA, PERGAMOS, AND THYATIRA

In the second, as in the third chapter, are set forth the revelations received by St John concerning each of the seven churches of Asia Minor, as well as corresponding instructions to them. These revelations contain praises of their Christian life and faith, a reproof of their insufficiencies, exhortations and consolations, and threats and promises. The content of these revelations and instructions has the closest relationship to the condition of church life in the churches of Asia Minor at the end of the first century. At the same time, it refers also to the whole Church in general for the whole course of its existence on earth. Some even see here an indication of seven periods in the life of the whole Christian Church from the time of the Apostles to the end of the world and the second coming of Christ.

TO THE CHURCH OF EPHESUS

2:1–7 *Unto the angel of the church of Ephesus write; These things saith he that holdeth the seven stars in his right hand, who walketh in the midst of the seven golden candlesticks; I know thy works, and thy labour, and thy patience, and how thou canst not bear them which are evil; and thou hast tried them which say they are apostles, and are not, and hast found them liars: and hast borne, and hast patience, and for my name's sake hast laboured, and hast not fainted. Nevertheless I have somewhat against thee, because thou hast left thy first love. Remember therefore from whence thou art fallen, and repent, and do the first works; or else I will come unto thee quickly, and will remove thy candlestick out of his place, except thou repent. But this thou hast, that thou hatest the deeds of the Nicolaitanes, which I also hate. He that hath an ear, let him hear what the Spirit saith unto the churches; To him that overcometh will I give to eat of the tree of life, which is in the midst of the paradise of God.*

First of all the Lord commands him to write to the angel of the Church of Ephesus. The Church of Ephesus is praised for its first works—for its labors, patience, and for opposing false teachers; but at the same time, it is condemned for leaving off its first love, and it hears the fearful threat that the candlestick will be taken away from its place if it does not repent. Furthermore, it was good that the Ephesians hated "the deeds of the Nicolaitans." To those who overcome temptations and passions, the Lord promises to vouchsafe the eating of the fruits of the tree of life.

Ephesus was a most ancient trading city on the shore of the Aegean Sea, famous for its wealth and immense population. There, the Holy Apostle Paul preached for more than two years, and toward the end of this period, he ordained as bishop of Ephesus his beloved disciple Timothy. There also the Holy Apostle John the Theologian lived for a long time and died. Subsequently in Ephesus there was the Third Ecumenical Council, which confessed the Most Holy Virgin Mary to be Theotokos. The threat to remove the candlestick of the Church of Ephesus was fulfilled. From a great world center Ephesus was soon turned into nothing: from a previously splendid city, there remained only a heap of ruins and a small Muslim village. The great candlestick of earliest Christianity was completely extinguished.

The Nicolaitans mentioned here were heretics who were a branch of the gnostics and were noted for their immoral life. They are also accused in the catholic epistles of the Holy Apostles Peter and Jude (2 Pet 2:1, Jude 4). The beginning of this heresy was made by the proselyte Nicholas of Antioch, who was one of the original seven deacons of Jerusalem (Acts 6:5), who fell away from the true faith. The reward for those among the Ephesian Christians who overcome is the tasting of the tree of life of paradise. By this one must understand in general the good things of the future blessed life of the righteous, a prefiguration of which was the tree of life in the original paradise, where our first ancestors lived (Gen 2:9).

> The removal of the candlestick of the church is the deprivation of Divine grace, to which it will be subjected in agitation and shaking from the spirits of malice and the evil men who help them. ... He that hath an ear, let him hear: Every man has a physical ear, but only the spiritual man acquires a spiritual ear. ... To such a man, who has overcome the temptations of the demons, He promises to give to taste of the tree of life, that is, to make him a participant in the good things of the future age. (St Andrew, chapter 3)

To the Church of Smyrna

> 2:8–11 *And unto the angel of the church in Smyrna write; These things saith the first and the last, which was dead, and is alive; I know thy works, and tribulation, and poverty (but thou art rich), and I know the blasphemy of them which say they are Jews, and are not, but are the synagogue of Satan. Fear none of those things which thou shalt suffer: behold, the devil shall cast some of you into prison, that ye may be tried; and ye shall have tribulation ten days: be thou faithful unto death, and I will give thee a crown of life. He that hath an ear, let him hear what the Spirit saith unto the churches; he that overcometh shall not be hurt of the second death.*

To the Church of Smyrna, which was composed of poor people who were, however, rich spiritually, there are foretold tribulations and persecutions from the Jews, whom the Lord calls "the synagogue of Satan" (compare Rom 2:28–29). The prophecy of tribulations is accompanied by an exhortation to endure to the end these tribulations, which will continue for "ten days"; and the promise is given of deliverance from "the second death."

Smyrna also was one of the most ancient cities of Asia Minor, renowned and glorious in pagan antiquity. Not less remarkable was Smyrna in the history of the earliest era of Christianity as a city which was very early illumined by the light of Christianity and kept in the midst of persecutions the pledge of faith and piety.

The Church of Smyrna, according to tradition, was founded by the Holy Apostle John the Theologian, and the disciple of the latter, St Polycarp, who was bishop there, glorified this church by his exploit of martyrdom. According to the information given by the church historian Eusebius, almost immediately after the prophecy given in the Apocalypse, the first persecution against Christians in Asia Minor broke out, during which St Polycarp of Smyrna also suffered.

Christ is "the first as God, and the last as having become man in the latter times and opened to us eternal life by His death of three days" (St Andrew, chapter 4; compare Isa 44:6).

According to some commentaries, the "ten days" signifies the shortness of the time of the persecutions; but according to others, it indicates a certain extended period, for the Lord commanded the people of Smyrna to be "faithful unto death," that is, for some long period. Some understand by this the persecution, which was under Domitian and continued for ten years. Others see in this a prophecy of the ten persecutions, which, altogether, the Christians endured from pagan emperors for the course of the first three centuries.

By the "second death," which is to come for unbelievers after the death of the body, is to be understood their condemnation to eternal torments (compare Rev 21:8, Matt 10:28).

To him that overcomes, that is, to him that endures all persecutions, is promised "a crown of life," or the inheritance of eternal good things.

Smyrna, to this day, remains a significant city and has the dignity of an Orthodox metropolis.

To the Church of Pergamos

> 2:12–13 *And to the angel of the church in Pergamos write; These things saith he which hath the sharp sword with two edges; I know thy works, and where thou dwellest, even where Satan's seat is; and thou holdest fast my name, and hast not denied my faith, even in those days wherein Antipas was my faithful martyr, who was slain among you, where Satan dwelleth.*

The Church of Pergamos is praised by the Lord for the fact that it holds fast His name and has not renounced faith in Him, even though the church was planted in the midst of a city extremely corrupted by paganism, which is the meaning of the figurative expression "thou dwellest, even where Satan's seat is," and it was sub-jected to a severe persecution, during which the Lord's martyr Antipas was slain. Although many have attempted to understand the name Antipas symbolically, it is known from the martyrologies that have come down to us that Antipas was bishop of Pergamos and, for his zealous confession of the Christian faith, was burned inside a heated bronze bull.[viii]

> 2:14–16 *But I have a few things against thee, because thou hast there them that hold the doctrine of Balaam, who taught Balac to cast a stumblingblock before the children of Israel, to eat things sacrificed unto idols, and to commit fornication. So hast thou also them that hold the doctrine of the Nicolaitanes, which thing I hate. Repent; or else I will come unto thee quickly, and will fight against them with the sword of my mouth.*

But then the Lord indicates also the negative manifestations in the life of the Church of Pergamos, namely, that there also the Nicolaitans have appeared, who have made lawful the eating of that which was offered to idols and every kind of fornication—things to which, in another epoch, the Israelites had been led by Balaam.

> 2:14–16 *Balaam, who taught Balac:*

"By these words He indicates the mental Balaam, the devil, who through the sensual Balaam taught Balac to tempt the Israelites to fornication and idol-wor-ship; for by the sweetness of this pleasure they fell so low that they offered sacrifices to Beelphegor" (see Num 25:1–3; St Andrew, chapter 5).

Pergamos is to the north of Smyrna and in antiquity it competed with Smyrna and Ephesus. In it there was a temple to the pagan god Aesculapius, the patron of physicians. Its sorcerers occupied themselves with medicine and offered great opposition to the preachers of Christianity. Pergamos, under the name of Bergamo, and the Christian church in it, have been preserved up to the present day, although in great poverty; since its previous splendor, nothing at all remains apart from the immense ruins of a once-splendid church in honor of St John the Theologian, erected by Emperor Theodosius (fourth century A.D.).

> 2:17 *He that hath an ear, let him hear what the Spirit saith unto the churches; To him that overcometh will I give to eat of the hidden manna, and will give him a white stone, and in the stone a new name written, which no man knoweth saving he that receiveth it.*

[viii] Hieromartyr Antipas, bishop of Pergamos, was a disciple of St John the Theologian. He died a martyr's death in the year A.D. 92 and was noted, both during his lifetime and after his death, for his healings of various afflictions, especially of the teeth. He is commemorated on April 11, when there is a church service to him. (S.R.)

The first image is taken from the Old Testament manna (Exod 16:14–15), which was a prefiguration of the bread which cometh down from heaven (John 6:50), that is, the Lord Jesus Christ Himself. By this manna, one must understand the living communion with the Lord in the future blessed age.

The metaphorical expression, "white stone," has its foundation in a custom of antiquity, according to which the victors at the public games and contests were given white stone tablets, which they later presented in order to receive the rewards conferred on them. Among Roman judges, it was the custom to collect votes by means of white and black stones. White signified freedom; black signified condemnation. In the mouth of the seer of mysteries, John, the white stone, symbolically signified the purity and innocence of Christians, for which they receive a reward in the future age.

To give names to new members of a kingdom is characteristic of kings and masters. The Heavenly King also will give to all the chosen sons of His Kingdom new names which will signify their inward qualities, their designation and service in the Kingdom of Glory. But since "the things of God knoweth no man, but the Spirit of God" (1 Cor 2:11), so also the new name given to a man by the All-knowing Master will be known only to the one who receives this name (compare Isa 62:2).

To the Church of Thyatira

> 2:18–20 *And unto the angel of the church in Thyatira write; These things saith the Son of God, who hath his eyes like unto a flame of fire, and his feet are like fine brass; I know thy works, and charity, and service, and faith, and thy patience, and thy works; and the last to be more than the first. Notwithstanding I have a few things against thee, because thou sufferest that woman Jezebel, which calleth herself a prophetess, to teach and to seduce my servants to commit fornication, and to eat things sacrificed unto idols.*

Thyatira was a small town in Lydia which has no particular significance in history, but it is known in the history of Christianity because from it there came Lydia, who was enlightened with the light of faith in Christ by the Holy Apostle Paul during his second journey of preaching in the city of Philippi (Acts 16:14, 15, 40). Probably this also aided the speedy establishment of Christianity in Thyatira. It is evident from the words, "thy last works are more than thy first," that all the good Christian qualities of the inhabitants of Thyatira, indicated before this in the text, are developing with time and becoming stronger.

The name Jezebel is used here evidently in the same metaphorical sense as the name Balaam earlier. It is known that Jezebel, the daughter of the king of Sidon, having entered into marriage with Ahab, the king of Israel, drew him into worshipping all the vile things of Tyre and Sidon and was the cause of the fall of the Israelites into idol worship (3 [1] Kings 16:31). We may suppose that the name "Jezebel" here indicates the same inclination toward idol worship and fornication of the Nicolaitans.

> *2:21–23 And I gave her space to repent of her fornication; and she repented not. Behold, I will cast her into a bed, and them that commit adultery with her into great tribulation, except they repent of their deeds. And I will kill her children with death; and all the churches shall know that I am he which searcheth the reins and hearts: and I will give unto every one of you according to your works.*

Continuing to speak in figurative manner, He compares the cunning and deception of the heretics to a harlot,[ix] threatening to strike her with death and afflictions, as well as all who have defiled themselves with her and committed fornication before God, unless they return to Him through repentance. This is addressed to the heretics who have been deceived and who seduce others. (St Andrew, chapter 6)

> *2:24–25 But unto you I say, and unto the rest in Thyatira, as many as have not this doctrine, and which have not known the depths of Satan, as they speak; I will put upon you none other burden. But that which ye have already hold fast till I come.*

"To the simple people He says: 'Since you, in your simplicity, are not able to stand against the cunning and clever, for, as you affirm, you do not fully know the depths of Satan—therefore I do not ask of you to wage battle by words, but only to preserve the teaching which you have received, until the time when I shall take you from here'"(St Andrew, chapter 6).

The "depths of Satan" is the name given here to the teaching of the Nicolaitans, as predecessors of the gnostics, who called their false teaching "the depths of God."

> *2:26–27 And he that overcometh, and keepeth my works unto the end, to him will I give power over the nations: And he shall rule them with a rod of iron; as the vessels of a potter shall they be broken to shivers: even as I received of my Father.*

To him who does My works will I give power, as promised in the Gospel, over five or ten cities (Luke 19:17–19). Or else this indicates the judgment of unbelievers, through which those who have been deceived, being judged by the believers in Christ, will be crushed as a crock is by the rod: The men of Nineveh shall rise in judgment with this generation, and shall condemn it (Matt 12:41). The words, "even as I received of My Father," are spoken of His human nature, because of His acceptance of flesh. (St Andrew, chapter 6)

[ix] In the Apocalypse, and in the Sacred Scripture in general, heresy is often indicated by the symbols of "fornication" and "adultery"—that is, "impurity" with regard to teaching—and heretics by the symbols of a "harlot" and those who commit fornication with her (see especially chapter 17). (S.R.)

Paganism fell (historically) as a result of the battle with Christianity. In this sense, the Lord promises (in general) "power over the nations" to the one who overcomes.

2:28 *And I will give him the morning star.*

There are two interpretations of these words. The Prophet Isaiah calls Satan the morning star (Lucifer) which fell from heaven (Isa 14:12). In that case, the words signify the dominion of the faithful Christian over Satan (compare Luke 10:18). On the other hand, the Holy Apostle Peter, in his second catholic epistle, by the "morning star," which shines forth in the hearts of men, means the Lord Jesus Christ (2 Pet 1:19). In this sense, the true Christian is promised the enlightenment of his soul by the light of Christ and participation in the future heavenly glory.[x]

2:29 *He that hath an ear, let him hear what the Spirit saith unto the churches.*

3. Instructions to the Churches of Asia Minor: Sardis, Philadelphia, and Laodicea

To the Church of Sardis

3:1–3 *And unto the angel of the church in Sardis write; These things saith he that hath the seven Spirits of God, and the seven stars; I know thy works, that thou hast a name that thou livest, and art dead. Be watchful, and strengthen the things which remain, that are ready to die: for I have not found thy works perfect before God. Remember therefore how thou hast received and heard, and hold fast, and repent. If therefore thou shalt not watch, I will come on thee as a thief, and thou shalt not know what hour I will come upon thee.*

To the angel of the Church of Sardis, the Lord commands to write in a tone more reproaching than consoling. This church has only the name of living faith, but in actual fact, it is spiritually dead. The Lord threatens the Christians of Sardis with sudden misfortune if they do not repent. There are, however, among them a very few who "have not defiled their garments." Those who overcome (the passions) the Lord promises to clothe in white garments, and their names will not be erased from the book of life, but they will be confessed by the Lord before His heavenly Father.

---

[x] St Andrew says of the "morning star," that there is nothing astonishing in the fact that it could have two opposite interpretations, a thing which happens often in Holy Scripture. What is important to understand is the *meaning* of the image. Here it means the same thing that victorious Christians have Christ the "morning star" shining in their hearts, and to say that they have dominion over Satan the "morning star" through the grace of Christ. (S.R.)

Sardis in antiquity was a large and wealthy city, the capital of the region of Lydia, and now it is the poor Turkish town of Sard. There are few Christians and they do not have their own church. Under the emperor Julian the Apostate (A.D. 360–363) the spiritual deadness of this city was clearly manifest: it quickly returned to idol worship, for which the chastisement of God overtook it; it was destroyed to its foundations.[xi]

> 3:4–5 *Thou hast a few names even in Sardis which have not defiled their garments; and they shall walk with me in white: for they are worthy. He that overcometh, the same shall be clothed in white raiment.*

By those who "have not defiled their garments" are metaphorically depicted here the defilements of the soul. Therefore, those who have not defiled their garments are those whose minds have not participated in the false teachings of heretics, while their lives were not spotted by passions and vices. By "white raiment" is to be understood the wedding garments in which the guests at the wedding banquet of the King's Son will be clothed; in this image, the Lord set forth in the parable the future blessedness of the righteous in His Heavenly Kingdom (Matt 22:11–12). These garments will be like the garments of the Saviour at the time of the Transfiguration, which became *white as the light* (Matt 17:2).

> 3:5 *And I will not blot out his name out of the book of life.*

The decrees of God concerning the fate of men are symbolically depicted in the image of a book in which the Lord, as the All-knowing and All-righteous Judge, records all the doings of men. This symbolical image is often used in Sacred Scripture (Pss 68:28, 138:16; Isa 4:3; Dan 7:10, 12:1; Mal 3:16; Exod 32:32–33; Luke 10:20; Phil 4:3; see also Rev 13:8, 17:8, 20:12, 15). According to this conception, he who lives worthy of the highest purpose is as it were inscribed in the book of life, while he who lives unworthily is as it were blotted out of this book, thereby being deprived of the right to eternal life. And therefore the promise to the one who overcomes sin, that his name will not be blotted out of the book of life, means the same thing as a promise not to deprive him of the heavenly goods which are prepared in the future life for the righteous.

> 3:5–6 *But I will confess his name before my Father, and before his angels. He that hath an ear, let him hear what the Spirit saith unto the churches.*

[xi] The image of the Lord's coming unexpectedly like a thief to chastise evil-doers is found elsewhere in the Apocalypse (16:15) and is used by the Lord also in the Gospel (see Matt 24:42–44, 1 Thess 5:2–4). (S.R.)

The promise to "confess his name" is the same thing that the Lord promised during His life on earth to His true followers (Matt 10:32, Luke 12:8), that is, "I will acknowledge and proclaim him to be my faithful disciple."

To the Church of Philadelphia

3:7–9 And to the angel of the church in Philadelphia write; These things saith he that is holy, he that is true, he that hath the key of David, he that openeth, and no man shutteth; and shutteth, and no man openeth. I know thy works: behold, I have set before thee an open door, and no man can shut it: for thou hast a little strength, and hast kept my word, and hast not denied my name. Behold, I will make them of the synagogue of Satan, which say they are Jews, and are not, but do lie; behold, I will make them to come and worship before thy feet, and to know that I have loved thee.

To the angel of the Church of Philadelphia, the Lord commands to write much that is consoling and praiseworthy. Despite its "little strength" (evidently referring to the fewness of its inhabitants), this church has not renounced the Name of Jesus before the satanic synagogue of its Jewish persecutors. For this the Lord will so arrange that they will come and bow down before her, and in the difficult time of temptation, for all the universe she will find defense and safekeeping in the Lord Himself. Therefore, the aim of the people of Philadelphia is to keep only that which they have, lest anyone take away their crown. The one who overcomes, the Lord, promises to make a pillar in the temple and to write upon him the Name of God and the name of the city of God—the New Jerusalem—and the new name of Jesus.

Philadelphia was the second-greatest city of Lydia and was named for its founder, Attalus Philadelphus, king of Pergamos. This city, alone of all the Asia Minor cities, for a long time did not give in to the Turks. It is remarkable that even at the present time Christianity in Philadelphia is in a more flourishing condition than in all of the other cities of Asia Minor. Here there has been preserved a numerous Christian population, having its own bishop and twenty-five churches. The inhabitants are distinguished by their great hospitality and kindness. The Turks call Philadelphia Alakh-Sher, that is, "city of God," and this name involuntarily reminds one of the promise of the Lord: "I will write upon him [that overcometh] the name of My God, and the name of the city of My God" (3:12).

The Son of God calls Himself He that has the key of David in the sense of having the highest authority in the house of David, for a key is a symbol of authority. The house of David or the kingdom of David means the same thing as the Kingdom of God, of which it was a prefiguration in the Old Testament (see Isa 22:22). Further, it is said that if the Lord deigns to open the doors of this kingdom to anyone, no one can hinder this, and the contrary likewise. Here also is contained a figurative indication of the firmness of the faith of the Philadelphians, which could not be broken by the Judaizing false teachers. The latter will come and bow down before the feet of the Philadelphians—that is, evidently they will acknowledge themselves to be defeated.

> 3:10–11 *Because thou hast kept the word of my patience, I also will keep thee from the hour of temptation, which shall come upon all the world, to try them that dwell upon the earth. Behold, I come quickly: hold that fast which thou hast, that no man take thy crown.*

By the "hour of temptation" during which the Lord promises to preserve His faithful Philadelphians, some understand the terrible persecutions against Christianity on the part of the pagan Roman emperors who seized "all of the world," as the Roman Empire was then called (compare Luke 2:1). Other commentators suppose that by Philadelphia one must understand one of the Christian churches, or all of the Christian Churches in general in the last times before the end of the world and the second coming of Christ. In this latter sense, especially understandable is the exhortation "Behold I come quickly: hold that fast which thou hast, that no man take thy crown." At that time, there will be an increased danger of losing faith because of the multitude of temptations, but thereby the reward for faithfulness will be, so to speak, right at hand, and therefore, we must be especially vigilant lest, out of light-mindedness, we lose the possibility of salvation—as, for example, the wife of Lot lost it.[xii]

> 3:12–13 *Him that overcometh will I make a pillar in the temple of my God, and he shall go no more out: and I will write upon him the name of my God, and the name of the city of my God, which is new Jerusalem, which cometh down out of heaven from my God: and I will write upon him my new name. He that hath an ear, let him hear what the Spirit saith unto the churches.*

The placing of a "pillar" in the Church of Christ, which has not been vanquished by the gates of hell (figuratively represented here in the form of a house), indicates that the one who overcomes temptations belongs to the Church of Christ inviolably; that is, he has a most solid position in the Kingdom of Heaven. The high reward for such a one will also be the writing upon him of a triple name: the name of a child of God, as belonging inseparably to God; the name of a citizen of the new or heavenly Jerusalem; and the name of Christian, as an authentic member of the Body of Christ. The New Jerusalem, beyond any doubt, is the heavenly triumphant Church (Rev 21:2, Gal 4:26), which cometh down out of heaven because the very origin of the Church from the Son of God, Who came down from heaven (John 3:13), is heavenly; it gives to people heavenly gifts and raises them to heaven.

[xii] In this second interpretation, the "hour of temptation" is virtually synonymous with the "great tribulation," which will come just before the end of the world, when "the days will be shortened" for the sake of the elect and "immediately after the tribulation of those days" the end of everything will come (Matt 24:21, 22, 29). (S.R.)

To the Church of Laodicea

> 3:14 *And unto the angel of the Laodiceans write; These things saith the Amen, the faithful and true witness, the beginning of the creation of God.*

To the angel of the Church of Laodicea, the seventh and last of the churches, he is commanded to write much by way of accusation. The Lord does not utter about it a single favorable word. He reproaches it for the fact that it is neither hot nor cold, and therefore He threatens to spit it forth from His mouth like lukewarm water which causes nausea. Despite the opinionated self-confidence of the Laodiceans in their moral perfections, the Lord calls them wretched, miserable, poor, blind, and naked, exhorting them to take care to cover their nakedness and to heal their blindness. At the same time, He calls them to repentance, saying that with love He stands at the doors of the heart of everyone who repents and is ready to come to Him with His mercies and forgiveness of everything. The one who overcomes his pride and in general his own moral infirmities the Lord promises to place together with Himself on His throne.

Laodicea, now called by the Turks, Eski-Gissar, that is, "Ancient Fortress," is in Phrygia on the river Lycus, near the city of Colossae. In antiquity it was famous for its trade, the fertility of its soil, and its domestic animals. Its population was numerous and wealthy; of this there are the testimonies of the excavations at which there have been found many precious pieces of sculpture, fragments of luxurious marble decorations, pedestals, and baskets, etc. One may suppose that it was its wealth that made the Laodiceans so lukewarm to the Christian faith, for which the city was subjected to the chastisement of God—its total destruction and desolation by the Turks.

The Lord is called "the beginning of the creation of God" not, of course, in the sense that He is the first creation of God, but in the sense that all things were made by Him, and "without Him was not any thing made that was made" (John 1:3), and likewise in the sense that He is the cause of the re-creation of fallen man (Gal 6:15; Col 1:15, 18; 3:10).

> 3:15–16 *I know thy works, that thou art neither cold nor hot: I would thou wert cold or hot. So then because thou art lukewarm, and neither cold nor hot, I will spue thee out of my mouth.*

The cold man, who has not known faith, can more easily believe and become a fervent believer than a cooled-off Christian who has become indifferent to the faith. Even an open sinner is better than a lukewarm Pharisee who is satisfied with his moral condition. This is why the Lord Jesus Christ reproached the Pharisees, preferring to them the repentant publicans and harlots. Open and evident sinners can more easily come to an awareness of their own sinfulness and to true repentance than people with a lukewarm conscience who do not acknowledge their moral infirmities.

> 3:17–18 *Because thou sayest, I am rich, and increased with goods, and have need of nothing; and knowest not that thou art wretched, and miserable, and poor, and blind, and naked: I counsel thee to buy of me gold tried in the fire, that thou mayest be rich; and white raiment, that thou mayest be clothed, and that the shame of thy nakedness do not appear; and anoint thine eyes with eyesalve, that thou mayest see.*

"Gold tried in the fire, white raiment, and eye salve," which the Lord advises the Laodiceans to buy from Him, signify, respectively, the love and good will of God acquired by repentance; good works and pure and undefiled conduct; and the highest heavenly wisdom which gives spiritual sight.

"If you wish to become rich, I counsel you, with flaming desire and a fervent heart, to acquire from Me, the Enricher, gold cleansed by the fire of temptations. From it you will have in your heart a treasure that cannot be stolen and will be clothed in a most bright garment of virtues, with which you will cover your nakedness of sin" (St Andrew, chapter 9).

We may suppose that the Laodiceans actually trusted excessively in their wealth, striving to join together the service of God and mammon. Some think that what is referred to here is pastors who are striving to enrich themselves by means of earthly wealth and have become of the opinion that, through wealth, they are called to lord it over the inheritance of God, overawing people through their wealth. The Lord advises such ones to buy from Him, that is, not merely to ask and receive freely, but to buy—that is, to acquire from Christ Himself at the price of labors of repentance—these things: "gold tried in the fire," that is, the authentic grace-given spiritual wealth, which for a pastor consists among other things in a word of instruction mixed with salt; "white raiment," that is, the gift of doing good to one's neighbor; and "eye salve," or the virtue of nonacquisitiveness, which opens one's eyes to the vanity and emptiness of all the wealth of this corruptible world.[xiii]

[xiii] St Cyprian of Carthage comments on this passage as follows: "You are mistaken, and are deceived, whosoever you are, that think yourself rich in this world. Listen to the voice of your Lord in the Apocalypse, rebuking men of your stamp with righteous reproaches: 'Thou sayest,' says He, 'I am rich, and increased with goods....' You therefore, who are rich and wealthy, buy for yourself of Christ gold tried by fire, that you may be pure gold, with your filth burnt out as if by fire, if you are purged by almsgiving and righteous works. Buy for yourself white raiment, that you who had been naked according to Adam, and were before frightful and unseemly, may be clothed with the white garment of Christ. And you who are a wealthy and rich matron in Christ's Church, anoint your eyes ... with Christ's eye salve, that you may be able to attain to see God, by deserving well of God, both by good works and

3:19 *As many as I love, I rebuke and chasten; be zealous therefore, and repent.* (See Prov 3:11–12; Heb 12:3–8.)

3:20 *Behold, I stand at the door, and knock: if any man hear my voice, and open the door, I will come in to him, and will sup with him, and he with me.*

"Not by compulsion, He says, is My presence: for I knock at the doors of the heart and rejoice with those who open over their salvation. This salvation I consider food and supper, and I eat what they eat, and thus they banish the famine of hearing the word of the Lord (Amos 8:11, Sept.) and the darkness of errors" (St Andrew, chapter 9).

3:21–22 *To him that overcometh will I grant to sit with me in my throne, even as I also overcame, and am set down with my Father in his throne. He that hath an ear, let him hear what the Spirit saith unto the churches.*

To him that overcomes is given the promise that he will sit on the throne of God, by which is to be understood the highest dignity of an inheritor of the Kingdom of Heaven, one who reigns together with Christ Himself, the Conqueror of the devil (see Matt 19:28, Luke 22:30).

The Seven Churches as Seven Christian Epochs

There is an opinion that the seven churches signify seven periods in the life of the whole Church of Christ, from its foundation to the end of the world:

1. The Church in Ephesus signifies the first period, the Apostolic Church, which labored and did not faint while fighting with the first heretics, the Nicolaitans, but soon abandoned the good custom of doing good to others—the "communion of goods" ("thy first love").
2. The Church of Smyrna signifies the second period, the period of persecutions against the Church, of which there were ten in all.
3. The Church of Pergamos signifies the third period, the epoch of the Ecumenical Councils and the battle with the heresies by the sword of the word of God.
4. The Church of Thyatira is the fourth period, the period of the blossoming of Christianity among the new peoples of Europe.
5. The Church of Sardis is the epoch of humanism and materialism of the sixteenth to the eighteenth centuries.
6. The Church of Philadelphia is the next-to-last period in the life of the Church of Christ, the epoch contemporary to us, when the Church will in fact have

character" (St Cyprian, *On Works and Alms*, English trans. in *Ante-Nicene Fathers*, vol. 5, pp. 479–80). (S.R.)

"little strength" in contemporary humanity and new persecutions will begin, when patience will be required.

7. The Church of Laodicea is the last, most frightful epoch before the end of the world, characterized by indifference to the faith and outward prosperity.[xiv]

4. THE SECOND VISION: THE VISION OF GOD SITTING ON THE THRONE, AND THE LAMB

4:1 After this I looked, and, behold, a door was opened in heaven: and the first voice which I heard was as it were of a trumpet talking with me; which said, Come up hither, and I will shew thee things which must be hereafter.

The fourth chapter contains the beginning of a new, a second vision. The depiction of a new and magnificent spectacle which opens before the gaze of St John begins with a commandment to him to ascend through an open door in heaven so as to see "things which must be hereafter." The opening of the door signifies the revelation of the hidden mysteries of the Spirit. By the words "Come hither," the hearer is commanded to put off entirely earthly thinking and be converted to heavenly thinking.

4:2–3 And immediately I was in the Spirit: and, behold, a throne was set in heaven, and One sat on the throne. And He that sat was to look upon like a jasper and a sardine stone: and there was a rainbow round about the throne, in sight like unto an emerald.

"And immediately I was in the Spirit"—that is, again in a state of ecstasy, St John saw this time God the Father Himself, sitting upon a throne. His appearance was like the precious stone jasper (a stone green like an emerald) and a sardine stone (sard, of a fiery color). The first of these colors, green, according to the commentary of St Andrew of Caesarea, signifies that the Divine nature is ever flourishing, life bearing, and gives nourishment. The second, the fiery yellow red, indicates purity and sanctity, which ever remain in God, and His threatening anger toward those who transgress His will. The union of these two colors indicates that God chastises sinners, but at the same time is always ready to forgive one who sincerely repents. The apparition of the One sitting on the throne was surrounded by a rainbow like an emerald, a stone of green color which signifies, as does also the rainbow which appeared after the Flood, the eternal mercy of God toward mankind.

[xiv] Has not this last epoch already begun in our midst in the 1980s? Judging from the indifference of Orthodox Christians who should be burning with faith and enlightening others, the widespread Phariseeism and satisfaction with the outward show of Orthodoxy, and the lukewarmness that so easily steals into the hearts of all of us who are not directly under persecution—this epoch has indeed begun. (S.R.)

The sitting on the throne itself signifies the opening of the Judgment of God, which is to be revealed in the last times. This is not yet the terrible Last Judgment, but a preparatory judgment like those judgments of God which have occurred many times in the history of mankind to people who have sinned. (For example, the universal Flood, the destruction of Sodom and Gomorrah, the destruction of Jerusalem, and many others.)

The precious stones jasper and sardine, and likewise the rainbow around the throne, being a symbol of the ceasing of the wrath of God and the renewal of the world, signify that the judgment of God upon the world, that is, its fiery destruction, is to end with its renewal. This is indicated also by the quality of jasper to heal wounds received by the sword.

"Since in this vision he presents the Father, he does not give to Him, as previously to the Son, the signs of a bodily image, but likens and compares Him to precious stones" (St Andrew, chapter 10; see Ezek 1:26–28).

4:4 And round about the throne were four and twenty seats: and upon the seats I saw four and twenty elders sitting, clothed in white raiment; and they had on their heads crowns of gold.

Around the throne on twenty-four other thrones sat twenty-four elders, clothed in white garments, with golden crowns on their heads. There are the most varied opinions and suppositions as to whom one must understand by these elders. One thing is certain: that these are representatives of humanity who have pleased the Lord. Many suppose, basing themselves on the promise given to the holy apostles, "ye ... also shall sit upon twelve thrones, judging the twelve tribes of Israel" (Matt 19:28), that by these twenty-four elders one must understand twelve representatives of the Old Testament humanity—the holy patriarchs and prophets—and twelve representatives of the New Testament humanity—namely, the twelve Apostles of Christ. The white garments are a symbol of purity and eternal feasting, and the golden crowns are a sign of victory over demons.

4:5 And out of the throne proceeded lightnings and thunderings and voices.

This indicates how frightful and terrible God is for unrepentant sinners who are unworthy of His mercy and forgiveness: compare the manifestation of God on Mt Sinai (Exod 19:16).

"But for those worthy of salvation, the lightnings and thunderings do not cause fear, but sweetness and enlightenment: the one enlightens their spiritual eyes, while the other gives pleasure to the hearing" (St Andrew, chapter 10).

4:5 And there were seven lamps of fire burning before the throne, which are the seven Spirits of God.

By these seven spirits one must understand either the seven chief angels, as St Irenaeus interprets it, or the seven gifts of the Holy Spirit, which are enumerated by the holy Prophet Isaiah (Isa 11:2; see the commentary on Apocalypse 1:4).

4:6 And before the throne there was a sea of glass like unto crystal.

The crystal sea, being unmoving and still, as opposed to the stormy sea seen later by St John (Rev 13:1), must signify, in the opinion of many interpreters, "the multitude of the holy heavenly powers," pure and immortal (St Andrew of Caesarea). These are the souls of men who have not been disturbed by the storms of the sea of life, but like crystal, reflect the seven colors of the rainbow, being penetrated by the seven gifts of the grace of the Holy Spirit.[xv]

4:6–8 And in the midst of the throne, and round about the throne, were four beasts [living creatures] full of eyes before and behind.[xvi] And the first beast [living creature] was like a lion, and the second beast [living creature] like a calf, and the third beast [living creature] had a face as a man, and the fourth beast [living creature] was like a flying eagle. And the four beasts [living creatures] had each of them six wings about him; and they were full of eyes within: and they rest not day and night, saying: Holy, Holy, Holy, Lord God Almighty, Which was, and is, and is to come.

Some think that by these living creatures should be understood the four elements and God's governance and preservation of them, or God's dominion over the regions of heaven, earth, sea, and the underworld. However, as is clear from the further description of the appearance of these living creatures, without doubt they are the very angelic powers who in the mystical vision of the holy prophet Ezekiel (Ezek 1:5–25) on the river Chobar, supported the mystical chariot on which the Lord God sits as a King.

These four living creatures have served as it were as emblems of the four Evangelists. The multitude of their eyes indicates the Divine omniscience, the

---

[xv] More simply, perhaps, as St Andrew also says (chapter 10), the sea of glass (which appears also in Rev 15:2, but nowhere else in Scripture) indicates the "undisturbability of the future life" as opposed to the changeability of the stormy sea of this life, from which Antichrist, being of earth, comes (Rev 13:1). (S.R.)

[xvi] Unfortunately, the KJV translates by the one word "beast" two entirely different Greek words: *zoôn*, which is more correctly translated in the Revised Standard Version as "living creature" (as also in the KJV when it appears in Ezek 1:5); and *thêrion* (Rev 6:8, 13:1, etc.) which is more properly "(wild) beast." Therefore, in the Apocalypse 4:6–9, we have replaced the KJV "beast" with the RSV "living creature." (S.R.)

knowing of everything past, present, and future. These are the highest angelic beings, closest to God [the Seraphim— S.R.] who ceaselessly glorify God (see also Isa 6:2–3).

"These symbols probably signify also the economy of Christ: the lion as king, the calf as chief priest or rather sacrifice, the man as incarnate for our sake, and the eagle as giver of the Life-giving Spirit which descends on us from above" (St Andrew, chapter 10).[xvii] "Which was, and is, and is to come signifies the Holy Trinity" (St Andrew, chapter 10).[xviii]

> 4:9–11 *And when those beasts [living creatures] give glory and honour and thanks to him that sat on the throne, who liveth forever and ever, the four and twenty elders fall down before him that sat on the throne, and worship him that liveth forever and ever, and cast their crowns before the throne, saying, Thou art worthy, O Lord, to receive glory and honour and power: for thou hast created all things, and for thy pleasure they are and were created.*

"The four and twenty elders fall down": These words signify that the elders are participants in the hymns of the heavenly powers and confess that they received from God the power of victory over spiritual enemies.

"They say: Inasmuch as Thou, O Master, art the Cause and Giver of the glorious victory, to Thee should be sent up thanksgiving from all creatures" (St Andrew, chapter 10).

5. CONTINUATION OF THE SECOND VISION: THE SEALED BOOK AND THE LAMB AS IT HAD BEEN SLAIN

> 5:1–3 *And I saw in the right hand of him that sat on the throne a book written within and on the backside, sealed with seven seals. And I saw a strong angel proclaiming with a loud voice, Who is worthy to open the book, and to loose the seals thereof? And no man in*

[xvii] St Irenaeus of Lyons (second century A.D.) was the first to identify the four living creatures with the four evangelists. According to early Orthodox icons (for example, the mosaics in the basilica of San Vitale in Ravenna) the lion is identified with St Mark, the calf with St Luke, the man with St Matthew, and the eagle with St John. (S.R.)

[xviii] St Athanasius the Great says also that "Holy, Holy, Holy" indicates the Holy Trinity and the equality of the Three Persons: "The Triad, praised, reverenced, and adored, is one and indivisible and without degrees. It is united without confusion, just as the Monad also is distinguished without separation. For the fact of those venerable living creatures (Isa 6, Rev 4:8) offering their praises three times, saying 'Holy, Holy, Holy,' proves that the Three Hypostases are perfect; just as in saying 'Lord' they declare the One Essence." (S.R.)

heaven, nor in earth, neither under the earth, was able to open the book, neither to look thereon.

The Lord Almighty Whom St John has seen sitting on the throne holds in His right hand a book written outside and inside with seven seals. Books in antiquity consisted of pieces of parchment rolled up in a roll or placed on a round stick. Inside such a scroll there was a kind of stick and the whole thing was bound outwardly and by a seal. Sometimes the book consisted of a piece of parchment which was folded in the form of a fan and tied from above with string, with seals on each bend or fold of the book. In such a case, the opening of one seal gave opportunity to open and read only one part of the book. The writing was usually made only on the inner side of the parchment, but in rare cases, both sides were written on. According to the explanation of St Andrew of Caesarea and other commentators, by the "book" which St John mentions one must understand "the most wise memory of God," in which are registered all things, likewise, "the depths of the decrees of God." In this book were consequently registered all the mystical decrees of the most wise providence of God concerning the salvation of men.

> The seven seals signify either the complete confirmation which is known to none, or the economy of Him Who tests the depth of the Divine Spirit, something which can be unsealed by no created being. The book is also to be understood as the prophecies concerning which Christ Himself has said that in part they were fulfilled in the Gospel (Luke 24:44), but that the others will be fulfilled in the last days. (St Andrew, chapter 11)

One of the mighty angels with a loud voice cries out that someone should open this book, taking off its seven seals, but there was found none worthy, no man in heaven, nor in earth, neither under the earth who would dare to do this. This signifies that to none of the created beings is accessible the knowledge of the mysteries of God. This inaccessibility is yet increased by the expression, "neither to look thereon," that is, even to look at it.

> *5:4–6 And I wept much, because no man was found worthy to open and to read the book, neither to look thereon. And one of the elders saith unto me, Weep not: behold the Lion of the tribe of Judah, the Root of David, hath prevailed to open the book, and to loose the seven seals thereof. And I beheld, and, lo, in the midst of the throne and of the four beasts [living creatures], and in the midst of the elders, stood a Lamb as it had been slain, having seven horns and seven eyes, which are the seven Spirits of God sent forth into all the earth.*

St John grieved much about this, but he was consoled by one of the elders who said: "Weep not. Behold the Lion of the tribe of Judah, the Root of David, hath prevailed to open the book and to loose the seven seals thereof." The lion signifies here a powerful one, a hero. By this is indicated the prophecy of the patriarch Jacob concerning the "lion from the tribe of Judah," by which is to be understood the Messiah, Christ (Gen 49:9–10).

Having looked, the seer of mysteries John beheld "a Lamb as it had been slain, having seven horns and seven eyes." This Lamb, carrying in himself the marks signifying that he had been offered in sacrifice, is, of course, the Lamb of God that taketh away the sin of the world (John 1:29), that is, Our Lord Jesus Christ. He alone is manifest as worthy to open the book of God's decrees; for He, having offered Himself as a sacrifice for the sins of men, is Himself revealed as the fulfiller of God's decrees for the salvation of the human race. Further, the later opening by Him of the seven seals of the book signifies the very fulfillment of the Divine decrees by the Only begotten Son of God as the Saviour of mankind. The seven horns are symbols of His power (Ps 74:11), and the seven eyes signify, as is immediately explained, "the seven Spirits of God sent forth into all the earth," that is, the seven gifts of the Holy Spirit which repose in Christ as the Anointed of God. The Prophet Isaiah already spoke of this (Isa 11:2), as did also the holy Prophet Zechariah (Zech 4). The seven eyes symbolize at the same time God's omniscience. "The Lamb stood in the midst of the throne," that is, there where the Son of God should be, at the right hand of God the Father.

> 5:7–8 *And he came and took the book out of the right hand of him that sat upon the throne. And when he had taken the book, the four beasts [living creatures] and four and twenty elder fell down before the Lamb, having every one of them harps, and golden vials full of odours, which are the prayers of the saints.*

The Lamb took the book from the One sitting on the throne and immediately the four creatures (the Seraphim) and the twenty-four elders falling down gave to Him divine worship. The harps which they had in their hands signify the harmonious singing of their souls. The golden cups, as is immediately explained, filled with incense, are the prayers of the saints.

"The odours, 'incense,' signify the fragrant sacrifice of the faithful which they offer by an undefiled life, for, as the divine Paul says, We are … a sweet savor of Christ (2 Cor 2:15). The vials are thoughts from which come the fragrance of good deeds and pure prayer" (St Andrew, chapter 12).

> 5:9–14 *And they sang a new song, saying, Thou art worthy to take the book, and to open the seals thereof: for thou wast slain, and hast redeemed us to God by thy blood out of every kindred, and tongue, and people, and nation; And hast made us unto our God kings and priests: and we shall reign on the earth. And I beheld, and I heard the voice of many angels round about the throne and the beasts [living creatures] and the elders: and the number of them was ten thousand times ten thousand, and thousands of thousands; saying with a loud*

voice, Worthy is the Lamb that was slain to receive power, and riches, and wisdom, and strength, and honour, and glory, and blessing. And every creature which is in heaven, and on earth, and under the earth, and such as are in the sea, and all that are in them, heard I saying, Blessing, and honour, and glory, and power, be unto him that sitteth upon the throne, and unto the Lamb for ever and ever. And the four beasts [living creatures] said, Amen. And the four and twenty elders fell down and worshipped him that liveth for ever and ever.

And they sang a hymn to the Son of God, the Redeemer of mankind, an authentically "new song" not heard from the creation of the world, concerning which the Psalmist King David already prophesies (Ps 97:1).

The new song is that which the Holy Spirit teaches to those who have been delivered from the oldness of the letter and who are enlightened from among all tribes and peoples. Of them, he (John) says that they will reign on that earth, which the Lord has promised to the meek (Matt 5:5).

In this song is glorified the new Kingdom of the Son of God, in which He reigns as the God-Man Who bought this Kingdom with the high price of His own blood. The redemption of mankind, although it refers only to man, still was so astonishing, so splendid, so touching and sacred, that it aroused the most lively participation in the whole choir of heaven so that all together angels and men glorify God for this work and "worshipped Him That liveth for ever and ever."

> By the four living creatures and the elders is signified the fact that from angels and men has been formed a single flesh and a single church through Christ God Who has joined together what was separate and has destroyed the middle wall of separation. And so, together with the four living creatures who surpass the other orders of angels, the elders also, who signify the fullness of those being saved, are worthy of the song and worship of God. May we also be vouchsafed this in Christ Himself the Giver of peace and our God, with Whom together with the Father and the Holy Spirit, may there be glory, dominion, honor, now and ever and unto the unending ages. Amen. (St Andrew, chapter 12)

6. THE OPENING BY THE LAMB OF THE SEALS OF THE MYSTICAL BOOK: THE FIRST TO SIXTH SEALS

6:1–2 And I saw when the Lamb opened one of the seals, and I heard, as it were the noise of thunder, one of the four beasts [living creatures] saying, Come and see. And I saw, and behold a white horse: and he that sat on him had a bow; and a crown was given unto him: and he went forth conquering, and to conquer.

In the sixth chapter there is related the taking away by the Lamb one by one of the first seals of the mystical book, and the signs that accompanied this. By the opening of the seals, one must understand the fulfillment of the Divine decrees by the Son of God Who has given Himself as a Lamb to be slaughtered.

In the explanation of St Andrew of Caesarea, the taking away of the first seal is the sending into the world of the holy apostles who, like a bow which directs the preaching of the Gospel against demons, by their saving arrows have brought the wounded ones to Christ and received a crown because by the Truth they have conquered the chief darkness. This is what is symbolized by the white horse and the one who sits upon it with a bow in his hands.

> Here among those in heaven is to be observed the good order which descends from the first choirs to the second. For the first voice, who commands the coming of the angel who mystically depicts the vision, was heard from one of the living creatures— the lion. It seems to me that the lion signifies the royal authority of the Apostles over the demons.... He went forth conquering, and to conquer: the first victory is the conversion of the pagans, and the second is (the Apostles') voluntary departure from the body joined with tortures. (St Andrew, chapter 13)

6:3–4 And when he had opened the second seal, I heard the second beast [living creature] say: Come and see. And here went out another horse that was red: and power was given to him that sat thereon to take peace from the earth, and that they should kill one another: and there was given unto him a great sword.

The taking away of the second seal and the appearance of the red horse, to the one sitting upon it to which "power was given to take peace from the earth," signifies the arousal of the unbelievers against the believers when peace was destroyed by the preaching of the Gospel in the fulfillment of the words of Christ: I came not to send peace but a sword (Matt 10:34); and then the earth was abundantly watered by the blood of the confessors and martyrs for Christ. "The 'red horse' is the sign either of the shedding of blood or of the heartfelt zeal of those who suffer for Christ" (St Andrew, chapter 14).

"Since the first living creature signifies apostolic authority, I suppose that the calf, the second living creature, indicates the sacred sacrifices of the holy martyrs" (St Andrew, chapter 14).

6:5–6 And when he had opened the third seal, I heard the third beast [living creature] say, Come and see. And I beheld, and lo a black horse; and he that sat on him had a pair of balances in his hand. And I heard a voice in the midst of the four beasts [living creatures] say, A measure of wheat for a penny, and three measures of barley for a penny; and see thou hurt not the oil and the wine.

The taking away of the third seal and the appearance right after this of the black horse with his rider who has "a pair of balances in his hand" signifies the falling away from Christ of those who do not have firm faith in Him. The black color of the horse symbolizes "lamentation over those who have fallen away from faith in Christ by reason of the difficulty of the torments" (St Andrew, chapter 15).

"A measure of wheat for a penny" signifies those who have lawfully struggled and carefully have preserved the image of God given to them. "And three measures of barley for a penny" signifies those who like cattle, because of lack of courage, have submitted to the persecutors out of fear, but later have repented and with tears have washed away their defiled image. "And see thou hurt not the oil and the wine" signifies that one should not out of fear renounce the healing of Christ or leave without Him those who are wounded and have fallen among thieves, but they should be brought the wine of consolation and the oil of compassion (St Andrew, chapter 15). Many by the black horse understand the misfortune of famine.

"By the third living creature I understand the man, which signifies the fall of men, and by the power of free will, the punishment for inclination to sin" (St Andrew, chapter 15).

We must help our brethren who have fallen in the persecutions, giving them consolation (wine) and compassion (oil). The wheat for a penny indicates good price for good wheat; the barley indicates cheaper goods.

> 6:7–8 *And when he had opened the fourth seal, I heard the voice of the fourth beast [living creature] say, Come and see. And I looked, and behold a pale horse: and his name that sat on him was Death, and Hell followed with him. And power was given unto them over the fourth part of the earth, to kill with sword, and with hunger, and with death, and with the beasts of the earth.*

The taking away of the fourth seal and the appearance of the pale horse with its rider whose name is Death signifies the manifestations of the wrath of God in revenge for the pious and the punishment of sinners. These are the various misfortunes of the last times prophesied by Christ the Saviour (Matt 24:6–7).

"The high flight and the swooping fall upon its prey of the fourth living creature, the eagle, indicates that the wounds come from above from the wrath of God for the revenge of the pious and the punishment of the impious, if only these latter will not be converted through correction to the better" (St Andrew, chapter 16).

> 6:9–11 *And when he had opened the fifth seal, I saw under the altar the souls of them that were slain for the word of God, and for the testimony which they held; And they cried with a loud voice, saying, How long, O Lord, holy and true, dost thou not judge and avenge our blood on them that dwell on the earth? And white robes were given unto every one of them; and it was said unto them, that they should rest yet for a little season, until their fellowservants also and their brethren, that should be killed as they were, should be fulfilled.*

The taking away of the fifth seal reveals the prayer of the holy martyrs at the throne of God for the hastening of the end of the world and the coming of the

Last Judgment. The souls of the righteous who have suffered for Christ, as is evident from this passage, are under the altar of the heavenly temple, just as on earth from the time of the martyrs there entered the custom of placing in the foundations of Christian temples and altars particles of the relics of the holy martyrs. The prayer of the righteous ones is explained, of course, not by a desire for any personal revenge but by a desire for the speeding up of God's righteousness on earth and His rewarding of each according to his works, which is to occur at the Last Judgment and will make them participants of eternal blessedness since they have given their lives for Christ and His Divine teaching. To them are given white garments, a symbol of their virtue, and it is told them to endure "yet for a little season" until their fellow laborers, and the brethren who will be killed just as they were, shall fill up the number so that all might receive the worthy reward from God.

> 6:12–17 *And I beheld when he had opened the sixth seal, and, lo, there was a great earthquake; and the sun became black as sackcloth of hair, and the moon became as blood; And the stars of heaven fell unto the earth, even as a fig tree casteth her untimely figs, when she is shaken of a mighty wind. And the heaven departed as a scroll when it is rolled together; and every mountain and island were moved out of their places. And the kings of the earth, and the great men, and the rich men, and the chief captains, and the mighty men, and every bondman, and every free man, hid themselves in the dens and in the rocks of the mountains; And said to the mountains and rocks, Fall on us and hide us from the face of him that sitteth on the throne, and from the wrath of the Lamb: For the great day of his wrath is come; and who shall be able to stand?*

The taking away of the sixth seal symbolizes those elemental misfortunes and horrors which will occur on earth in the last period of its existence immediately before the end of the world, before the second coming of Christ and the Last Judgment.

These will be those very signs concerning which the Lord Jesus Christ Himself prophesied not long before His suffering on the Cross (Matt 24:29, Luke 21:25–26).

These signs will evoke mortal fear and terror among people of all conditions who will live then on the earth, beginning with kings, nobles, and generals and ending with slaves. All will tremble with the coming of "the great day of His wrath" and will entreat the mountains and stones: "Hide us from the face of Him Who sitteth on the throne and from the wrath of the Lamb." Similar horrors were experienced by the murderers of Christ at the destruction of Jerusalem. On a yet greater scale such horrors will overtake the whole of mankind before the end of the world.

The earthquake, of which we often read in Scripture, is a change of things; wherefore also, the expression yet once more *I will shake all nations* (Hag 2:7) signifies as the apostle says, *the removing of those things that are shaken* (Heb 12:26–27).

The blackness of the sun and the darkness and bloody appearance of the moon indicate, as the Blessed Cyril has often expressed it, the darkness of soul of those upon whom the wrath of God will come. And that "the stars fell," as has been written also of those deceived by Antiochus, indicate that those who think themselves to be the lights of the world will fall, being crushed and defeated by what will happen at that time, when as the Lord has said, If it were possible they shall deceive the very elect by reason of the great tribulation (Matt 24:24). This is perhaps why there is given here the indication of the fig tree, which, at the blowing of the wind of the devil, casts down its fruit while still unripe, since they have not ripened in the heat of temptations and are not sweetened by grace.... Whether all this will turn out in a physical form at the glorious Coming of Christ the King is known by Him Who possesses the mystical treasury of knowledge and wisdom. (St Andrew, chapter 18)

The heaven is not to be subject to corruption and destruction but, as it were, to a certain rolling up and change for the better. Irenaeus, in his fifth accusatory treatise against the knowledge falsely so-called, says: "Neither the essence nor the being of the creation will perish or will be destroyed, for true and strong is He Who created it, but the 'fashion of this world passeth away' (1 Cor 7:31), the world in which the transgression was performed." (St Andrew, chapter 18)[223]

At the coming of Antichrist, those (called here symbolically mountains) who are leaders either over the good order of the Church or over the worldly dominions, and the churches of the faithful which are presented here under the image of islands ... will fall from their places, changing them one for another—something which we too experienced and underwent according to His love for mankind on account of our sins before His Coming. (St Andrew, chapter 18)

7. The Appearance After the Opening of the Sixth Seal of the One Hundred and Forty-Four Thousand Sealed upon the Earth and Clothed in White Garments in Heaven

7:1 And after these things I saw four angels standing on the four corners of the earth, holding the four winds of the earth, that the wind should not blow on the earth, nor on the sea, nor on any tree.

These four angels appeared evidently as the fulfillers of the chastisement of God upon the world. One of the purposes set before them is "holding the four winds." As St Andrew of Caesarea explains, this

clearly testifies concerning the end of the submissiveness (natural order) of the creation and the inevitability of evil because everything growing upon the earth sprouts and is nourished by winds; and with their cooperation men also sail on the sea, ... we think that all this in the greatest possible degree will occur at the coming of Antichrist, and not in the Jewish land only, but over the whole earth, on the four corners of which, he says, there will stand angels as the performers of a service pre-assigned to them by God, but for us unknown. (St Andrew, chapter 19)

7:2–3 And I saw another angel ascending from the east, having the seal of the living God: and he cried with a loud voice to the four angels, to whom it was given to hurt the earth and the sea, Saying, Hurt not the earth, neither the sea, nor the trees, till we have sealed the servants of our God in their foreheads.

But here there appeared also "another angel" who had the "seal of the living God" in order to place this seal on the foreheads of the servants of God and thereby deliver them from the approaching chastisements. This is something like what was revealed once to the holy Prophet Ezekiel about the man clothed in a podir, that is, a long linen garment, who places a seal upon those who groan (Ezek 9:4) so as not to destroy the righteous together with the unrighteous (for the hidden virtues of the saints are unknown even to the angels).

In what this seal consists we do not know, and there is no need to seek this out. Perhaps this will be the sign of the Precious Cross of the Lord, by which it will be possible to distinguish believers from unbelievers and apostates; or perhaps it will be the seal of martyrdom for Christ.

This will primarily be fulfilled during the time of the coming of Antichrist, when the seal of the Life-giving Cross will distinguish the unfaithful from the faithful, who will bear the sign of Christ before them unashamed and with boldness … the virtuous will need the angelic help before the coming of disasters, and this will be by the power of the seal of the Spirit which will be given us; but this seal will reveal its power only to the extent that we show our own activity. (St Andrew, chapter 19)

7:4–8 And I heard the number of them which were sealed: and there were sealed an hundred and forty and four thousand of all the tribes of the children of Israel. Of the tribe of Juda were sealed twelve thousand. Of the tribe of Reuben were sealed twelve thousand. Of the tribe of Gad were sealed twelve thousand. Of the tribe of Aser were sealed twelve thousand. Of the tribe of Nephthalim were sealed twelve thousand. Of the tribe of Manasses were sealed twelve thousand. Of the tribe of Simeon were sealed twelve thousand. Of the tribe of Levi were sealed twelve thousand. Of the tribe of Issachar were sealed twelve thousand. Of the tribe of Zabulon were sealed twelve thousand. Of the tribe of Joseph were sealed twelve thousand. Of the tribe of Benjamin were sealed twelve thousand.

This sealing will be with the Israelites, who before the end of the world will be converted to Christ, as St Paul predicts (Rom 9:27, 11:26). In each of the twelve tribes there will be twelve thousand sealed, and 144,000 in all. Of these tribes only the tribe of Dan is not mentioned, because from it, according to tradition, will come the antichrist. In place of the tribe of Dan is mentioned the priestly tribe of Levi, which previously had not entered into the twelve tribes. Such a limited number is mentioned, perhaps, in order to show how small is the number of the sons of Israel who are saved in comparison with the uncountable multitudes of those who have loved the Lord Jesus Christ from among all the other peoples of the earth who had been pagans.

> The precise equality of the numbers of those saved from each tribe, it seems to me, indicates the fruitfulness of apostolic seed, because the number twelve taken twelve times and multiplied by a thousand gives the number indicated here, for they were the disciples of the seed which fell on the ground and brought forth the multiple fruit of universal salvation. (St Andrew, chapter 19)

> 7:9–14 *After this I beheld, and lo, a great multitude, which no man could number, of all nations, and kindreds, and people, and tongues, stood before the throne, and before the Lamb, clothed with white robes, and palms in their hands; And cried with a loud voice, saying, Salvation to our God which sitteth upon the throne, and unto the Lamb. And all the angels stood round about the throne, and about the elders and the four beasts [living creatures], and fell before the throne on their faces, and worshipped God, Saying, Amen: Blessing, and glory, and wisdom, and thanksgiving, and honour, and power, and might, be unto our God for ever and ever. Amen. And one of the elders answered saying unto me, What are these which are arrayed in white robes? and whence came they? And I said unto him, Sir, thou knowest. And he said to me, These are they which came out of great tribulation, and have washed their robes, and made them white in the blood of the Lamb.*

According to St Andrew of Caesarea, those in white robes "are those of whom David speaks: 'I will count them, and they will be more in number than the sand' (Ps 138:18 LXX)—those who earlier suffered as martyrs for Christ and those who, from every tribe and people, are to receive sufferings with courage in the last times. By the pouring out of their blood for Christ some of them have made white, and others will make white, the garment of their deeds" (St Andrew, chapter 20).

In their hands they have palm branches—signs of victory over the devil. Their lot is one of eternal rejoicing before the throne of God.

One of the heavenly elders explains to St John that *these are they which came out of great tribulation, and have washed their robes; and have made them white in the blood of the Lamb.* All these signs indicate clearly that these are martyrs for Christ, and the reference to great tribulation causes some commentators to suppose that these are the Christians who will be killed by the antichrist in the last period of the world's existence. For Christ the Saviour Himself has declared concerning this tribulation: "For then shall be great tribulation, such as was not since the beginning of the world to this time, no, nor ever shall be" (Matt 24:21). This will be in addition to the number of the martyrs mentioned in Apocalypse (Rev 6:11).

> 7:15 *Therefore are they before the throne of God, and serve him day and night in his temple: and he that sitteth on the throne shall dwell among them.*

As the highest award that they will receive, it is indicated that they shall remain before the throne of God, serving Him "day and night"—indicating figuratively the uninterruptedness of this service; for, as St Andrew says,

> There will be no night there, but a single day, illuminated not by a material sun, but by the spiritual Sun of Righteousness. And perhaps by "night" is to be understood hidden and profound mysteries, and by "day" what is clear and easy to receive. The temple of God is the creation which has been renewed by the Spirit, or, more precisely, those who have preserved the pledge of the Spirit whole and unquenched; in which ones God has promised to dwell and walk (cf. 2 Cor 6:16). (St Andrew, chapter 20)

7:16 They shall hunger no more, neither thirst any more, neither shall the sun light on them, nor any heat.

These words, indicating the characteristics of the blessedness of these righteous ones, mean that they will not endure any kind of misfortunes. "They shall have the bread of heaven and the water of life, and they will have no pain and will endure no misfortunes such as are depicted in the form of the sun and heat, for the time of sufferings has passed" (St Andrew, chapter 20).

7:17 For the Lamb which is in the midst of the throne shall feed them, and shall lead them unto living fountains of waters: and God shall wipe away all tears from their eyes.

The "Lamb" Himself "shall feed them," that is, guide them, and they shall be vouchsafed an abundant outpouring of the Holy Spirit ("living fountains of waters"). The Lord said also of the believer that out of his belly shall flow rivers of living water (John 7:38). The saints, being then abundantly nourished by it, having acquired perfect knowledge after the cessation of private knowledge, and being delivered from corruption and change, will remain in endless rejoicing and joy.[xix]

8. The Taking Away of the Seventh Seal: The Voices of the Angelic Trumpets: The First to Fourth

8:1 And when he had opened the seventh seal, there was silence in heaven about the space of half an hour.

Thus, it is also in the physical world: the coming of a storm is often preceded by profound silence. This silence in heaven signifies the concentration of reverent attention on the part of the angels and men who stand before the throne of God in expectation of the fearful signs of the wrath of God before the end of this age and the manifestation of the kingdom of Christ.

[xix] This is the Kingdom of Heaven. (S.R.)

8:2–3 And I saw the seven angels which stood before God; and to them were given seven trumpets. And another angel came and stood at the altar, having a golden censer; and there was given unto him much incense, that he should offer it with the prayers of all saints upon the golden altar which was before the throne.

Before the first seven angels, as chastisers of the erring human race, the saints, with an angel at their head, stand before God in prayer for men. St Andrew of Caesarea says that the saints will entreat God that "after the disasters which strike at the end of the world, the torments of impious and lawless men might be lessened in the future age and by His coming He might reward those who have labored" (St Andrew, chapter 21).

At the same time, the saints again and again will entreat God, just as they entreated Him at the taking away of the fifth seal (Rev 6:9–11), that God might manifest His righteous judgment against the lawless and the persecutors of the faith of Christ and might cause to cease the fierceness of the torturers.

"The golden altar, on which is established every ministering holy power and on which the sacrifices of martyrdom are offered, is Christ the prefiguration of Whom was shown to Moses on the mountain together with the tabernacle (Exod 25:9, Heb 8:5)" (St Andrew, chapter 21).

8:4–5 And the smoke of the incense, which came with the prayers of the saints, ascended up before God out of the angel's hand. And the angel took the censer, and filled it with fire of the altar, and cast it into the earth: and there were voices, and thunderings, and lightnings, and an earthquake.

The punishments described immediately after this are without doubt the consequences of this prayer. The Lord shows here that He does not leave without attention the prayers of His faithful servants. The voices and thunderings and the rest "indicate the horrors which are to occur before the end (of the world), just as on Mt Sinai they served as symbols of the Divine Presence which frightened everyone and brought the most sensible of them to conversion" (St Andrew, chapter 21).[xx]

8:6 And the seven angels which had the seven trumpets prepared themselves to sound.

Here there follow the sounding of the trumpets one after the other, of all seven angels, which are accompanied each time by great disasters and punishments for the earth and its inhabitants.

8:7 The first angel sounded, and there followed hail and fire mingled with blood, and they were cast upon the earth: and the third part of trees was burnt up, and all green grass was burnt up.

[xx] The casting of the fire of the censer on the earth indicates the Divine Judgment manifested on earth. See Ezekiel 10:2 where the coals of fire scattered over the city indicate the chastisement of Jerusalem. (S.R.)

The chastisements of God follow gradually, indicating the mercy and long-suffering of God, calling sinners to repentance. At first the chastisement of God strikes a third of the trees and all the green grass. Wheat and other grasses are burned to the root—those things which are necessary for the feeding of men and animals. By "hail and fire mingled with blood ... cast upon the earth," many commentators understand a war of extermination. Does this not refer to an aerial bombardment with its destructive and incendiary bombs?

> The fire mingled with blood indicates the destruction of cities ... their fires and blood-letting, during which, as we see, there will be killed not less then a third part of all the creatures living on earth: wars exterminate not only men, but also everything produced on earth. Our supposition and opinion regarding this is confirmed by the blessed Joel, for he says that before the coming of the great day there will be sent on earth blood and fire and vapour of smoke (Joel 2:30). (St Andrew, chapter 22)

> *8:8–9 And the second angel sounded, as it were a great mountain burning with fire was cast into the sea: and the third part of the sea became blood; And a third part of the creatures which were in the sea, and had life, died; and the third part of the ships were destroyed.*

One may suppose that on the bottom of one of the oceans there will open up a volcano whose fiery lava will fill the third part of the water basins of the earth, bringing death to everything alive. Others think that what is referred to here are fearful bloody sea battles with the help of newly invented murderous weapons.

> *8:10–11 And the third angel sounded, and there fell a great star from heaven, burning as it were a lamp, and it fell upon the third part of the rivers, and upon the fountains of waters; And the name of the star is called Wormwood: and the third part of the waters became wormwood; and many men died of the waters, because they were made bitter.*

Some think that this is a meteor which will fall upon earth and will cause the poisoning of the sources of waters on the earth, which will become fatal. But perhaps this is also one of the newly discovered weapons of a fearful war of the future.

> The star indicates either that all this comes upon men from the heavens, or it signifies the devil, of whom Isaiah says: "How has Lucifer, that rose in the morning, fallen from heaven!" (Isa 14:12). For he, making men drunk through pleasures by his stormy and bitter corruption, is allowed by God to bring a tormenting tribulation, if not upon all, then at least upon the third part. (St Andrew, chapter 24).[xxi]

[xxi] Wormwood, it would seem, indicates in general the sorrows and bitterness of the last times. (S.R.)

8:12 And the fourth angel sounded, and the third part of the sun was smitten, and the third part of the moon, and the third part of the stars; so as the third part of them was darkened, and the day shone not for a third part of it, and the night likewise.

It is not possible for us to understand this at the present time. One thing is clear, that this is to be accompanied by various disasters for men—bad harvest, famine, and so forth.

We think that this is akin to what is said about the sun and the moon by Joel (Joel 2:10) and which has already been ordained by the decree of the Master for the end. We repeat that the third part of the luminaries and stars indicates the third part of the duration of the day and night. From this we understand that God at that time will bring about disasters not all at once; for, allowing to be damaged only a third part of time, in the remaining and large part he secretly calls to repentance. Indeed, who can bear the cup of Divine wrath unmingled? (St Andrew, chapter 25)

8:13 And I beheld, and heard an angel flying through the midst of heaven, saying with a loud voice, Woe, woe, woe, to the inhabiters of the earth by reason of the other voices of the trumpet of the three angels, which are yet to sound!

This voice of the angel indicates the love of mankind and the compassion of the Divine angels, who have pity for the unrepentant men who are subjected to such disasters. By angels with trumpets some commentators understand Christian preachers who call to correction and repentance.

"For those who have their dwelling in the heavens, the disasters and sufferings are the cause of receiving unfading crowns and rewards" (St Andrew, chapter 25).

9. THE SOUNDING OF THE FIFTH AND SIXTH OF THE ANGELIC TRUMPETS: THE LOCUSTS AND THE ARMY OF HORSEMEN

9:1–3 And the fifth angel sounded, and I saw a star fall from heaven unto the earth: and to him was given the key of the bottomless pit. And he opened the bottomless pit; and there arose a smoke out of the pit, as the smoke of a great furnace; and the sun and the air were darkened by reason of the smoke of the pit. And there came out of the smoke locusts upon the earth: and unto them was given power, as the scorpions of the earth have power.

St Andrew of Caesarea by this star understands an angel for the chastisement of men, by the "bottomless pit" he understands Gehenna, and by the locusts he understands the worms of whom the prophet said, "Their worm shall not die" (Isa 66:24); the darkening of the sun and air indicates the blindness of the souls of men.

"Of the star I think it is an angel of God: by God's allowance he leads out of the pit the evil demons who have been condemned, those whom Christ bound when

He was Incarnate, so that they might do their work before the end and then be subjected to endless torment" (St Andrew, chapter 26).

On the binding of the devil and his loosing see Rev 20:7; compare also John 12:31. The smoke indicates the darkness which precedes the evil deeds done at their (the demons') instigation, after the performance of which they will be given authority to torment men.

> 9:4–5 *And it was commanded them that they should not hurt the grass of the earth, neither any green thing, neither any tree; but only those men which have not the seal of God in their foreheads. And to them it was given that they should not kill them, but that they should be tormented five months: and their torment was as the torment of a scorpion, when he striketh a man.*

According to St Andrew the "five months" indicate the shortness of this chastisement, since "except those days should be shortened, there should no flesh be saved" (Matt 24:22). One may see here also a correspondence to the five outward senses, through which sin enters the soul of a man. And that these locusts "should not hurt the grass of the earth ... but only men is because the whole creation will be delivered from corruption, being now in bondage to corruption because of us" (St Andrew, chapter 26).

"And that the mental locusts sting men like scorpions signifies that at the end of evil deeds there is hidden the death of the soul" (St Andrew, chapter 26).

"That death does not come even though men desire it, indicates that this depends upon the decree of God, Who by the bitterness of the disasters which are sent considers it profitable to make hateful to men the sin which is the very cause and consequence of such disasters" (St Andrew, chapter 26).

> 9:7–10 *And the shapes of the locusts were like unto horses prepared unto battle; and on their heads were as it were crowns like gold, and their faces were as the faces of men. And they had hair as the hair of women, and their teeth were as the teeth of lions. And they had breastplates, as it were breastplates of iron; and the sound of their wings was as the sound of chariots of many horses running to battle. And they had tails like unto scorpions, and there were stings in their tails: and their power was to hurt men five months.*

This description of the monstrous locusts causes some commentators to think that these locusts are nothing else than an allegorical description of human passions. Each of such passions, when it reaches a certain limit, has all the signs of these monstrous locusts. In describing the coming of the day of the Lord, the holy prophet Joel describes also the appearance before it of destroyers who in part remind one of these locusts.

I suppose that by these locusts one should most likely understand the evil demons who have prepared themselves for battle with us and, as signs of victory, wear on their heads crowns like gold with which we also think to be crowned when we submit to them as having received an evil victory through pleasure. The hair of women testifies of the demons' love of pleasure and arousal to fornication; the teeth of lions indicate their hardheartedness; their tails, which are likened to those of scorpions indicate the consequences of sins, which produce the death of the soul, for *sin, when it is finished, bringeth forth death* (Jas 1:15). (St Andrew, chapter 26)

Contemporary commentators, not without a certain reasonableness, find a kinship of these locusts with airplanes and their bombing attacks.

9:11 *And they had a king over them, which is the angel of the bottomless pit, whose name in the Hebrew tongue is Abaddon, but in the Greek tongue hath his name Apollyon.*

By the king of these locusts, who bears the name "angel of the bottomless pit"—Abaddon in Hebrew, or Apollyon in Greek—the commentators understand the devil.

9:12 *One woe is past; and, behold, there come two woes more hereafter.*

"So that we might wage an uncompromising battle against the devil, it is said by way of threatening that after this two more woes will come upon us" (St Andrew, chapter 26).

9:13–16 *And the sixth angel sounded, and I heard a voice from the four horns of the golden altar which is before God, Saying to the sixth angel which had the trumpet, Loose the four angels which are bound in the great river Euphrates. And the four angels were loosed, which were prepared for an hour, and a day, and a month, and a year, for to slay the third part of men. And the number of the army of the horsemen were two hundred thousand thousand: and I heard the number of them.*

I think that these four angels are the most cunning demons who were bound at the coming of Christ and who, by the command of God which comes from the heavenly altar (an image of which was the ancient tabernacle), are loosed by the Divine angel to agitate the peoples not only against Christians, but also against each other, so that through this some might be manifested as tested, faithful, and worthy of the best rewards, the highest mansions and dwellings like ripe wheat; while others, like tares, the impious, constant sinners and unrepentant and here justly punished, might receive a yet harder condemnation at the judgment. And that they were bound at the Euphrates is nothing strange, for, by God's allowance, some were condemned until the time in the bottomless pit, others in wine, and some in other places, so that after the final end of the battle against men they might be subjected to eternal torments. Perhaps the mention of the Euphrates is an indication that Antichrist will come from those lands. (St Andrew, chapter 27)

9:17–18 And thus I saw the horses in the vision, and them that sat on them, having breast-plates of fire, and of jacinth, and brimstone: and the heads of the horses were as the heads of lions; and out of their mouths issued fire and smoke and brimstone. By these three was the third part of men killed, by the fire, and by the smoke, and by the brimstone, which issued out of their mouths.

The horses signify either men who are like beasts and lust after women, or those who are subject and under the authority of the demons. Those that sit on them are those that govern them. The breastplates of fire, and of jacinth, and brimstone indicate, we believe, the aerial being and devouring activity of evil spirits, the murderousness and bestiality of which are described by the image of the heads of lions. Out of their mouths issued fire and smoke and brimstone by which a third part of men will be killed indicate either sins which burn the fruits of the heart by the poisonousness of the demons' instigations, instructions, and temptations; or (it may be), by God's allowance, the laying waste by barbarians of cities and the shedding of blood. (St Andrew, chapter 27)

9:19 For their power is in their mouth, and in their tails: for their tails were like unto serpents, and had heads, and with them they do hurt.

Their tails are like serpents which have heads, for the end of the sowing of demons is poisonous, in which is the death of the soul.

Some commentators understand by these depictions an allegorical representation of a frightful war of bloodshed, a monstrous and pitiless one. Truly rare in its terrors and pitilessness was indeed, the Second World War, which we have not long ago endured. Some people see also in this frightful mounted army tanks which spurt forth fire.

9:20–21 And the rest of the men which were not killed by these plagues yet repented not of the works of their hands, that they should not worship devils, and idols of gold, and silver, and brass, and stone, and of wood: which neither can see, nor hear, nor walk: Neither repented they of their murders, nor of their sorceries, nor of their fornication, nor of their thefts.

Such will be the end of the world, the general cruelty and stony insensibility of which are already to be observed now.

10. THE ANGEL CLOTHED WITH A CLOUD AND A RAINBOW WHO PROCLAIMS THE END

10:1–2 And I saw another mighty angel come down from heaven, clothed with a cloud: and a rainbow was upon his head, and his face was as it were the sun, and his feet as pillars of fire: And he had in his hand a little book open: and he set his right foot upon the sea, and his left foot on the earth.

This appearance has the form of an introductory account before the seventh and final trumpet. It stops the continuation of the prophetic allegories but does not interrupt them.

Some think that this angel is the Lord Jesus Christ Himself, or the Holy Spirit, but St John calls him "an angel" and St Andrew of Caesarea considers that this is precisely an angel, perhaps one of the Seraphim adorned with the glory of the Lord. His standing on the sea and on the earth signifies the dominion over the elements of the earthly world: "The pillars of fire signify the fear and punishment brought by the angel upon the impious who have robbed on the earth and on the sea" (St Andrew, chapter 28).

The little book which he holds in his hand, according to St Andrew, contains "the names and deeds of those of the evil ones who have lived by thievery or in some other way have done lawless deeds on earth and have killed on the sea" (St Andrew, chapter 28). According to other commentators, the book contains in general the prophecy concerning the future fate of the world and mankind.

> 10:3–4 *And cried with a loud voice, as when a lion roareth: and when he had cried, seven thunders uttered their voices. And when the seven thunders had uttered their voices, I was about to write: and I heard a voice from heaven saying unto me, Seal up those things which the seven thunders uttered, and write them not.*

St Andrew of Caesarea supposes that these seven thunders should be understood as either "seven voices of one thundering angel or of seven other angels who declare concerning the future." That which they say "is now unknown but will be revealed later by experience and the course of events themselves.... The final knowledge and explanation of what they declare belongs to the last times" (St Andrew, chapter 28).

Some suppose that these are seven periods in the history of mankind: (1) the triumph of Christianity over paganism; (2) the great migration period and the fall of the Roman Empire, in whose place there arise new Christian governments; (3) the appearance of Islam and the collapse of the Byzantine Empire; (4) the epoch of the Crusades; (5) the fall of piety in Byzantium already subjected to Islam and in the old Rome where the spirit of papism came to dominate as a result of which there appeared apostasy from the Church in the form of the Reformation; (6) the revolution and the installing everywhere of social anarchy out of which the son of perdition, the antichrist, is to come; and (7) the restoration of the Roman, that is, the worldwide empire, with Antichrist at its head, and the end of the world. There was no need to depict in advance all these events for they will be revealed in time.

> 10:5–6 *And the angel which I saw stand upon the sea and upon the earth lifted up his hand to heaven, And sware by him that liveth for ever and ever, who created heaven, and the*

things that therein are, and the earth, and the things that therein are, and the sea, and the things which are therein, that there should be time no longer.

"There should be time no longer," **i.e.,** the usual cycle of the elements of the world is to cease; there will be no time as measured by the sun and there should begin eternity. Here it is important that the angel swore "by Him that liveth for ever and ever," that is, by God Himself. Consequently those sectarians are wrong who consider that no oath whatsoever is to be allowed.

10:7 *But in the days of the voice of the seventh angel, when he shall begin to sound, the mystery of God should be finished, as he hath declared to his servants the prophets.*

That is, there shall soon begin the last of the seven epochs of the existence of the world and the seventh angel shall trumpet. Then there will be finished "the mystery of God" prophesied by our prophets, that is, the end of the world and everything that is to occur in connection with it.

10:8–11 *And the voice which I heard from heaven spake unto me again, and said, Go and take the little book which is open in the hand of the angel which standeth upon the sea and upon the earth. And I went unto the angel, and said unto him, Give me the little book. And he said unto me, Take it, and eat it up; and it shall make thy belly bitter, but it shall be in thy mouth sweet as honey. And I took the little book out of the angel's hand, and ate it up; and it was in my mouth sweet as honey: and as soon as I had eaten it, my belly was bitter. And he said unto me, Thou must prophesy again before many peoples, and nations, and tongues, and kings.*

Here is indicated the fact that St John has received the prophetic gift just as the Old Testament prophets received it: for example, the holy prophet Ezekiel to whom likewise it was commanded to eat a scroll of a book before he was sent by the Lord to preach to the house of Israel (Ezek 2:8–10; 3:1–4).

The sweetness and bitterness in the explanation of St Andrew signify the following:

Sweet for you, he says, is the knowledge of the future; at the same time it is bitter for the belly, i.e., the heart, the dwelling place of the food of the Word because of compassion for those who will have to endure the punishments sent down by God's decrees. This is also to be interpreted in another way inasmuch as the holy Evangelist had not experienced evil deeds; by this swallowing of the book which contained the deeds of the impious is indicated to him that at the beginning of sin there is sweetness, and after the accomplishment, bitterness, by reason of revenge and reward. (St Andrew, chapter 29)

The compassionate heart of the apostle could not but feel the whole bitterness of the grief which awaits sinful mankind. The chapter concludes with St John receiving the command to prophesy.

11. THE PROPHECY OF THE TEMPLE, OF ENOCH AND ELIJAH, THE VOICE OF THE TRUMPET OF THE SEVENTH ANGEL

> 11:1–2 *And there was given me a reed like unto a rod: and the angel stood, saying, Rise, and measure the temple of God, and the altar, and them that worship therein. But the court which is without the temple leave out, and measure it not; for it is given unto the Gentiles: and the holy city shall they tread under foot forty and two months.*

According to the commentary of St Andrew, "the temple of the living God is the Church in which the rational sacrifices are offered by us. The *court which is without* is the society of unbelievers and Jews who are unworthy of the angelic measuring (i.e., the definition of the degree of their moral perfection and corresponding blessedness) because of their impiety" (St Andrew, chapter 30).

The treading underfoot of the Holy City, Jerusalem, or the universal Church for the course of forty-two months signifies that at the coming of the antichrist, the faithful will be persecuted for the course of three and a half years.

Some interpreters suppose that this measurement of the temple signifies the speedy destruction of the Old Testament temple in Jerusalem on the site of which there is to be raised a New Testament Christian church, just like a similar measurement of the temple by means of a reed was given in a vision to the prophet Ezekiel (chapters 40–45), signifying the restoration of the destroyed temple. Others consider that the inner court which was measured by the Apostle signifies the "church of the firstborn" in heaven (cf. Heb 12:23), the heavenly sanctuary; and that the outer court left without measurement is the Church of Christ on earth, which must endure persecution at first from the pagans and then, in the last times, from the antichrist. The miserable condition of the earthly Church is limited, however, to this period of forty-two months. The fulfillment of the prophecy of forty-two months some interpreters have seen in the persecution of Diocletian, which was distinguished by its great cruelty and lasted from February 23, 305, to July 25, 308, which is about three and a half years. The persecution touches only the outward court; that is, the outer side of the life of Christians whose property will be taken away. They will be subjected to torture, while the inner sanctuary of their souls will remain untouched.

> 11:3–6 *And I will give power unto my two witnesses, and they shall prophesy a thousand two hundred and threescore days, clothed in sackcloth. These are the two olive trees, and the two candlesticks standing before the God of the earth. And if any man will hurt them, fire proceedeth out of their mouth, and devoureth their enemies: and if any man will hurt*

The Book of Revelation of St John the Theologian 281

them, he must in this manner be killed. These have power to shut heaven, that it rain not in the days of their prophecy: and have power over waters to turn them to blood, and to smite the earth with all plagues, as often as they will.

For the course of this whole time, 1,260 days, "two witnesses of God" will preach repentance to men and convert them from the deception of the antichrist. By these two witnesses, all the Holy Fathers and teachers of the Church understand almost unanimously the Old Testament righteous ones, Enoch and Elijah, who were taken alive into heaven. During their preaching, while possessing authority and power over the elements in order to chastise and bring to their senses the impious, they themselves will be unharmed.

O wondrous grace of God! for He offers a treatment equal in power to the wound. Just as the false Christ will possess every diabolical activity and all false signs and miracles, and will be more glorious than all sorcerers and deceivers, so also will God arm these saints with the power of true signs and miracles, so that by offering truth and light they might overthrow the lie and darkness and convert the deceived either by the word of teaching or by the blows of chastisement (drought, fire, changes in the elements, and so forth), and might expose the deceiver himself without themselves suffering in the least either through him or others. (St Andrew, chapter 30)

11:7–8 And when they shall have finished their testimony, the beast that ascendeth out of the bottomless pit shall make war against them, and shall overcome them, and kill them. And their dead bodies shall lie in the street of the great city, which spiritually is called Sodom and Egypt, where also our Lord was crucified.

Only at the end of their mission, after a course of three and a half years, "the beast that ascendeth from the bottomless pit" (i.e., Antichrist) will be allowed by God to kill the preachers, and their corpses will be thrown into the streets of the great city, which is evidently the city of Jerusalem where the antichrist will found his kingdom, giving himself off as the messiah who was prophesied by the prophets.

"In this city he will establish his kingdom and royal throne in the likeness of David ... so as to prove that he is Christ who fulfills the Prophet's word: I will raise up the tabernacle of David that is fallen and will rebuild the ruins of it (Amos 9:11, LXX). These words the Jews will accept and refer to his coming" (St Andrew, chapter 30).

11:9–10 And they of the people and kindreds and tongues and nations shall see their dead bodies three days and a half, and shall not suffer their dead bodies to be put in graves. And they that dwell upon the earth shall rejoice over them, and make merry, and shall send gifts one to another; because these two prophets tormented them that dwelt on the earth.

These people will be deceived by the false miracles of the antichrist who, with the cooperation of the devil, will be the most glorious of all sorcerers and deceivers; he will not allow for the prophets to be given over to burial, and the people will rejoice in their death, "because these two prophets tormented them that dwelt upon the earth," arousing their conscience.

> 11:11–12 *And after three days and an half the spirit of life from God entered into them, and they stood upon their feet; and great fear fell upon them which saw them. And they heard a great voice from heaven saying unto them, Come up hither. And they ascended up to heaven in a cloud; and their enemies beheld them.*

The evil joy of the impious will not be long in duration. In three and a half days, the holy prophets will be brought to life by God and raised up to heaven.

> 11:13 *And the same hour was there a great earthquake, and the tenth part of the city fell, and in the earthquake were slain of men seven thousand: and the remnant were affrighted, and gave glory to the God of heaven.*

At the same time a great earthquake will occur, a tenth part of the city will be destroyed, and seven thousand men will perish, and the remainder being seized with fear will send up glory to the God of heaven. Thus, the work of the antichrist will be given a decisive blow.

"When the impious will be punished, the martyrs of Christ will be glorified, and those worthy of salvation will glorify God" (St Andrew, chapter 31).

> 11:14–17 *The second woe is past; and, behold, the third woe cometh quickly. And the seventh angel sounded; and there were great voices in heaven, saying, The kingdoms of this world are become the kingdoms of our Lord, and of his Christ; and he shall reign for ever and ever. And the four and twenty elders, which sat before God on their seats, fell upon their faces, and worshipped God, Saying, We give thee thanks, O Lord God Almighty, which art, and wast, and art to come; because thou hast taken to thee thy great power, and hast reigned.*[xxii]

"Here he again says that the angels and those who have lived like angels will send up thanksgiving to God. For our sake, He has willed as man to receive the kingdom which as God He possessed from the beginning" (St Andrew, chapter 32).

> 11:18 *And the nations were angry, and thy wrath is come, and the time of the dead, that they should be judged, and that thou shouldest give reward unto thy servants the prophets,*

[xxii] The seventh trumpet indicates the end of this world and the beginning of the kingdom of Christ. (S.R.)

and to the saints, and them that fear thy name, small and great; and shouldest destroy them which destroy the earth.

Finally, after having been long-suffering, He sends against the unbelieving nations, which are angry at this as if it were a new or strange teaching, their punishment. The time of the dead indicates the time of the resurrection of the dead, in which to each will be given a reward corresponding to his deeds.

By prophets, saints, and them that fear His name, one may understand three degrees of men: those who offer fruit a hundredfold, sixtyfold, and thirtyfold (Matt 13:23). The prophets, however, will receive the first place and sit on twelve thrones. Small and great, we think, refer either to the lesser saints and those who surpass them; or else the small are sinners who have been belittled, and the great are the righteous. (St Andrew, chapter 32)

11:19 *And the temple of God was opened in heaven, and there was seen in his temple the ark of his testament: and there were lightnings, and voices, and thunderings, and an earthquake, and great hail.*[xxiii]

By the opening of heaven and the appearance of the ark, in the interpretation of St Andrew, is indicated "the revelation of the good things prepared for the saints, which things, according to the Apostle, are all hidden in Christ, in Whom *dwelleth all the fulness of the Godhead bodily* (Col 2:9). These things will be revealed at the same time that the lawless and impious ones will be sent frightful voices, lightnings, thunderings, and hail; the change of the present world in the earthquake symbolizes the torments of Gehenna" (St Andrew, chapter 33).

12. The Third Vision: The Battle of the Kingdom of God with the Power Hostile to It of Antichrist: The Church of Christ Under the Image of the Woman Travailing in Birth

12:1–2 *And there appeared a great wonder in heaven; a woman clothed with the sun, and the moon under her feet, and upon her head a crown of twelve stars: And she being with child cried, travailing in birth, and pained to be delivered.*

Certain commentators have seen in this mystical woman the Most Holy Theotokos, but such outstanding commentators as St Hippolytus of Rome, St Methodius of Olympus, and St Andrew of Caesarea find that this is "the Church clothed in the Word of the Father, shining more brightly than the sun." This brilliance of the sun signifies likewise that she possesses the true knowledge of God and His laws and contains His revelations. The moon under her feet signifies that she is

---

[xxiii] Compare the heavens opening to St Stephen, Acts 7:55–56. (S.R.)

above everything that changes. St Methodius considers the moon allegorically as the "faith of those cleansed of corruption by the bath, that is, baptism, since upon the moon depends the nature of moisture."

On her head is a crown of twelve stars that, being originally gathered together from the twelve tribes of Israel, she subsequently was guided by the twelve apostles who comprise her light-bearing glory.

From the fact that she is in pain during childbirth, it is evident that it is incorrect to see in this woman the Most Holy Theotokos, for the giving birth from Her of the Son of God was without pain. These torments of birthgiving signify the difficulties that had to be overcome by the Church of Christ when it was being established in the world (martyrdom, the spreading of heresies). At the same time, it signifies, in the explanation of St Andrew, that "the Church is pained for each one of those who is reborn by water and the Spirit until, as the divine Apostle has said, 'until Christ shall be formed in you' (Gal 4:19). St Methodius says, 'The Church is pained giving rebirth from natural to spiritual men and transforming them in appearance and image in the likeness of Christ'" (St Andrew, chapter 33).

> 12:3 *And there appeared another wonder in heaven; and behold a great red dragon, having seven heads and ten horns, and seven crowns upon his heads.*

In this image of the dragon one cannot but see the ancient serpent called the devil or Satan, of whom it will be spoken (12:9). The red color signifies his bloodthirsty cruelty; the seven heads signify his extreme slyness and cunning, as opposed to the seven spirits of God, the gifts of the Holy Spirit; the ten horns are his evil power and might, which are directed against the Ten Commandments of the Law of God. The crowns on his head signify the royal authority of the devil in his dark kingdom. As applied to the history of the Church, some see in these seven crowns seven kings who rise up against the Church; and in the ten horns, ten persecutions against the Church.

> 12:4 *And his tail drew the third part of the stars of heaven, and did cast them to the earth: and the dragon stood before the woman which was ready to be delivered, for to devour her child as soon as it was born.*

By these stars which the devil draws after himself in his fall, commentators understand the fallen angels or demons. By them are also understood representatives of the churches and teachers who are corrupted by satanic power. As for the dragon standing before the woman, St Andrew writes: "The devil always arms himself against the Church and increasingly strives to make those reborn by her his food" (St Andrew, chapter 33).

> 12:5a *And she brought forth a man child, who was to rule all nations with a rod of iron.*

This is an image of Jesus Christ, as St Andrew says, "In the person of those who are baptized, the Church ceaselessly gives birth to Christ; just as, according to the Apostle, we come 'unto the measure of the stature of the fulness of Christ' (Eph 4:13)" (St Andrew, chapter 33). St Hippolytus says likewise, "The Church will not cease to give birth from its heart to the Word which is persecuted in the world by unbelievers." The Church always gives birth to Christ through men, and from the very beginning Satan has striven to devour Christ as he did in the person of Herod.

12:5b *And her child was caught up unto God, and to his throne.*

Thus, the Lord Jesus Christ was caught up to heaven on the day of His glorious ascension and sat upon the throne of His Father at His right hand; so also all the saints in whom Christ is depicted are caught up unto God so as not to be conquered by temptations which surpass their powers. So also are all Christians of the last times to be caught up to meet the Lord in the air (1 Thess 4:17).

12:6 *And the woman fled into the wilderness, where she hath a place prepared of God, that they should feed her there a thousand two hundred and threescore days.*

By this flight of the woman into the wilderness, many see the flight of Christians from Jerusalem, which had been besieged by the Romans at the time of the great Jewish War, A.D. 66–70. Then people fled into Pella and the desert beyond the Jordan. This indeed lasted for three and a half years. By this wilderness one may see also that wilderness where the first Christians saved themselves from the persecutors, and also that wilderness in which the holy ascetics saved themselves from the nets of the devil. It is not improbable that the literal wilderness, as it did before for the martyrs, will save those who flee from the attacks of the apostate and false Christ into mountains, caves, and holes of the earth. The three and one-half years, signified by the twelve hundred sixty days, is the time for the course of which the apostasy will reign.

12:7–9 *And there was war in heaven: Michael and his angels fought against the dragon; and the dragon fought and his angels, And prevailed not; neither was their place found any more in heaven.*

In the commentary of St Andrew of Caesarea, these words "may refer to the first casting out of the devil for his pride and envy from the angelic order; likewise to his defeat by the Cross of the Master when the Lord said, Now is the judgment of this world; now shall the prince of this world be cast out (John 12:31; see Ezek 28:16)" (St Andrew, chapter 34).

Under the image of this battle likewise, commentators see the victory of Christianity over paganism, insofar as the devil and his demons have aroused and armed with all their power the pagans to battle against the Church of Christ.

12:10–12 And I heard a loud voice saying in heaven, Now is come salvation, and strength, and the kingdom of our God, and the power of his Christ: for the accuser of our brethren is cast down, which accused them before our God day and night. And they overcame him by the blood of the Lamb, and by the word of their testimony; and they loved not their lives unto the death. Therefore rejoice, ye heavens, and ye that dwell in them. Woe to the inhabiters of the earth and of the sea! for the devil is come down unto you, having great wrath, because he knoweth that he hath but a short time.

In this victory over the devil, an active part was taken by Christians themselves who "overcame him by the blood of the Lamb, and by the word of their testimony; and they loved not their lives unto the death." Such were the holy martyrs. Being conquered in two battles, one with the Archangel Michael and his heavenly host in the heavens, and the other with the martyrs of Christ on earth—Satan has preserved yet a certain appearance of authority on earth, crawling about it like a serpent, living out his last days on earth devising ways in which to wage a final and decisive battle with God and believing Christians with the help of the antichrist and his helper, the false prophet.

12:13–14 And when the dragon saw that he was cast unto the earth, he persecuted the woman which brought forth the man child. And to the woman were given two wings of a great eagle, that she might fly into the wilderness, into her place, where she is nourished for a time, and times, and half a time, from the face of the serpent.

The devil does not cease to persecute the Church, but the Church, having two wings of an eagle, the Old and New Testaments, hides from the devil in the wilderness; by which one may understand both the spiritual and the literal wilderness in which the true Christian ascetics have hid themselves and are hiding themselves now. St Andrew of Caesarea says, "And so it is always, but especially at the coming of the antichrist who will reign for three and one-half years. At that time it may be there will escape from him those who have hidden in the literal wilderness—the mountains, holes, and caves" (St Andrew, chapter 35).

12:15–16 And the serpent cast out of his mouth water as a flood after the woman, that he might cause her to be carried away of the flood. And the earth helped the woman, and the earth opened her mouth, and swallowed up the flood which the dragon cast out of his mouth.

By this "water" St Andrew understands "a multitude either of evil demons or of various temptations." By the earth which swallows up this water he understands "the humility of wisdom of the saints who, saying from all their heart, I am but earth and ashes (Gen 18:27), by this very confession rip apart all the nets of the devil. For, as was revealed by the angel to the divine Anthony, nothing so crushes and cuts off the power of the devil as humility" (St Andrew, chapter 35). By this, certain people understand the frightful persecutions against the Church from the pagan emperors and the streams of Christian blood which flowed at that time. Like a river which overflows upon the earth and is swallowed up by it, all the malicious powers of Satan were destroyed and vanished without a trace when Christianity triumphed over paganism under Emperor Constantine the Great.

> 12:17 *And the dragon was wroth with the woman, and went to make war with the remnant of her seed, which keep the commandments of God, and have the testimony of Jesus Christ.*

This refers to that unceasing and age-old battle which the devil has waged against all true sons of the Church from the time of the foundation of Christianity upon the earth, and that he will wage with an ever-increasing degree to the end of the world until his efforts will be worn out and will end in the person of the antichrist.

13. The Beast: The Antichrist and the Beast: The Antichrist and His Helper the False Prophet

> 13:1–2 *And I stood upon the sand of the sea, and saw a beast rise up out of the sea, having seven heads and ten horns, and upon his horns ten crowns, and upon his heads the name of blasphemy. And the beast which I saw was like unto a leopard, and his feet were as the feet of a bear, and his mouth as the mouth of a lion: and the dragon gave him his power, and his seat and great authority.*

By this "beast which rises up out of the sea" almost all interpreters understand the antichrist who comes out of the "sea of life," that is in the midst of the human race, which is agitated like a sea. From this it is clear that the antichrist will not be some kind of spirit or demon, but rather a heinous offspring of the human race. He will not be an incarnate devil as some have thought, but a man. Some by this beast have understood a God-fighting government, such as during early Christian times was the Roman Empire and in the last times will be the worldwide kingdom of the antichrist in the last times. The holy seer of mysteries, John, depicts in dark colors this last enemy of the Church of Christ. He is like unto a leopard with feet like a bear's and with the mouth of a lion. Thus, in the person of the antichrist is united the characteristics, the qualities of the most wild beasts. He has likewise seven heads just like the devil, the dragon himself, and these heads are crowned with names, blasphemous names, for the open depiction of his inward impiety and his despising of everything holy. His ten horns are crowned by diadems as a sign of the fact that he will make use of his God-fighting power with the authority of a king on earth. This authority he will receive with the help of the dragon or the devil who will give him his throne (compare Dan 7:2–6 and the three empires).

13:3–4 And I saw one of his heads as it were wounded to death; and his deadly wound was healed: and all the world wondered after the beast. And they worshipped the dragon which gave power unto the beast: and they worshipped the beast, saying, Who is like unto the beast? who is able to make war with him?

St John notes that one of the heads of the beast is, as it were, mortally wounded. But this mortal wound has been healed, and this has astonished the whole earth, which follows after the beast. And this has caused frightened people to submit both to the dragon who gives power to the beast and to the beast himself. All bow down to him saying, "Who is like unto this beast? Who can compare with him?" All this signifies that it will not be easy for the antichrist to acquire authority over all mankind; but at the beginning, he will have to wage fierce wars and even experience a mighty defeat. But then there will follow his astonishing victories and his reign over the world.

The words, "I saw one of his heads as it were wounded to death" indicates either that one of his princes, being put to death, through the magic charms of the antichrist will be falsely shown as resurrected, in a way similar to what Simon the sorcerer did for which he was accused by the chief apostle Peter; or that the Roman Empire, having endured a kind of death through a division from the autocracy of the antichrist, will be seen to be restored as was Caesar Augustus. (St Andrew, chapter 36)[xxiv]

13:5–6 And there was given unto him a mouth speaking great things and blasphemies; and power was given unto him to continue forty and two months. And he opened his mouth in blasphemy against God, to blaspheme his name, and his tabernacle, and them that dwell in heaven.

Thus, his reign will not be long, as otherwise, in the words of the Saviour, "there should be no flesh saved" (Matt 24:22).

"The tabernacle of God is the dwelling of God the Word in the flesh—that is, His incarnation and repose in the saints, against whom—just as against the angels—the beast will direct his blasphemy" (St Andrew, chapter 36).

And he said,

The fourth beast shall be the fourth kingdom upon earth, which shall be diverse from all other kingdoms, and shall devour the whole earth, and shall tread it down, and break it in pieces. And his ten horns out of this kingdom are ten kings that shall arise: and another shall arise after them; and he shall be diverse from the first, and he shall subdue three kings. And he shall speak great words against the Most High,

---

This false resurrection is a kind of parody of Christ's Resurrection, a part of the imitation of Christ by Antichrist. (S.R.)

and shall wear out the saints of the Most High, and think to change time and laws: and they shall be given into his hand until a time and times and the dividing of time. (Dan 7:23–25)

13:7–10 And it was given unto him to make war with the saints, and to overcome them: and power was given him over all kindreds, and tongues, and nations. And all that dwell upon the earth shall worship him, whose names are not written in the book of life of the Lamb slain from the foundation of the world. If any man have an ear, let him hear. He that leadeth into captivity shall go into captivity: he that killeth with the sword must be killed with the sword. Here is the patience and the faith of the saints.

In these verses is indicated the manner of the activity of the antichrist. He will be distinguished by blasphemy, by violence against men who do not submit to him and "it was given to him to make war with the saints and to overcome them," that is, the power to force them to submit to him—of course in a purely outward fashion—for only those will bow down to Antichrist whose names are not written in the Book of Life of the Lamb. Only by patience and faith will the saints be able to defend themselves against the antichrist. And they are consoled by St John with the assurance that "He that killeth with the sword must be killed with the sword," that is, that a righteous recompense awaits the antichrist. (cf. Matt 10:22: "He that endureth to the end shall be saved.")

13:11–13 And I beheld another beast coming up out of the earth; and he had two horns like a lamb, and he spake as a dragon. And he exerciseth all the power of the first beast before him, and causeth the earth and them which dwell therein to worship the first beast, whose deadly wound was healed. And he doeth great wonders, so that he maketh fire come down from heaven on the earth in the sight of men.

In these verses St John speaks of the helper of the antichrist—the false prophet—and his activity. This is also a beast, in Greek *thêrion*, which signifies a beast whose beastly nature is especially manifest, as for example in wild animals—hyena, jackal, tiger. But he is depicted not as coming out of the sea like the first one, but out of the earth. This signifies that all his feelings and conceptions are entirely earthly, of a sensuous character. He will have "two horns like a lamb."

In the explanation of St. St Andrew's this is so as to

cover with lamb's skin the murderous nature of a hidden wolf, and because in the beginning he will strive to have an image of piety. St Irenaeus of Lyons says that this is "the weapon-bearer of the antichrist and the false prophet. To him will be given a power of signs and miracles so that going before the antichrist he might prepare his path of perdition. The healing of the wound of the beast we say is either a seeming union for a short time of the divided kingdom, or a swiftly passing-away restoration by the antichrist of the dominion of Satan which was destroyed by the Cross of the

Lord; or a false resurrection of someone from the dead who was close to him. He will speak like a serpent, for he acts and speaks according to the qualities of the founder of evil, the devil." (St Andrew, chapter 37)

Imitating the Lord Jesus Christ, he will use for the establishment of authority of the antichrist, two powers—the power of the word and the power of miracles. But he will speak "like a dragon," that is, blasphemously, and the fruit of his talking will be atheism and extreme impiety. For the deception of men, he will begin to perform "great wonders," such as bringing down fire from heaven.

The forerunner of the apostate—the false christ—will perform everything through sorcery and deceit for the deception of men, so that Antichrist might be considered as God. He will be the glorious performer of such miracles and worthy of undoubted glory, like St John the Baptist who brought believers to the Saviour; for the lie also, for the deception of men, will strive to imitate the truth. Therefore it is not at all astonishing that for deceived eyes fire will be seen coming down from heaven, since from the history of Job we know that, by God's allowance, fire came down from heaven by the activity of Satan and burnt his flock. (St Andrew, chapter 37)

But these will be not true miracles, as God alone performs, but "false miracles" (cf. 2 Thess 2:9). They will consist of cunningness, of the deception of the senses, and of the use of natural but hidden powers of nature, with the help of the devil, within the limits of the authority of his diabolic powers.

"He will deceive those whose hearts have their constant dwellings upon earth; but he will not deceive the senses of those who have acquired a dwelling in the heavens—they will be made perfectly firm by the prophecy of his coming" (St Andrew, chapter 37).

13:14–15 And deceiveth them that dwell on the earth by the means of those miracles which he had power to do in the sight of the beast; saying to them that dwell on the earth, that they should make an image to the beast, which had the wound by a sword, and did live. And he had power to give life unto the image of the beast, that the image of the beast should both speak, and cause that as many as would not worship the image of the beast should be killed.

There are accounts of how the demons, by sorcery, have often spoken by means of images, statues, trees, water, etc., and even perhaps through dead bodies.... Therefore, there is nothing unfitting in the fact that the weapon-bearer or forerunner of Antichrist, acting with the help of demons, should make an image of the beast and falsely show it to be speaking, or that he should command that those who do not worship him should be killed. (St Andrew, chapter 37)

13:16–17 And he causeth all, both small and great, rich and poor, free and bond, to receive a mark in their right hand, or in their foreheads: and that no man might buy or sell, save he that had the mark, or the name of the beast, or the number of his name.

All who bow down to the antichrist will receive "a mark on the right hand or in their foreheads," just as slaves in antiquity once bore marks branded on their foreheads and soldiers upon their hands.

He will strive to place upon all the outline of the ruinous name of the apostate and deceiver, in their right hands, in order to cut off the doing of right and good deeds, and likewise in their foreheads, in order to instruct the deceived to be bold in deception and darkness. But it will not be received by those sealed in their faces with the Divine Light. And the seal of the beast will be spread everywhere, in buying and selling, so that those who do not receive it will suffer a violent death from the want of necessities. (St Andrew, chapter 37)

13:18 *Here is wisdom. Let him that hath understanding count the number of the beast: for it is the number of a man: and his number is Six hundred threescore and six.*

An extraordinary mysteriousness is bound up with the name of Antichrist and with the "number of his name." There have been many attempts even in ancient times to unriddle the significance and the meaning of these words, but they have not resulted in anything positive. Most frequently of all, there have been attempts to seek out the name of Antichrist by putting together letters which have a numerical significance. In various alphabets, for example, according to the guess of St Irenaeus, the number of the beast, 666, is formed from combining the numerical value of the letters of the name "Latinos" or "Titan." Certain others have found the number of the beast in the name of Julian the Apostate; later in the title of the Pope of Rome—Vicarius Filii Dei, vicar of the Son of God; in the name of Napoleon, and so on. Our sectarians in Russia strove to find the number 666 in the name of Patriarch Nikon. Reflecting on the name of Antichrist, St Andrew says, "If it were needed for us to know this name, the seer of mysteries St John would have revealed it. But the grace of God did not will that this ruinous name should be written in the Divine Book." If we examine words, then, in the opinion of St Hippolytus, one might find a multitude of names—both personal names and titles—which correspond to this number. "A careful examination of the number, and likewise of everything else written about him, will reveal the time of temptation to those who think soundly and are vigilant by the time of temptation" (St Andrew, chapter 38).

14. PREPARATORY EVENTS BEFORE THE GENERAL RESURRECTION AND THE LAST JUDGMENT; THE HYMN OF PRAISE OF THE ONE HUNDRED FORTY-FOUR THOUSAND RIGHTEOUS ONES; AND THE ANGELS WHO ANNOUNCE THE FATE OF THE WORLD

14:1–5 *And I looked, and, lo, a Lamb stood on the mount Sion, and with him an hundred forty and four thousand, having his Father's name written in their foreheads. And I heard a voice from heaven, as the voice of many waters, and as the voice of a great thunder: and I heard the voice of harpers harping with their harps: And they sung as it were a new song before the throne, and before the four beasts [living creatures], and the elders: and no man could learn that song but the hundred and forty and four thousand, which were redeemed from the earth. These are they which were not defiled with women; for they are virgins. These are they which follow the Lamb whithersoever he goeth. These were redeemed from among men, being the firstfruits unto God and to the Lamb. And in their mouth was found no guile: for they are without fault before the throne of God.*

In this vision is depicted the Church, the pure bride of Christ, at the time of the flourishing of the empire of the beast. The number 144,000 here has a similar significance as in chapter 7:2–8. In this instance, the chosen of God are from all the peoples of the earth, presented figuratively in the form of the twelve tribes of Israel. That the name of the Father of the Lamb is written upon their brows signifies the distinguishing qualities of their inward attitude: their moral character and form of life, their entire dedication to the service of God. To them is joined the choir of those playing upon harps "as it were a new song." This is the song of the new creation of God, the song of the redemption and renewal of mankind by the blood of the Lamb of God. Only that part of mankind which has been redeemed sings this song. Therefore "no man could learn that song but the hundred and forty and four thousand, which were redeemed from the earth." By "virgins," certain commentators understand here not virgins in the literal meaning of the word but those who were saved from the grasp of paganism and idol worship, in as much as in the Holy Scripture of the Old Testament, idol worship is often called adultery.

14:6–7 And I saw another angel fly in the midst of heaven, having the everlasting gospel to preach unto them that dwell on the earth, and to every nation, and kindred, and tongue, and people, Saying with a loud voice, Fear God, and give glory to him; for the hour of his judgment is come: and worship him that made heaven, and earth, and the sea, and the fountains of waters.

Immediately after this, there appears to St John a second vision of three angels soaring in the heavens. One declares to men the "everlasting gospel" and as it were says: "Fear God and do not be afraid of Antichrist who cannot destroy your souls together with your bodies, and oppose him with boldness for judgment and reward is close and he has power only for a short time" (St Andrew, chapter 40). Certain exegetes by this angel understand the preachers of the gospel in general.

14:8 And there followed another angel saying, Babylon is fallen, is fallen, that great city, because she made all nations drink of the wine of the wrath of her fornication.

Another angel declares the fall of Babylon by which is usually understood the kingdom of evil and sin in the world. Some commentators understand by this Babylon ancient pagan Rome, which gave all the people to drink "the wine of fornication" or idol worship. Others understand by this symbol the false Christian empire; and by the wine of fornication the false teaching of religion (compare Jer 51:7).

14:9–12 And the third angel followed them, saying with a loud voice, If any man worship the beast and his image, and receive his mark in his forehead, or in his hand, The same shall drink of the wine of the wrath of God, which is poured out without mixture into the cup of his indignation; and he shall be tormented with fire and brimstone in the presence of the holy angels, and in the presence of the Lamb: And the smoke of their torment ascendeth up for ever and ever: and they have no rest day nor night, who worship the beast and his image, and whosoever receiveth the mark of his name. Here is the patience of the saints: here are they that keep the commandments of God, and the faith of Jesus.

The third angel threatens with eternal torments all those who serve the beast and bow down to him and his image and receive his mark upon their brow or hand. By the "wine of the wrath of God" one must understand the difficult decrees of God that bring people into a state of almost unconsciousness and, like drunken people, into a state of disturbing spirit. In Palestine, wine was never used whole, unmixed with water. Therefore the wrath of God in its powerful activity is likened here to unmixed wine. The impious will be subjected to eternal torments and the saints will be saved by their own patience.

By the smoke of their torment is to be understood either the sighing of those being tormented which ascends from below together with lamentation, or the smoke which proceeds from the fire by which the fallen will be punished. From the fact that the smoke ascendeth up for ever and ever we see that the torments of sinners are just as endless as the blessedness of the righteous is eternal. (St Andrew, chapter 42)

14:13 And I heard a voice from heaven saying unto me, Write, Blessed are the dead which die in the Lord from henceforth: Yea, saith the Spirit, that they may rest from their labours; and their works do follow them.

The "heavenly voice" St Andrew explains, "does not bless everyone, but only those who, mortifying themselves to the world, die for the Lord and bear in their bodies the death of Jesus, and suffer together with Christ. For these, the departure from the body in truth is a rest from labors" (St Andrew, chapter 42). Here we find yet another testimony of the significance of good deeds for salvation—something that is denied by Protestants.

14:14 And I looked, and behold a white cloud, and upon the cloud one sat like unto the Son of man, having on his head a golden crown, and in his hand a sharp sickle.

By the cloud we understand either a perceptible cloud like the one that hid our Lord Jesus Christ from the eyes of the apostles, or else a certain angelic power which is called "cloud" by reason of its purity and lightness.... The One sitting on the cloud and like unto the Son of Man is Christ. The crown upon His head signifies His royal authority over everything visible and invisible; it is golden by reason of the high value of this material among us. The sharp sickle indicates the end of the world, which the Lord Himself has called a harvest. (St Andrew, chapter 43)

14:15–16 *And another angel came out of the temple, crying with a loud voice to him that sat on the cloud, Thrust in thy sickle, and reap: for the time is come for thee to reap; for the harvest of the earth is ripe. And he that sat on the cloud thrust in his sickle on the earth; and the earth was reaped.*

By this harvest one must understand the end of the world (Matt 13:39). "That the harvest of the earth is ripe indicates that the final time has come when the seed of piety, which has matured like ripe wheat and has offered to the husbandman fruit thirtyfold, sixtyfold, and a hundredfold will be vouchsafed the heavenly granaries" (St Andrew, chapter 43).

14:17 *And another angel came out of the temple which is in heaven, he also having a sharp sickle.*

"He is come out to perform the cutting off of the most impious" (St Andrew, chapter 44).

14:18 *And another angel came out from the altar, which had power over fire; and cried with a loud cry to him that had the sharp sickle, saying, Thrust in thy sharp sickle, and gather the clusters of the vine of the earth; for her grapes are fully ripe.*

"From this we learn that some of the angelic powers which are placed over creatures are in charge of waters, others of fire, and others of some other part of creation; that this one is placed over fire indicates that he is one of the highest angels and his duty is to punish, for with a loud voice he commands the one having a sickle to cut off the clusters of the vine of the earth" (St Andrew, chapter 44). By "clusters of grapes," we are to understand the enemies of the Church whose iniquity has reached an extreme ("are fully ripe"), so that the measure of their crimes overflows.

14:19–20 *And the angel thrust in his sickle into the earth, and gathered the vine of the earth, and cast it into the great winepress of the wrath of God. And the winepress was trodden without the city, and the blood came out of the winepress, even unto the horse bridles, by the space of a thousand and six hundred furlongs.*

Here there is a reference to the city of Jerusalem outside of which, on the Mount of Olives, there were many wine presses in which were pressed olives and grapes (cf. Joel 3:13). The abundance of the harvest of grapes is described in the fact that the wine poured out on the earth in such abundance that it reached the horses' bridles. The hyperbolic expression used here by the holy seer of mysteries indicates that the defeat of the enemies of God will be so terrible that the blood will flow as if in rivers. Sixteen hundred furlongs is a definite number taken in place of an indefinite one and signifies in general the abundant field of battle.

> Inasmuch as those who gave themselves over to pleasures became ferocious horses, therefore they will be taken by tortures up to the bridles—that is, they will be restrained by torments, for they knew no bridling in their pleasures. 1,000 signifies the multitude of evil, and 600 the fervent pursuit of sin through the misuse of creation which was made in six days, and also that in the 600th year of Noah the earth was inundated. (St Andrew, chapter 44)

15. The Fourth Vision: The Seven Angels Who Have the Seven Last Plagues

> 15:1 *And I saw another sign in heaven, great and marvelous, seven angels having the seven last plagues; for in them is filled up the wrath of God.*

With this chapter begins the final, fourth vision, which embraces in itself the eight final chapters of the Apocalypse, chapters 15–22.

"Everywhere he takes the number 7, signifying thereby that what has been brazenly done in the seven days of this present life of unrighteousness will be bridled by the seven plagues and the seven angels" (St Andrew, chapter 45).

> 15:2 *And I saw as it were a sea of glass mingled with fire: and them that had gotten the victory over the beast, and over his image, and over his mark, and over the number of his name, stand on the sea of glass, having the harps of God.*

The sea of glass, in the interpretation of St Andrew of Caesarea,

signifies the multitude of those being saved, the purity of the future repose, and the brightness of the saints, by the virtuous rays of which brightness they shine like the sun (cf. Matt 13:43) and the fact that the fire is mixed in with the glass may be understood by what has been written by the Apostle. Every man's work shall be made manifest: for the day shall declare it, because it shall be revealed by fire; and the fire shall try every man's work of what sort it is (1 Cor 3:13). It does not in the least harm those who are pure, undefiled because, in the phrase of the Psalmist (Ps 28:7), it has two attributes: one scorches the sinner and the other, as St Basil the Great has understood, illumines the righteous. It is likely that by fire is to be understood the Divine knowledge and the grace of the Life-giving Spirit, for God revealed himself in the fire unto Moses and in the form of fiery tongues the Holy Spirit descended on the Apostles. (St Andrew, chapter 45)

The harps signify the harmony of virtues in the well-ordered spiritual life of the righteous or the harmony which is to be observed in them between the word of truth and the deeds of righteousness.

> *15:3–4 And they sing the song of Moses the servant of God, and the song of the Lamb, saying, Great and marvellous are thy works, Lord God Almighty; just and true are thy ways, thou King of saints. Who shall not fear thee, O Lord, and glorify thy name? for thou only art holy: for all nations shall come and worship before thee; for thy judgments are made manifest.*

"By the song of Moses we suppose that hymns are sent up to God from those justified before grace under the law; and by the song of the Lamb that those who lived righteously after the coming of Christ offer up to Him unceasing hymns and thanksgiving" (St Andrew, chapter 45). The song of Moses is likewise sung as a hymn of victory: "It is fitting for those who are celebrating the last most important victory over the enemy to remember the first successes of their battle, such as in the history of the chosen people of God, in the victory of Moses over Pharaoh. It is his song that is sung now by Christian victors."[224] This hymn sounds most triumphant: "Let us sing unto the Lord for gloriously has He been glorified," and in the present case it is most fitting.[xxv] The righteous, in their song, glorify God also for the manifestation of His Judgment: "for Thy judgments are made manifest."

> *15:5–6 And after that I looked, and, behold, the temple of the tabernacle of the testimony in heaven was opened: And the seven angels came out of the temple, having the seven plagues, clothed in pure and white linen, and having their breasts girded with golden girdles.*

It is in this image, that God commanded Moses in the Old Testament to build the earthly tabernacle.… The seer of mysteries says that the angels were clothed in pure white linen garments, as a sign of the purity and brightness of their virtue. And they were girded on their breast with golden girdles, as a sign of might, and the purity of their being, their honesty and the limitlessness of their service. (St Andrew, chapter 45)

> *15:7 And one of the four beasts [living creatures] gave unto the seven angels seven golden vials full of the wrath of God, who liveth for ever and ever.*

From one of the four "living creatures," that is, the eldest angels, they receive "seven golden vials full of the wrath of God, Who liveth for ever and ever." These "living creatures," the Cherubim or Seraphim, are the highest zealots of the glory of God, filled with the most profound knowledge of the decrees of God, both of the

---

[xxv] The song of Moses, which is sung in the Orthodox Church at the Vesperal Liturgy of Great and Holy Saturday, is found in Exodus 15:1–21. (S.R.)

past and of the future, which is indicated by the very appearance of these blessed beings who are filled with eyes before and behind. It is they who receive the commandment of God to assign the seven other angels to pour out upon the earth the seven vials of the wrath of God, before the end of the world and the final judgment of the living and the dead (see Ezek 5:13).

15:8 *And the temple was filled with smoke from the glory of God, and from his power; and no man was able to enter into the temple, till the seven plagues of the seven angels were fulfilled.*

Through this smoke, says St Andrew,

we recognize that the wrath of God is frightful, terrible and tormenting, and it, filling the temple, in the day of Judgment, visits those who are worthy of it and above all those who have submitted to Antichrist and done the deeds of apostasy. This is confirmed also by what follows, for he says and no man was able to enter into the temple, till the seven plagues of the seven angels were fulfilled. First the plagues had to be completed, [that is, the punishment of sinners] and then it was to be given to the saints to dwell in the city on high. (St Andrew, chapter 45)

16. The Seven Angels Pouring Out the Seven Vials of the Wrath of God upon the Earth

16:1 *And I heard a great voice out of the temple saying to the seven angels, Go your ways, and pour out the vials of the wrath of God upon the earth.*

In this chapter there is depicted God's judgment upon the enemies of the Church under the symbol of the seven vials or seven cups of the wrath of God poured out by the seven angels. The symbol of these plagues is taken from the plagues which struck ancient Egypt, whose defeat was the prefiguration of the defeat of the false Christian kingdom, which has been called Egypt (see Rev. 11:8) and then Babylon.

16:2 *And the first went, and poured out his vial upon the earth; and there fell a noisome and grievous sore upon the men which had the mark of the beast, and upon them which worshipped his image.*

This symbol is taken evidently from the sixth plague which struck Egypt. According to the interpretations of some, here one should understand this to be a physical epidemic. In the interpretation of St Andrew of Caesarea, the noisome sores are "the grief which occurs in the hearts of the apostates, and which torment them in the likeness of affliction of the heart; for those who are punished by God receive no help from the antichrist which they have deified" (St Andrew, chapter 46).

16:3 And the second angel poured out his vial upon the sea; and it became as the blood of a dead man: and every living soul died in the sea.

Here is to be understood international and civil wars, with much shedding of blood.

It is not astonishing that in order to expose the weakness of Antichrist and the light-mindedness of the deceived, the Divine power through the prophets Enoch and Elijah will turn the sea, as it were, into the blood of one who has been killed, and will destroy everything in the sea as God once did in Exodus 7:18.... Another supposition is also possible, in that by this is signified a defeat during battles at his coming; for when Gog and Magog will attack each other in all parts of the world and when the kings who did not submit to Antichrist will be exterminated with their armies and there will be many murders, then, as the result of sea battles, the sea will be defiled by blood and the rivers also will become red from those who are killed there. (St Andrew, chapter 47)

16:4–6 And the third angel poured out his vial upon the rivers and fountains of waters; and they became blood. And I heard the angel of the waters say, thou art righteous, O Lord, which art, and wast, and shalt be, because thou hast judged thus. For they have shed the blood of saints and prophets, and thou hast given them blood to drink; for they are worthy.

To this St Andrew says, "From this it is evident that angels have been placed over the elements" (St Andrew, chapter 48). What is referred to here is likewise the frightful shedding of blood which will occur before the end of the world, during the time of the antichrist.

16:7 And I heard another out of the altar say, Even so, Lord God Almighty, true and righteous are thy judgments.

Thus he says that from this altar was heard a voice praising the righteousness of God's judgment, which surpasses every mind in word. From the Gospels we know that the mental powers are glad and rejoice over the salvation of those who are converted through repentance, while they grieve over the seduction from the true path and give thanks to God for the punishment of those who have transgressed the Divine commandments, so that at least in part they may receive the forgiveness of sins. (St Andrew, chapter 48)

16:8–9 And the fourth angel poured out his vial upon the sun; and power was given unto him to scorch men with fire. And men were scorched with great heat, and blasphemed the name of God, which hath power over these plagues: and they repented not to give him glory.

St Andrew says this punishment may be understood either literally or that by this "heat" one should understand "the heat of temptations so that men through enduring sorrows might hate their cause which is sin" (St Andrew, chapter 49). The people who have become senseless, however, in their hardness of heart, will not be capable of repentance.

> 16:10–11 *And the fifth angel poured out his vial upon the seat of the beast; and his kingdom was full of darkness; and they gnawed their tongues for pain, And blasphemed the God of heaven because of their pains and their sores, and repented not of their deeds.*

This reminds one of the ninth plague in Egypt (Exodus 10:21). By this plague one must understand the significant decrease of the greatness and authority of the antichrist whose magnificence up until then had struck people, and at the same time, one must understand the stubborn lack of repentance of those who worshipped the antichrist.

> 16:12 *And the sixth angel poured out his vial upon the great river Euphrates; and the water thereof was dried up, that the way of the kings of the east might be prepared.*

Here the Euphrates is depicted as a hindrance, which prevented the kings with their armies from coming for the completion of the decrees of God upon the kingdom of the antichrist. This symbol is taken from the position of the ancient Roman Empire for which the Euphrates served as a barrier against attacks of the eastern peoples.

> 16:13–14 *And I saw three unclean spirits like frogs come out of the mouth of the dragon, and out of the mouth of the beast, and out of the mouth of the false prophet. For they are the spirits of devils, working miracles, which go forth unto the kings of the earth and of the whole world, to gather them to the battle of that great day of God Almighty.*

By these spirits of devils one is to understand false teachers, chatterers, and intruders, who are lovers of their stomachs, shameless, and puffed up, and who will attract the people to themselves by false miracles. The great day of God Almighty is the time when God will reveal His glory for the punishments of the enemies of the Church.

> 16:15 *Behold, I come as a thief. Blessed is he that watcheth, and keepeth his garments, lest he walk naked, and they see his shame.*

What is meant here is the suddenness of the second coming of Christ (compare Matt 24:43–44).

"To watch and keep one's garments means to be vigilant and to be unwaveringly concerned for good deeds, which comprise the garment of the saints" (St Andrew, chapter 51).

> 16:16 *And he gathered them together into a place called in the Hebrew tongue Armageddon.*

"Armageddon" signifies cutting up or murder. St Andrew says, "in this place let us suppose the peoples who have been gathered and led by the devil will be killed, for he, the devil, is comforted by the blood of men" (St Andrew, chapter 51). This name is taken from the valley of Mageddo, where King Josias fell in battle with Pharaoh Nechao (2 Chron 35:22).

16:17–18 *And the seventh angel poured out his vial into the air; and there came a great voice out of the temple of heaven, from the throne, saying, It is done. And there were voices, and thunders, and lightnings; and there was a great earthquake, such as was not since men were upon the earth, so mighty an earthquake, and so great.*

By the pouring out of the seventh vial, the kingdom of the beast will receive its final defeat.

"The earthquake signifies a change in the existing world as the Apostle has said: 'Yet once more I shake not the earth only, but also the heaven' (Heb 12:26)" (St Andrew, chapter 52).

16:19 *And the great city was divided into three parts, and the cities of the nations fell: and great Babylon came in remembrance before God, to give unto her the cup of the wine of the fierceness of his wrath.*

By this great city, St Andrew understands the capital of the kingdom of the antichrist, which will be Jerusalem.

The division of the city into three parts indicates, we suppose, the Christians, Jews, and Samaritans living in it.... There will occur their division into three parts: the pious, the impious, and sinners; and all will go to those one in mind with themselves. The falling of the cities of the nations signifies either their destruction or decrease and the ceasing of pagan life with the coming of the Divine Kingdom. Great Babylon, as if forgotten by reason of [God's] long-suffering, will come into remembrance, and for trampling on the righteous and her impious words and deeds, will drink the cup of God's wrath. (St Andrew, chapter 52)

16:20 *And every island fled away, and the mountains were not found.*

St Andrew explains this:

From the Divine Scripture we are instructed to understand, by islands, the holy Churches, and by mountains, those who are the heads of them. That they flee away at the coming of everything that has been preordained, this we have heard from the Lord Who said, Those who are in the east will flee to the west, and those who are in the west will flee to the east, "for then shall be great tribulation, such as there was not since the beginning of the world to this time, no, nor ever shall be" (Matt 24:21)—when some as a punishment for sins and others for a testing of virtue will endure misfortunes and unhappiness, not only from the antichrist in torments for Christ, but also in flight, in torments and sufferings in mountains and caves, which for the preservation of piety they will prefer to living in cities. (St Andrew, chapter 52)

If one is to understand these words in a literal sense, this will be a picture of frightful destruction which in our times—when atomic and hydrogen bombs have been discovered—is not difficult to imagine.

16:21 *And there fell upon men a great hail out of heaven, every stone about the weight of a talent: and men blasphemed God because of the plague of the hail; for the plague thereof was exceeding great.*

Is it not bombs we should understand by this murderous hail? In our times also we often observe such a hardness of heart when nothing causes men to come to their senses, but they only blaspheme God.

"By the hail coming down from heaven we understand God's wrath sent by Him and coming down from above. And that this hail is the size of a talent indicates the fullness of wrath by reason of the full weight and extremity of sin; an indication of this is the talent which Zechariah saw (Zech 5:7)" (St Andrew, chapter 52).

17. THE JUDGMENT ON THE GREAT HARLOT WHO SITS ON MANY WATERS

17:1–3 *And there came one of the seven angels which had the seven vials, and talked with me, saying unto me, Come hither; I will shew unto thee the judgment of the great whore that sitteth upon many waters: With whom the kings of the earth have committed fornication, and the inhabitants of the earth have been made drunk with the wine of her fornication. So he carried me away in the spirit into the wilderness; and I saw a woman sit upon a scarlet-coloured beast, full of names of blasphemy, having seven heads and ten horns.*

One of the seven angels offered to St John to show him the judgment on the great harlot who sits on many waters, with whom the kings of the earth committed fornication and with the wine of whose fornication those upon the earth became drunk.

Some have understood this harlot to be ancient Rome, as being disposed upon seven hills; they consider the seven heads of the beast as the seven most impious of all the emperors who, from Domitian to Diocletian, persecuted the Church (first to fourth centuries A.D.). St Andrew, citing this opinion says further: "But we, being guided and forming our conception according to the sequence of events, think that the harlot is in general the earthly kingdom, represented as it were in one body, or the city which is to reign even unto the coming of Antichrist" (St Andrew, chapter 53).

Some commentators see in this harlot the church which is unfaithful to Christ, which is bowed down to Antichrist, or the society of the apostates of God—that part of Christian humanity, which will enter into close contact with the world of sin, will serve it and depend entirely upon its crude power—the power of the beast, Antichrist, which is why this woman is shown to the seer of mysteries as sitting on a scarlet beast. "For the beast himself and his scarlet appearance serve as an indication of severity, cruelty, and a predisposition to murder" (St Andrew, chapter 53).

> 17:4 *And the woman was arrayed in purple and scarlet colour, and decked with gold and precious stones and pearls, having a golden cup in her hand full of abominations and filthiness of her fornication:*

The purple, scarlet, and gold are symbols of her royal authority and dominion. St Andrew says to this, "The cup signifies the sweetness of evil deeds before they are tasted and the gold indicates their preciousness" (St Andrew, chapter 53).

The members of this church which is unfaithful to Christ, or the society of the apostates of God, will be fleshly men given over to sensuality. As one of the commentators says, "Being filled with outward piety and at the same time not foreign to feelings of a crude love of honors, and a vainglorious love of fame, the members of the unfaithful church will love luxury and comfort, and will begin to arrange luxurious ceremonies for the powerful of the world (see Rev 17:2, 18:3–9) to attain holy aims by sinful means and they will preach exclusively by the sword and gold" (N. Vinogradov).

> 17:5 *And upon her forehead was a name written, Mystery, Babylon The Great, The Mother Of Harlots And Abominations Of The Earth.*

St Andrew says to this, "The writing upon the forehead indicates the shamelessness of unrighteousness, the fullness of sins and disturbance of heart; she is a mother for she leads those in the cities under her by her fornication of soul, giving birth thereby to iniquities which are vile before God" (St Andrew, chapter 53).

A more general commentary is inclined to see in this harlot—who bears the name of Babylon—the whole crudely sensual and anti-Christian culture of mankind in the last times in general, for which is prepared a frightful universal catastrophe at the end of the world in the second coming of Christ. The fall of this "Babylon" is presented in the Apocalypse as the first act of victory in the worldwide battle of the Church of Christ with the sinful kingdom of the devil.

> 17:6 *And I saw the woman drunken with the blood of the saints, and with the blood of the martyrs of Jesus: and when I saw her, I wondered with great admiration.*

Here is meant all the martyrs for Christ who have suffered in the course of the history of the world, especially during the time of the antichrist.

> 17:7–8 *And the angel said unto me, Wherefore didst thou marvel? I will tell thee the mystery of the woman, and of the beast that carrieth her, which hath the seven heads and ten*

*horns. The beast that thou sawest was, and is not; and shall ascend out of the bottomless
pit, and go into perdition:*

Further, the angel who showed the harlot to St John gives him an explanation
of the whole vision. St Andrew says that

> this beast is Satan who, having been put to death by the Cross of Christ, will again,
> as it is said, come back to life at the end. By false signs and miracles he will, through
> the antichrist, act for the overthrowing of the Cross. Therefore he was and acted up
> to the time of the Cross and then he was no longer, inasmuch as by the saving pas-
> sion he was made powerless and was deprived of the authority which he had over the
> peoples through idol worship. (St Andrew, chapter 54)

At the end of the world, Satan again

> will come in the way indicated by us, coming out of the pit, or from the place where
> he was condemned and where the demons, banished by Christ, begged him not to
> send them, but rather into the swine (Luke 8:30–32); or he shall come out of the pres-
> ent life which is called the pit metaphorically by reason of the depth of sin in this life,
> which is tossed about and agitated by the winds of the passions. For the destruction
> of men, Antichrist will also come out from this place, having Satan in himself, so as
> to receive his perdition quickly in the age to come. (St Andrew, chapter 54)

> 17:8 *And they that dwell on the earth shall wonder, whose names were not written in the
> book of life from the foundation of the world, when they behold the beast that was, and is
> not, and yet is.*

"By reason of the false miracles, he says those that are not written in the book
of those who live eternally and who have not studied this in accordance with the
prophecies of Christ, will be astonished at the coming of the beast. They will be
astonished also, reflecting on how he has again received his previous authority" (St
Andrew, chapter 54). (See also Rev 13:8.)

> 17:9–10 *And here is the mind which hath wisdom. The seven heads are seven mountains,
> on which the woman sitteth. And there are seven kings: five are fallen, and one is, and the
> other is not yet come; and when he cometh, he must continue a short space.*

Inasmuch as this is said spiritually, he says, to understand it requires spiritual
wisdom.

In these seven heads and seven mountains, St Andrew sees seven kingdoms
which have a special worldwide significance and power: Assyria, the Medes, Babylon, Persia, Macedonia, Rome, and its two periods—the period of the Republic

and the period of the Empire, or the ancient Roman period and the newer Roman period that began with Emperor Constantine.

> Under the name of five kings who have fallen out of the seven, Blessed Hippolytus understands ages, of which five have already passed. The sixth, in which the Apostle saw this, is still going on, and the seventh age which follows upon the sixth has not yet come, but when it comes will not continue long … or [the kings] are the seven kingdoms which have been from the beginning of the world until now; five have already fallen, the sixth—under which the revelation was made—was ancient Rome, and the seventh is yet to come—this is the new Rome. (St Andrew, chapter 54)

> 17:11 *And the beast that was, and is not, even he is the eighth, and is of the seven, and goeth into perdition.*

This beast is the antichrist. He is called the eighth because: "After the seven kingdoms, he will arise for the deception and laying waste of the earth" (St Andrew, chapter 54). He is "of the seven," because he has made his appearance from one of these kingdoms.

> 17:12–14 *And the ten horns which thou sawest are ten kings, which have received no kingdom as yet; but receive power as kings one hour with the beast. These have one mind, and shall give their power and strength unto the beast. These shall make war with the Lamb, and the Lamb shall overcome them: for he is Lord of lords, and King of kings: and they that are with him are called, and chosen, and faithful.*

Here, no amount of guessing or supposition can lead anywhere. Some have wished to see in all these kings, as in the beast, Roman emperors, but all of these are forced interpretations. What is being discussed here is, of course, the last times. All these kings who are of one mind with the beast, that is, Antichrist, will wage war with the Lamb, that is, Christ, and will be conquered. "Daniel also saw seven horns coming before Antichrist, which were altogether uprooted by the cursed one, and the others submitted to him (Dan 7:20–24). One hour indicates either the shortness of time or a single part of the year, that is, the three-month period after which they will submit to Antichrist as their chief" (St Andrew, chapter 54).

> 17:15–18 *And he saith unto me, The waters which thou sawest, where the whore sitteth, are peoples, and multitudes, and nations, and tongues. And the ten horns which thou sawest upon the beast, these shall hate the whore, and shall make her desolate and naked, and shall eat her flesh, and burn her with fire. For God hath put in their hearts to fulfil his will, and to agree, and give their kingdom unto the beast, until the words of God shall be fulfilled. And the woman which thou sawest is that great city, which reigneth over the kings of the earth.*

It is noteworthy that the harlot bears the name of Babylon, of whom the holy seer of mysteries says directly in 17:18 that she "is that great city, which reigneth over the kings of the earth," and that the waters upon which she sits are "peoples; and multitudes, and nations, and tongues." She will be punished and annihilated by the beast, the antichrist himself, whose ten horns will do this work.

18. THE FALL OF BABYLON, THE GREAT HARLOT

This chapter depicts in a most vivid way the destruction of Babylon, the great harlot, which is accompanied on the one hand by the lamentations of the kings of the earth who had committed fornication with her, and of the merchants of the earth who had sold her various precious goods. On the other hand, it is accompanied by rejoicing in heaven because of the righteous judgment of God.

Certain contemporary interpreters suppose that this Babylon will actually be some kind of immense city, a world center, the capital of the Kingdom of Antichrist, which will be distinguished for its wealth and at the same time for the extreme corruption of its morals, which has generally been characteristic of large and wealthy cities.

18:1 *And after these things I saw another angel come down from heaven, having great power; and the earth was lightened with his glory.*

Here is shown the brightness of the heavenly powers and their purity—several times more superior in radiance and beauty than the stars and their light (St Andrew, chapter 55).

18:2 *And he cried mightily with a strong voice, saying, Babylon the great is fallen, is fallen, and is become the habitation of devils, and the hold of every foul spirit, and a cage of every unclean and hateful bird.*

"About the Chaldean capital of Babylon, captured by Cyrus and the Persians, something similar was foretold by Isaiah (Isa 13:21–22, 21:9), that by reason of its utter desolation, it would be filled with wild beasts and unclean spirits" (St Andrew, chapter 55).

18:3 *For all nations have drunk of the wine of the wrath of her fornication, and the kings of the earth have committed fornication with her, and the merchants of the earth are waxed rich through the abundance of her delicacies.*

And how did Babylon make the nations drink the wine of its fornication? It was their leader in all manner of lawlessness, and it sent gifts to those cities which were obedient—to their chiefs and rulers who were enemies of truth.

18:4–5 *And I heard another voice from heaven, saying, Come out of her, my people, that ye be not partakers of her sins, and that ye receive not of her plagues. For her sins have reached unto heaven, and God hath remembered her iniquities.*

"Come out of her, My people."

"As it was spoken to Lot in Sodom, 'Escape for thy life' (Gen 19:17), and in Isaiah (Isa 52:11), so it is said here; for one should avoid contact and cohabitation with those who offend God" (St Andrew, chapter 55).

> 18:6 *Reward her even as she rewarded you, and double unto her double according to her works: in the cup which she hath filled fill to her double.*

This speaks of those who, although innocent, suffered here from the rulers of that city, and whose endurance of sorrows elicited a most cruel punishment of their tormentors. It may also indicate one's transition from one state to another, i.e., from one who is being punished to one who is a holy punishing force. The chalice is called double either because the sinners and lawless will receive terrible punishments both here and in the future life; or because both the soul and body will suffer torments for their common deeds; or because sin will be punished not only through outward suffering, but even more so inwardly, through the conscience. (St Andrew, chapter 55)

> 18:7 *How much she hath glorified herself, and lived deliciously, so much torment and sorrow give her: for she saith in her heart, I sit a queen, and am no widow, and shall see no sorrow.*

"If there is no fear of God in them, those living in complacency and glory are wont to say, 'I shall never be removed' (Ps 29:7 LXX). So also does this city speak of itself" (St Andrew, chapter 55).

> 18:8 *Therefore shall her plagues come in one day, death, and mourning, and famine; and she shall be utterly burned with fire: for strong is the Lord God who judgeth her.*

One day means either the suddenness and shortness of time in which—from the sword, sores and hunger—a wailing will arise from this city which will be overtaken by destruction and consuming flames; or, the course of that same day in which, according to the prophecy, it will suffer. When the enemies seize the city, one day will suffice to defeat the people through all manner of provocation and various forms of death. God is almighty to save those who please Him, and likewise to punish unrepentant sinners. (St Andrew, chapter 55)

> 18:9–10 *And the kings of the earth, who have committed fornication and lived deliciously with her, shall bewail her, and lament for her, when they shall see the smoke of her burning, Standing afar off for fear of her torment, saying, Alas, alas that great city Babylon, that mighty city! for in one hour is thy judgment come.*

Here, we think, "kings of the earth" indicates the rulers, just as the Psalmist said of Jerusalem: "The rulers gathered together" (Ps 2:2 LXX). Of those who have forsaken the Divine commandments it is said that they will burst into weeping, looking at its desolation and listening to its burning, being terrified by the sudden change which occurred in such a short time. (St Andrew, chapter 55)

18:11–14 *And the merchants of the earth shall weep and mourn over her; for no man buyeth their merchandise any more: The merchandise of gold, and silver, and precious stones, and of pearls, and fine linen, and purple, and silk, and scarlet, and all thyine wood, and all manner vessels of ivory, and all manner vessels of most precious wood, and of brass, and iron, and marble, And cinnamon, and odours, and ointments, and frankincense, and wine, and oil, and fine flour, and wheat, and beasts, and sheep, and horses, and chariots, and slaves, and souls of men. And the fruits that thy soul lusted after are departed from thee, and all things which were dainty and goodly are departed from thee, and thou shalt find them no more at all.*

Through these expressions it should be understood that no one will buy.... We should re-examine and re-evaluate that which is traded in the cities and what articles and goods are acquired for excessive pleasure.

The use of horses, chariots, and the bodies of men will be unnecessary.... There will not be an enslaving free trade of men's souls; neither will there be a return to the enjoyment of the previous prosperity and magnificence. (St Andrew, chapter 55)

18:15–17 *The merchants of these things, which were made rich by her, shall stand afar off for the fear of her torment, weeping and wailing, And saying, Alas, alas that great city, that was clothed in fine linen, and purple, and scarlet, and decked with gold, and precious stones, and pearls! For in one hour so great riches is come to nought. And every shipmaster and all the company in ships, and sailors, and as many as trade by sea, stood afar off.*

Here attention is turned to the sufferings of this Babylon, the weeping over it indicating the great misfortune and frightful destiny, which will punish the city, once they boast of royal favor.

18:18–19 *And cried when they saw the smoke of her burning, saying, What city is like unto this great city! And they cast dust on their heads, and cried, weeping and wailing, saying, Alas, alas that great city, wherein were made rich all that had ships in the sea by reason of her costliness! for in one hour is she made desolate. Rejoice over her, thou heaven, and ye holy apostles and prophets; for God hath avenged you on her.*

It is very possible that the sea in a figurative sense indicates the present life, as it is subject to constant agitation; and merchants are swimmers, like fish, amid the worldly agitation.... The merchants of the worldwide Babylon—i.e., Confusion (cf. Gen 11:9)—at the demise of the visible world will likewise suffer and sob inconsolably, both on account of being deprived of the pleasures of this present life, and also on account of the reproach of their conscience. (St Andrew, chapter 55)

The word "heaven" indicates here either angels or saints, who dwell therein. With these the apostles and prophets are enjoined to rejoice, thus avenging those who were reproached or offended, or those who—however unsuccessful their preaching among the inhabitants of the aforementioned city—were often subject to dishonor; or those who were dispersed through all the earth and were slaughtered for the sake of God, as servants of His Word. So also were the prophets killed by the Jews, and the apostles by the pagans to whom they gave precedence in their preaching.

"They rejoice in the coming punishments, not with a perverse joy, but ardently desiring to cut off sin. Furthermore, these temporal punishments serve that there might be less suffering in the age to come" (St Andrew, chapter 55).

> 18:21–24 *And a mighty angel took up a stone like a great millstone, and cast it into the sea, saying, Thus with violence shall that great city Babylon be thrown down, and shall be found no more at all. And the voice of harpers, and musicians, and of pipers, and trumpeters, shall be heard no more at all in thee; and no craftsman, of whatsoever craft he be, shall be found any more in thee; and the sound of a millstone shall be heard no more at all in thee; And the light of a candle shall shine no more at all in thee; and the voice of the bridegroom and of the bride shall be heard no more at all in thee: for thy merchants were the great men of the earth; for by thy sorceries were all nations deceived. And in her was found the blood of prophets, and of saints, and of all that were slain upon the earth.*

In the last verses of this chapter there is indicated the suddenness of God's chastisement which will overtake this city. St Andrew says that its perdition will occur just as swiftly as a millstone sinks into the sea, and this perdition will be so extraordinary that there will remain not a single trace of this city. This is indicated figuratively: "and the voice of harpers, and musicians, and of pipers and trumpeters, shall be heard no more at all in thee."

In the final verse there is indicated another reason for the destruction of Babylon—that in her was found "the blood of prophets, and of saints, and of all that were slain upon the earth."

19. The Battle of the Word of God with the Beast and His Army, and the Destruction of the Latter

> 19:1–4 *And after these things I heard a great voice of much people in heaven, saying, Alleluia; Salvation, and glory, and honour, and power, unto the Lord our God: For true and righteous are his judgments: for he hath judged the great whore, which did corrupt the earth with her fornication, and hath avenged the blood of his servants at her hand. And again they said, Alleluia. And her smoke rose up for ever and ever. And the four and twenty elders and the four beasts [living creatures] fell down and worshipped God that sat on the throne, saying, Amen; Alleluia.*

In the first ten verses of this chapter there is described also very vividly the rejoicing in heaven in the midst of numerous choirs of saints on account of the destruction of the hostile kingdom of Antichrist and the coming Kingdom of Christ. The latter is depicted in the form of the wedding feast of the Lamb and the participation therein of the righteous (cf. Matt 22:1–14; Luke 14:16–24).

In the explanation of St Andrew of Caesarea, "Alleluia" signifies "divine glorification" and "Amen" means "truly, may it be." This, he says, is sung in praise unto God by the angelic powers together with men equal to the angels. It is sung thricely by reason of the three Hypostases of Father, Son, and Holy Spirit, the One God, Who has avenged the blood of His servants upon Babylon and has done good by punishing its inhabitants and cutting off sin. "Alleluia" is from the Hebrew *hallelu yah*, and means literally, "Praise ye the Lord."

"And her smoke rose up for ever and ever." This refers to the fact that the punishment which has overtaken Babylon the harlot will endure forever.

> 19:5–7 *And a voice came out of the throne, saying, Praise our God, all ye his servants, and ye that fear him, both small and great. And I heard as it were the voice of a great multitude, and as the voice of many waters, and as the voice of mighty thunderings, saying, Alleluia: for the Lord God omnipotent reigneth. Let us be glad and rejoice, and give honour to him: for the marriage of the Lamb is come, and his wife hath made herself ready.*

"Let us be glad and rejoice and give honour to Him, for the marriage of the Lamb has come." The reason for rejoicing lies in the fact that the time has come to celebrate the marriage of the Lamb. By "marriage" or "wedding banquet" in general the state of spiritual rejoicing of the Church is to be understood. By the Bridegroom of the Church, we are to understand the Lamb, the Lord Jesus Christ, the Head of His Mystical Body. By the bride and wife of the Lamb we are to understand the Church (cf. Eph 5:25). The wedding itself signifies the intimate union of the Lord Jesus Christ and His Church, which is sealed by faithfulness and confirmed on both sides by the Covenant, as by mutual agreement (cf. Hos 2:18–20). The wedding feast signifies the enjoyment of the fullness of God's grace which, by virtue of the redeeming merits of Christ, will be abundantly given to all true members of Christ's Church, that they may rejoice and be glad in these unutterably good things.

> 19:8–9 *And to her was granted that she should be arrayed in fine linen, clean and white: for the fine linen is the righteousness of the saints. And he saith unto me, Write, Blessed are they which are called unto the marriage supper of the Lamb. And he saith unto me, These are the true sayings of God.*

"That the Church is adorned in fine linen signifies her brightness in virtues, her refined understanding and the height of her reflection and contemplation of the Divine judgments" (St Andrew, chapter 57).

"Blessed are they that are called unto the marriage supper of the Lamb." "The marriage supper of Christ," explains St Andrew,

> is the triumph of those that are saved and the joy in harmony with it, which the blessed will receive when they, being pure in soul, enter into the eternal Bridal Chamber with the Holy Bridegroom, for He Who has promised is faithful (Heb 10:23). Just as there is a multitude of good things in the future age which surpass every thought, so also there are many and varied names by which they are named. They are sometimes called "Kingdom of Heaven," because of its glory and uprightness; sometimes "paradise" by reason of the never-ending repast of delights; sometimes the "bosom of Abraham" because of the consolation there of those that have reposed; and sometimes "bridal chamber" and "marriage," not only by reason of the eternal rejoicing, but also because of the pure, true and unutterable union of God with His servants, a union which surpasses bodily communion one with another, in the same measure as light is distinct from darkness, and fragrance from foul odor. (St Andrew, chapter 57)

19:10 *And I fell at his feet to worship him. And he said unto me, See thou do it not: I am thy fellowservant, and of thy brethren that have the testimony of Jesus: worship God: for the testimony of Jesus is the spirit of prophecy.*

The angel, to whom St John wished to bow down, forbade him to do this, saying, "I am thy fellowservant, and of thy brethren that have the testimony of Jesus: worship God, for the testimony of Jesus is the spirit of prophecy." The meaning of these words is as follows: Do not bow down to me for I am only your fellowservant. But that Holy Spirit Who speaks and acts through the Apostles, and in particular through St John who has preached the testimony of Jesus, speaks also through the angels as through the same kind of emissaries of God. "Your dignity is the same as mine," the angel, as it were, says. "Having been given the gifts of the Holy Spirit, you testify of the words and deeds of Jesus Christ; and I, receiving from that same Holy Spirit the revelation of future events, communicate them to you and to the Church." In other words, the Spirit of the testimony of Christ is also the Spirit of prophecy, that is, having the same dignity and the same purpose. St Andrew of Caesarea notes here the humility of the angels "who do not ascribe to themselves—like the evil demons—any divine glory, but ascribe it to the Master" (St Andrew, chapter 57).

19:11–12 *And I saw heaven opened, and behold a white horse; and He that sat upon him was called Faithful and True, and in righteousness he doth judge and make war. His eyes were as a flame of fire, and on his head were many crowns; and he had a name written, that no man knew, but he himself.*

These verses describe the appearance of the Divine Bridegroom Himself—the Word of God, His battle with the beast and his army, and His final victory over them. St John saw the heaven open, from whence descended on a white horse the Lord Jesus Christ in the form of a horseman, after Whom followed the heavenly hosts likewise seated on white horses. The white horse, according to St Andrew,

> signifies the brightness of the saints upon whom is seated the One Who will judge the nations, emitting from His flaming and fiery eyes, that is, from His all-seeing power, a fiery flame which does not scorch the righteous but illumines them. Sinners, however, are devoured by the flame without being illumined. Like a king, He appears with a multitude of crowns on His head, which signifies that to Him "is given all authority in heaven and on earth" (cf. Matt 28:18) and over all the kingdoms of the world. (St Andrew, chapter 58)

"And He had a name written, that no man knew, but He Himself." The fact that the name is unknown indicates the incomprehensibility of His Divine Essence.

> 19:13 *And he was clothed with a vesture dipped in blood: and his name is called The Word of God.*

Here this name is revealed: "The Word of God." This indeed is incomprehensible to men, for it refers to the essence and origin of the Divine nature of Jesus Christ, which cannot be understood by any mortal. In the Old Testament Scriptures, the name of God is therefore called wondrous (cf. Judg 13:18, Isa 9:6, Prov 30:4).

"And He was clothed with a vesture dipped in blood."

"The vesture of the Word of God," says St. St Andrew, "is His most pure and incorrupt flesh made purple with His Blood during the time of His voluntary sufferings" (St. St Andrew, chapter 58).

> 19:14 *And the armies which were in heaven followed him upon white horses, clothed in fine linen, white and clean.*

"These are the heavenly powers who are distinguished by the refinement of their nature, the height of their understanding, and the brightness of their virtues, and who are revered for the inseparability of their strong and intimate union with Christ" (St Andrew, chapter 58).

> 19:15 *And out of His mouth goeth a sharp sword, that with it he should smite the nations: and he shall rule them with a rod of iron: and he treadeth the winepress of the fierceness and wrath of Almighty God.*

The "sharp sword" is the sword of Christ Who, in the present case, appears not so much as a teacher (cf. Rev 1:16), but more as a King Who wields His judgments like weapons for the punishment of the impious (Isa 11:4). They will be ruled with a rod of iron—this expression is taken from Psalm 2:9 and is explained in Revelation 2:27 and 12:5.

> 19:16 *And he hath on his vesture and on his thigh a name written, KING OF KINGS, AND LORD OF LORDS.*

This name, testifying to the Divine dignity of its bearer, was written on His thigh, that is, on the royal cloth near that part of the body where, in the custom of the eastern people, a sword hung from the belt.

> 19:17–19 *And I saw an angel standing in the sun; and he cried with a loud voice, saying to all the fowls that fly in the midst of heaven, Come and gather yourselves together unto the supper of the great God; That ye may eat the flesh of kings, and the flesh of captains, and the flesh of mighty men, and the flesh of horses, and of them that sit on them, and the flesh of all men, both free and bond, both small and great. And I saw the beast, and the kings of the earth, and their armies, gathered together to make war against him that sat on the horse, and against his army.*

Further, the seer of mysteries saw an angel standing in the sun, who, calling all to rejoice over the punishment of sinners and the cutting off of sin, cried out, "Come and gather yourselves together, unto the supper of the great God, that ye may eat the flesh of kings and the flesh of mighty men." This appeal of the angel to birds of prey symbolically signifies that the defeat of the enemies of God will be most frightful, as in a bloody battle, when the bodies of the dead, because of their great number, will remain unburied and will be devoured by the birds.

> 19:20 *And the beast was taken, and with him the false prophet that wrought miracles before him, with which he deceived them that had received the mark of the beast, and them that worshipped his image. These both were cast alive into a lake of fire burning with brimstone.*

Such is the result of the ensuing battle. St Andrew says,

It may be that they will not be subjected to the common death, but being killed in the twinkling of an eye, they will be condemned to a second death in the fiery lake. In the same way the Apostle Paul says about those going to judgment, that those who remain among the living will be changed "in the twinkling of an eye" (1 Cor 15:52). But these two enemies of God will, on the contrary, go not to judgment but to condemnation. This supposition is based on the words of the Apostle that the antichrist will be killed by the spirit of the mouth of God (2 Thess 2:8), and on the opinion of a certain teacher that some men will remain alive after the killing of the antichrist (although some understand this differently). But we affirm that the living will be those whom Daniel blesses, while these two, after God cuts off their power, will be cast with their incorruptible bodies into the fire of Gehenna, which for them will comprise death and their being killed by Christ's Divine command. (St Andrew, chapter 59)

Just as the blessed life begins already in this life, so also the hell for the hard-hearted and those torn by evil conscience begins already in this life and continues to a greater extent in the life to come.

19:21 *And the remnant were slain with the sword of him that sat upon the horse, which sword proceeded out of his mouth: and all the fowls were filled with their flesh.*

"There are two deaths," explains St Andrew,

one is the separation of the soul from the body; the other is being cast into Gehenna. Applying this to those who battle together with Antichrist, we have reason to suppose that with the sword, or by the commandment of God, they will be brought to the first death—the death of the body, and only after it will follow the second; and this is correct. If they are not brought to the first death, then they, together with those by whom they were deceived, will be participants of the second death, i.e., eternal torment. (St Andrew, chapter 59)

20. THE GENERAL RESURRECTION AND THE LAST JUDGMENT

20:1–3 *And I saw an angel come down from heaven, having the key of the bottomless pit and a great chain in his hand. And he laid hold on the dragon, that old serpent, which is the Devil, and Satan, and bound him a thousand years, And cast him into the bottomless pit, and shut him up, and set a seal upon him, that he should deceive the nations no more, till the thousand years should be fulfilled: and after that he must be loosed a little season.*

After the defeat of Antichrist, St John saw an angel descending from heaven who had a key to the abyss and a great chain in his hand. This angel "laid hold on the dragon, that old serpent … and bound him a thousand years…." St Andrew of Caesarea interprets this passage in this way: by this "thousand years" one must understand the whole time "from the incarnation of Christ to the coming of Antichrist" (St Andrew, chapter 60). With the coming of the Incarnate Son of God on earth—and in particular from the moment of His redemption of mankind through His death on the Cross—Satan was bound, paganism was cast down, and there came upon earth the thousand-year reign of Christ. The thousand-year Kingdom of Christ on earth is to be understood as the victory of Christianity over paganism and the establishment on earth of the Church of Christ. The definite number one thousand is used here in place of an indefinite number, signifying the long period of time until the second coming of Christ.

20:4 And I saw thrones, and they sat upon them, and judgment was given unto them: and I saw the souls of them that were beheaded for the witness of Jesus, and for the word of God, and which had not worshipped the beast, neither his image, neither had received his mark upon their foreheads, or in their hands; and they lived and reigned with Christ a thousand years.

This picture symbolically depicts the kingdom of the Christian faith after the overthrow of paganism. Those who have assumed judgment and sit on the thrones are all Christians who have attained salvation, for to them has been given the promise of the Kingdom and the glory of Christ (1 Thess 2:12). From this choir, the holy seer of mysteries singles out in particular "those that were beheaded for the witness of Jesus and for the Word of God," that is, the holy martyrs. St John says, "I saw the souls of them that were beheaded." From this it is clear that these saints who participate in the thousand-year reign of Christ are reigning with Christ and performing judgment not on earth but in heaven, for it speaks here only concerning their souls, which are not yet united with their bodies. From these words, it is evident that the saints take part in the governing of the Church of Christ on earth, and therefore it is natural and proper to appeal to them with prayers, asking their intercession before Christ with Whom they reign.

"And they lived and reigned with Christ a thousand years." Their "living" is of a moral and spiritual nature. The holy seer of mysteries calls this "the first resurrection" (Rev 20:5), while further on he speaks of the second bodily resurrection. This reigning of the saints with Christ will continue until the final victory over the dark impious powers under Antichrist. Then the resurrection of bodies will occur, and the last frightful Judgment will begin, when the souls of the saints will be reunited with their bodies and will reign with Christ forever.

20:5 But the rest of the dead lived not again until the thousand years were finished. This is the first resurrection.

The expression "lived not again" means the dark and difficult condition of the souls of the impious sinners after bodily death. It continues "until the thousand years were finished." As in many other places in Sacred Scripture, this particle "until" (in Greek *eos*) does not signify the continuation of an action only to a certain boundary; on the contrary, it is a complete denial of any limit (see Matt 1:25). In other words, it means that the impious dead are denied forever the blessed life.

20:6 Blessed and holy is he that hath part in the first resurrection: on such the second death hath no power, but they shall be priests of God and of Christ, and shall reign with him a thousand years.

From the Divine Scripture we know that there are two lives and two deaths: the first life is temporal and fleshly because of the transgression of the commandments, while the second is the eternal life promised to the saints for the keeping of the Divine commandments. Corresponding to these there are two kinds of death: one fleshly and temporal, and the other eternal as chastisement for sins, which is the fiery Gehenna. (St Andrew, chapter 62)

Consequently, it is understood that if here on earth one has lived in Christ Jesus and has come before Him after the first death (that is, bodily death) with fervent faith in Him and filled with His grace, then one has no need to fear the second death, that is, the fiery Gehenna.

These first six verses of the twentieth chapter of the Apocalypse have served as a pretext for the development of a false teaching concerning the "thousand-year reign of Christ on earth," which has received the name of Chiliasm. In essence it teaches that not long before the end of the world, Christ the Saviour will come again to earth, defeat Antichrist, resurrect the righteous, and make a new kingdom on earth. As a reward for their struggles and sufferings, the righteous will reign together with Christ for the course of a thousand years and will enjoy all the good things of temporal life. Only then will there follow the second, universal resurrection of the dead, the universal judgment, and the general giving of eternal rewards. This teaching is known in two forms. Some say that Christ will restore Jerusalem in all its beauty and reinitiate the fulfillment of Moses's ritual law with all its sacrifices, and that the blessedness of the righteous will consist in all manner of sensual enjoyments. In the first century, this teaching was held by the heretic Cerinthus and other Judaizing heretics, including the Ebionites and the Montanists, and in the fourth century, by the Apollinarians. Others, on the contrary, have affirmed that this blessedness will consist in purely spiritual delights. In this latter form, chiliastic ideas were expressed first by Papias of Hieropolis; later they are to be found in the works of St Justin Martyr, St Irenaeus, Hippolytus, Methodius, and Lactantius. In recent times, it has been revived with certain peculiarities by the Anabaptists, the followers of Swedenborg, the Illuminati, and Adventists. One must be aware, however, that neither in its first nor in its second form can the teaching of Chiliasm be accepted by an Orthodox Christian for the following reasons:

1. According to the chiliast teaching, the resurrection of the dead will take place twice: the first, a thousand years before the end of the world—when only the righteous will be resurrected; and the second, at the very end of the world, when sinners also will be resurrected. However, Christ the Saviour clearly taught only one universal resurrection of the dead, when both the righteous and the sinners will be resurrected and all will receive their final recompense (John 6:39–40, Matt 13:37–43).
2. The word of God speaks of only two comings of Christ in the world: the first in lowliness, when He came to redeem us; and the second in glory, when He will appear to judge the living and the dead. Chiliasm introduces one more—a

third coming of Christ a thousand years before the end of the world. The word of God knows no such thing.

3. The word of God teaches only of two kingdoms of Christ: the Kingdom of Grace, which will continue until the end of the world (1 Cor 15:23–26), and the Kingdom of Glory, which will begin after the Last Judgment and will have no end (Luke 1:33, 2 Peter 1:11). Chiliasm, however, allows yet a third, as it were, a middle kingdom of Christ, which will last only a thousand years.

4. The teaching of a sensual kingdom of Christ clearly contradicts the word of God, according to which the Kingdom of God is not "meat and drink" (Rom 14:17); in the resurrection of the dead, they do not marry nor are given in marriage (Matt 22:30); the rites of the law of Moses had only a prefiguring significance and were forever done away with by the more perfect New Testament Law (Acts 15:23–30, Rom 6:14, Gal 5:6, Heb 10:1).

Certain ancient teachers of the Church—Justin, Irenaeus, and Methodius—held Chiliasm only as a personal opinion. At the same time, there were those who decidedly rose up against it, such as Caius the Presbyter of Rome, St Dionysius of Alexandria, Origen, Eusebius of Caesarea, St Basil the Great, St Gregory the Theologian, St Epiphanius, Blessed Jerome, and Blessed Augustine. To hold Chiliasm even as a private opinion was no longer permissible after the Church, at the Second Ecumenical Council in 381, condemned the teaching of the heretic Apollinarius concerning the thousand-year reign of Christ. At the same time this was confirmed by the introduction into the Symbol of Faith of the words "of His Kingdom there will be no end."

One must likewise know that the Apocalypse is a book which is profoundly mystical, and therefore, to understand and interpret literally the prophecies contained in it—especially if such a literal understanding contradicts other passages of Sacred Scripture—is entirely opposed to the rules of hermeneutics. In such cases, it is correct to seek in perplexing passages a metaphorical or allegorical meaning.

> 20:7–8 *And when the thousand years are expired, Satan shall be loosed out of his prison, And shall go out to deceive the nations which are in the four quarters of the earth, Gog and Magog, to gather them together to battle: the number of whom is as the sand of the sea.*

By the "loosing of Satan out of his prison" is to be understood the appearance of Antichrist before the end of the world. The liberated Satan will strive in the person of Antichrist to deceive all the nations of the earth, and will raise up Gog and Magog in battle against the Christian Church. St Andrew says: "Some people think that Gog and Magog are the northern and most remote Scythian peoples or, as we call them, Huns, the most militant and numerous peoples of the earth. They are restrained from taking possession of the whole world only by the Divine right hand, until the liberation of the devil. Others, translating from the Hebrew, say that Gog signifies 'one who gathers' or 'a gathering' and that Magog signifies 'one who is exalted' or 'exaltation.' And so, these names signify either a gathering of peoples or their exaltation" (St Andrew, chapter 63). One must suppose that these names are used in a metaphorical sense to denote those fierce hordes who, at the end of the world, will arm themselves under the leadership of the antichrist against the Church of Christ.

> 20:9 *And they went up on the breadth of the earth, and compassed the camp of the saints about, and the beloved city.*

This means that the enemies of Christ will spread over the whole earth and will begin everywhere the persecution of Christianity.

> 20:9 *And fire came down from God out of heaven, and devoured them.*

The holy prophet Ezekiel drew a similar picture of the defeat of the wild hordes of Gog (Ezek 38:18–22, 39:1–6). This is a depiction of God's wrath which will be poured out upon the enemies of God at the second coming of Christ.

> 20:10 *And the devil that deceived them was cast into the lake of fire and brimstone, where the beast and the false prophet are, and shall be tormented day and night for ever and ever.*

Such will be the eternal lot of the devil and his servants—Antichrist and the false prophet; they will be condemned to the unending torments of hell. After this final victory over the devil, there will follow the universal resurrection of the dead and the Last Judgment.

> 20:11 *And I saw a great white throne, and him that sat on it.*

This is a picture of the universal judgment of God upon the human race. The whiteness of the throne upon which the Chief Judge of the universe sits signifies the sanctity and righteousness of this Judge.

> 20:11 *From whose face the earth and the heaven fled away; and there was found no place for them.*

Here is depicted the great and frightful changes in the universe, which will occur before the final and Dread Judgment (cf. 2 Pet 3:10).

> 20:12 *And I saw the dead, small and great, stand before God; and the books were opened: and another book was opened, which is the book of life: and the dead were judged out of those things which were written in the books, according to their works.*

The opened books symbolically signify the omniscience of God Who knows all the works of men. That there is only one book of life is a sign of the small number of the chosen ones of God, who are to inherit salvation. St Andrew says, "The opened books represent the acts and conscience of each person. One of them is the book of life in which are written the names of the saints" (St Andrew, chapter 64).

20:13 *And the sea gave up the dead which were in it; and death and hell delivered up the dead which were in them: and they were judged every man according to their works.*

The meaning here is that all men, without exception, will be resurrected and stand before God's Judgment.

20:14–15 *And death and hell were cast into the lake of fire. This is the second death. And whosoever was not found written in the book of life was cast into the lake of fire.*

This is said in the sense that those people who are glorified and saved will no longer fear either hell or death; for them, death and hell will cease to exist forever. By the "lake of fire" and the "second death" are to be understood the eternal condemnation of sinners whose names did not appear to be written in the Lord's book of life.

21. *The Opening of the New Heaven and the New Earth: The New Jerusalem*
Immediately after this, St John was shown the spiritual beauty and grandeur of the New Jerusalem, that is, the Kingdom of Christ, which is to be revealed in all its glory in the second coming of Christ, after the victory over the devil.

21:1 *And I saw a new heaven and a new earth: for the first heaven and the first earth were passed away; and there was no more sea.*

Here is meant not the nonexistence of the creation, but its change for the better as the apostle testifies: "The creature itself also shall be delivered from the bondage of corruption into the glorious liberty of the children of God" (Rom 8:21). The divine Psalmist says, "and as a vesture shalt Thou change them, and they shall be changed" (Ps 101:27 LXX). "The renewal of what is grown old does not signify its obliteration and annihilation, but the putting away of its agedness and wrinkles" (St Andrew, chapter 65). This newness of heaven and earth will consist of their transformation through fire and the newness of their forms and attributes, but not in the changing of the essence itself. The sea, whose nature is inconstant and agitated, will vanish.

21:2 *And I John saw the holy city, new Jerusalem, coming down from God out of heaven, prepared as a bride adorned for her husband.*

The image of this "new Jerusalem" represents the triumphant Church of Christ, adorned as the Lord's Bride in the purity and virtues of the saints. St Andrew says of this: "This city, which has Christ as its cornerstone, is composed of the saints concerning whom it is written: 'They shall be as the stones of a crown, lifted up as an ensign upon His land' (Zech 9:16)" (St Andrew, chapter 65).

21:3–4 *And I heard a great voice out of heaven saying, Behold, the tabernacle of God is with men, and he will dwell with them, and they shall be his people, and God himself shall be with them and be their God. And God shall wipe away all tears from their eyes; and there shall be no more death, neither sorrow, nor crying, neither shall there be any more pain: for the former things are passed away.*

The Old Testament tabernacle was only a prefiguration of the dwelling of God with men, which begins in the future, eternal blessed life, and will be a source of blessedness for those who are liberated from all the sorrows of the present earthly life. The Church is presently the image of the true tabernacle.

21:5–6 *And he that sat upon the throne said, Behold, I make all things new. And he said unto me, Write: for these words are true and faithful. And he said unto me, It is done. I am Alpha and Omega, the beginning and the end. I will give unto him that is athirst of the fountain of the water of life freely.*

By the water of life is understood the grace of the Holy Spirit which is presented figuratively in Holy Scripture under the image of living water (cf. John 4:10–14, 7:37–39).

21:7 *He that overcometh shall inherit all things; and I will be his God, and he shall be my son.*

"He that overcometh shall inherit all things"—that is, those who overcome the invisible demons in battle will receive all these good things, and they will become sons of God.

21:8 *But the fearful, and unbelieving, and the abominable, and murderers, and whoremongers, and sorcerers, and idolaters, and all liars, shall have their part in the lake which burneth with fire and brimstone: which is the second death.*

The fearful, and those who lack courage in the battle with the devil, and sinners who are given over to passions and vices, will be condemned to the "second death," that is, the eternal torments of hell (see St Andrew, chapter 66).

21:9 *And there came unto me one of the seven angels which had the seven vials full of the seven last plagues, and talked with me, saying, Come hither, I will shew thee the bride, the Lamb's wife.*

From what follows, it is evident that the bride, "the Lamb's wife," named here is the Church of Christ. St Andrew says:

He correctly calls the bride "the Lamb's wife," for when Christ was slaughtered like a lamb, He betrothed the Church to Himself by His own blood. Just as a wife was created for Adam during his sleep through the taking of a rib, so also the Church, fashioned by the shedding of blood from the side of Christ at the time of His voluntary repose on the Cross in the sleep of death, was united with Him Who was wounded for our sakes. (St Andrew, chapter 67)

21:10–14 And he carried me away in the spirit to a great and high mountain, and shewed me that great city, the holy Jerusalem, descending out of heaven from God, Having the glory of God: and her light was like unto a stone most precious, even like a jasper stone, clear as crystal; And had a wall great and high, and had twelve gates, and at the gates twelve angels, and names written thereon, which are the names of the twelve tribes of the children of Israel: On the east three gates; on the north three gates; on the south three gates; and on the west three gates. And the wall of the city had twelve foundations, and in them the names of the twelve apostles of the Lamb.

The wife of the Lamb, the holy Church, appeared before the spiritual gaze of the holy seer of mysteries in the form of a splendid great city descending from heaven—Jerusalem. The rest of the chapter is devoted to a detailed description of this wondrous city. Shining with precious stones, this city had twelve gates named for the twelve tribes of Israel, and twelve foundations bearing the names of the twelve apostles. It is characteristic of this city that "her light was like unto a stone most precious, even like a jasper stone." St Andrew says, "The light of the Church is Christ who is called Jasper as one who is always alive, blossoming, giving of life, pure" (St Andrew, chapter 67). A high wall surrounds the city as a sign that not a single unworthy person can enter therein. This same idea is expressed by the angels of God, who stand guard on the twelve gates. The gates bear the names of the twelve tribes of Israel, for just as on earth tribes comprise the society of the chosen people of God, so these same names are used by the chosen ones of heaven—the new Israel.

On the twelve foundations of the wall are written the names of the apostles of the Lamb; this, of course, is a sign that the Apostles are the foundation on which the Church is established, as the founders of the Christian faith among all peoples of the earth. Here one cannot help but see a refutation of the Latin dogma that the Church of Christ is founded solely upon the Apostle Peter.

21:15–18 And he that talked with me had a golden reed to measure the city, and the gates thereof, and the wall thereof. And the city lieth foursquare, and the length is as large as the breadth: and he measured the city with the reed, twelve thousand furlongs. The length and the breadth and the height of it are equal. And he measured the wall thereof, an hundred and forty and four cubits, according to the measure of a man, that is, of the angel. And the building of the wall of it was of jasper: and the city was pure gold, like unto clear glass.

The city is measured by an angel before the holy seer of mysteries with the aid of a golden reed. St Andrew says, "The golden reed indicates the honesty of the measuring angel, whom he saw in human form, and likewise the dignity of the measured city by whose wall we are to understand Christ" (St Andrew, chapter 67).

The city has the form of a right angle square; the equality of its height, length and breadth—twelve thousand furlongs each—indicates the form of a cube, which signifies its firmness and solidity. The height of the wall of the city is 144 cubits. All these numerical expressions are used, one must suppose, to signify the perfection, solidity, and astonishing symmetry of the whole building of the Church of God.

21:19–21 And the foundations of the wall of the city were garnished with all manner of precious stones. The first foundation was jasper; the second, sapphire; the third, a chalcedony; the fourth, an emerald; The fifth, sardonyx; the sixth, sardius; the seventh, chrysolyte; the eighth, beryl; the ninth, a topaz; the tenth, a chrysoprasus; the eleventh, a jacinth; the twelfth, an amethyst. And the twelve gates were twelve pearls; every several gate was of one pearl: and the street of the city was pure gold, as it were transparent glass.

The wall of the city is built of jasper, symbolizing the divine glory (cf. 21:11), and the ever-blossoming and unfading life of the saints. The city itself was of pure gold, like clear glass, symbolic of the honor and brightness of its inhabitants. The foundations of the wall of the city are adorned with all kinds of precious stones; in particular, each of the twelve foundations had the appearance of being formed of a single precious stone. As St Andrew notes, eight of the twelve stones were worn in the mantle of the chief priest; the other four are added to show the harmony of the New Testament with the Old, and the preeminence of those who shone forth in it. And this is true, for the Apostles—symbolized by the precious stones—were adorned with every virtue.

According to the interpretation of St Andrew, the significance of these twelve stones is as follows:

The first foundation, jasper, is a stone of greenish color and symbolizes the chief Apostle Peter, who bore in his body the death of Christ and showed a blossoming and unfading love toward Him. The second stone is sapphire from which comes the color azure; it symbolizes the blessed Paul, who was raised up even to the third heaven. The third, chalcedony, evidently the same as anthracite which was on the mantle of the chief priest, symbolizes the blessed Apostle Andrew, who is like a coal ignited by the Spirit.

The fourth, emerald, is of a green color and is mixed with oil which gives it a shine and beauty; it symbolizes the holy Evangelist John, who softens with divine oil the grief and despondency which occur in us through sin, and by the precious gift of theology grants us faith which never grows faint. The fifth, sardonyx, a stone which has the color of a shining human fingernail, symbolizes James, who was first to endure bodily death for the sake of Christ. The sixth, sardius, is a brilliant stone, orange in color, which has healing properties against swellings and wounds from irons; it symbolizes the beauty of the virtues of the blessed Philip, a beauty which was illumined by the fire of the Divine Spirit and which heals the wounds of those souls who have been deceived. The seventh, chrysolite, shines like gold and symbolizes, perhaps, Bartholomew, who shone with precious virtues and Divine preaching. The eighth, beryl, the color of the sea and air, symbolizes Thomas, who undertook distant voyages for the salvation of the Indians. The ninth, topaz, is a black stone which, they say, gushes forth a milky substance containing properties beneficial to those suffering from eye diseases; it symbolizes the blessed Matthew, who heals by means of the Gospel those who are blind in heart and gives milk to those newly born in the Faith. The tenth, chrysoprasus, surpassing in its brilliance gold itself, symbolizes the blessed Thaddeus, who preached to Abgar the King of Edessa the Kingdom of Christ—signified by gold, and the death in it—signified by ashes. The eleventh, jacinth, an azure or sky-colored hyacinth, probably symbolizes Simon, the zealot of the gifts of Christ, who possessed heavenly wisdom. The twelfth, amethyst, a purple stone, symbolizes Matthias, who was vouchsafed the Divine fire at the distribution of tongues, for his fiery desire to please the One Who chose him to take the place of the one who had fallen away. (St Andrew, chapter 67)

The twelve gates of the city were built of twelve whole precious stones. St Andrew says:

The twelve gates are evidently the twelve disciples of Christ, through whom we have come to know the door and the path of life. They are also the twelve precious pearls, having received their light and brilliant luster from the one precious pearl of great price, which is Christ. The street of the city is of pure gold, like transparent glass. All these details express one and the same idea: everything in the heavenly Church of God is holy, pure, beauteous and constant; everything is magnificent, spiritual and precious. (St Andrew, chapter 67)

21:22–23 And I saw no temple therein: for the Lord God Almighty and the Lamb are the temple of it. And the city had no need of the sun, neither of the moon, to shine in it: for the glory of God did lighten it, and the Lamb is the light thereof.

Further there is described the inner way of life of the inhabitants of this marvelous heavenly city. First of all, there is no visible temple in it, "for the Lord God

Almighty and the Lamb are the temple of it." Since worship will be given there to the Lord God without intermediary, there is no need either of a material temple or of any kind of rites or sacred activities. Second, this heavenly city will have no need of any kind of illumination, "for the glory of God did lighten it and the Lamb is the light thereof." Where the noetic Sun of Righteousness is, there is no need for the material sun (St Andrew, chapter 67). Third, the population will be the most various and mixed, for "all who have been crowned with victory over the passions will offer there the glory and honor of good deeds" (St Andrew, chapter 67). Fourth, the gates of the heavenly city will not be closed all day, and there will be no night (cf. Isa 60:11). All this means that the heavenly Church will not be threatened by any danger from attack of any kind of enemies.

> *21:24–27 And the nations of them which are saved shall walk in the light of it: and the kings of the earth do bring their glory and honour into it. And the gates of it shall not be shut at all by day: for there shall be no night there. And they shall bring the glory and honour of the nations into it. And there shall in no wise enter into it any thing that defileth, neither whatsoever worketh abomination, or maketh a lie: but they which are written in the Lamb's book of life.*

The general inner sign, which distinguishes this heavenly Church from the earthly, is the fact that while in the earthly Church good exists along with evil and tares grow together with good wheat, in the heavenly Church, only what is good, pure and holy is gathered together from all the peoples of the earth. Everything evil, defiled, and unclean, which has accumulated over the whole period of the world's history, will be separated and, as it were, poured out together into a single, foul-smelling cistern, whose impurity cannot in any way come into contact with this wondrous dwelling place that belongs to the blessed alone.

22. The Final Features of the Image of the New Jerusalem. The Confirmation of Everything Said, The Command to Keep the Commandments of God and to Expect the Second Coming of Christ Which Will Be Soon

> *22:1 And he shewed me a pure river of water of life, clear as crystal, proceeding out of the throne of God and of the Lamb.*

The unceasing blessedness of the members of the heavenly Church is depicted in a series of symbols. The first symbol is "a pure river of water of life." This symbolically depicts the grace of the Life-giving Spirit, which fills the streets of the holy city, that is, the multitude of its inhabitants who, in the words of the Psalmist, are more in number than the sand (Ps 138:18 LXX). This is the grace and mercy of God, which will always be poured out inexhaustibly upon the inhabitants of the heavenly city, filling their hearts with unutterable blessedness (cf. Isa 35:9–10).

22:2 In the midst of the street of it, and on either side of the river, was there the tree of life, which bare twelve manner of fruits, and yielded her fruit every month: and the leaves of the tree were for the healing of the nations.

The second symbol is the "tree of life," just as there was one in the earthly paradise before the fall of our first ancestors. The tree of life in the heavenly Jerusalem will possess special qualities of surpassing excellence: twelve times a year it will bring forth fruit, and its leaves will serve to heal nations.

St Andrew considers "the tree of life to signify Christ, understood through the Holy Spirit, for in Him is the Spirit, and He is worshipped in the Spirit and is the giver of the Spirit; through Him also the twelve fruits [i.e., the Apostles] give us the inexhaustible nourishment of the knowledge of God."

The leaves of the tree of life [that is, of Christ] signify the most refined, exalted, and enlightened understanding of the decrees of God, and its fruits are the most perfect knowledge revealed in the age to come. These leaves will be for healing, that is, for the cleansing of the ignorances of those people who are lower than others in the accomplishment of virtues, for "there is one glory of the sun, and another glory of the moon, and another glory of the stars" (1 Cor 15:41), and "In My Fathers house are many mansions" (John 14:2). So it is that according to the character of their works, one shall be granted less and another greater brightness. (St Andrew, chapter 68)

22:3–4 And there shall be no more curse: but the throne of God and of the Lamb shall be in it; and his servants shall serve him: And they shall see his face; and his name shall be in their foreheads.

Every curse shall be taken away from the inhabitants of this holy city, and those that are vouchsafed to become inhabitants of the city will behold God face to face,

not in riddles but, as the great Dionysius testifies, in the same form in which He was beheld by the holy Apostles on the holy mountain. Instead of the plate of gold worn by the ancient high priest (Exod 28:36–37), they will have the mark of the name of God—not on their foreheads only, but also in their hearts: that is, firm, unchanging and bold love for Him, for the mark on the forehead signifies an adornment of boldness. (St Andrew, chapter 68)

22:5 And there shall be no night there; and they need no candle, neither light of the sun; for the Lord God giveth them light: and they shall reign for ever and ever.

All these features indicate the unceasing and most complete communion of the members of the heavenly Church with their Master Whom they behold face to face. This will be for them a source of inexhaustible blessedness (cf. Ezek 47:12).

In the concluding verses of the Apocalypse, the holy Apostle John confirms the truth and faithfulness of everything said, and speaks of the nearness of the fulfillment of all that which was shown to him, and likewise the nearness of the second coming of Christ when each will be rewarded according to his deeds.

22:6–11 And he said unto me, These sayings are faithful and true: and the Lord God of the holy prophets sent his angel to shew unto his servants the things which must shortly be done. Behold, I come quickly: blessed is he that keepeth the sayings of the prophecy of this book. And I John saw these things, and heard them. And when I had heard and seen, I fell down to worship before the feet of the angel which shewed me these things. Then saith he unto me, See thou do it not: for I am thy fellowservant, and of thy brethren the prophets, and of them which keep the sayings of this book: worship God. And he saith unto me, Seal not the sayings of the prophecy of this book: for the time is at hand. He that is unjust, let him be unjust still: and he which is filthy, let him be filthy still: and he that is righteous, let him be righteous still: and he that is holy, let him be holy still.

"Behold, I come quickly." In the explanation of St Andrew, "these words indicate either the shortness of the present life in comparison with the future, or the suddenness or quickness of the end of each person, since departure from here comprises the end for each individual. Inasmuch as one does not know in what hour the thief will come, we are commanded to watch and have our loins girded and our lamps lit (cf. Luke 12:35–39)" (St Andrew, chapter 69). One must remember that for God there is no time, that one day before Him is as a thousand years and a thousand years is as a single day (cf. 2 Pet 3:8).

22:12–17 And behold, I come quickly; and my reward is with me, to give every man according as his work shall be. I am Alpha and Omega, the beginning and the end, the first and the last. Blessed are they that do his commandments, that they may have right to the tree of life, and may enter in through the gates into the city. For without are dogs, and sorcerers, and whoremongers, and murderers, and idolaters, and whosoever loveth and maketh a lie. I Jesus have sent mine angel to testify unto you these things in the churches. I am the root and the offspring of David, and the bright and morning star. And the Spirit and the bride say, Come. And let him that heareth say, Come. And let him that is athirst come. And whosoever will, let him take the water of life freely.

He will come soon, because He comes without delay—nothing will stop His coming, just as nothing will stop or destroy His unchanging decrees and promises. Men count days, months, and years, while the Lord counts not time, but the righteousness and unrighteousness of men; and by the measuring stick of His chosen ones He decrees the measure of the coming of that great and bright day, when "there should be time no longer" (cf. Rev 10:6) and there begins the unsetting day of His Kingdom. The Spirit and the Bride —(that is the Church of Christ) call everyone to come and freely scoop up the water of life, so as to be vouchsafed to become citizens of the heavenly Jerusalem.

> 22:18–21 *For I testify unto every man that heareth the words of the prophecy of this book, If any man shall add unto these things, God shall add unto him the plagues that are written in this book: And if any man shall take away from the words of the book of this prophecy, God shall take away his part out of the book of life, and out of the holy city, and from the things which are written in this book. He which testifieth these things saith, Surely I come quickly: Amen. Even so, come, Lord Jesus. The grace of our Lord Jesus Christ be with you all. Amen.*

St John concludes the Apocalypse with a blessing upon those who fulfill the commandments of God and a strict warning not to distort the words of the prophecy under threat of the application of those plagues that are written in this book. In conclusion St John expresses the desire for the speedy coming of Christ in the words, "Amen. Even so, come, Lord Jesus." Then he gives the customary apostolic blessing, from which it is evident that the Apocalypse was originally intended as an epistle to the churches of Asia Minor (cf. Rev 1:4).

The content of the Apocalypse clearly indicates that it has an historical foundation and great significance for the Church of all times. It represents the natural culmination of the canon of the sacred books and, in depicting the future and final fate of the Church and the world, it places us, as it were, immediately before the face of the coming Judge.

The end, and glory be to God!

 **BIBLIOGRAPHY**

This series, *Commentary on the Holy Scriptures of the New Testament*, is based on the published lectures for the courses taught by the late Archbishop Averky (Taushev) for the students of Holy Trinity Orthodox Seminary between 1951 and 1953. These lectures were intended to provide a synthesis of various pre-Revolutionary works and textbooks on the New Testament Scriptures, which were published in Russia and used both as a means for self-education and as part of the curricula of theological academies and seminaries. The following sources were either used by Archbishop Averky when writing his lectures or added by the editorial staff of Holy Trinity Seminary Press to the endnotes created for the English edition of Archbishop Averky's book. For the convenience of the readers, the editors have separated this bibliography into primary sources ("Sources") and secondary literature ("Studies"), and when possible, have cited modern editions of these works. A few more recently published studies and commentaries were added to the bibliography to assist the reader in further exploration of the treasury of Orthodox scriptural exegesis.

ABBREVIATIONS

ANF: *The Ante-Nicene Fathers*. Edited by Alexander Roberts and James Donaldson. 1885–1887. 10 vols. Repr. Peabody, Mass.: Hendrickson, 1994.

ET: English translation.

NPNF: *The Nicene and Post-Nicene Fathers*, Series 1. Edited by Philip Schaff. 1886–1889. 14 vols. Repr. Peabody, Mass.: Hendrickson, 1989.

   The Nicene and Post-Nicene Fathers, Series 2. Translated and edited by Philip Schaff and Henry Wace. 1890–1898. 14 vols. Repr. Peabody, Mass.: Hendrickson, 1994.

PG: *Patrologia graeca*. Edited by J.-P. Migne. 162 vols. Paris, 1857–1886.

PL: *Patrologia latina*. Edited by J.-P. Migne. 217 vols. Paris, 1844–1864.

Sources

Ambrosiaster. *Commentaries on the Epistles of St Paul*. PL 17, col. 45–508.

St Andrew of Caesarea. *Commentary on the Apocalypse*. Translated by Eugenia Scarvelis Constantinou, Fathers of the Church 123. Washington, D.C.: Catholic University of America Press, 2012.

St Athanasius of Alexandria. *Discourses Against the Arians*. ET in NPNF, Series 2, vol. 4.306–447.

St Augustine. *The City of God, Books XVII-XXII*. Translated by Gerald G. Walsh and Daniel J. Honan, Fathers of the Church 24. Washington, D.C.: Catholic University of America Press, 1981.

St Augustine. *On Faith and Works*. Translated by Gregory J. Lombardo, Ancient Christian Writers 48. New York: Newman Press, 1988.

St Basil the Great. *On the Holy Spirit*. Translated by Stephen Hildebrand, Popular Patristics 42. Yonkers, N.Y.: St Vladimir's Seminary Press, 2011.

St Cyprian of Carthage. *On Works and Alms*. ET in ANF, vol. 5.476–84.

St Dimitry of Rostov. *Минеи-Четьи на русском языке* [The Lives of Saints in the Russian Language] [in Russian]. Vol. 1–12. Moscow: Synodal Printing Press, 1906.

The Divine Liturgy of Our Father Among the Saints John Chrysostom: Slavonic-English Parallel Text. 4th ed. Jordanville, N.Y.: Holy Trinity Publications, Printshop of St Job of Pochaev, 2015.

Eusebius of Caesarea. *The Ecclesiastical History*. Translated by J. E. L. Oulton, Loeb Classical Library 265. London: Heinemann; Cambridge, Mass.: Harvard University Press, 1942.

St Ignatius of Antioch. *The Letters*. Edited and translated by Bart D. Ehrman in *The Apostolic Fathers*, vol. 1, Loeb Classical Library 24. Cambridge, Mass.: Harvard University Press, 2003.

St Irenaeus of Lyons. *Against the Heresies*. ET in ANF, vol. 1.309–567.

St Isidore of Pelusium. *Letters*. PG 78, col. 178–1674.

Blessed Jerome of Stridon. *Commentary on the Epistle to Titus*. PL 26, col. 555–600.

Blessed Jerome of Stridon. *Letter 133 to Ctesiphon*. ET in NPNF, Series 2, vol. 6.272–80.

St John Chrysostom. *Commentary on Galatians*. ET in NPNF, Series 1, vol. 13.1–48.

St John Chrysostom. *Homilies on the Epistle to the Hebrews*. ET in NPNF, Series 1, vol. 14.363–522.

St John Chrysostom. *Homilies on Colossians*. ET in NPNF, Series 1, vol. 13.257–321.

St John Chrysostom. *Homilies on First Corinthians*. ET in NPNF, Series 1, vol. 12.3–269.

St John Chrysostom. *Homilies on Second Corinthians*. ET in NPNF, Series 1, vol. 12.271–420.

St John Chrysostom. *Homilies on Ephesians*. ET in NPNF, Series 1, vol. 13.49–172.

St John Chrysostom. *Homilies on Philemon*. ET in NPNF, Series 1, vol. 13.545–57.

St John Chrysostom. *Homilies on Philippians*. ET in NPNF, Series 1, vol. 13.181–255.

St John Chrysostom. *Homilies on First Thessalonians*. ET in NPNF, Series 1, vol. 13.323–75.

St John Chrysostom. *Homilies on Second Thessalonians*. ET in NPNF, Series 1, vol. 13.377–98.

St John Chrysostom. *Homilies on First Timothy*. ET in NPNF, Series 1, vol. 13.407–73.

St John Chrysostom. *Homilies on Second Timothy*. ET in NPNF, Series 1, vol. 13.475–518.

St John Chrysostom. *Homilies on Titus*. ET in NPNF, Series 1, vol. 13.519–543.

[Ps.-] St John of Damascus. *Exposition on the Epistles of St Paul*. PG 95, col. 439–1034.

St John of Kronstadt. *Новые слова, произнесенные в 1902 году* [New Sermons Spoken in 1902]. 1903.

Oecumenius of Tricca. *Commentary on the New Testament*. PG 118–19.

St Theophan the Recluse. *Толкование Первого Послания Апостола Павла к Коринфянам* [The Commentary on the First Epistle of St Paul to Corinthians]. In *Полное собрание творений* [Complete Collected Works]. Moscow: Publication Council of the Russian Orthodox Church, 2013.

St Theophan the Recluse. *Толкование послания св. апостола Павла к Галатам* [The Commentary on the Epistle of St Paul to Galatians]. In *Полное собрание творений* [Complete Collected Works]. Vol. 15. Moscow: Publication Council of the Russian Orthodox Church, 2013.

St Theophan the Recluse. *Толкование послания св. апостола Павла к Ефесеям* [The Commentary on the Epistle of St Paul to the Ephesians]. 2nd ed. Moscow: St Panteleimon Russian Monastery on Mt Athos, 1893.

St Theophan the Recluse. *Толкования посланий апостола Павла к Колоссянам, к Филиппийцам* [The Commentaries on the Epistles of St Paul to Colossians and Philippians]. Moscow: Pravilo Very, 2005.

St Theophan the Recluse. *Толкования Посланий апостола Павла к Солунянам, к Филимону, к Евреям* [The Commentaries on the Epistles of St Paul to the Thessalonians, to Philemon, to the Hebrews]. Moscow: Pravilo Very, 2005.

St Theophan the Recluse. *Мысли на каждый день года по церковным чтениям из Слова Божия* [Thoughts for Every Day of the Year According to the Ecclesiastical Lessons from the Word of God]. Moscow: Sretensky Monastery/Pravilo Very, 1995.

Blessed Theodoret of Cyrus. *Interpretation of the Epistle to Colossians*. PG 82, col. 591–628.

Blessed Theodoret of Cyrus. *Interpretation of the First Epistle to Corinthians*. PG 82, col. 225–376.

Blessed Theodoret of Cyrus. *Interpretation of the Epistle to Ephesians*. PG 82, col. 505–58.

Blessed Theodoret of Cyrus. *Interpretation of the Epistle to the Hebrews*. PG 82, col. 673–786.

Blessed Theodoret of Cyrus. *Interpretation of the Second Epistle to Thessalonians*. PG 82, col. 657–74.

Blessed Theodoret of Cyrus. *Interpretation of the First Epistle to Timothy*. PG 82, col. 787–830.

Blessed Theodoret of Cyrus. *Interpretation of the Second Epistle to Timothy*. PG 82, col. 831–58.

Blessed Theodoret of Cyrus. *Interpretation of the Epistle to Titus*. PG 82, col. 857–70.

Blessed Theophylact of Ochrid. *Exposition in the Epistle of James*. PG 125, col. 1131–90.

Blessed Theophylact of Ochrid. *Exposition in the Second Epistle of John*. PG 126, col. 67–78.

Blessed Theophylact of Ochrid. *Exposition in the Second Epistle to Thessalonians*. PG 124, col. 1327–58.

Blessed Theophylact of Ochrid. *Exposition in the First Epistle to Timothy*. PG 125, col. 9–90.

Blessed Theophylact of Ochrid. *Exposition in the Second Epistle to Timothy*. PG 125, col. 89–140.

Blessed Theophylact of Ochrid. *Exposition in the Epistle to Titus*. PG 125, col. 141–72.

STUDIES

Alexandrov, Archpriest Nikolai S. *Пособие к изучению Священного Писания Нового Завета для школы и семьи* [A Manual for the Study of the New Testament Scriptures for the School and Family]. St Petersburg: Synodal Printing Press, 1910.

Archbishop Averky (Taushev). *The Apocalypse*. Translated by Fr. Seraphim Rose. Platina, Calif.: St Herman of Alaska Brotherhood, 1985.

Barsov, Matvei V. *Сборник статей по истолковательному и назидательному чтению Деяний святых апостолов* [A Collection of Articles on Exegetical and Instructive Reading of the Acts of the Apostles]. Simbirsk, 1890.

Archbishop Dmitri (Royster). *The Epistle to the Hebrews: A Commentary*. Crestwood, N.Y.: St Vladimir's Seminary Press, 2003.

Archbishop Dmitri (Royster). *St Paul's Epistle to the Romans: A Pastoral Commentary*. Crestwood, N.Y.: St Vladimir's Seminary Press, 2008.

Archbishop Dmitri (Royster). *The Epistle of Saint James: A Commentary*. Yonkers, N.Y.: St Vladimir's Seminary Press, 2010.

Farley, Archpriest Lawrence R. *The Apocalypse of St John: A Revelation of Love and Power*. Chesterton, Ind.: Conciliar Press, 2011.

Farley, Archpriest Lawrence R. *The Epistle to the Hebrews: High Priest in Heaven*. Chesterton, Ind.: Ancient Faith Publishing, 2013.

Farley, Archpriest Lawrence R. *Shepherding the Flock: The Pastoral Epistles of St Paul the Apostle to Timothy and Titus*. Chesterton, Ind.: Conciliar Press, 2008.

Farley, Archpriest Lawrence R. *Words of Fire: The Early Epistles of St Paul to the Thessalonians and the Galatians*. Chesterton, Ind.: Conciliar Press, 2010.

Gwynn, John, ed. *The Apocalypse of St John in A Syriac Version Hitherto Unknown*. Dublin: Hodges, Figgis and Co.; London: Longmans, Green and Co., 1897.

Ivanov, Alexander V. *Руководство к изучению Священного Писания Нового Завета* [A Handbook for the Study of the New Testament Scriptures]. Reprint. St Petersburg: St Trinity Sergius Lavra, 2008.

Kheraskov, Archpriest Mikhail I. *Послания Апостольские и Апокалипсис: истолковательное обозрение* [The Epistles of the Apostles and the Revelation: An Exegetical Survey]. Vladimir, 1893.

Bishop Mikhail (Luzin). *Деяния и Послания апостолов с Апокалипсисом на славянском и русском наречии, с предисловиями и подробными объяснительными примечаниями* [The Acts and the Epistles in Slavonic and Russian, with introductions and detailed commentary]. Vols. 1–2. Moscow, 1886; Kiev, 1890.

Sysoev, Priest Daniel. *Explanation of the Apocalypse*. Translated by Deacon Nathan Williams. New Jersey: Daniel Sysoev Inc., 2017.

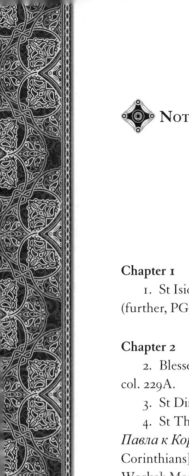

 Notes

Chapter 1

1. St Isidore of Pelusium, *Letter* 2.216 (to Dionysius), *Patrologia Graeca* (further, PG) 78, col. 660B.

Chapter 2

2. Blessed Theodoret of Cyrus, *Interpretation of 1 Corinthians* 1, PG 82, col. 229A.

3. St Dimitry of Rostov, *Lives of Saints* (*Chetii Minei*), December 8.

4. St Theophan the Recluse, *Толкование Первого Послания Апостола Павла к Коринфянам* [Commentary on the First Epistle of St Paul to Corinthians] (vol. 17.1 of *Полное собрание творений* [Complete Collected Works]; Moscow: Publication Council of the Russian Orthodox Church, 2013), 55–56.

5. Blessed Theodoret, *Interpretation of 1 Corinthians* 1:27, PG 82, col. 237D.

6. See, e.g., St Augustine, *On Faith and Works* 14.22; ET by Gregory J. Lombardo, Ancient Christian Writers 48 (New York: Newman Press, 1988), 29–30.

7. St Theophan the Recluse, *Толкование Первого Послания Апостола Павла к Коринфянам* [Commentary on the First Epistle of St Paul to Corinthians], in *Полное собрание творений* [Complete Collected Works], vol. 17.1, p. 236.

8. Blessed Theodoret, *Interpretation of 1 Corinthians* 4:8, PG 82, col. 257A.

9. St Theophan the Recluse, *Толкование Первого Послания Апостола Павла к Коринфянам* [Commentary on the First Epistle of St Paul to Corinthians], 281.

10. St John Chrysostom, *Homilies on First Corinthians* 15.2; ET in *Nicene and Post-Nicene Fathers* (further, NPNF), vol. 12, p. 85.

11. St Theophan the Recluse, *Толкование Первого Послания Апостола Павла к Коринфянам* [Commentary on the First Epistle of St Paul to Corinthians], 322.

12. See St John Chrysostom, *Homilies on the First Corinthians* 15.

13. St Theophan the Recluse, *Толкование Первого Послания Апостола Павла к Коринфянам* [Commentary on the First Epistle of St Paul to Corinthians], 410.

14. St John Chrysostom, *Homilies on First Corinthians* 26.1; ET in NPNF, vol. 12, p. 149.

15. St Theophan the Recluse, *Толкование Первого Послания Апостола Павла к Коринфянам* [Commentary on the First Epistle of St Paul to Corinthians].

16. St John Chrysostom, *Homilies on First Corinthians* 26.4; ET in NPNF, vol. 12, p. 153.

17. In distinguishing between the Eucharistic liturgy and the "agape meal" in the life of the first-century early Christian churches, Archbishop Averky reflects the assumption prevalent in the New Testament and liturgical scholarship of the nineteenth and twentieth centuries. Recent studies in liturgical history have concluded that in early Christian churches, no distinction was made between the "agape meal" and the Eucharist, and the latter was celebrated in the context of a communal meal, which in various sources could bear the name of either "Eucharist" or "agape," as seen in *Didache* 9–10. See M. Zheltov and V. Vasilik, "*Arana*" [Agape Meal] in *Православная Энциклопедия* [Orthodox Encyclopedia] (Moscow: Moscow Patriarchate, 2005), 1.214–19.

18. St John Chrysostom, *Homilies on First Corinthians* 34.3; ET in NPNF, vol. 12, p. 203.

19. Blessed Theodoret, *Interpretation in First Corinthians* 13:13, PG 82, col. 337B–C.

Chapter 3

20. St John Chrysostom, *Homilies on Second Corinthians* 6.3; ET in NPNF, vol. 12, p. 307.

21. St Theophan the Recluse, *Толкование Второго Послания Апостола Павла к Коринфянам* [Commentary on the Second Epistle of St Paul to Corinthians] (vol. 17.2 in *Полное собрание творений* [Complete Collected Works]; Moscow: Publication Council of the Russian Orthodox Church, 2013.

22. St John Chrysostom, *Homilies on Second Corinthians* 26.1; ET in NPNF, vol. 12, p. 398.

23. St Theophan the Recluse, *Толкование Второго Послания Апостола Павла к Коринфянам* [Commentary on the Second Epistle of St Paul to Corinthians], in *Полное собрание творений* [Complete Collected Works], vol. 17.2, p. 467.

24. St John Chrysostom, *Homilies on Second Corinthians* 26.2; ET in NPNF, vol. 12, p. 400.

25. Ibid.

26. St Theophan the Recluse, *Толкование Второго Послания Апостола Павла к Коринфянам* [Commentary on the Second Epistle of St Paul to Corinthians], 498.

Chapter 4

27. Oecumenius, *Commentary on the Epistle to Galatians* 1.17–19, PG 118, col. 1100D–1101A.

28. St John Chrysostom, *Commentary on Galatians* 2.4; ET in NPNF, vol. 13, p. 15.

29. Ibid., 3.1; NPNF, vol. 13, p. 23.

30. Cited in St Theophan the Recluse, *Толкование послания св. апостола Павла к Галатам* [Commentary on St Paul's Epistle to Galatians] in *Collected Works*, vol. 15 (Moscow, 2013), 294.

31. Ibid., 294.

32. Ibid., 295.

33. Ibid., 317.

34. St John Chrysostom, *Commentary on Galatians* 3.4; ET in NPNF, vol. 13, p. 29.

35. St Theophan the Recluse, *Толкование послания св. апостола Павла к Галатам* [Commentary on St Paul's Epistle to Galatians], 345.

36. Ibid., 346.

37. St John Chrysostom, *Commentary on Galatians* 4:20; ET in NPNF, vol. 13, p. 33.

38. St Theophan the Recluse, *Толкование послания св. апостола Павла к Галатам* [Commentary on St Paul's Epistle to Galatians], 400.

39. Ibid., 401.

Chapter 5

40. See St Ignatius, *Epistle to the Ephesians* 12.2: "You [i.e., the Ephesians] are fellow initiates with Paul who was sanctified, martyred, and became worthy of blessedness. When I attain to God, may I be found in the footsteps of him, who remembers you in every epistle in Christ Jesus" (ed. and trans. Bart D. Ehrman, *The Apostolic Fathers*, vol. 1, Loeb Classical Library 24 [Cambridge, Mass.: Harvard University Press, 2003], 232–33).

41. St Theophan the Recluse, *Толкование послания св. апостола Павла к Ефесеям* [Commentary on the Epistle of St Paul to the Ephesians] (2nd ed.; Moscow: St Panteleimon Russian Monastery on Mt Athos, 1893), 123.

42. Ibid., 125.

43. St John Chrysostom, *Homily 3 on Ephesians*; ET in NPNF, vol. 13, p. 62.

44. St Theophan the Recluse, *Толкование послания св. апостола Павла к Ефесеям* [Commentary on the Epistle of St Paul to the Ephesians], 157.

45. Blessed Theodoret of Cyrus, *Interpretation of the Epistle to Ephesians* 2:17, PG 82, col. 524C.

46. Ibid. 3:19, PG 82, col. 532B.

47. St Theophan the Recluse, *Толкование послания св. апостола Павла к Ефесеям* [Commentary on the Epistle of St Paul to the Ephesians], 298.

48. St John Chrysostom, *Homilies on Ephesians* 20; ET in NPNF, vol. 13, p. 146.

Chapter 6

49. St John Chrysostom, *Homilies on Philippians* 9; ET in NPNF, vol. 13, p. 224.

50. St John Chrysostom, *Homilies on Philippians* 12; ET in NPNF, vol. 13, p. 240.

51. Ibid.

52. Cited in St Theophan the Recluse, *Толкования посланий апостола Павла к Колоссянам, к Филиппийцам* [The Commentaries on the Epistles of St Paul to Colossians and Philippians] (Moscow: Pravilo Very, 2005), 550.

Chapter 7

53. St Theophan the Recluse, *Толкования посланий апостола Павла к Колоссянам, к Филиппийцам* [The Commentaries on the Epistles of St Paul to Colossians and Philippians] (Moscow: Pravilo Very, 2005), 63.

54. St John Chrysostom, *Homilies on Colossians* 3; ET in NPNF, vol. 13, p. 271.

55. Blessed Theodoret of Cyrus, *Interpretation of the Epistle to Colossians* 1:17, PG 82, col. 600D.

56. St John Chrysostom, *Homilies on Colossians* 3.2; ET in NPNF, vol. 13, p. 271.

57. Ibid.

58. Ibid., 271–72.

59. See Blessed Theodoret, *Interpretation of the Epistle to Colossians* 1:18, PG 82, col. 601A.

60. St Theophan the Recluse, *Толкования посланий апостола Павла к Колоссянам, к Филиппийцам* [The Commentaries on the Epistles of St Paul to Colossians and Philippians], 78.

61. Ibid., 79.

62. St John Chrysostom, *Homilies on Colossians* 3; ET in NPNF, vol. 13, p. 272.

63. Ibid., vol. 13, p. 281.

64. St Theophan the Recluse, *Толкования посланий апостола Павла к Колоссянам, к Филиппийцам* [The Commentaries on the Epistles of St Paul to Colossians and Philippians], 131.

65. See Ibid., 132.

66. See Ibid., 151.

67. St John Chrysostom, *Homilies on Colossians* 3; ET in NPNF, vol. 13, p. 286.

68. St Theophan the Recluse, *Толкования посланий апостола Павла к Колоссянам, к Филиппийцам* [The Commentaries on the Epistles of St Paul to Colossians and Philippians], 189–90.

69. Cited in Ibid., 206.

70. Ibid., 208.

71. Ibid., 246–47.

72. Ibid., 252–53.

73. Ibid., 253.

Chapter 8

74. St Theophan the Recluse, *Толкования Посланий апостола Павла к Солунянам, к Филимону, к Евреям* [The Commentaries on the Epistles of St Paul to the Thessalonians, to Philemon, to the Hebrews] (Moscow: Pravilo Very), 30.

75. St John Chrysostom, *Homilies on First Thessalonians* 1.1; ET in NPNF, vol. 13, p. 323.

76. See St Theophan the Recluse, *Толкования Посланий апостола Павла к Солунянам, к Филимону, к Евреям*, 73–74.

77. Cited after Ibid., p. 134.

78. St John Chrysostom, *Homilies on First Thessalonians* 5; ET in NPNF, vol. 13, p. 345.

79. St Theophan the Recluse, *Толкования Посланий апостола Павла к Солунянам, к Филимону, к Евреям*, 189.

80. St Theophan the Recluse, *Толкования Посланий апостола Павла к Солунянам, к Филимону, к Евреям*, 203.

81. Theocritus, "Idylls 4," in *The Greek Bucolic Poets* (ed. and trans. J. M. Edmonds, Loeb Classical Library 28; London: Heinemann; New York: Macmillan, 1912), 56–57.

82. Catullus, "Carmen 5," in *The Poems and Fragments of Catullus* (ET in the meters of the original by Robinson Ellis; London: John Murray, 1871), 4.

83. St John of Damascus, *Commentaries on the Epistles of St Paul*, PG 95, col. 913. Archbishop Averky cites this text, included among the *dubia* (probably inauthentic

writings) of St John in *Patrologia Graeca*, after the commentary of St Theophan the Recluse (*Толкования Посланий апостола Павла к Солунянам, к Филимону, к Евреям*, 208).

84. St John Chrysostom, *Homilies on First Thessalonians* 8; ET in NPNF, vol. 13, p. 356.

85. St Theophan the Recluse, *Толкования Посланий апостола Павла к Солунянам, к Филимону, к Евреям*, 220.

86. Ibid., 229.

87. St John Chrysostom, *Homilies on First Thessalonians* 9; ET in NPNF, vol. 13, p. 360.

88. Ibid., 362.

89. St Theophan the Recluse, *Толкования Посланий апостола Павла к Солунянам, к Филимону, к Евреям*, 231.

Chapter 9

90. St Theophan the Recluse, *Толкования Посланий апостола Павла к Солунянам, к Филимону, к Евреям* [The Commentaries on the Epistles of St Paul to the Thessalonians, to Philemon, to the Hebrews] (Moscow: Pravilo Very, 2005), 390–92.

91. See St John Chrysostom, *Homilies on Second Thessalonians* 2; ET in NPNF, vol. 13, p. 386; Blessed Theodoret of Cyrus, *Interpretation of the Second Epistle to Thessalonians* 2:3, PG 82, col. 664A; see also Augustine, *The City of God* 20.19.

92. See St Theophan the Recluse, *Толкования Посланий апостола Павла к Солунянам, к Филимону, к Евреям*, 393.

93. St John Chrysostom, *Homilies on Second Thessalonians* 2; ET in NPNF, vol. 13, p. 386.

94. Cited in St Theophan the Recluse, *Толкования Посланий апостола Павла к Солунянам, к Филимону, к Евреям*, 393–94.

95. Ibid., 393.

96. St John Chrysostom, *Homilies on Second Thessalonians* 3.2; ET in NPNF, vol. 13, p. 386.

97. St Theophan the Recluse, *Толкования Посланий апостола Павла к Солунянам, к Филимону, к Евреям*, 398.

98. St John Chrysostom, *Homilies on Second Thessalonians* 3.2; ET in NPNF, vol. 13, p. 386.

99. Cited in St Theophan the Recluse, *Толкования Посланий апостола Павла к Солунянам, к Филимону, к Евреям*, 399.

100. St John Chrysostom, *Homilies on Second Thessalonians* 4.1; ET in NPNF, vol. 13, p. 388.

101. In his commentary, Blessed Theophylact of Ochrid makes a reference to Chrysostom's view that "what is restraining" (*katechon*) indicates either the grace of the Spirit or the Roman empire; just as Chrysostom, Theophylact seems to be inclined to the latter option (*Exposition on the Second Epistle to Thessalonians* 2:6, PG 124, col. 1341B).

102. Blessed Theodoret, *Interpretation of the Second Epistle to Thessalonians* 2:6, PG 82, col. 665A.

103. Oecumenius of Tricca, *Commentary on the New Testament*, PG 119, col. 120C.

104. Possibly, Severus of Antioch; Ibid., col. 120D.

105. St Theophan the Recluse, *Толкования Посланий апостола Павла к Солунянам, к Филимону, к Евреям*, 406–407.

106. St John of Kronstadt, *Новые слова, произнесенные в 1902 году* [New Sermons Spoken in 1902] (1903), 47; cited after I. K. Surskiy, *Отец Иоанн Кронштадтский* [Father John of Kronstadt] (Belgrade, 1938), 1.326.

107. St Theophan the Recluse, *Толкования Посланий апостола Павла к Солунянам, к Филимону, к Евреям*, 409.

108. See Bishop Mikhail (Luzin), *Толковый Апостол: Соборные послания* [The Apostle with the Commentary: General Epistles] (Moscow: Pravilo Very, 2009).

109. Blessed Theodoret, *Interpretation of the Second Epistle to Thessalonians* 2:7, PG 82, col. 665B.

110. (Ps.-) St John of Damascus, *Commentary on the Epistles of St Paul*, PG 95, col. 924.

111. St Theophan the Recluse, *Толкования Посланий апостола Павла к Солунянам, к Филимону, к Евреям*, 420.

112. Theophylact of Ochrid, *Exposition on the Second Epistle to Thessalonians* 2:11, PG 124, col. 1345A.

113. St Theophan the Recluse, *Толкования Посланий апостола Павла к Солунянам, к Филимону, к Евреям*, 424.

114. St John Chrysostom, *Homilies on Second Thessalonians* 4; ET in NPNF, vol. 13, p. 390.

115. Ibid., 390.

116. St Theophan the Recluse, *Толкования Посланий апостола Павла к Солунянам, к Филимону, к Евреям*, 438–39.

117. Ibid., 492.

Chapter 10

118. St John Chrysostom, *Homilies on First Timothy* 2; ET in NPNF, vol. 13, p. 414.

119. Blessed Theodoret of Cyrus, *Interpretation of the First Epistle to Timothy*, PG 82, col. 793A.

120. St Theophan the Recluse, *Толкования Посланий апостола Павла к Титу, к Тимофею* [The Commentary on the Epistles of St Paul to Titus, to Timothy (Pastoral Epistles)] (Moscow: Pravilo Very, 2005), 281.

121. See *The Divine Liturgy of Our Father Among the Saints John Chrysostom: Slavonic-English Parallel Text* (4th ed., Jordanville, N.Y.: Holy Trinity Publications, Printshop of St Job of Pochaev, 2015), 212–13.

122. St Theophan the Recluse, *Толкования Посланий апостола Павла к Титу, к Тимофею*, 294.

123. See St John Chrysostom, *Homilies on First Timothy* 5; ET in NPNF, vol. 13, p. 425.

124. St John Chrysostom, *Homilies on First Timothy* 6; ET in NPNF, vol. 13, p. 426.

125. Theophylact of Ochrid, *Exposition in the First Epistle to Timothy* 2:12, PG 125, col. 37C.

126. Oecumenius, *Commentary on the New Testament*, PG 119, col. 156B.

127. St John Chrysostom, *Homilies on First Timothy* 9; ET in NPNF, vol. 13, p. 436.

128. Theophylact of Ochrid, *Exposition in the First Epistle to Timothy* 2:15, PG 125, col. 40C.

129. Blessed Theodoret, *Interpretation of the First Epistle to Timothy* 3:1, PG 82, col. 804B–C.

130. St Theophan the Recluse, *Толкования Посланий апостола Павла к Титу, к Тимофею*, 363.

131. Cited after Ibid., 363.

132. Theophylact of Ochrid, *Exposition in the First Epistle to Timothy* 3:2, PG 125, col. 41C.

133. Blessed Theodoret, *Interpretation of the First Epistle to Timothy* 3:2, PG 82, col. 804D.

134. Theophylact of Ochrid, *Exposition in the First Epistle to Timothy* 3:9, PG 125, col. 48B.

135. St Theophan the Recluse, *Толкования Посланий апостола Павла к Титу, к Тимофею*, 402.

136. Theophylact of Ochrid, *Exposition in the First Epistle to Timothy* 3:16, PG 125, col. 52B.

137. The NKJV translation renders this part of 1 Timothy 3:16 as "received up in glory"; however, we have to consider that in the Orthodox tradition this verse (*anelêmphthê en doxêi*) is paraphrased in the opening phrase of the troparion for the feast of the Lord's Ascension (*Anelêmphthês en doxêi* … "Thou hast ascended in glory … "). Thus, the proper contextual translation for this segment of 3:16, especially for the purposes of this commentary, would be "ascended in glory."

138. St Theophan the Recluse, *Толкования Посланий апостола Павла к Титу, к Тимофею*, 410.

139. Ibid., 410–11.

140. Blessed Theodoret, *Interpretation of the First Epistle to Timothy* 4:2, PG 82, col. 812D.

141. St John Chrysostom, *Homilies on First Timothy* 12.3; ET in NPNF, vol. 13, p. 446.

142. Ibid., 13.1; vol. 13, p. 449.

143. Ambrosiaster, *Commentary on the Epistles of St Paul* in *Patrologia Latina* (further, PL) 17, col. 476B.

144. "But if any widow has children or grandchildren, let them first learn to show piety at home and to repay their parents; for this is good and acceptable before God."

145. Oecumenius of Tricca, *Commentary on the New Testament*, PG 119, col. 173D.

146. See St John Chrysostom, *Homilies on First Timothy* 15.1; ET in NPNF, vol. 13, p. 459.

147. Ibid., 460.

148. St John Chrysostom, *Homilies on First Timothy* 15; ET in NPNF, vol. 13, p. 461.

149. Blessed Theodoret, *Interpretation of the First Epistle to Timothy* 5:22, PG 82, col. 821C.

150. Oecumenius, *Commentary on the New Testament*, PG 119, col. 184B.

151. Ibid., col. 184C.

152. Theophylact of Ochrid, *Exposition in the First Epistle to Timothy* 5:22, PG 125, col. 73B.

153. Theophan the Recluse, *Толкования Посланий апостола Павла к Титу, к Тимофею*, 519.

154. Ibid., 520.

Chapter 11

155. St Theophan the Recluse, *Толкования Посланий апостола Павла к Титу, к Тимофею* [The Commentary on the Epistles of St Paul to Titus, to Timothy (Pastoral Epistles)] (Moscow: Pravilo Very, 2005), 222.

156. See St Basil the Great, *On the Holy Spirit* 27 (trans. Stephen Hildebrand, Popular Patristics 42; Yonkers, N.Y.: St Vladimir's Seminary Press, 2011), 66.

157. Cited in Oecumenius, *Commentary on the New Testament*, PG 119, col. 209C.

158. Blessed Theodoret of Cyrus, *Interpretation of the Second Epistle to Timothy* 2:2, PG 82, col. 840A.

159. St Theophan the Recluse, *Толкования Посланий апостола Павла к Титу, к Тимофею*, 684–85.

160. Ibid., 686.

161. Jerome of Stridon, *Letter 133 to Ctesiphon* 4; ET in NPNF, Series 2, vol. 6, p. 275.

162. St Theophan the Recluse, *Толкования Посланий апостола Павла к Титу, к Тимофею*, 772.

163. Ibid., 780.

164. St John Chrysostom, *Homilies on Second Timothy* 8; ET in NPNF, vol. 13, p. 506.

165. Ibid., 9; vol. 13, p. 510.

166. See Ibid., 510.

167. Theophylact of Ochrid, *Exposition in the Second Epistle to Timothy* 4:3, PG 125, col. 128D–129A.

168. St Theophan the Recluse, *Толкования Посланий апостола Павла к Титу, к Тимофею*, 806.

169. Ibid., 808.

170. Ibid., 810.

171. St John Chrysostom, *Homilies on Second Timothy* 9; ET in NPNF, vol. 13, p. 511.

172. See St John Chrysostom, *Homilies on Second Timothy* 10; ET in NPNF, vol. 13, p. 514; Blessed Theodoret, *Interpretation of the Second Epistle to Timothy* 4:17, PG 82, col. 856B.

Chapter 12

173. "Virgins, have Christ alone before your eyes … May I have pleasure in your purity, … as of Timothy, as of Titus, as of Evodius, as of Clement, who departed this life in chastity"—*Philad.* 4 (longer recension); see Ignatius of Antioch, *The Letters* (trans. Alistair Stewart, Popular Patristics Series 49; Yonkers, N.Y.: St Vladimir's Seminary Press, 2013).

174. St John Chrysostom, *Homilies on Titus* 1.1; ET in NPNF, vol. 13, p. 519–20.

175. St John Chrysostom, *Homilies on Titus* 2; ET in NPNF, vol. 13, p. 524.

176. Ibid.

177. Blessed Jerome, *Commentary on Titus* 1:6, PL 26, col. 556C; cited in St Theophan the Recluse, *Толкования Посланий апостола Павла к Титу, к Тимофею*, 72.

178. Theophylact of Ochrid, *Exposition in the Epistle to Titus* 1:8, PG 125, col. 149D.

179. St Jerome, *Commentary on Titus* 1:8–9, PL 26, col. 559B; cited after St Theophan the Recluse, *Толкования Посланий апостола Павла к Титу, к Тимофею*, 85.

180. Blessed Theodoret of Cyrus, *Interpretation of the Epistle to Titus* 1:14, PG 82, col. 861C.

Chapter 13

181. St John Chrysostom, *Homilies on Philemon* 1; ET in NPNF, vol. 13, p. 547.

182. Ibid, Argument, 545.

183. St Theophan the Recluse, *Толкования Посланий апостола Павла к Солунянам, к Филимону, к Евреям* [The Commentaries on the Epistles of St Paul to the Thessalonians, to Philemon, to the Hebrews] (Moscow: Pravilo Very), 562–63.

184. Ibid., 561–62. Compare, how St John Chrysostom expounds this passage: "that it might not appear insulting to him, whom he requests, if he had not the confidence to ask and obtain in behalf of a theft, he in some measure relieves this, saying, 'Not to mention to you that you owe me even your own self besides.' Not only thine own things, but thyself also. And this proceeded from love, and was according to the rule of friendship, and was a proof

of his great confidence. See how he everywhere provides for both, that he may ask with great security, and that this may not seem a sign of too little confidence in him" (*Homilies on Philemon* 3; ET in NPNF, vol. 13, p. 555).

185. St Theophan the Recluse, *Толкования Посланий апостола Павла к Солунянам, к Филимону, к Евреям*, 565.

Chapter 14

186. Eusebius, *Church History* 6.25; ET in Eusebius, *The Ecclesiastical History* (trans. J. E. L. Oulton, Loeb Classical Library 265; London: Heinemann; Cambridge, MA: Harvard University Press, 1942), 79.

187. See Canon 27 of the Council of Carthage (A.D. 419), in NPNF, Series 2, vol. 14, p. 453–54.

188. Eusebius, *Church History* 6.14; ET in Eusebius, *Ecclesiastical History* (trans. Oulton), 47.

189. St Theophan the Recluse, *Толкования Посланий апостола Павла к Солунянам, к Филимону, к Евреям* [The Commentaries on the Epistles of St Paul to the Thessalonians, to Philemon, to the Hebrews] (Moscow: Pravilo Very, 2005), 606.

190. Ibid., p. 615–16.

191. Blessed Theodoret of Cyrus, *Interpretation of the Epistle to the Hebrews* 1:1–2, PG 82, col. 680A.

192. See St John Chrysostom, *Homilies on the Epistle to the Hebrews* 3.6; ET in NPNF, vol. 14, p. 378: "And everywhere he says [the Law] was given by angels. Some indeed say that Moses is signified; but without reason. For here he says angels in the plural: and the angels too which he here speaks of, are those in heaven. What then is it? Either he means the Decalogue only (for there Moses spake, and God answered him [Exod. 19:19]), or that angels were present, God disposing them in order, or that he speaks thus in regard of all things said and done in the old Covenant, as if angels had part in them. But how is it said in another place, 'The Law was given by Moses' (John 1:17), and here 'by angels'? For it is said, 'And God came down in thick darkness' (Exod 19:16, 20)."

193. See Blessed Theodoret, *Interpretation of the Epistle to the Hebrews* 2:5, PG 82, col. 692A.

194. St John Chrysostom, *Homilies on the Epistle to the Hebrews* 17.4; ET in NPNF, vol. 14, p. 447.

195. Blessed Theodoret, *Interpretation of the Epistle to the Hebrews* 11:1, PG 82, col. 757A–B.

196. St John Chrysostom, *Homilies on the Epistle to the Hebrews* 26.3; ET in NPNF, vol. 14, p. 483.

197. Ibid., 26.5, vol. 14, p. 484.

198. Blessed Theodoret, *Interpretation of the Epistle to the Hebrews* 11:28, PG 82, col. 765C.

199. St John Chrysostom, *Homilies on the Epistle to the Hebrews* 27.3; ET in NPNF, vol. 14, p. 487.

200. Ibid., 488.

201. Blessed Theodoret, *Interpretation of the Epistle to the Hebrews* 12:34–37, PG 82, col. 768C–769B.

202. St John Chrysostom, *Homilies on the Epistle to the Hebrews* 28.2; ET in NPNF, vol. 14, p. 492.

Part III

203. Eusebius, *Church History* 5.18.5; ET in Eusebius, *The Ecclesiastical History* (trans. Kirsopp Lake, Loeb Classical Library 153; London: Heinemann; New York: Putnam, 1926), 489.

204. See Eusebius, *Church History* 7.24.5–9 (trans. Oulton), 199.

205. See Ibid. 6.14.1; 47.

Chapter 15

206. The Divine Liturgy ascribed to St James, the Lord's brother and the first bishop of Jerusalem, was celebrated as a main Eucharistic service in Jerusalem and Palestine until about the eleventh or twelfth century. It was revived and restored for liturgical use at the end of the nineteenth century in Zakynthos and Jerusalem. In the 1930s, Hegumen Philip (Gardner) completed the translation of the Liturgy of St James into Church Slavonic; this translation was published by the Printshop of St Job of Pochaev in Ladomirova (Slovakia) in 1938. The Liturgy of St James is celebrated annually in Jerusalem, Zakynthos, at Holy Trinity Monastery (Jordanville, N.Y.) and in other places throughout the world.

207. Blessed Theophylact of Ochrid, *Exposition in the Epistle of St James* 2:10-13, PG 125, col. 1153D–1156A.

Chapter 16

208. See *Life of Venerable Zosimas, Bishop of Babylon*, in St Dimitry of Rostov, *The Lives of Saints* (in Russian), June 4.

209. Eusebius, *Church History* 2.15.2; (trans. Lake), 145.

210. "… Wherefore, having contested for the truth, thou didst rejoice to announce the good tidings even to those in Hades: that God hath appeared in the flesh …" (*The Unabbreviated Horologion or Book of Hours* [Jordanville, N.Y.: Holy Trinity Monastery, 1997]).

211. Most likely, this is a reference to the apostle and evangelist Mark.

Chapter 17

212. See notes 232–233.

Chapter 18

213. Eusebius includes 1 John among the canonical ("recognized") books of the Scriptures, while adding 2 John and 3 John to the "disputed" list; see *Church History* 3.25.1-2; ET in Eusebius, *Ecclesiastical History* (trans. Lake), 257.

214. Eusebius, *Church History* 7.25.18-21; ET in Eusebius, *Ecclesiastical History* (trans. Oulton), 203–7.

Chapter 19

215. See Eusebius, *Church History* 7.25.1–7.

216. Theophylact of Ochrid, *Exposition of the Second Epistle of John*, PG 126, col. 80A.

Chapter 21

217. According to Origen, the Apostle Jude derives this story from an apocryphal work entitled *Ascension of Moses* (*On the First Principles* 3.2.1; ET in *Ante-Nicene Fathers*, vol. 4, p. 328), which is no longer extant. Other contemporary scholars suggest that St Jude may have been referring to a lost apocryphal treatise *Testament of Moses* or another pseudoepigraphical or apocryphal book.

218. Compare Jude 14–15 with the apocryphal Book of Enoch 1:9: "And behold! He cometh with ten thousands of His holy ones to execute judgment upon all, and to destroy all the ungodly: and to convict all flesh of all the works of their ungodliness which they have ungodly committed, and of all the hard things which ungodly sinners have spoken against Him" (*The Apocrypha and Pseudepigrapha of the Old Testament in English* [vol. 2; ed. R. H. Charles; Oxford: Clarendon Press, 1913], 189).

Part IV

219. First published in *The Orthodox Word*, nos. 100-11, 113-18, 120, 122, 125-26, and in Archbishop Averky Taushev, *The Apocalypse* (trans. Fr Seraphim Rose; Platina, Calif.: St Herman of Alaska Brotherhood, 1985, 1995, 3rd ed. forthcoming). Reprinted with permission. Here and further bibliographical references were completed by the editors of Holy Trinity Seminary Press and are found in the endnotes. The footnotes marked by "S.R." were completed by Fr Seraphim (Rose) for his translation of Archbishop Averky's commentary.

Chapter 22

220. St Irenaeus of Lyons, *Against Heresies* 5.30.3; ET in ANF, vol. 1, p. 560.

221. See *The Apocalypse of St John in A Syriac Version Hitherto Unknown* (ed. John Gwynn; Dublin: Hodges, Figgis and Co.; London: Longmans, Green and Co., 1897), 1.

222. In this edition we have preserved the translation of St Andrew of Caesarea's *Commentary on the Apocalypse*, completed by Hieromonk Seraphim (Rose) in the course of his work on translating Archbishop Averky's commentary. Just as with Archbishop Averky's text, St Andrew's commentary was also translated from the Russian edition. For a more recent English translation of St Andrew's commentary from the original Greek, see Andrew of Caesarea, *Commentary on the Apocalypse* (trans. Eugenia Scarvelis Constantinou, Fathers of the Church 123; Washington, D.C.: Catholic University of America Press, 2012).

223. St Irenaeus of Lyons, *Against Heresies* 5.36.1; ANF, vol. 1, p. 566.

224. Alexander Ivanov, *Руководство к изучению священных книг Нового Завета* [A Manual for the Study of the Sacred Writings of the New Testament] (St Petersburg, 1907).

SUBJECT INDEX

Scripture Index